MICROPROCESSOR ARCHITECTURE

This book gives a comprehensive description of the architecture of microprocessors from simple in-order short pipeline designs to out-of-order superscalars. It discusses topics such as

- The policies and mechanisms needed for out-of-order processing, such as register renaming, reservation stations, and reorder buffers
- Optimizations for high performance, such as branch predictors, instruction scheduling, and load–store speculations
- Design choices and enhancements to tolerate latency in the cache hierarchy of single and multiple processors
- State-of-the-art multithreading and multiprocessing, emphasizing single-chip implementations

Topics are presented as conceptual ideas, with metrics to assess the effects on performance, if appropriate, and examples of realization. The emphasis is on how things work at a black box and algorithmic level. The author also provides sufficient detail at the register transfer level so that readers can appreciate how design features enhance performance as well as complexity.

Jean-Loup Baer is Professor Emeritus of Computer Science and Engineering at the University of Washington, where he has been since 1969. Professor Baer is the author of *Computer Systems Architecture* and of more than 100 refereed papers. He is a Guggenheim Fellow, an ACM Fellow, and an IEEE Fellow. Baer has held several editorial positions, including editor-in-chief of the *Journal of VLSI and Computer Systems* and editor of the *IEEE Transactions on Computers*, the *IEEE Transactions on Parallel and Distributed Systems*, and the *Journal of Parallel and Distributed Computing*. He has served as General Chair and Program Chair of several conferences, including ISCA and HPCA.

Microprocessor Architecture

FROM SIMPLE PIPELINES TO CHIP MULTIPROCESSORS

Jean-Loup Baer

University of Washington, Seattle

CAMBRIDGE
UNIVERSITY PRESS

CAMBRIDGE UNIVERSITY PRESS
Cambridge, New York, Melbourne, Madrid, Cape Town, Singapore,
São Paulo, Delhi, Dubai, Tokyo

Cambridge University Press
32 Avenue of the Americas, New York, NY 10013-2473, USA

www.cambridge.org
Information on this title: www.cambridge.org/9780521769921

First published 2010

Printed in the United States of America

A catalog record for this publication is available from the British Library.

Library of Congress Cataloging in Publication data

Baer, Jean-Loup.
Microprocessor architecture: from simple pipelines to chip multiprocessors /
Jean-Loup Baer.
    p.   cm.
Includes bibliographical references and index.
ISBN 978-0-521-76992-1 (hardback)
1. Microprocessors.   2. Computer architecture.   I. Title.
QA76.5.B227   2009
004.2′2 – dc22   2009025686

ISBN 978-0-521-76992-1 Hardback

To Diane, Marc, Shawn, and Danielle

Contents

Preface

Computer architecture is at a turning point. Radical changes occurred in the 1980s when the Reduced Instruction Set Computer (RISC) philosophy, spurred in good part by academic research, permeated the industry as a reaction to the Complex Instruction Set Computer (CISC) complexities. Today, three decades later, we have reached a point where physical limitations such as power dissipation and design complexity limit the speed and the performance of single-processor systems. The era of chip multiprocessors (CMP), or multicores, has arrived.

Besides the uncertainty on the structure of CMPs, it is not known yet whether the future CMPs will be composed of simple or complex processors or a combination of both and how the on-chip and off-chip memory hierarchy will be managed. It is important for computer scientists and engineers to look at the possible options for the modules that will compose the new generations of multicores. In this book, we describe the architecture of microprocessors from simple in-order short pipe designs to out-of-order superscalars with many optimizations. We also present choices and enhancements in the cache hierarchy of single processors. The last part of this book introduces readers to the state-of-the-art in multithreading and multiprocessing, emphasizing single-chip implementations and their cache hierarchy.

The emphasis in this book is on "how things work" at a black box and algorithmic level. It is not as close to the hardware as books that explain features at the register transfer level. However, it provides sufficient detail, say at the "bit level" and through pseudocode, so that the reader can appreciate design features that have or will enhance performance as well as their complexity.

As much as possible we present topics as conceptual ideas, define metrics to assess the performance impact if appropriate, show alternate (if any) ways of implementing them, and provide examples of realization.

Synopsis

This book has three main parts. Chapter 1 and Chapter 2 review material that should have been taught in a prerequisite class. Chapters 3 through 6 describe single-processor systems and their memory hierarchy. Chapter 7 and Chapter 8 are devoted to parallelism. The last (short) chapter, Chapter 9, introduces limitations due to technology and presents challenges for future CMPs.

More specifically:

- Chapter 1 reviews Moore's law and its influence as well as current limitations to ever faster processors. Performance metrics such as *cycles per instruction* (CPI), *instruction per cycle* (IPC), and speedup are defined. A section on performance evaluation introduces benchmarks and simulators. Chapter 2 summarizes the main concepts behind pipelining, including data and control hazards. Two versions of the "classical" 5-stage pipeline are contrasted. The basics of cache organization and performance are reviewed. Virtual memory (paging) and *Translation Look-Aside Buffers* (TLBs) are presented from the computer architecture (not the operating system) viewpoint.
- Chapter 3 describes two landmark "families" in the history of modern multiple-issue microprocessors: in-order processors represented by the DEC Alpha 21164 and out-of-order processors represented by the Intel Pentium P6 micro-architecure. In order to ease the description of the latter, a first look at register renaming is provided, with a sidebar showing the classical Tomasulo algorithm. This chapter ends with an introduction to the Very Long Instruction Word (VLIW) / Explicitly Parallel Instruction Computing (EPIC) philosophy and a brief overview of its most well-known industrial realization, the Intel Itanium. Chapter 4 and Chapter 5 are devoted to detailed explanations of, respectively, the front end and the back end of the pipeline. Because many advances in super-scalar performance have been attained through speculation, we start Chapter 4 with a "model" of a branch predictor. This model will be referred to in the book when other speculative schemes are explored. We then describe actual branch predictors and branch target predictors. A sidebar describes the sophisticated Alpha 21264 tournament predictor. The remainder of the chapter deals with instruction fetching, including trace caches, and presents another view of register renaming that has become more popular than Tomasulo's. Chapter 5 looks at another potential bottleneck in the pipeline, namely the wakeup-select cycle. Load speculation and other back-end optimizations are introduced. Chapter 6 deals with the cache hierarchy: how to improve access times for first-level caches (another critical potential source of slowdown); methods to hide latency from higher-level caches and main memory such as prefetching and lock-up free caches; and, in a more research-oriented way, design and performance issues for large caches. We conclude this chapter with a look at main memory.
- Chapter 7 and Chapter 8 present multiprocessors and multithreading. In Chapter 7, we first introduce taxonomies that will set the stage for the two chapters. Cache coherence is then treated with both snoopy protocols and directory protocols, because it is likely that both types of protocols will be used in future parallel processing systems, whether on-chip or between chips. The next topic is synchronization, in which, in addition to the existing lock mechanisms, we mention approaches that might replace or complement them, such as transactional

memory. We also briefly introduce relaxed memory models, a topic that may become more important in the near future. The chapter concludes with a description of multimedia instruction set extensions because this is a (limited) form of parallelism. In Chapter 8, we start by looking at various flavors of multithreading: fine-grained, coarse-grained, and SMT. This leads us to the description of some current CMPs. We start with two examples of general-purpose CMPs: the Sun Niagara, a CMP using fine-grained multithreaded simple processors, and the Intel Core Duo, a representative of Intel multicores using complex superscalar processors. We conclude with two special-purpose CMPs: the IBM Cell, intended for games and scientific computation, and the Intel IXP, a network processor using coarse-grained multithreaded microengines.

- Finally, Chapter 9 gives a brief introduction to the factors that have capped the exponential performance curve of single processors, namely power issues, wire lengths, and pipeline depths. We end the chapter with an (incomplete) list of challenges for future CMPs.

Use of the book

This book grew out of courses given over the last ten years at the senior undergraduate and first-year graduate level for computer science and computer engineering students at the University of Washington. It is intended as a book for a second course in computer architecture. In an undergraduate class, we typically spend 10% of the time on review and presentation of simulators. We spend 60% of the time on single processors. About 25% is spent on multiprocessors and multithreading, and the remainder on some research presentations by colleagues and advanced graduate students. At the graduate level, the choice of topics depends more on the instructor. For example, one possible approach would be to assign the first two chapters as required reading and start directly with topics of the instructor's choice. A rule of thumb that we have followed is to have a 50–50 split in classroom time between single-processor (Chapters 3 through 6) and CMPs (Chapters 7 through 9).

Acknowledgments

I am indebted to students who took my classes and to many colleagues, including my doctoral students, for their help and comments. I want especially to recognize the leaders and participants of the weekly CSE "Computer Architecture Lunch," which Wen-Hann Wang and I created more than two decades ago. Their choice of the topics in this seminar and their constructive criticism of the importance of specific areas have influenced the contents of this book. Their patient explanations of what were for me obscure points has hopefully led to clearer exposition. In particular, I thank my faculty colleagues Luis Ceze, Carl Ebeling, Susan Eggers, Mark Oskin, and Larry Snyder and my research collaborators Craig Anderson, Tien-Fu Chen, Patrick Crowley, Dennis Lee, Douglas Low, Sang-Lyul Min, Xiaohan Qin, Taylor VanVleet, Wen-Hann Wang, Wayne Wong, and Rick Zucker.

I thank Lauren Cowles and David Jou at Cambridge University Press for providing me with excellent anonymous reviews, and Shana Meyer and colleagues at Aptara, Inc. – in particular, copy editor Joseph C. Fineman – for a smooth and timely production process.

Jean-Loup Baer
Seattle, WA
August 2009

1 Introduction

Modern computer systems built from the most sophisticated microprocessors and extensive memory hierarchies achieve their high performance through a combination of dramatic improvements in technology and advances in computer architecture. Advances in technology have resulted in exponential growth rates in raw speed (i.e., clock frequency) and in the amount of logic (number of transistors) that can be put on a chip. Computer architects have exploited these factors in order to further enhance performance using architectural techniques, which are the main subject of this book.

Microprocessors are over 30 years old: the Intel 4004 was introduced in 1971. The functionality of the 4004 compared to that of the mainframes of that period (for example, the IBM System/370) was minuscule. Today, just over thirty years later, workstations powered by engines such as (in alphabetical order and without specific processor numbers) the AMD Athlon, IBM PowerPC, Intel Pentium, and Sun UltraSPARC can rival or surpass in both performance and functionality the few remaining mainframes and at a much lower cost. Servers and supercomputers are more often than not made up of collections of microprocessor systems.

It would be wrong to assume, though, that the three tenets that computer architects have followed, namely *pipelining, parallelism,* and the *principle of locality,* were discovered with the birth of microprocessors. They were all at the basis of the design of previous (super)computers. The advances in technology made their implementations more practical and spurred further refinements. The microarchitectural techniques that are presented in this book rely on these three tenets to translate the architectural specification – the *instruction set architecture* – into a partition of *static* blocks whose *dynamic* interaction leads to their intended behavior.

In the next few pages, we give an extremely brief overview of the advances in technology that have led to the development of current microprocessors. Then, the remainder of this chapter is devoted to defining performance and means to measure it.

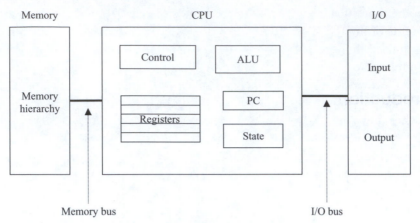

Figure 1.1. The von Neumann machine model.

1.1 A Quick View of Technological Advances

1.1.1 The von Neumann Machine Model

Modern microprocessors have sophisticated engineering features. Nonetheless, they still follow essentially the conventional von Neumann machine model shown in Figure 1.1. The von Neumann model of a stored program computer consists of four blocks:

- A *central processing unit* (CPU) containing an arithmetic–logical unit (ALU) that performs arithmetic and logical operations, registers whose main function is to be used for high-speed storage of operands, a control unit that interprets instructions and causes them to be executed, and a program counter (PC) that indicates the address of the next instruction to be executed (for some authors the ALU and the control unit constitute separate blocks).
- A *memory* that stores instructions, data, and intermediate and final results. Memory is now implemented as a hierarchy.
- An *input* that transmits data and instructions from the outside world to the memory.
- An *output* that transmits final results and messages to the outside world.

Under the von Neumann model, the *instruction execution cycle* proceeds as follows:

1. The next instruction (as pointed to by the PC) is fetched from memory.
2. The control unit decodes the instruction.
3. The instruction is executed. It can be an ALU-based instruction, a load from a memory location to a register, a store from a register to the memory, or a testing condition for a potential branch.
4. The PC is updated (incremented in all cases but a successful branch).
5. Go back to step 1.

Of course, in the more than sixty years of existence of stored program computers, both the contents of the blocks and the basic instruction execution cycle sequence have been optimized thoroughly. In this book, we shall look primarily at what can be found on a microprocessor chip. At the outset, a microprocessor chip contained the CPU. Over the years, the CPU has been enhanced so that it could be pipelined. Several functional units have replaced the single ALU. Lower levels of the memory hierarchy (caches) have been integrated on the chip. Recently, several microprocessors and their low-level caches coexist on a single chip, forming *chip multiprocessors* (CMPs). Along with these (micro)architectural advances, the strict sequential execution cycle has been extended so that we can have several instructions proceed concurrently in each of the basic steps. In Chapters 2 through 6, we examine the evolution of single processor chips; Chapters 7 and 8 are devoted to multiprocessors.

1.1.2 Technological Advances

The two domains in which technological advances have had the most impact on the performance of microprocessor systems have been the increases in clock frequency and the shrinking of the transistor features leading to higher logic density. In a simplistic way, we can state that increasing clock frequency leads to faster execution, and more logic yields implementation of more functionality on the chip.

Figure 1.2 shows the evolution of the clock frequencies of the Intel microprocessors from the inception of the 4004 in 1971 to the chip multiprocessors of 2003 and beyond. From 1971 to 2002, we see that processor raw speeds increased at an exponential rate. The frequency of the 4004, a speck on the figure that cannot be seen because of the scaling effect, was 1.08 MHz, a factor of 3,000 less than the 3.4 GHz of the Pentium 4. This corresponds roughly to a doubling of the frequency every 2.5 years. To be fair, though, although the Pentium 4 was the fastest processor in 2003, there were many mainframes in 1971 that were faster than the 4004. Some supercomputers in the late 1960s, such as the IBM System 360/91 and Control Data 6600/7600 – two machines that will be mentioned again in this book – had frequencies of over 100 MHz. However, if they were two orders of magnitude faster than the 4004, they were about six orders of magnitude more expensive. After 2003, the frequencies stabilize in the 3 GHz range. We shall see very shortly the reason for such a plateau.

The number of transistors that can be put on a chip has risen at the same pace as the frequency, but without any leveling off. In 1965, Gordon Moore, one of the founders of Intel, predicted that "the number of transistors on a given piece of silicon would double every couple of years." Although one can quibble over the "couple of years" by a few months or so, this prediction has remained essentially true and is now known as *Moore's law*. Figure 1.3 shows the exponential progression of transistors in the Intel microprocessors (notice the log scale). There is a growth factor of over 2,000 between the 2,300 transistors of the Intel 4004 and the 1.7 billion transistors of the 2006 Intel dual-core Itanium (the largest number of transistors in the

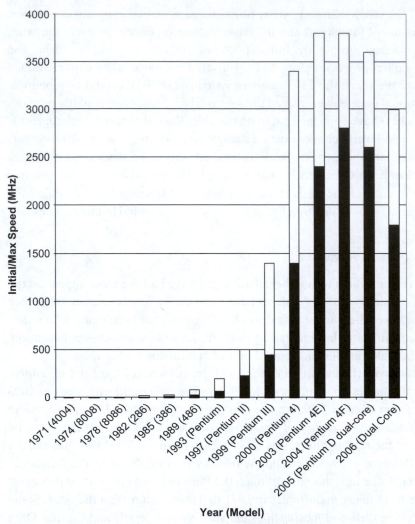

Figure 1.2. Evolution of Intel microprocessors speeds (black bars: frequency at introduction; white bars: peak frequency).

microprocessors of Figure 1.2 is a little over half a billion for a dual-core Extreme). It is widely believed that Moore's law can be sustained until 2025.

Besides allowing implementers to use more logic (i.e., provide more functionality) or more storage (i.e., mitigate the imbalance between processor speed and memory latency), consequences of Moore's law include reduced costs and better reliability.

However, the exponential growths in speed and logic density do not come without challenges. First, of course, the feature size of the manufacturing process, which is closely related to transistor sizes, cannot be reduced indefinitely, and the number of transistors that can be put on a chip is physically bounded. Second, and of primary importance now, is the amount of power that is dissipated. Figure 1.4 illustrates this point vividly (again, notice the log scale). Third, at multigigahertz frequencies, the on-chip distance (i.e., sum of wire lengths) between producer and consumer of

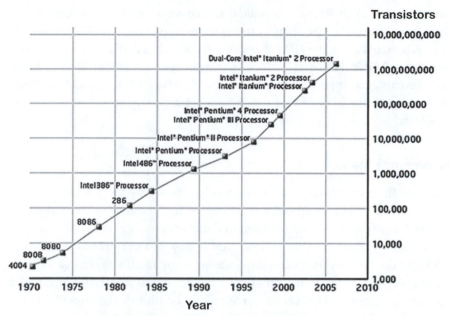

Figure 1.3. Illustration of Moore's law for the Intel microprocessors.

information becomes a factor and influences microarchitectural design decisions. We will elaborate more on these design problems in Chapter 9.

Now we can come back to the source of the leveling of speeds in Figure 1.2 after 2002. The power requirements as shown in Figure 1.4 and the growth in the number of transistors as shown by Moore's law limit the speeds that can be attained, because the switching (or dynamic) power dissipation is related to the frequency, and the

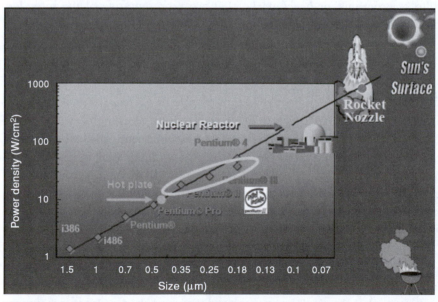

Figure 1.4. Power dissipation in selected Intel microprocessors (from Fred Pollack, Micro32 keynote).

static power (leakage) dissipation is related to the number of transistors on the chip. Therefore, Intel and other manufacturers have capped the frequencies at their 2003 level. An exception is the IBM Power6, introduced in 2007, which is clocked at slightly over 4.7 GHz. However, even with this latest development, the exponential speed increase has stopped. The persistence of Moore's law and the resulting increase in the amount of logic that can be put on a chip have led to the emergence of CMPs.

1.2 Performance Metrics

Raw speed and the number of transistors on a chip give a good feel for the progress that has been made. However, in order to assess the performance of computer systems, we need more precise metrics related to the execution of programs.

From a user's viewpoint, what is important is how fast her programs execute. Often, though, this time of execution depends on many factors that have little to do with the processor on which the programs execute. For example, it may depend on the operating system (which version of Windows or Linux), the compiler (how well optimized it is), and network conditions (if the user's workstation is sharing I/O devices with other workstations on a local area network). Moreover, the programs that user A is interested in can be completely different from those of interest to programmer B. Thus, to perform meaningful architectural comparisons between processors and their memory hierarchies or to assess the benefits of some components of the design, we need:

- Metrics that reflect the underlying architecture in a program-independent fashion.
- A suite of programs, or *benchmarks*, that are representative of the intended load of the processor.

Neither of these goals is easy to attain in a scientific manner.

1.2.1 Instructions Per Cycle (*IPC*)

Metrics to assess the microarchitecture of a processor and of its memory hierarchy, (i.e., caches and main memory), should be defined independently of the I/O subsystem. The execution time of a program whose code and data reside in the memory hierarchy will be denoted EX_{CPU} to indicate the context in which it is valid.

The execution time of a program depends on the number of instructions executed and the time to execute each instruction. In a first approximation, if we assume that all instructions take the same time to execute, we have

$$EX_{CPU} = \textit{Number of instructions} \times \textit{Time to execute one instruction} \qquad (1)$$

Now, *Time to execute one instruction* can be expressed as a function of the cycle time (the reciprocal of the clock frequency) and the number of cycles to execute an instruction, or *CPI* (for "cycles per instruction"). Equation (1) can then be rewritten as:

$$EX_{CPU} = Number\ of\ instructions \times CPI \times cycle\ time \qquad (2)$$

CPI is a program-independent, clock-frequency-independent metric. Recently, computer architects have preferred to quote figures related to its reciprocal, *IPC* (for "instructions per cycle.") The main reason for this cosmetic change is that it is psychologically more appealing to strive for increases in *IPC* than for decreases in *CPI*. Thus, we can rewrite Equation (2) as

$$EX_{CPU} = (Number\ of\ instructions \times cycle\ time)/IPC \qquad (2')$$

and define *IPC* as

$$IPC = (Number\ of\ instructions \times cycle\ time)/EX_{CPU} \qquad (3)$$

or

$$IPC = Number\ of\ instructions/(clock\ frequency \times EX_{CPU)} \qquad (3')$$

or, if we express EX_{CPU} as *Total number of cycles × cycle time*,

$$IPC = Number\ of\ instructions/Total\ number\ of\ cycles \qquad (3'')$$

Another reason to use *IPC* as a metric is that it represents *throughput*, (i.e., the amount of work per unit of time). This is in contrast to $EX_{CPU,}$ which represents *latency*, which is an amount of time.

In an ideal single-pipeline situation, when there are no hazards and all memory operations hit in a first-level cache, one instruction completes its execution at every cycle. Thus, both *CPI* and *IPC* are equal to one. We can forget about the overhead of filling the pipeline, for this operation takes only a few cycles, a negligible amount compared to the billions – or trillions – of cycles needed to execute a program. However, when there are hazards – for example, branches, load dependencies, or cache misses (we will review these hazards and the basics of the memory hierarchy in Chapter 2) – then *CPI* will increase (it is easier to reason about *CPI* than about *IPC*, although for the reasons mentioned above we shall often refer to *IPC*). More specifically, assuming that the only disruptions to the ideal pipeline are those that we just listed, *CPI* can be rewritten as

$$CPI = 1 + CPI_{load\ latency} + CPI_{branches} + CPI_{cache} \qquad (4)$$

where CPI_x refers to the extra number of cycles contributed by cause x. This yields the formula for *IPC*:

$$IPC = \frac{1}{1 + \sum_{x} CPI_x} \qquad (4')$$

EXAMPLE 1: Assume that 15% of instructions are loads and that 20% of the instructions following a load depend on its results and are stalled for 1 cycle. All instructions and all loads hit in their respective first-level caches. Assume further that 20% of instructions are branches, with 60% of them being taken and 40% being not taken. The penalty is 2 cycles if the branch is not taken, and it is 3 cycles if the branch is taken. Then, 1 cycle is lost for 20% of the loads, 2 cycles are lost when a conditional branch is not taken, and 3 cycles are lost for taken branches. This can be written as

$$CPI_{load\ latency} = 0.15 \times 0.2 \times 1 = 0.03$$

and

$$CPI_{branches} = 0.2 \times 0.6 \times 3 + 0.2 \times 0.4 \times 2 = 0.52$$

Thus

$$CPI = 1.55 \quad \text{and} \quad IPC = 0.65.$$

A very simple optimization implementation for branches is to assume that they are not taken. There will be no penalty if indeed the branch is not taken, and there will still be a 3 cycle penalty if it is taken. In this case, we have

$$CPI_{branches} = 0.2 \times 0.6 \times 3 = 0.36, \quad \text{yielding } CPI = 1.39 \quad \text{and} \quad IPC = 0.72$$

Of course, it would have been more profitable to try optimizing the branch-taken case, for it occurs more frequently and has a higher penalty. However, its optimization is more difficult to implement. We shall return to the subject of branch prediction in detail in Chapter 4.

Let us assume now that the hit ratio of loads in the first level cache is 95%. On a miss, the penalty is 20 cycles. Then

$$CPI_{cache} = (1 - 0.95) \times 20 = 1$$

yielding (in the case of the branch-not-taken optimization) $CPI = 2.39$ and $IPC = 0.42$.

We could ask whether it is fair to charge both the potential load dependency and the cache miss penalty for the 5% of loads that result in a cache miss. Even in a very simple implementation, we could make sure that on a cache miss the result is forwarded to the execution unit and to the cache simultaneously. Therefore, a better formulation for the load dependency penalty would be $CPI_{load\ latency} = 0.15 \times 0.2 \times 1 \times 0.95 = 0.029$. The overall CPI and IPC are not changed significantly (in these types of performance approximation, results that differ by less than 1% should be taken with a large grain of salt). Although this optimization does not bring any tangible improvement, such small benefits can add up quickly when the engines become more complex, as will be seen in forthcoming chapters, and should not be scorned when there is no cost in implementing them. This example also indicates that the memory hierarchy contributions to CPI could be dominating. We shall treat techniques to reduce the penalty due to the memory hierarchy in Chapter 6.

There exist other metrics related to execution time and, more loosely, to IPC. One of them – *MIPS,* or millions of instructions per second – was quite popular in the 1970s and the 1980s, but has now fallen into desuetude because it is not very representative of the architecture of contemporary microprocessors. *MIPS* is defined as

$$MIPS = \frac{Number\ of\ instructions}{EX_{CPU} \times 10^6} \qquad (5)$$

The main problem with this metric is that all instructions are considered to be equal and neither classes of instructions nor explicit decreases in *IPC* (hazards) are taken into account. This can lead to discrepancies such as a system having a higher *MIPS* rating (*MIPS* is a rate inversely proportional to execution time, so the higher, the better) than another while having a larger execution time because, for example, it executes fewer instructions but some of these instructions have much higher latency (see the exercises at the end of the chapter).

MFLOPS, the number of millions of floating-point operations per second, has a definition similar to that of *MIPS*, except that only floating-point operations are counted in *Number of instructions*. It can be argued that it is a representative measure for systems whose main goal is to execute scientific workloads where most of the computation time is spent in tight loops with many floating-point operations. However, it does suffer from some of the same shortcomings as *MIPS*, mainly compiler-dependent and algorithm-dependent optimizations. Reaching *teraflops*, that is, 1,000 megaflops, was for a long time the goal of supercomputer manufacturers; it was achieved in 1996 by a massively parallel computer (i.e., a system composed of thousands of microprocessors). The next Holy Grail is to achieve *pentaflops* (a million megaflops): it is not the subject of this book.

1.2.2 Performance, Speedup, and Efficiency

Equation (2) is *the* rule that governs *performance*, which can be defined as the reciprocal of the execution time. A smaller execution time implies better performance. The three factors that affect performance are therefore:

- The number of instructions executed. The smaller the number of instructions executed, the smaller the execution time, and therefore the better the performance. Note that reducing the number of instructions executed for a given program and a given instruction set architecture (ISA) is a *compiler*-dependent function.
- *CPI* or *IPC*. The smaller the *CPI* (the larger the *IPC*), the better the performance. It is the goal of computer architects to improve *IPC*, (i.e., this is a question of *microarchitecture* design and implementation).
- The clock cycle time or frequency. The smaller the cycle time (the higher the frequency), the better the performance. Improving the cycle time is *technology*-dependent.

Improvement in any of these three factors will improve performance. However, in practice these factors are not completely independent. For example, minimizing the number of instructions executed can be counterproductive. A case in point is that a multiplication can be sometimes replaced by a small sequence of add-and-shift operations. Though more instructions are executed, the time to execute the add–shift sequence may be smaller than that of the multiply. The apparent contradiction is that in Equation (2) the factor *CPI* was assumed to be the same for all instructions. In fact, in the same way as we introduced CPI_x for showing specific penalties due to cause x, we should make sure that *CPI* reflects the mix of instructions and their execution times. If we have c classes of instructions with frequencies $f_1, f_2, \ldots, f_c$ and with cycles per instruction $CPI_1, CPI_2, \ldots, CPI_c$, then Equation (4) should be rewritten as

$$CPI = \sum_{i=1}^{c} f_i \times CPI_i + \sum_x CPI_x \tag{6}$$

or

$$IPC = \frac{1}{\sum_{i=1}^{c} f_i \times CPI_i + \sum_x CPI_x} \tag{6'}$$

Similarly, *IPC* and clock cycle time are related. With smaller cycle times, fewer operations can be performed in a single stage of the pipeline, and the latter becomes deeper. Hazards now can inflict larger penalties when these are expressed in terms of number of cycles. Thus, *IPC* might decrease with a smaller cycle time. However, recall from Equation (2′) that what is important is decreasing the ratio *cycle time/IPC*.

IPC is a useful metric when assessing enhancements to a given microarchitecture or memory latency hiding technique. We will often make use of it in subsequent chapters. However, using *IPC* as a basis for comparison between systems that have different ISAs is not as satisfactory, because the choice of ISA affects and is affected by all three components of performance listed above.

When comparing the performance of two systems, what we are interested in is their relative performance, not their absolute ones. Thus, we will say that system A has better (worse) performance than system B if the execution time of A – on some set of programs (cf. Section 1.2.3) – is less (more) than the execution time of B:

$$\frac{Performance_A}{Performance_B} = \frac{EX_{CPU-B}}{EX_{CPU-A}} \tag{7}$$

A particularly interesting ratio of performance is *Speedup*, which is the ratio of performance between an enhanced system and its original implementation:

$$Speedup = \frac{Enhanced\ performance}{Original\ performance} = \frac{EX_{CPU-original}}{EX_{CPU-enhanced}} \tag{8}$$

Historically, the speedup was defined for parallel processors. Let T_i denote the time to execute on i processors ($i = 1, 2, \ldots, n$); then the speedup for n processors is

$$Speedup_n = \frac{T_1}{T_n}$$

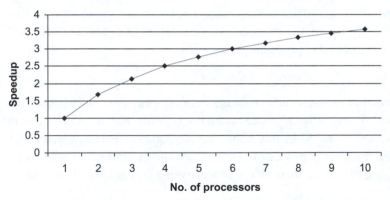

Figure 1.5. Illustration of Amdahl's law. The sequential portion of the program is 20%.

At first glance, we could expect to reach linear speedup, that is, $T_n = T_1/n$, on some programs that exhibit a lot of parallelism. However, even for "embarrassingly parallel" programs, there is always a certain amount of sequential execution and synchronization. This observation has led Amdahl to the formulation of his famous law. As Amdahl states, the execution of a program consists of a *sequential* part of execution time s, followed by a *parallel* part, which, in the case of a single processor, has an execution time p. Then $T_1 = s + p$ and $T_n = s + p/n$, yielding a speedup

$$Speedup_n = \frac{s + p}{s + p/n} \tag{9}$$

If we normalize $T_1 = s + p$ to 1, what *Amdahl's law* says is that at the limit (n very large), the maximum speedup $1/s$ is limited by the fraction of time spent in sequential execution. For example, if 20% of the time were spent in sequential execution, the maximum speedup would be 5.

This is shown in Figure 1.5, where the speedup grows slowly as soon as the number of processors exceeds 6 or 7. For example, to reach a speedup of 4 we would need 16 processors; with 64 processors the speedup would be 4.7; with 128 processors it would be 4.85. Note also that Amdahl's law gives a slightly optimistic result for speedup in that it assumes that all processors can perform parallel work at all times, except during the time where one processor performs sequential execution.

Amdahl's law clearly indicates that linear speedup is an upper bound (it requires $s = 0$). How then could some superlinear speedups be reported? The ambiguity is in what we define as a "processor." If it includes the memory hierarchy, in addition to the computational unit itself, then a problem that does not fit in the cache or the main memory hierarchy of a single processor could fit in the combination of caches or main memories of several processors. If cache-to-cache transfers are faster than cache-to-memory transfers, or if fewer transfers from disks are necessary in the multiprocessor case, then we can very well obtain a superlinear speedup.

Amdahl's law covers more situations than parallel execution. In general terms, it says that optimizing one part of the system used a fraction p of the time can yield at a maximum a speedup of $1/(1-p)$.

While the speedup shows the performance improvement gained by adding resources, the *efficiency* is a metric related to the utilization of these resources and is defined in the case of parallel processing as

$$Efficiency_n = Speedup_n/n \qquad (10)$$

where n is the number of processors. In the same example as above, the efficiency for 4 processors is a little over 0.6; for 16 processors it has become 0.25; for 64 processors it has dwindled down to 0.075. In this book, we shall almost exclusively look at systems with a small number of processors, or a small number of identical arithmetic units within a single CPU. Thus, we shall not concern ourselves much with efficiency.

1.3 Performance Evaluation

Evaluating the performance of computer systems can take several forms. We can (1) rely on queuing theoretical or analytical models, or (2) measure the execution time of a suite of programs, called benchmarks, or (3) simulate, at various levels of detail, the whole system or some of its components. Of course, nothing prevents us from using a combination of these approaches.

Queuing theoretical models are most useful when the system under consideration can be described at a rather abstract level. A typical example would be to assess the throughput of a disk subsystem where the input rate and the service time can be expressed as functions of well-known statistical distributions. The level of detail at which this book covers processors and memory hierarchies does not lend itself to such abstractions; therefore, we do not use queuing systems in this book. However, in some instances, for example to estimate contention on a shared resource, we might make use, or quote the results, of analytical models. In this introductory chapter, though, we focus on the description and use of benchmarks, and on simulation methodology.

1.3.1 Benchmarks

Our intent is to study the design of microprocessor systems that, by essence, are general-purpose machines. Hence, the relative performances of such systems may depend on the workloads that they execute. Consider the following three examples, among many: for a single user, the best system is the one that executes the fastest the programs that he uses most often; for the manager of a Web server farm, the best system might be the one that gives the lowest mean response time, within a tolerable variance, to the customers' queries; for the designer of a database system, the metric of interest might be the number of transactions that can be processed in some unit of time. More generally, a suite of test programs, or *benchmarks*, should be available for each category of users. In our case, we restrict ourselves to benchmarks that are used to evaluate the processor and its memory hierarchy in a computation-intensive fashion (i.e., where the effects of I/O, operating system, and networking are either absent or negligible).

Benchmark Classification

We can distinguish between three kinds of benchmarks:

1. *Synthetic benchmarks*. These are artificial programs that are specially written to measure the performance of specific architectural factors. The first such synthetic benchmark was Whetstone. It contains a very large proportion of floating-point instructions. Over half of the execution time is spent in mathematical library routines. The original benchmark, written 30 years ago in Algol and then in FORTRAN, and since then rewritten in C, is sometimes used as an alternative to *MFLOPS* (with the same drawbacks!). By contrast, Dhrystone, introduced about ten years later, was intended for nonnumeric applications. It contains a high proportion of string-handling operations, no tight loops, and no floating-point operations. It is written in C (a Java version is available). It has been abandoned for contemporary microprocessors but is still used for rating embedded processors – to the dismay of its own inventor, who considers this benchmark obsolete because it does not take into account the realities of modern (embedded) processors. The use of synthetic benchmarks is not recommended, and will not be mentioned further.

2. *Kernels*. Kernels are small portions of real programs that exercise principally a certain feature of the system. Two well-known kernels are the Livermore loops and Linpack. The Livermore loops are a set of 24 FORTRAN DO loops extracted from real programs used at Lawrence Livermore National Laboratory in the mid seventies. They were recoded in C about 10 years ago. They were used mostly for testing the potential vectorization of the loops themselves, whether by hardware or by compilers. Linpack (Linear Algebra Package) is a collection of FORTRAN subroutines that are used to solve dense systems of linear equations. It was designed in the mid 1970s for calibrating vector and parallel processors. Linpack has been replaced by Lapack (same acronym definition as Linpack), which uses block-oriented matrix operations, thus taking into account the improvements in speed and capacity of memory hierarchies present in contemporary (parallel) systems. According to its authors, Lapack is "a library of FORTRAN 77 subroutines for solving the most commonly occurring problems in numerical linear algebra." Similar to kernels are *microbenchmarks*, which are small programs designed to isolate and measure special characteristics of the architecture. Two examples of use of microbenchmarks are the quantification of overhead in synchronization primitives and the effect of memory latency on streaming operations.

3. *Complete programs*. The suite of selected programs depends on the intended use of the benchmarks. The nonprofit organization SPEC (System Performance Evaluation Corporation) was founded in the late 1980s and has for charter to "establish, maintain and endorse a standardized set of relevant benchmarks that can be applied to the newest generation of high-performance computers." Whereas SPEC now publishes benchmarks for a variety of applications (e.g., Web servers, graphic applications, Java client/server), the next section

describes the two suites most relevant to microprocessor vendors and designers, named collectively SPEC CPU*XXXX*, where *XXXX* is a year. Here, mention is made of two other suites that are used often to extend the range of SPEC CPU*XXXX*. One is the Olden suite, which comprises 10 programs with extensive linked list processing and thus offers significant challenges to the exploitation of instruction-level parallelism and to techniques to hide memory latency. The second is a collection of programs for commercial workloads gathered by the TPC (Transaction Processing Council), a nonprofit organization that has the same goals as SPEC. However, the TPC's interest lies in the evaluation of servers whose main functions are to perform transaction processing and database tasks.

SPEC CPU2000 and SPEC CPU2006

The drawbacks of the MIPS metric and the claims attached to it regarding the "fastest" computers led a number of vendors to create the nonprofit organization SPEC. The first SPEC benchmark suite was announced in 1989. It expressed the performance of a system relative to that of a VAX 11/780, which, by definition, had a SPEC rating of 1. It was modified a first time in 1992 and then again in 1995. Since by then the VAX 11/780 was obsolete, this latter version gave performance relative to a newer machine, a 40 MHz Sun SPARCstation without a second-level cache and with 64 megabytes (MB) of memory. The next version, in 2000, modified the SPEC95 suite and supplemented it. An enhanced version SPEC CPU2006 is now available. The normalizing machine for the CPU2000 was a Sun Ultra5_10 SparcStation that ran at 300 MHz and that has a two-level cache hierarchy and 256 MB of memory. This machine had a SPEC rating of 100. In 2006, the processor is similar but the caches and main memory are larger.

The CPU2000 benchmark consists of 12 integer programs SPEC CINT 2000 (11 written in C, and 1 in C++), and 14 floating-point programs SPEC CFP 2000 (11 written in FORTRAN 77 or 90, and 3 in C). They are shown in Table 1.1. The first column gives the name of the program (the numerical prefix serves as an identifier to distinguish versions of programs, some of which are updated versions from SPEC CPU95). The second column gives the source language in which the program is written, and the third a one-liner describing the intent of the program. Three data sets are provided with each program: *test* for a quick functional test, *train* for medium-length runs, and *reference*, which should be the one used for reporting results. With the *reference* data sets the programs run for tens or even hundreds of billions of instructions. Thus on a 3 GHz machine with an *IPC* of 1 (a reasonable figure in modern out-of-order processors; cf. Chapter 3), it would take of the order of 10 seconds to run a 30 billion instruction benchmark and 2 minutes to run one an order of magnitude longer. The procedure to run SPEC benchmarks is well documented and must be adhered to by vendors if they wish to see publication of their results. In particular, since compiler technology can play a big role in reducing execution time (recall Equation (2)), compiler optimizations specific to a single

Table 1.1. The SPEC CPU2000 12 integer benchmarks (CINT2000) and
the 14 floating-point benchmarks (CFP2000)

Benchmark	Language	Description
164.gzip	C	Compression
175.vpr	C	FPGA circuit placement and routing
176.gcc	C	C programming language compiler
181.mcf	C	Combinatorial optimization
186.crafty	C	Game playing: chess
197.parser	C	Word processing
252.eon	C++	Computer visualization
253.perlbmk	C	PERL programming language
254.gap	C	Group theory, interpreter
255.vortex	C	Object-oriented database
256.bzip2	C	Compression
300.twolf	C	Place and route simulator
168.wupwise	F77	Physics: quantum chromodynamics
171.swim	F77	Shallow-water modeling
172.mgrid	F77	Multi-grid Solver
173.applu	F77	Parabolic/elliptic PDEs
177.mesa	C	3-D graphics library
178.galgel	F90	Computational fluid dynamics
179.art	C	Image recognition, neural networks
183.equake	F90	Seismic wave propagation simulation
187.facerec	F90	Image processing: face recognition
188.ammp	C	Computational chemistry
189.lucas	F90	Number theory: primality testing
191.fma3d	F90	Finite element crash simulation
200.sixtrack	F77	High-energy nuclear physics: accelerator design
301.apsi	F77	Meteorology: pollutant distribution

program in the suite are disallowed. The programs for SPEC CPU2006 are shown
in Table 1.2. About half of the integer programs are the same as those in SPEC
CPU2000. Note, however, that there are more C++ programs, both in the integer
and in the floating-point suites.

We could ask ourselves whether the SPEC CPU2000 or CPU2006 benchmarks
are representative of the use of microprocessors. For example, in SPEC CINT 2000
there is only one program mildly representative of desktop applications (*parser*),
and it is not present any longer in 2006. Similarly, there is only one interpreter program (*perl*). Some efforts have been made to include C++ programs in the 2006
version, but there is no program written in Java. However, studies of desktop applications and of interpreters have shown that their instruction mixes and the way they
exercise the lower levels of the memory hierarchy are pretty similar to what is happening with the integer programs represented in SPEC benchmarks. On the other
hand, commercial workloads to be run on servers, consisting potentially of several
processors, attach more importance to the interactions with the operating system
and I/O devices. Comparison with the SPEC suite is not meaningful, and for this

Table 1.2. The SPEC CPU2006 12 integer benchmarks and 17 floating-point benchmarks

Benchmark	Language	Description
400.perlbench	C	PERL programming language
401.bzip2	C	Compression
403.gcc	C	C compiler
429.mcf	C	Combinatorial optimization
445.gobmk	C	Artificial intelligence: go
456.hmmer	C	Search gene sequence
458.sjeng	C	Artificial intelligence: chess
462.libquantum	C	Physics: quantum computing
464.h264ref	C	Video compression
471.omnetpp	C++	Discrete-event simulation
473.astar	C++	Path-finding algorithms
483.xalancbmk	C++	XML processing
410.bwaves	FORTRAN	Fluid dynamics
416.gamess	FORTRAN	Quantum chemistry
423.milc	C	Physics: quantum chromodynamics
434.zeusmp	FORTRAN	Physics: computation fluid dynamics
435.gromacs	C, FORTRAN	Biochemistry, molecular dynamics
436.cactusADM	C, FORTRAN	Physics: general relativity
437.leslie3D	FORTRAN	Fluid dynamics
444.namd	C++	Biology, molecular dynamics
447.dealII	C++	Finite element analysis
450.soplex	C++	Linear programming, optimization
453.povray	C++	Image ray tracing
454.calculix	C, FORTRAN	Structural mechanics
459.GemsFDTD	FORTRAN	Computational electromagnetics
465.tonto	FORTRAN	Quantum chemistry
470.lbm	C	Fluid dynamics
481.wrf	C, FORTRAN	Weather prediction
482.sphinx3	C	Speech recognition

reason TPC and SPEC themselves have developed specific benchmarks for these types of applications.

Reporting Benchmarking Results

Several ways of reporting measurements of benchmark execution times have been advocated. The easiest way, and maybe the most significant way, is to simply add the execution times of the programs, or, equivalently, report their *arithmetic mean*. That is, if T_i is the time to execute the ith of n programs, the mean execution time is

$$T = \frac{1}{n} \sum_i T_i \tag{11}$$

If, instead of measuring execution times, we were reporting on a series of experiments measuring rates, such as *IPC*, we would use the *harmonic mean*. In this case,

Equation (11) would become

$$IPC = \frac{n}{\sum_i \frac{1}{IPC_i}} \tag{11'}$$

Because in some instances some programs are more important than others, we can weight a program according to its probable use. In contrast, because some programs execute longer than others, we might want to adjust their contributions so that each of them has equal weight in the final arithmetic mean. With a weight w_i associated with the ith program, Equation (11) becomes the *weighted arithmetic mean* (of course, we can modify Equation (11') similarly for a *weighted harmonic mean*):

$$T_w = \frac{1}{n} \sum_i T_i \times w_i \tag{12}$$

As mentioned earlier, SPEC does not use a (weighted) arithmetic mean of execution times, but instead asks that results of the benchmarks runs be normalized to that of a reference machine. Then the *geometric mean* of the ratios of the execution time of the runs – or, more precisely, of the median of an odd number of runs (greater than three) – to the execution time of the same program on the reference machine is the metric that gives the SPEC rating (except that the reference machine has a rating of 100). Note that all programs are given the same weight, so that the geometric mean is

$$G = \sqrt[n]{\prod_i \frac{T_i}{S_i}} \tag{13}$$

where T_i is the execution time for the ith program on the machine to be rated, and S_i the corresponding time on the reference machine. We could easily extend the definition of the geometric mean to that of a weighted geometric mean.

The geometric mean of normalized execution times has a nice property, namely, performance relationships between two machines are independent of the normalizing machine. This can easily be derived by noticing that Equation (13) can be rewritten as

$$G = \frac{\sqrt[n]{\prod_i T_i}}{\sqrt[n]{\prod_i S_i}} \tag{13}$$

so that the ratio between the geometric means G_1 and G_2 of runs on two machines is independent of the normalizing factor. Practically, what this means is that if comparisons were made between two machines using a VAX 11/780 as a normalizing factor, these experiments would not have to be rerun if the normalizing factor had become a Sun SPARCstation.

Alas, the geometric mean of normalized execution times also has a significant drawback: it can give the wrong result. This is shown in Table 1.3, where machine M1 executes programs P1 and P2 each in 5 (normalized) units of time, for a total

Table 1.3. *Example of the drawback of the geometric mean*

	Normalized time on reference machine	Normalized time on M1	Normalized time on M2
Program P1	1	5	10
Program P2	1	5	2
Arithmetic mean	1	5	6
Geometric mean	1	5	4.5

of 10, and machine M2 executes them in 10 and 2 units, respectively, for a total of 12. However, the normalized geometric mean is higher for M1 (5) than for M2 (4.5).

This example shows how benchmarks can be manipulated. If the time to execute P2 on M2 had been 3 units, the geometric mean for M2 would have been greater than the one for M1, and the ratings given by the arithmetic and geometric means would have been consistent. By "optimizing" the short program by one unit of time, we have exposed the anomalous behavior of the geometric mean. Fortunately, the opportunity for such optimizations does not exist in the SPEC 2000 and 2006 benchmarks, because the number of instructions executed in each program is of the same order of magnitude. Nonetheless, the only faithful metric for execution times is the (weighted) arithmetic mean, and for rates it is the (weighted) harmonic mean.

1.3.2 Performance Simulators

Measuring the execution time of programs on existing machines is easy, especially if the precision that is desired is of the order of milliseconds. In this case, it is sufficient to call on library routines to read the internal clock of the machine. If more detail is required, such as knowledge of *CPI* or *IPC,* programmable counters available in most current microprocessors can be set up to record the total number of cycles used during execution as well as the number of instructions that have been committed.[1] Since the cycle time is known, the *IPC* can then be deduced (recall Equation (3″)). However, when the machine is in the design stage, or when we want to assess the performance of potential enhancements of an existing machine, we need to have recourse to simulation.

Simulation can be used during design for functional and behavioral correctness verification and for performance assessment. Classes of simulators exist for the various levels of design. Without going into too much detail, we can distinguish between:

- Circuit design: The key words here would be wires, gates, CMOS, and so on. This is the domain of electrical engineers, with Spice being the simulator of choice. This topic is outside the scope of the book.

---

[1] Committed instructions are those that ultimately modify the processor state. The distinction between committed and fetched instructions will become apparent when we cover speculative schemes such as branch prediction.

- Logical design: This is the level at which gates and wires are put together to build combinational circuits such as ALUs or PLAs and at which stable storage primitives such as flip-flops and latches are combined to implement registers and hard-wired control. It is assumed that the readers know how to build these basic blocks. Hardware description languages (HDLs) such as Verilog and VHDL are used for simulation as well as for design and synthesis. Newer languages such as System C, which is closer to the C–C++ class of procedural languages, are gaining in popularity.
- Register transfer level (RTL): This is the microarchitecture level, where the data flow between the basic blocks and the setting of control lines are described. It is the level to which we will direct most of our attention in this book. HDLs can also be used at this level.
- Processor and memory hierarchy description: The definition of the ISA belongs to this level, and, naturally, it will also be a focus in subsequent chapters.
- System issues: I/O, multithreading, and multiprocessing are to be included at this level. Although the system level is not at the center of our interests here, we shall deal with granularities of parallelism above that of the ISA level.

From the performance viewpoint, the last three levels are the ones that are most often targeted. Depending on the desired results, simulations can be performed cycle by cycle (the usual case), or instruction by instruction (or memory reference by memory reference). Simulators are written in a high-level language such as C or C++, because such languages are more portable and better known than HDLs, and synthesis capabilities are not required. Simulators come in two flavors: *trace-driven simulators* and *execution-driven simulators*. Both share the same back end, (i.e., a cycle-based simulation of the events that occur in the microarchitecture). The difference comes in what is fed to the back end. In the case of trace-driven simulation the input is a trace (i.e., a sequence of the instructions that have been executed by the program). In the execution-driven case, the input mechanism and the performance simulator are closely intertwined: The input mechanism is a functional simulator (i.e., a program interpreter). After each instruction has been recognized, and its results computed, it is passed on to the performance simulator.

Trace-driven simulation requires trace collection, which is the determination and storing of the instruction sequences. Hardware monitors can be used to that effect, but there are limitations due to their restricted storage capacities and to the difficulties of inserting probes at the right places in the currently very integrated chips. Software traces can be collected by inserting extra instructions in the workload so that the sequence of instructions being executed can be recorded. Both processes are slow: hardware collection because of the need for frequently emptying buffers in safe storage, and software tracing because of the extra instructions being executed, as well as the buffering process. The great advantage of traces is that the slow process of recording the traces needs to be done only once and the same trace can be used for all further simulations of the same workload. The disadvantages are that the trace requires extensive storage space (although this can be mitigated

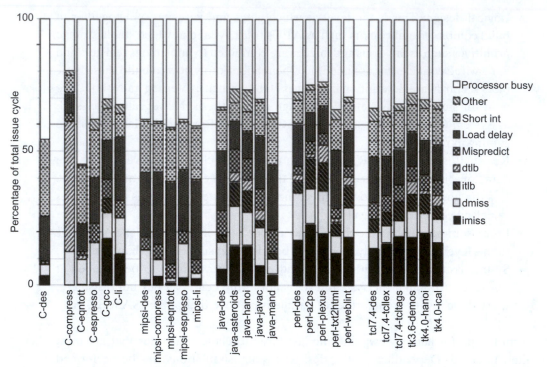

Figure 1.6. Typical output of an execution-driven simulator (from Romer et al., ASPLOS 1996).

somewhat by trace reduction techniques) and that the trace may not be a faithful image of all the actions that were performed at the microarchitecture level. Prevalent among those are the actions that pertain to the wrongly predicted speculative paths, for the wrongly predicted instructions will not appear in the trace.

In execution-driven simulation, the internal workings of the processor can be reproduced faithfully. Since there is a close link with the functional simulator that "computes" results, intermediate or temporary data can be generated. This property permits the capability to simulate, for example, the use of resources during the execution of mispredicted speculative paths or the timing of cache line prefetches. Moreover, the study of power consumption, part of which depends on the amount of bit switching during execution, can be added on to the performance simulation. A typical output of an execution-driven simulation is shown in Figure 1.6. Each bar corresponds to the simulation of a particular program. In this example, one can see the proportion of cycles for which the processor is busy, the impact of cache misses, the proportion of cycles spent on the wrong path, and so on.

Execution-driven simulators, and to a lesser extent trace-driven simulators, share two drawbacks. First, real-time events such as those triggered by I/O cannot be simulated directly. A possible option is to insert markers in the traces (not too difficult) or to add such events in a trace-directed manner to the functional simulation. Second – and this is more detrimental – execution-driven simulations, and again to a lesser extent trace-driven simulations, take an inordinate amount of CPU execution time. A ratio of three to four orders of magnitude of the CPU time required for simulation to the CPU time of execution in the normal setting is to be expected, depending on the desired level of detail. For example, the most popular simulator used in academic circles is SimpleScalar, originally developed at the University of Wisconsin. According to its authors, SimpleScalar can simulate 350,000 instructions per second on a 1.7 GHz Pentium 4. If we assume that the simulator and the program simulated have *IPC*s that are both close to 1, then the slowdown of the simulator compared to native execution on the 1.7 GHz Pentium is indeed between 3 and 4 orders of magnitude ($1.7 \times 10^9 / 0.35 \times 10^6$) Thus, if we follow our previous estimate of 10 seconds to 2 minutes to execute one of the SPEC benchmarks on a real machine, then it would take between 3 minutes and 5 hours to simulate it in its entirety, depending on the length of the benchmark and the speed of the simulator. Because, to be complete, we want to look at all the components of the benchmarks, and because in general we want to look at several design options, we can see that it might take of the order of several days or even years of CPU time to get results.

Several methods have been proposed to scale down the simulation time. A first approach would be to simulate only a contiguous portion of the program, say the first one billion instructions. Because most programs spend a large part of the beginning of their execution initializing data structures and performing setup tasks, this naive shortcut has a large probability of yielding architectural metrics that are not representative of the execution of the full program.

A potential improvement would be to *fast-forward* the first billion instructions (i.e., just simulate enough of the initial part of the program to warm up data structures such as caches and branch predictors). Then the next billion instructions would be simulated in detail, and statistics would be gathered. Although this method removes the drawback linked to the initialization, it is flawed in the same way as the first one, for only one contiguous portion of the program is simulated and there is no guarantee that it is representative of the whole execution.

The next improvement then would be to sample intervals – say 10 intervals of 100 million instructions each – at various points of the execution. Though certainly more of the program execution would then be covered, it is again not possible to be assured that it is representative of the full execution.

A better way is to detect similar *phases* in the program, (i.e., sequences of consecutive instructions that have similar behavior independent of their relative time positioning). The difficulty, of course, is to define what is meant by similar. The similarity measure must be independent of the architectural factors that will be measured; otherwise, the phase detection would be biased. It is therefore better to rely only on the execution paths. For the purpose of subsequent simulations, the phase detection can be performed offline, that is, with a (fast) preprocessing of the whole program. Each interval of, say, 100 million instructions can be given a signature that depends only on the instructions that it executes. For example, the signature could be the frequency of execution of each basic block[2] in the program. Then signatures

---

[2] A program basic block is a sequence of consecutive instructions with the first instruction being reached via a branch and the last instruction being a branch and no instructions in between being branches.

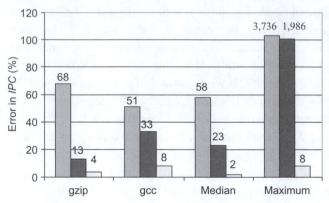

Figure 1.7. Simulation accuracy using the first one billion instructions (left bar), fast forwarding (medium bar), and phase selection (right bar) (data from Sherwood et al., *IEEE Micro*, Nov. 2003).

of intervals are compared, and intervals can be grouped according to some clustering algorithm. By giving a bound on the number of clusters, we can limit the number of phases that need to be simulated. For example, if this bound is 10, we will detect at most 10 phases. We can then simulate intervals within each phase. This method has been successfully applied to the SPEC CPU2000 suite with excellent results. Figure 1.7 (median results) shows that simulating one billion instructions from the start leads to errors in *IPC* that are over 58% in half of the cases (with a maximum error of 3 orders of magnitude). Fast forwarding gives results that are improved by a factor of 2 to 3 but are still far from being close, especially in the worst case. When phases are used, with the same number of simulated instructions, the errors become very small even in the worst case.

An alternative approach is to handcraft smaller input sets and run the benchmark programs to completion. The runs with the reduced data sets should be statistically equivalent to those with the longer runs in terms of the number of times each function is called and the mix of instructions. The advantage of this method is that there is no sampling, whereas in the phase method there is a potential source of error in that only samples are simulated and the warm-up of some structures such as caches might induce some error. The drawbacks of the reduced-data-set method are that it cannot be automated (i.e., each program and data set constitute a specific case) and that it is quite difficult to find good fits.

1.4 Summary

Microprocessors are based on the von Neumann model of a stored program computer. Over more than three decades, the contents of a single chip have grown from a simple CPU with one ALU to multiple complex processors with their own cache hierarchies. Within each processor instructions are pipelined, and several instructions can occupy the same stage of the pipe simultaneously.

Technological advances have produced exponential increases in speed and in the amount of logic that can be put on a chip. Frequencies have been capped since the beginning of the twenty-first century, mostly because of heating problems due to power dissipation. Moore's law, which predicts that the number of transistors on a chip will double every two years, is still valid and will remain so until at least 2025. The speed limitations and Moore's law are two of the main factors that have led to the emergence of chip multiprocessors.

The performance of a microprocessor system and of its main memory hierarchy is inversely proportional to the execution time, which is given by the canonical expression

$$EX_{CPU} = Number\ of\ instructions \times CPI \times cycle\ time$$

where *CPI* is the number of cycles per instruction. *CPI*, or its reciprocal *IPC* (the number of instructions per cycle), is the main metric of interest for computer architects, whose goal is to decrease *CPI* (increase *IPC*).

The performance of computer systems is measured with the use of benchmarks. The SPEC CPU benchmarks suites are widely used for microprocessors. Execution-driven simulators are the norm when components of *CPI* need to be assessed. Execution-driven simulation is a (computer-)time-consuming process that can be reduced by judicious selection of representative samples in the benchmarks.

1.5 Further Reading and Bibliographical Notes

Advances in technology are posted frequently on the Web. Figure 1.2 is abstracted from several sources on the Web, such as Wikipedia and Intel sites.

Moore's law was formulated in 1965 by Gordon Moore in a 4-page paper [M65] entitled "Cramming More Components onto Integrated Circuits." Moore went on to found Intel with Bob Noyce in 1968. Their first product was a memory chip. In 1971, they decided that memory was not the growth business they were looking for, and they developed the first microprocessor, the 4004. The rest is history. Figure 1.3 or an equivalent can be seen on many Web sites (just search for "Moore's law graph"). Figure 1.4 comes from a presentation by Fred Pollack at Micro32 (http://www.lri.fr/~de/lowpower.pdf).

Good introductions to performance metrics can be found in the books of Hennessy and Patterson [HP07, PH04] (Chapter 2 in the 2004 undergraduate text, Chapter 1 in the 2007 graduate one). Amdahl's law [A67] was first formulated during a panel at the Spring Joint Computer Conference in 1967. Gene Amdahl was the advocate for the (fast) single-processor approach, while other panelists touted various forms of parallelism. Culler, Singh, and Gupta [CSG99] discuss superlinear speedup and scaling in general (Chapter 4). When to use means or rates, and some ill-conceived ideas about the geometric mean as applied to benchmark results, were first discussed by James Smith [S88]. A follow-up on how to apply weights to arithmetic and harmonic means is given by Lizy John [J04] (cf. Exercise 14). Citron et al.

[CHG06] argue that in most cases the choice of what mean to use is of little consequence.

All the benchmarks listed in Section 1.3.1 are available on the Web. Information on many currently used benchmarks can be found at http://www.netlib.org/benchmark/. The original Whetstone benchmark was written in Algol (1976) by Curnow and Wichman [CW76], and then in FORTRAN for greater dissemination and for double-precision floating-point experiments. It was rewritten in C ten years later. Weicker [W84] developed Dhrystone in 1984. The first set of 14 Livermore loops was introduced in the early 1970s. A new set of 24 FORTRAN loops became available in the early 1980s (see the paper by McMahon [M88]). The Linpack benchmark was created under Jack Dongarra's leadership in 1979 [DBMS79]. It has been used to maintain a list of the 500 most powerful computer systems, the *Top 500*. A retrospective on its use can be found in a paper by Dongarra et al. [DLP03].

A wealth of information on the SPEC benchmarks, including the benchmarks themselves, how to obtain them, and how to use them, can be found at http://www.specbench.org/. A description of each benchmark in the 2006 CPU suite can be found in Henning [H06]. The TPC council's home page is at http://www.tpc.org/.

Many research papers have charts of the form given in Figure 1.6. The latter is extracted from Romer et al. [RLVWWBBL96]. A special issue of *IEEE Computer Magazine* (February 2002) reports on four different execution-driven simulators, including SimpleScalar [ALE02], the one most often used in academia. Information on Superscalar (tutorials, how to download it, etc.) is on the WWW at http://www.simplescalar.com/. Sherwood et al. [SPHSC03] describe phase selection. How to craft smaller input sets for SPEC CPU2000 was investigated at the University of Minnesota [KL02] (see the MinneSPEC project: http://www.arctic.umn.edu/minnespec/index.shtml).

EXERCISES

1. (Section 1.1) Draw a chart similar to the one in Figure 1.2 indicating the maximum number of transistors put on an Intel Pentium chip in a given year. Start your chart in 1993 and end it in the current year. Does the trend follow Moore's law?

2. (Section 1.2.1) Of the three factors in Eq. (2) ($EX_{CPU} = Number\ of\ instructions \times CPI \times cycle\ time$), which is most influenced by:

   (a) The technology

   (b) The compiler

   (c) The computer architect

3. (Section 1.2.1) In Example 1 of Section 1.2.1, we assumed that we had a "short" pipeline, because the branch misprediction cost was only 3 cycles in the case of a mispredicted branch taken. As we shall see, modern microprocessors have penalties that may be as large as 15 or 20 cycles. Keeping all other parameters the same as in the example and assuming that a branch-not-taken strategy has been implemented, plot *CPI* vs. branch misprediction cost when the latter varies between 3 and

20 cycles. Do your computations argue for sophisticated branch predictors when the pipelines become "deeper"?

4. (Section 1.2.1) In Example 1 of Section 1.2.1, we assumed that the cache miss penalty was 20 cycles. With modern processors running at a frequency of 1 to 3 GHz, the cache miss penalty can reach several hundred cycles (we will see how this can be somewhat mitigated by a cache hierarchy). Keeping all other parameters the same as in the example, plot *CPI* vs. cache miss penalty cost when the latter varies between 20 and 500 cycles (choose appropriate intervals). Do your computations argue for the threat of a "memory wall" whereby loading instructions and data could potentially dominate the execution time?

5. (Section 1.2.1) When running an integer benchmark on a RISC machine, the average instruction mix was as follows:

Instructions	Average Frequency
Load	26%
Store	9%
Arithmetic	14%
Compare	13%
Cond. branch	16%
Uncond. branch	1%
Call/returns	2%
Shift	4%
Logical	9%
Misc.	6%

The following measurements of average *CPI* for individual instruction categories were made:

Instruction type	Average CPI (clock cycles)
All ALU instructions	1
Load–store	1.4
Conditional branches:	
Taken	2.0
Not taken	1.5
Jumps	1.2

Assume that 60% of the conditional branches are taken and that all instructions in the Misc. category are ALU instructions. What are the *CPI* and *IPC* of the benchmark on this RISC machine?

6. (Section 1.2.1) Give an equation relating the performance measure *MIPS*, *IPC*, and the cycle time c. If from one generation of processors to the next c decreases by 50%, how should the value of *IPC* change so that *MIPS* is doubled? In view of the results of Exercises 3 and 4, do you think this is possible?

7. (Section 1.2.1) Machine M runs at 3 GHz. When running program P, its $CPI =$ 1.5.

    (a) How many instructions will be executed during 1 second while running program P?

    (b) While running program P, the mouse has to be polled 30 times per second. The polling routine requires executing 200 instructions with a CPI of 2. What is the overhead, that is, the fraction of time used in polling the mouse? Is it significant?

8. (Section 1.2.1) Consider two implementations M1 and M2 of the same ISA. We are interested in the performances of two programs P1 and P2, which have the following instruction mixes:

Operations	P1	P2
Load/store	40%	50%
ALU	50%	20%
Branches	10%	30%

The CPIs for each machine are:

Operations	M1	M2
Load–store	2	2
ALU	1	2
Branches	3	2

    (a) Assume that the clock rate of M1 is 2 GHz. What should be the clock rate of M2 so that both machines have the same execution time for P1?

    (b) Assume now that both machines have the same clock rate and that P1 and P2 execute the same number of instructions. Which machine is faster for a workload consisting of equal runs of P1 and P2?

    (c) Find a workload (using only P1 and P2) that makes M1 and M2 have the same performance when they have the same clock rate.

9. (Section 1.2.1) A processor M-5 has a five-stage pipeline and a clock cycle time of 10 ns. A newer implementation of the same instruction set in a processor M-7 uses a seven-stage pipeline and a cycle time of 7.5 ns.

    (a) Define the maximum throughput of a pipeline. Which of M-5 and M-7 has better maximum throughput?

    (b) Consider now a loop of five instructions (four arithmetic instructions and a branch to the beginning of the loop). There is a dependency between two consecutive arithmetic instructions in the loop. This dependency induces a 1 cycle stall in M-5 and a 2 cycle stall in M-7. The branch induces a 2 cycle stall on M-5 and a 4 cycle stall on M-7. Which processor executes the loop faster in "steady state" (i.e., you don't have to consider the time it takes to start up the pipeline in the first iteration and/or drain it in the last iteration)?

(c) Assume now that the loop is unrolled once, that is, instead of n iterations of four instructions and a branch, we have now $n/2$ iterations of eight instructions and a branch. Instead of one data dependency per loop, we now have two data dependencies per unrolled loop. Which processor executes the unrolled loop faster?

10. (Section 1.2.1) [PH04] Construct an example whereby two systems have the same *MIPS* rating but one of them has an EX_{CPU} smaller than the other one.

11. (Section 1.2.2) Illustrate Amdahl's law in terms of speedup vs. sequential portion of program by showing the speedup for $N = 8$ processors when the sequential portion of the program grows from 1% to 25%.

12. (Section 1.2.2 – Amdahl's law) With sequential execution occurring 15% of the time:

(a) What is the maximum speedup with an infinite number of processors?
(b) How many processors are required to be within 20% of the maximum speedup?
(c) How many processors are required to be within 2% of the maximum speedup?

13. (Section 1.3.1) For each of the metrics specified, indicate which of the (weighted) arithmetic, harmonic, or geometric mean you would use:

(a) An experiment where you have run the SPEC CPU2006 integer benchmark on your laptop and noted the execution times of each program in the suite.
(b) Same experiment as in (a), but now you also run the suite on a computer in your lab at the University. How do you compare the speeds of the two machines?
(c) An experiment where you have simulated 100 million instructions in each of 12 programs and measured *CPI* for each simulation.
(d) Same experiment as in (c), but now you report in terms of *IPC*.

14. (Section 1.3.10) [J04] It can be shown that weighted arithmetic mean (WAM) and weighted harmonic mean (WHM) can lead to the same results if correct weights are applied. Consider the *MIPS* measure where $MIPS_i = I_i/t_i$ (I_i is the number of instructions for program i in millions, and t_i is the execution time Ex_i times 10^6). Consider a benchmark of n programs with instructions counts I_i and execution times $t_i, i = 1, \ldots, n$. Let N be the total number of instructions, and T the total execution time for all programs.

(a) Show that if the weights for the arithmetic mean are t_i/T and those for the harmonic mean are I_i/N, then the WAM and WHM of the $MIPS_i$ are the same.
(b) Show that for the *CPI* metric a WAM weighted with I_i and a WHM weighted with c_i, the number of cycles simulated in each program, will yield the same result.
(c) How would you weigh the WAM and the WHM if you were measuring *IPC* rather than *CPI*?

(d) Show that for the speedup, a WAM weighted with execution time ratios in the enhanced system and a WHM weighted with execution time ratios in the base system will yield the same result.

(e) In general, given a metric *A/B* how should the arithmetic mean be weighted in order to give the correct result? How should the harmonic mean be weighted?

REFERENCES

[A67] G. Amdahl, "Validity of the Single Processor Approach to Achieving Large Scale Computing Capabilities," *Proc. AFIPS SJCC*, 30, Apr. 1967, 483–485

[ALE02] T. Austin, E. Larson, and D. Ernst, "SimpleScalar: An Infrastructure for Computer System Modeling," *IEEE Computer*, 35, 2, Feb. 2002, 59–67

[CW76] H. Curnow and B. Wichman, "Synthetic Benchmark," *Computer Journal*, 19, 1, Feb. 1976

[CHG06] D. Citron, A. Hurani, and A. Gnadrey, "The Harmonic or Geometric Mean: Does it Really Matter," *Computer Architecture News*, 34, 6, Sep. 2006, 19–26

[CSG99] D. Culler and J. P. Singh with A. Gupta, *Parallel Computer Architecture: A Hardware/Software Approach*, Morgan Kaufman Publishers, San Francisco, 1999

[DBMS79] J. Dongarra, J. Bunch, C. Moler, and G. Stewart, *LINPACK User's Guide*, SIAM, Philadelphia, 1979

[DLP03] J. Dongarra, P. Luszczek, and A. Petitet, "The LINPACK Benchmark: Past, Present, and Future," *Concurrency and Computation: Practice and Experience*, 15, 2003, 1–18

[H06] J. Henning, Ed., "SPEC CPU2006 Benchmark Descriptions," *Computer Architecture News*, 36, 4, Sep. 2006, 1–17

[HP07] J. Hennessy and D. Patterson, *Computer Architecture: A Quantitative Approach*, Fourth Edition, Elsevier Inc., San Francisco, 2007

[J04] L. John, "More on Finding a Single Number to Indicate Overall Performance of a Benchmark Suite," *Computer Architecture News*, 32, 1, Mar. 2004, 3–8

[KL02] A. KleinOsowski and D. Lilja, "MinneSPEC: A New SPEC Benchmark Workload for Simulation-Based Computer Architecture Research," *Computer Architecture Letters*, 1, Jun. 2002

[M65] G. Moore, "Cramming More Components onto Integrated Circuits," *Electronics*, 38, 8, Apr. 1965

[M88] F. H. McMahon, "The Livermore Fortran Kernels Test of the Numerical Performance Range," in J. L. Martin, Ed., *Performance Evaluation of Supercomputers*, Elsevier Science B.V., North-Holland, Amsterdam, 1988, 143–186

[PH04] D. Patterson and J. Hennessy, *Computer Organization & Design: The Hardware/Software Interface*, Third Edition, Morgan Kaufman Publishers, San Francisco, 2004

[RLVWWBBL96] T. Romer, D. Lee, G. Volker, A. Wolman, W. Wong, J.-L. Baer, B. Bershad, and H. Levy, "The Structure and Performance of Interpreters," *Proc. 7th Int. Conf. on Architectural Support for Programming Languages and Operating Systems*, Oct. 1996, 150–159

[S88] J. Smith, "Characterizing Computer Performance with a Single Number," *Communications of the ACM*, 31, 10, Oct. 1988, 1201–1206

[SPHSC03] T. Sherwood, E. Perelman, G. Hamerly, S. Sair, and B. Calder, "Discovering and Exploiting Program Phases," *IEEE Micro*, 23, 6, Nov.–Dec. 2003, 84–93

[W84] R. Weicker, "Dhrystone: A Synthetic Systems Programming Benchmark," *Communications of the ACM*, 27, Oct. 1984, 1013–1030

2 The Basics

This chapter reviews features that are found in all modern microprocessors: (i) instruction pipelining and (ii) a main memory hierarchy with caches, including the virtual-to-physical memory translation. It does not dwell on many details – that is what subsequent chapters will do. It provides solely a basis on which we can build later on.

2.1 Pipelining

Consider the steps required to execute an arithmetic instruction in the von Neumann machine model, namely:

1. Fetch the (next) instruction (the one at the address given by the program counter).
2. Decode it.
3. Execute it.
4. Store the result and increment the program counter.

In the case of a load or a store instruction, step 3 becomes two steps: calculate a memory address, and activate the memory for a read or for a write. In the latter case, no subsequent storing is needed. In the case of a branch, step 3 sets the program counter to point to the next instruction, and step 4 is voided.

Early on in the design of processors, it was recognized that complete sequentiality between the executions of instructions was often too restrictive and that parallel execution was possible. One of the first forms of parallelism that was investigated was the overlap of the mentioned steps between consecutive instructions. This led to what is now called *pipelining*.[1]

---

[1] In early computer architecture texts, the terms *overlap* and *look-ahead* were often used instead of *pipelining*, which was used for the pipelining of functional units (cf. Section 2.1.6).

2.1.1 The Pipelining Process

In concept, pipelining is similar to an assembly line process. Jobs A, B, and so on, are split into n sequential subjobs $A_1, A_2, \ldots, A_n$ ($B_1, B_2, \ldots, B_n$, etc.) with each A_i (B_i, etc.) taking approximately the same amount of processing time. Each subjob is processed by a different station, or equivalently the job passes through a series of *stages*, where each stage processes a different A_i. Subjobs of different jobs overlap in their execution: when subjob A_1 of job A is finished in stage 1, subjob A_2 will start executing in stage 2 while subjob B_1 of job B will start executing in stage 1. If t_i is the time to process A_i and $t_M = \max_i t_i$, then in steady state one job completes every t_M. Throughput (the number of instructions executed per unit time) is therefore enhanced. On the other hand, the latency (total execution time) of a given job, say L_A for A, becomes

$$L_A = nt_M, \quad \text{which may be greater than} \sum_{i=1}^{n} t_i.$$

Before applying the pipelining concept to the instruction execution cycle, let us look at a real-life situation. Although there won't be a complete correspondence between this example and pipelining as implemented in contemporary processors, it will allow us to see the advantages and some potential difficulties brought forth by pipelining.

Assume that you have had some friends over for dinner and now it's time to clean up. The first solution would be for you to do all the work: bringing the dishes to the sink, scraping them, washing them, drying them, and putting them back where they belong. Each of these five steps takes the same order of magnitude of time, say 30 seconds, but bringing the dishes is slightly faster (20 seconds) and storing them slightly slower (40 seconds). The time to clean one dish (the latency) is therefore 150 seconds. If there are 4 dishes per guest and 8 guests, the total cleanup time is $150 \times 4 \times 8 = 4800$ seconds, or 1 hour and 20 minutes. The throughput is 1 dish per 150 seconds. Now, if you enlist four of your guests to help you and, among the five of you, you distribute the tasks so that one person brings the dishes, one by one, to the second, who scrapes them and who in turn passes them, still one by one, to the washer, and so on to the dryer and finally to the person who stores them (you, because you know where they belong). Now the latency is that of the longest stage (storing) multiplied by the number of stages, or $40 \times 5 = 200$ seconds. However, the throughput is 1 dish per longest stage time, or 1 dish per 40 seconds. The total execution time is $40 \times 8 \times 4 + 4 \times 40 = 1360$ seconds, or a little less than 23 minutes. This is an appreciable savings of time.

Without stretching the analogy too far, this example highlights the following points about pipelining:

- In order to be effective, the pipeline must be *balanced*, that is, all stages must take approximately the same time. It makes no sense to optimize a stage whose processing time is not the longest. For example, if drying took 25 seconds instead of 30, this would not change the overall cleanup time.

- A job must pass through all stages, and the order is the same for all jobs. Even if a dish does not need scraping, it must pass through that stage (one of your friends will be idle during that time).
- *Buffering* (holding a dish in its current partially processed state) between stages is required, because not all stages take exactly the same time.
- Each stage must have all the resources it needs allocated to it. For example, if you have only one brush and it is needed some of the time, by both the scraper and the washer there will be some stalling in the pipeline. This situation is a form of (structural) *hazard*.
- The pipeline may be disrupted by some internal event (e.g., someone drops a dish and it breaks) or some external event (one of your coworkers is called on the phone and has to leave her station). In these cases of *exception* or *interrupt*, the pipeline must be flushed and the state of the process must be saved so that when the exception or interrupt is removed, the operation can start anew in a consistent state.

Other forms of hazards exist in processor pipelines that do not fit well in our example: they are *data hazards* due to dependencies between instructions and *control hazards* caused by transfers of control (branches, function calls). We shall return to these shortly.

2.1.2 A Basic Five-stage Instruction Execution Pipeline

Our presentation of the instruction execution pipeline will use a RISC processor as the underlying execution engine. The processor in question consists of a set of registers (the register file), a program counter PC, a (pipelined) CPU, an instruction cache (I-cache), and a data cache (D-cache). The caches are backed up by a memory hierarchy, but in this section we shall assume that the caches are perfect (i.e., there will be no cache misses). For our purposes in this section, the state of a running process is the contents of the registers and of the program counter PC. Each register and the PC are 32 bits long (4 bytes, or 1 word).

Recall that a RISC processor is a load–store architecture, that is, all instructions except those involving access to memory have register or immediate operands. The instructions are of same length (4 bytes in our case) and can be of one of three types:

- Arithmetic–logical instructions, of the form $R_i \leftarrow R_j op R_k$ (one of the source registers R_j or R_k can be replaced by an immediate constant encoded in the instruction itself).
- Load–store instructions, of the form $R_i \leftarrow Mem[R_j + disp]$ or $Mem[R_j + disp] \leftarrow R_i$.
- Control instructions such as (conditional) branches of the form $br\ (R_j op R_k)$ *displ*, where a taken branch ($R_j\ op\ R_k$ is true) sets the PC to its current value plus the *displ* rather than having the PC point to the next sequential instruction.

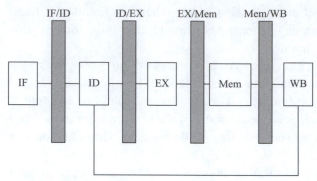

Figure 2.1. Highly abstracted pipeline.

As we saw at the beginning of this chapter, the instruction that requires the most steps is a load instruction, which requires five steps. Each step is executed on a different stage, namely:

1. Instruction fetch (IF). The instruction is fetched from the memory (I-cache) at the address indicated by the PC. At this point we assume that the instruction is not a branch, and we can increment the PC so that it will point to the next instruction in sequence.
2. Instruction decode (ID). The instruction is decoded, and its type is recognized. Some other tasks, such as the extension of immediate constants into 32 bits, are performed. More details are given in the following.
3. Execution (EX). In the case of an arithmetic instruction, an ALU performs the arithmetic or logical operation. In the case of a load or store instruction, the address $addr = R_j + disp$ is computed ($disp$ will have been extended to 32 bits in the ID stage). In the case of a branch, the PC will be set to its correct value for the next instruction (and other actions might be taken, as will be seen in Section 2.1.4).
4. Memory access (Mem). In the case of a load, the contents of $Mem[addr]$ are fetched (from the D-cache). If the instruction is a store, the contents of that location are modified. If the instruction is neither a load nor a store, nothing happens during that stage, but the instruction, unless it is a branch, must pass through it.
5. Writeback (WB). If the instruction is neither a branch nor a store, the result of the operation (or of the load) is stored in the result register.

In a highly abstracted way, the pipeline looks like Figure 2.1. In between each stage and the next are the pipeline registers, which are named after the left and right stages that they separate. A pipeline register stores all the information needed for completion of the execution of the instruction after it has passed through the stage at its left.

If we assume that accessing the caches takes slightly longer than the operations in the three other stages, that is, that the cache access takes 1 cycle, then a snapshot

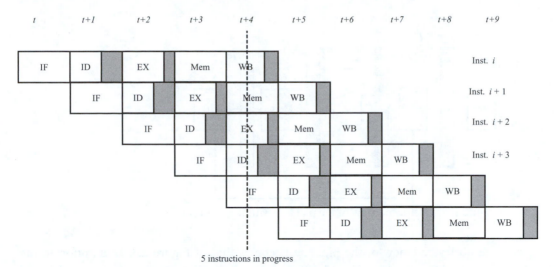

5 instructions in progress

Figure 2.2. Snapshot of sequential program execution.

of the execution of a sequential program (no branches) is shown in Figure 2.2 (the shaded parts indicate that some stages are shorter than the IF and Mem stages).

As can be seen, as soon as the pipeline is full (time $t+4$), five instructions are executing concurrently. A consequence of this parallelism is that resources cannot be shared between stages. For example, we could not have a single cache unified for instruction and data, because instruction fetches, that is, accesses to the I-cache during the IF stage, occur every cycle and would therefore interfere with a load or a store (i.e., with access to the D-cache during the Mem stage). This interference would be present about 25% of the time (the average frequency of load–store operations). As mentioned earlier, some stage might be idle. For example, if instruction $i+1$ were an add, then at time $t+4$ the only action in the Mem stage would be to pass the result computed at time $t+3$ from the pipeline register EX/Mem where it was stored to the pipeline register Mem/WB.

It is not the intention to give a detailed description of the implementation of the pipeline. In order to do so, one would need to define more precisely the ISA of the target architecture. However, we shall briefly consider the resources needed for each stage and indicate what needs to be stored in the respective pipeline registers. In this section, we only look at arithmetic–logical and load–store instructions. We will look at control instructions in Section 2.1.4.

The first two stages, fetch (IF) and decode (ID), are common to all instructions. In the IF stage, the next instruction, whose address is in the PC, is fetched, and the PC is incremented to point to the next instruction. Both the instruction and the incremented PC are stored in the IF/ID register. The required resources are the I-cache and an adder (or counter) to increment the PC. In the ID stage, the opcode of the instruction found in the IF/ID register is sent to the unit that controls the settings of the various control lines that will activate selected circuits or registers and cache read or write in the subsequent three stages. With the presence of this control unit (implemented, for example, as a programmable logic array (PLA)),

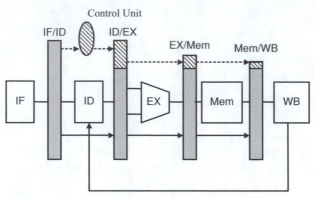

Figure 2.3. Abstracted view of the pipeline with the control unit.

the abstracted view of the pipeline becomes that of Figure 2.3. In addition to the opcode decoding performed by the control unit, all possible data required in the forthcoming stages, whether the instruction is an arithmetic–logical one or a load–store, are stored in the ID/EX register. This includes the contents of source registers, the extension to 32 bits of immediate constants and displacements (a sign extender is needed), the name of the potential result register, and the setting of control lines. The PC is also passed along.

After the IF and ID stages, the actions in the three remaining stages depend on the instruction type. In the EX stage, either an arithmetic result is computed with sources selected via settings of adequate control lines, or an address is computed. The main resource is therefore an ALU, and an ALU symbol for that stage is introduced in Figure 2.3. For both types of instruction the results are stored in the EX/Mem register. The EX/Mem register will also receive from the ID/EX register the name of the result register, the contents of a result register in the case of a store instruction, and the settings of control lines for the two remaining stages. Although passing the PC seems to be unnecessary, it is nonetheless stored in the pipeline registers. The reason for this will become clear when we deal with exceptions (Section 2.1.4). In the Mem stage, either a read (to the D-cache) is performed if the instruction is a load, or a write is performed if the instruction is a store, or else nothing is done. The last pipeline register, Mem/WB, will receive the result of an arithmetic operation, passed directly from the EX/Mem register, or the contents of the D-cache access, or nothing (in the case of a store), and, again, the value of the PC. In the WB stage the result of the instruction, if any, is stored in the result register. It is important to note that the contents of the register file are modified only in the last stage of the pipeline.

2.1.3 Data Hazards and Forwarding

In Figure 2.2, the pipeline is ideal. A result is generated every cycle. However, such smooth operation cannot be sustained forever. Even in the absence of exceptional conditions, three forms of hazards can disrupt the functioning of the pipeline. They are:

1. *Structural* hazards, when stages compete for shared resources or when buffers (e.g., pipeline registers between stages) overflow. In our simple case, we have avoided this form of hazards.
2. *Data hazards*, when an instruction in the pipeline depends on an instruction that has not yet completed its operation.
3. *Control hazards*, when the flow of control is not sequential.

Data hazards occur because of data dependencies between instructions that are concurrently in the pipeline. More specifically, assume that the execution of instruction i must precede that of instruction j in order to respect the semantics of the program order. We say that instruction j is data-dependent on instruction i if the output of instruction i is an input operand for instruction j. Such a dependency is called a *read-after-write*, or RAW, dependency. Consider the following example:

EXAMPLE 1:

i: $R7 \leftarrow R12 + R15$
$i + 1$: $R8 \leftarrow R7 - R12$
$i + 2$: $R15 \leftarrow R8 + R7$

There are three RAW dependencies:

- Instruction $i + 1$ has a RAW dependency with instruction i, because one of its input registers, register R7, is the output register of instruction i.
- Instruction $i + 2$ has a RAW dependency with instruction i, for the same reason.
- Instruction $i + 2$ has a RAW dependency with instruction $i + 1$, because one of its input registers, register R8, is the output register of instruction $i + 1$.

Register R12, which is a common source register for instructions i and $i + 1$, does not cause any dependency.

Another form of dependency, called *write-after-read*, or WAR, dependency, (or also called anti-dependency) appears in Example 1, in that register R15, an input operand of instruction i, is the output register of instruction $i + 2$. This will not cause any problem for our simple pipeline – nor would have an output dependency, or *write-after-write*, or WAW, dependency, which occurs when two instructions have the same output register. However, these dependencies will have to be remedied when we look at more complex machines (Chapter 3). We simply note at this point that a RAW dependency is a procedural matter: the algorithm (program) that is running dictates it. On the other hand, WAR and WAW are naming dependencies. If the compiler had been smarter, or if there were more registers, one instance of R15 could have been named, say, R16, and thus the WAR would have been avoided.

Consider now the execution of this sample program on the pipeline. If instruction i starts at time t, the result register R7 will be written at time $t + 4$. However, it

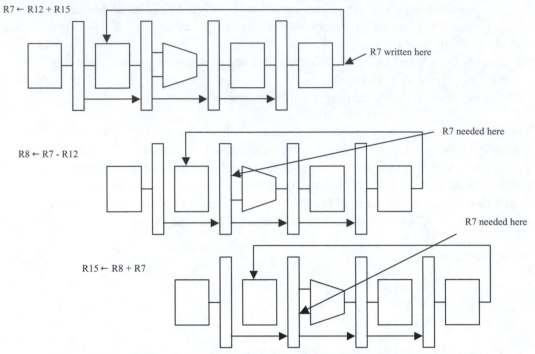

R7 ← R12 + R15

R7 written here

R8 ← R7 - R12

R7 needed here

R7 needed here

R15 ← R8 + R7

Figure 2.4. Illustration of RAW data hazards.

needs to be read from the register file to the ID/EX register at time $t+2$ for instruction $i+1$ and at time $t+3$ for instruction $i+2$. This is illustrated in Figure 2.4. (The RAW for register R8 is not shown in the figure.)

A possible solution would be to stall the pipeline until the result is available. Fortunately, this stalling can be avoided, for the needed result is already present in a stable form in the pipeline. As can be seen, the result at time $t+2$ is present in the ID/EX register, and at time $t+3$ is present in the EX/Mem register. It is therefore sufficient to provide paths (and multiplexer settings) so that the result can be *forwarded* as inputs to the ALU. This is shown in Figure 2.5.

Note that if instruction $i+3$ had R7 as an input operand, it would be available from the register file if the implementation is such that writing of the register file occurs in the first half of a cycle and reading of it occurs in the second half.

The forwarding paths from EX/Mem and Mem/WB to the inputs of the ALU and the associated control logic resolve RAW dependencies for arithmetic–logical operations. However, there are other instances of RAW dependencies that must be taken care of, namely those involving load–store operations. Consider the following sequence of two instructions:

EXAMPLE 2:

i: R6 ← Mem[R2]
$i+1$:   R7 ← R6 + R4

There is a RAW dependency between these two instructions, because register R6 is the output register of instruction i and an input register to instruction $i+1$.

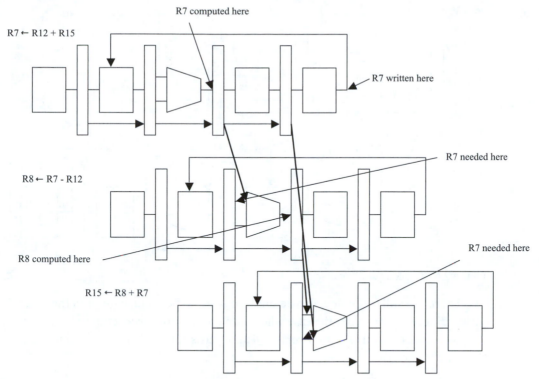

Figure 2.5. Forwarding to resolve RAW hazards.

No in-time forwarding is possible in this case, because the result of the load in the pipeline will be available at the end of the Mem stage (say, time $t+3$ if instruction i starts at time t), and the content of that register is needed as an input to the EX stage of instruction $i+1$ at time $t+2$. There is no choice at this point. The pipeline must be stalled for one cycle (graphically, as shown in Figure 2.6, a *bubble* is inserted in the pipe). Forwarding will still occur, but one cycle later. So we need to expand the forwarding control unit to include the case of a load followed by a dependent instruction and include a stalling control unit.

Stalling entails impeding the progress of one instruction (instruction $i+1$ in Example 2) as well as preventing a new instruction from being fetched, because we want the contents of the IF/ID register to remain the same. This can be implemented via a *stalling unit* which will detect at the ID stage of instruction $i+1$ that the previous instruction is a load (information available in the ID/EX register) and that the result register of the load is the same as one of the input registers of the current instruction. In that case a no-op is inserted in the pipeline (for example, by setting control lines so that neither memory nor the register file will be modified), and the reading of the I-cache and increment of the PC are disabled for the next cycle.

Schematically, the pipeline now looks like Figure 2.7. The "Stalling unit" is drawn close to the control unit, and the "Forwarding unit" close to the pipeline registers that contain the information and the data needed for forwarding.

R6 ← Mem [R2]   R6 available here

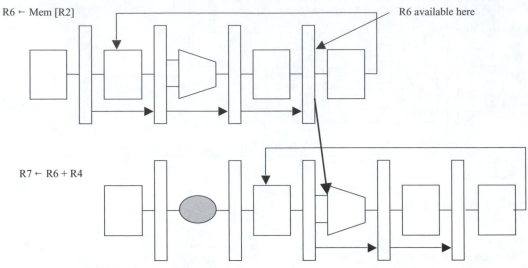

R7 ← R6 + R4

Figure 2.6. The load stalling case.

There are still a couple more details that need to be taken care of in the case of forwarding. First, consider the case where two consecutive instructions use the same output register and this output register is the basis for a RAW dependency in the third instruction, as in

i: $R10 \leftarrow R4 + R5$
$i + 1$: $R10 \leftarrow R4 + R10$
$i + 2$: $R8 \leftarrow R10 + R7$

Instruction $i + 2$ has RAW dependencies with instruction i and with instruction $i + 1$. Clearly the semantics of the program argue for the result of instruction $i + 1$ to be forwarded to instruction $i + 2$. This priority must be encoded in the logic of the forwarding unit. Second, a common sequence of two instructions, found frequently in

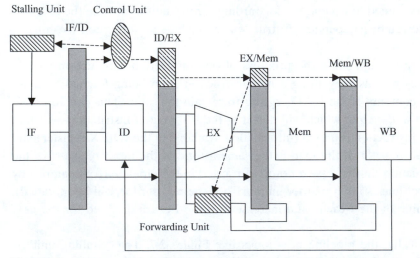

Figure 2.7. Abstracted view of the pipeline after resolving data hazards.

routines where some part of memory is to be copied to another part, consists of a load of some data followed by a store of the same data, as in

i: $R5 \leftarrow Mem[R6]$
$i + 1$: $Mem[R8] \leftarrow R5$

The forwarding unit must recognize this case so that the contents of the Mem/WB register after the load are forwarded as the data to be written in memory in the next cycle, rather than the contents of register R5.

2.1.4 Control Hazards; Branches, Exceptions, and Interrupts

Pipelining works well when there is no transfer of control, because the IF stage is based on the PC being incremented at each cycle to fetch the next instruction. Transfer of control – such as conditional branches that are taken, unconditional branches, function calls, and returns – disrupts the sequential flow. A break in the sequential flow creates *control hazards*. In this chapter we consider only conditional branches; we shall treat transfer of control more completely when we look in depth at branch prediction in Chapter 4.

Let us first analyze the steps required after IF and ID when a branch of the form *br (R_j op R_k) displ* is encountered, namely:

- Comparison between registers R_j and R_k and setting of a flag for the outcome of the comparison.
- Computation of the target address PC + *displ* (if necessary).
- Modification of the PC (if necessary).

The "if necessary" steps are required when the conditional branch is taken. We first notice that if the branch is taken, we need to use an ALU twice: once to perform the comparison, and once to compute the target address. In our pipeline, so far, there is only one ALU in the EX stage. The adder or counter used to increment the PC in the IF stage cannot be reused for other purposes, because it is accessed on every cycle.

A first solution is to reuse the ALU in the EX stage. This implies modifications to the data path and the control unit (see the exercises). Since ALUs are not expensive, we discard this solution and introduce a new ALU. Following the precept that data for different instruction types are prepared in the ID stage, we perform the branch target calculation in the ID stage for every instruction and store the result in the ID/EX register. Therefore, the new ALU will be activated in the ID stage. If the instruction is not a branch, the information will not be used. If the instruction is a branch, the Boolean operation on the source registers will be done in the EX stage, so that the outcome of the branch will be known during that stage and the PC can be modified during that cycle.

Figure 2.8 illustrates what happens. If the branch is not taken, the two instructions fetched after the branch are the correct ones. If the branch is taken, they are wrong and their potential results must be voided.

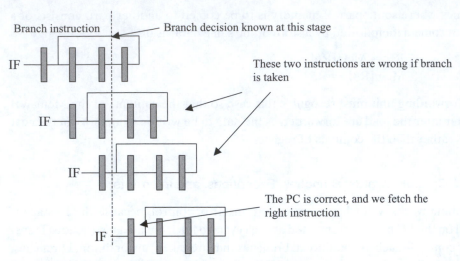

Figure 2.8. Control hazard: the branch is taken.

A first solution to remedy the situation is to always stall 2 cycles when a branch is encountered. A branch will be identified during the ID cycle. For the next 2 cycles no-ops are inserted in the pipe, as was done for the case of the 1 cycle load dependency, and fetching of new instructions is prevented. At the end of this second cycle, either the PC is left unchanged (the branch was not taken) or the PC is loaded with the target address that was computed in the ID stage and passed along to the EX/Mem pipeline register.

A better solution can be implemented at no extra cost. Since in the case of a not-taken branch the two instructions following the branch were the correct ones, we can predict that the branch is not taken. If we mispredict, that is, the branch is taken, we shall have to nullify the actions of the two instructions following the branch. Since at that point these two instructions following the branch have not yet reached a stage where either memory or registers can be modified, we can again no-op them.

Unfortunately, branches are taken slightly more often than not. So it would be better to have a branch-taken strategy. Better yet would be a predictive strategy yielding either a "taken" or a "not taken" outcome with a high probability of being right. The importance of such a strategy is not evident in the five-stage pipeline design. However, with deeper pipelines, where the outcome of the branch is not known until 10 to 20 cycles after it has been decoded, branch prediction has a great influence on performance. A full section of Chapter 4 is devoted to this topic.

So far, we have only considered control hazards generated as consequences of program flow. Two other types of control hazard can occur: *exceptions* and *interrupts*. Exceptions, sometimes called program or internal interrupts, arise as direct consequences of instruction execution. In our simple pipeline they can occur at any stage except the last one. For example, on removing the assumption of a perfect memory hierarchy, page faults can happen during the IF for instruction fetching or during Mem for either load or store instructions. Illegal opcodes are detected during the ID stage. Arithmetic exceptions, such as division by zero, underflow, and overflow, are recognized during the EX stage. Interrupts, on the other hand, are not linked to a specific program. They are external stimuli, asynchronous with program execution. Examples of interrupts are I/O termination, time-outs, and power failures.

Upon detection of an exception or an interrupt, the process state[2] must be saved by the operating system. Then the exception or interrupt condition must be cleared by a handler routine, which can take various forms such as aborting the program (e.g., for a division by zero), "correcting" the exception (e.g., for page faults), or performing tasks totally independent of the process (e.g., I/O termination). If the program has not been aborted, it will be scheduled to be restarted sometime in the future. When it is time for the program to restart, its state is restored and execution resumes.

Let us look at how pipelining affects the treatment of exceptions. Assume that the exception is produced by the execution of instruction i. We say that we have a *precise exception* mechanism if:

- instructions before i in program order currently in the pipeline (i.e., instructions $i - 1, i - 2, \ldots$) complete normally, and their results are part of the saved process state;
- instruction i and instructions after it already in the pipe (i.e., instructions $i, i + 1, i + 2, \ldots$) will be no-opped;
- the PC of the saved process state is the PC corresponding to instruction i: when the process is restarted, it will be restarted at instruction i.

This last condition shows why we kept the PCs of instructions in the pipeline moving from stage to stage.

In terms of implementation, precise exceptions are easy to handle in the case of a simple pipeline like the one we have presented so far. When the exception is detected, a flag is inserted in the pipeline register at the right of the stage where the exception occurred, and all other control lines in that pipeline register are set as for a no-op. Fetching of new instructions is prevented. When the flag reaches the Mem/WB pipeline register, the PC found in that pipeline register is saved in an *exception PC* register. All pipeline registers are then zeroed out, and transfer of control is given to the exception handler, whose first task will be to save the process state (registers and *exception PC*). Note that with this scheme exceptions are handled in program order, the desired effect, and not necessarily in temporal order. To see why, consider the case of instruction i having a divide-by-zero exception (stage EX) and instruction $i + 1$ generating an instruction page fault (stage IF). If instruction i is fetched at time t, its exception will happen at time $t + 2$, whereas that of instruction $i + 1$ will happen at time $t + 1$. At time $t + 1$ an exception flag will be inserted in the IF/ID pipeline register. This will be propagated to the ID/EX register at time $t + 2$,

---

[2] At this point, no distinction is made between *process* and *program*. We elaborate on this point in Section 2.3.

but at that time another exception flag will be set in the EX/Mem register because of instruction i's exception. This second flag will be the first one checked (at time $t + 3$), and therefore the exceptions will be treated in program order.

Handling of precise exceptions becomes more complex in processors with multiple pipelines and with some stages in these pipelines spanning several cycles. We shall return to this topic in Chapter 3.

Handling of interrupts is quite similar. The presence of interrupts is checked at every cycle. If an interrupt is pending (indicated, for example, by the setting of a special bit as part of the process state), the fetching of instructions of the running program is prevented. The pipeline is flushed, that is, all instructions currently in the pipe are completed. When the last one is done, the process state is saved with the exception PC register containing the PC of the first instruction that was not fetched. Now the interrupt handler can be activated as was the exception handler.

Detailed methods of handling an exception or interrupt are outside the scope of this book. Suffice it to say that there are two general ways to transfer control to the right routine in the operating system (O.S.). In both cases, the cause of the exception or interrupt is encoded by the hardware. In the first method, the encoding is saved as part of a *status register* that is included in the process state. When the O.S. is called to treat the exception, it will decode the contents of that register and transfer them to the appropriate routine. Note that the address of the entry routine in the O.S. must itself be available as an input to the PC. In the second method, called *vector interrupt*, the encoding serves as an index to a vector of addresses, of which each element is an address of a specific O.S. routine that can treat the exception. Once the process state has been saved, the PC is loaded with the appropriate vector element.

2.1.5 Alternative Five-Stage Pipeline Designs

If we step back and look at the design of the five-stage pipeline as presented in the previous sections, we can see that the ordering and functionality of some of the stages are mandated by the sequence of actions needed to execute an instruction, whereas others are left to the will of the designer or may be dependent on the ISA of the target architecture. More specifically, the instruction and decode stages (IF and ID) cannot be moved around, and if we adhere to the philosophy that the process state can only be modified in the last stage, the writeback stage (WB) has to remain at its place. Moreover, the load–store operations require the EX stage to be able to perform address generation (AG) computations and to be followed by the Mem stage to access the D-cache. So, a better name for the EX stage would be EX-AG to indicate its double function. With this ordering we saw that:

1. We could avoid RAW dependencies between arithmetic instructions at the cost of forwarding paths between the EX-AG/Mem and Mem/WB pipeline registers and the inputs of the ALU of the EX-AG stage (cf. Figure 2.7).
2. We could not avoid a 1 cycle load latency penalty when the result of a load operation was a source operand for the next instruction.

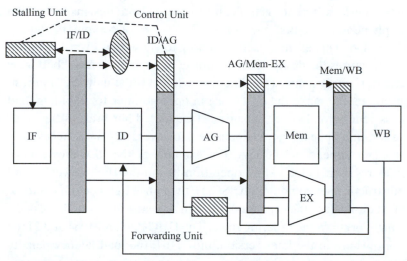

Figure 2.9. Alternative five-stage pipeline design.

3. Branch resolution could be performed during the EX-AG stage, resulting in a 2 cycle branch penalty on a taken branch (with a branch-not-taken prediction policy).
4. The Mem stage was not used for arithmetic–logical instructions.

Suppose that there are many two-instruction sequences of the following form:

Load variable x in register R.
Use register R as a source operand.

Then the 1 cycle load latency penalty can be a serious impediment to performance. A possible alternative is to have the five stages be IF, ID, AG, EX/Mem, and WB, that is, the third stage devoted only to addressing generation computations, whereas D-cache accesses for load–store operations and general ALU operations for arithmetic–logical instructions are performed in the fourth stage. An abstracted view of this pipeline is shown in Figure 2.9.
With respect to the four points just listed:

1. We still avoid RAW dependencies between arithmetic–logical instructions, but this is at the cost of one extra ALU. On the other hand, the forwarding unit is slightly simplified.
2. The 1 cycle load latency is avoided, but we have created a 1 cycle address generation latency penalty in the case where an arithmetic instruction generates a result for a register used in an address computation, as in

i: $R5 \leftarrow R6 + R7$
$i + 1$: $R9 \leftarrow \text{Mem}[R5]$

Note that a stalling control unit is still required, although its logic is different.
3. The branch resolution that used to be done in the EX stage needs to be done now in the AG stage, but this should not be a problem, for we need an adder (ALU) for the address computation in that stage.
4. Now it is the AG stage that is unused for arithmetic–logical operations.

Which of these two designs is better is difficult to answer. Both designs have been commercially implemented, the first one in the MIPS series of computers and the second in the Intel 486. This example serves simply to show that even for rather simple hardware structures the design space is subject to choices. In fact, "better" is itself hard to define. If performance (pipeline throughput) is the metric of interest, compiler optimizations can make the difference in opportunities for avoiding load latency or address generation latency penalties. If expanded hardware is the criterion, the second solution appears more expensive. However, this is not necessarily the case, and it might depend on the ISA. For example, if the ISA allows auto-increment of index registers in load–store operations (as in the IBM PowerPC and many complex instruction set computers (CISCs)), then an ALU would have to be included in the first design (see the exercises). Even in the same family of processors, subtle changes might occur in the ordering stage. The DEC Alphas 21064 and 21164 are a case in point, where in the later version, the 21164, the load latency penalty was decreased from 2 to 1 cycle at the expense of a branch-taken penalty increase of 1 cycle. It was felt that more accurate branch prediction techniques in the 21164 would compensate for the increase in branch penalty, thus making the decrease in load latency penalty more valuable.

2.1.6 Pipelined Functional Units

The instruction execution pipelines that we have presented so far can be considered as *first-generation*. They are shallow and they are simple. In current processors the pipelines are much deeper, and each of the five stages is itself decomposed into several stages. How IF, ID, and WB are expanded and designed is treated in Chapters 4 and 5. The memory hierarchy and the Mem stage will be presented first in the forthcoming sections in this chapter and in more detail in Chapter 6. Our interest in this section is centered on the EX stage.

EX stages are executed in functional units. In modern microprocessors, there exist functional units for:

- Fast integer arithmetic and logical operations.
- Slow integer arithmetic operations, essentially multiply, multiply–add (for dot products), and divide.
- Floating-point operations such as add, multiply, divide, and square root.

Fast integer arithmetic can be done in a single cycle. In first-generation pipelined processors, the slow arithmetic and the floating-point (f-p) operations were implemented either in software or by using a coprocessor or by a combination of both. In current microprocessors, all these operations are performed in hardware with specialized functional units for the major categories of instructions. In general these functional units are pipelined, the exceptions being nonpipelined division and square root (if present). When the unit is pipelined, there are two parameters of interest: the number of stages, and the minimum number of cycles before two independent (no RAW dependency) instructions of the same type can enter the functional unit. For example, in some implementations of the Intel P6 (Pentium Pro and followers) microarchitecture, integer multiplies (four stages) and f-p adds (three stages) can enter their respective units at every cycle, whereas 2 cycles must separate f-p multiplies (five stages).

We briefly describe how f-p adds and f-p multiplies can be pipelined. Recall that the IEEE standard representation for f-p arithmetic requires that single-precision and double-precision numbers be represented respectively with 32 and 64 bits. In the following, we limit ourselves to single precision, although most scientific computations use double precision. However, the principles are the same regardless of the precision. In single precision, the representation of a number consists of three fields:

- A sign bit S ($S = 0$ for positive and $S = 1$ for negative numbers).
- 8 bits of exponent E. The base[3] for the exponent is 2. The exponent is *biased*, that is, the real value of the exponent is the difference between E and 127 (01111111 in binary).
- A *normalized* mantissa F of $32 - 1 - 8 = 23$ bits, where the normalization implies that the most significant bit of the mantissa does not need to be represented. Under usual conditions, all arithmetic must result in normalized numbers.

Thus, the value of a normalized f-p number V is $V = (-1)^S \times 2^{E-127} \times 1.F$

Special patterns are reserved for plus and minus infinity (overflow and underflow) as well as for NaN (Not a Number) occurrences that result from incorrect operations such as division by zero (cf. the nonprecise exceptions in Chapter 3). Zero is represented by 32 null bits, although a -0 is possible ($S = 1$ and all other bits 0). There are specific rules for rounding, such as rounding to the nearest even, toward 0, and toward plus or minus infinity. Details are beyond the scope of this section.

Let us start with f-p addition, which, conceptually, is slightly more complex than multiplication because of the inherent sign and magnitude representation of the mantissas. Let (S_1, E_1, F_1) and (S_2, E_2, F_2) be the two numbers to be added. Addition (and subtraction with trivial changes) proceeds as follows:

1. *Compare exponents.* Find the larger number by comparing E_1 and E_2. If $E_1 < E_2$, swap the two operands so that $D = E_1 - E_2$ is positive. Tentatively set the result exponent to E_1 and the result sign to S_1.
2. *Prepare and align mantissas.* Insert a 1 at the left of F_1 and at the left of F_2. If $S_1 \neq S_2$, then replace F_2 by its 2's complement. Perform a right arithmetic shift for F_2 of D bits.
3. Add mantissas.

---

[3] Some older machines used a different representation. In particular, IBM System/360 and 370 (and successors) used base 16, thus allowing a wider range of values to be represented – with a concomitant loss in precision, because each digit was 4 bits wide.

4. *Normalize and round off.* Shift the result mantissa right by one bit if there was a carry-out in the preceding step, and decrease the result exponent by 1. Otherwise, shift left until the most significant bit is a 1, increasing the result exponent by 1 for each bit shifted. Suppress the leftmost 1 for the result mantissa. Round off.

Step 3 (add mantissas) is a little more complex than it appears. Not only does a carry-out need to be detected when both operands are of the same sign, but also, when $D = 0$ and the two operands are of different signs, the resulting mantissa may be of the wrong sign. Its 2's complement must then be taken, and the sign of the result must be flipped.

This algorithm lends itself quite well to pipelining in three (or possibly four) stages: compare exponents, shift and add mantissas (in either one or two stages), and normalize and round off.

The algorithm for multiplication is straightforward:

1. *Add exponents.* The resulting exponent is $E = E_1 + E_2 - 127$ (we need to subtract one of the two biases). The resulting sign is positive if $S_1 = S_2$ and negative otherwise.
2. *Prepare and multiply mantissas.* The preparation simply means inserting 1's at the left of F_1 and F_2. We don't have to worry about signs.
3. *Normalize and round off.* As in addition, but without having to worry about a potential right shift.

Because the multiplication takes longer than the other two steps, we must find a way to break it into stages. The usual technique is to use a Wallace tree of carry–save adders (CSAs).[4] If the number of CSAs is deemed too large, as for example for double-precision f-p arithmetic, a feedback loop must be inserted in the "tree." In that case, consecutive multiplications cannot occur on every cycle, and the delay depends on the depth of the feedback.

With the increase in clock frequencies, the tendency will be to have deeper pipelines for these operations, because less gate logic can be activated in a single cycle. The optimal depth of a pipeline depends on many microarchitectural factors besides the requirement that stages must be separated by stable state components, that is, the pipeline registers. We shall return briefly to this topic in Chapter 9.

2.2 Caches

In our pipeline design we have assumed that the IF and Mem stages were always taking a single cycle. In this section, we take a first look at the design of the memory hierarchy of microprocessor systems and, in particular, at the various organizations

---

[4] CSAs take three inputs and generate two outputs in two levels of AND–OR logic. By using a log–sum process we can reduce the number of operands by a factor 2/3 at each level of the tree. For a multiplier and a multiplicand of n bits each, we need $n - 2$ CSAs before proceeding to the last regular addition with a carry–lookahead adder. Such a structure is called a Wallace tree.

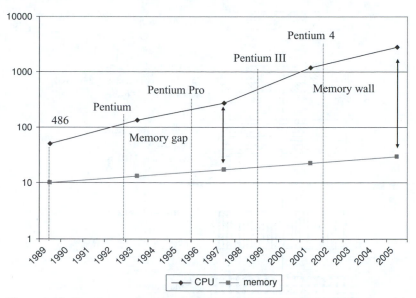

Figure 2.10. Processor–memory performance gap (note the logarithmic scale).

and performance of caches, the highest levels in the hierarchy. Our assumption was that caches were always perfect. Naturally, this is not the reality.

In early computers, there was only one level of memory, the so-called primary memory. The secondary memory, used for permanent storage, consisted of rotating devices, such as disks, and some aspects of it are discussed in the next section. Nowadays primary memory is a hierarchy of components of various speeds and costs. This hierarchy came about because of the rising discrepancy between processor speeds and memory latencies. As early as the late 1960s, the need for a memory buffer between high-performance CPUs and main memory was recognized. Thus, caches were introduced. As the gap between processor and memory performance increased, multilevel caches became the norm. Figure 2.10 gives an idea of the processor and memory performance trends during the 1990s. While processor speeds increased by 60% per year, memory latencies decreased by only 7% per year. The ratio of memory latency to cycle time, which was about 5:1 in 1990, became more than one order of magnitude in the middle of the decade (the *memory gap*) and more than two orders of magnitude by 2000 (the *memory wall*). Couched in terms of latencies, the access time for a DRAM (main memory) is of the order of 40 ns, that is, 100 processor cycles for a 2.5 GHz processor.

The goal of a memory hierarchy is to keep close to the ALU the information that is needed presently and in the near future. Ideally, this information should be reachable in a single cycle, and this necessitates that part of the memory hierarchy, a cache, be on chip with the ALU. However, the capacity of this on-chip SRAM memory must not be too large, because the time to access it is, in a first approximation, proportional to its size. Therefore, modern computer systems have multiple levels of caches. A typical hierarchy is shown in Figure 2.11 with two levels of

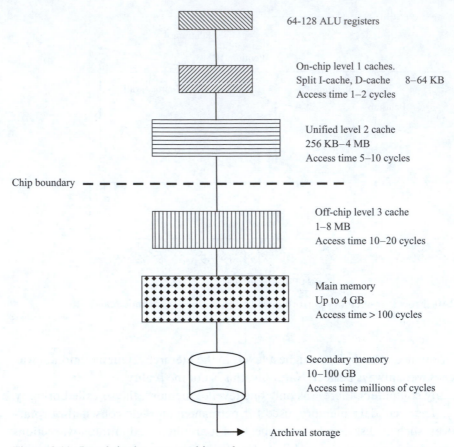

Figure 2.11. Levels in the memory hierarchy.

on-chip caches (SRAM) and one level of off-chip cache (often a combination of SRAM and DRAM), and main memory (DRAM).

Note that the concept of caching is used in many other aspects of computer systems: disk caches, network server caches, Web caches, and so on. Caching works because information at all these levels is not accessed randomly. Specifically, computer programs exhibit the *principle of locality*, consisting of *temporal locality*, whereby data and code used in the past are likely to be reused in the near future (e.g., data in stack, code in loops), and *spatial locality*, whereby data and code close (in terms of memory addresses) to the data and code currently referenced will be referenced again in the near future (e.g., traversing a data array, straight-line code sequences).

Caches are much smaller than main memory, so, at a given time, they cannot contain all the code and data of the executing program. When a memory reference is generated, there is a lookup in the cache corresponding to that reference: the I-cache for instructions, and the D-cache for data. If the memory location is mapped in the cache, we have a *cache hit*; otherwise, we have a *cache miss*. In the case of a hit, the content of the memory location is loaded either in the IF/EX pipeline register in the case of an instruction, or in the Mem/WB register in the case of a load, or else the content of the cache is modified in the case of a store. In the case of a miss, we have to recursively probe the next levels of the memory hierarchy until the missing item is found. For ease of explanation, in the remainder of this section we only consider a single-level cache unless noted otherwise. In addition, we first restrict ourselves to data cache reads (i.e., loads). Reads for I-caches are similar to those for D-caches, and we shall look at writes (i.e., stores) separately.

2.2.1 Cache Organizations

Caches serve as high-speed buffers between main memory and the CPU. Because their storage capacity is much less than that of primary memory, there are four basic questions on cache design that need to be answered, namely:

1. When do we bring the content of a memory location into the cache?
2. Where do we put it?
3. How do we know it's there?
4. What happens if the cache is full and we want to bring the content of a location that is not cached? As we shall see in answering question 2, a better formulation is: "What happens if we want to bring the content of a location that is not cached and the place where it should go is already occupied?"

Some top-level answers follow. These answers may be slightly modified because of optimizations, as we shall see in Chapter 6. For example, our answer to the first question will be modified when we introduce prefetching. With this caveat in mind, the answers are:

1. The contents of a memory location are brought into the cache *on demand*, that is, when the request for the data results in a cache miss.
2. Basically the cache is divided into a number of cache entries. The mapping of a memory location to a specific cache entry depends on the *cache organization* (to be described).
3. Each cache entry contains its name, or *tag*, in addition to the data contents. Whether a memory reference results in a hit or a miss involves checking the appropriate tag(s).
4. Upon a cache miss, if the new entry conflicts with an entry already there, one entry in the cache will be replaced by the one causing the miss. The choice, if any, will be resolved by a replacement algorithm.

A generic cache organization is shown in Figure 2.12. A cache entry consists of an address, or tag, and of data. The usual terminology is to call the data content of an entry a *cache line* or a *cache block*.[5] These lines are in general several words (bytes) long; hence, a parameter of the cache is its *line size*. The overall cache capacity, or *cache size*, given in kilobytes (KB) or megabytes (MB), is the product of the number of lines and the line size, that is, the tags are not counted in the overall

---

[5] We will use *line* for the part of a cache entry and *block* for the corresponding memory image.

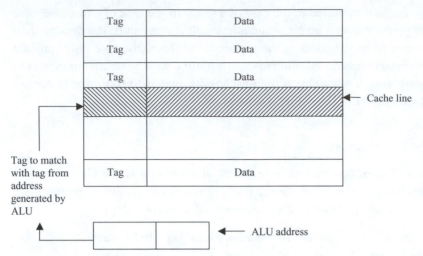

Figure 2.12. Generic cache organization. If (part of) the address generated by the ALU matches a tag, we have a hit; otherwise, we have a miss.

cache size. A good reason for discarding the tags in the terminology (but not in the actual hardware) is that from a performance viewpoint they are overhead, that is, they do not contribute to the buffering effect.

Mapping of a memory location, or rather of a sequence of memory words of line-size width that we will call a *memory block*, to a cache entry can range from full generality to very restrictive. If a memory block can be mapped to any cache entry, we have a *fully associative* cache. If the mapping is restricted to a single entry, we have a *direct-mapped* cache. If the mapping is to one of several cache entries, we have a *set-associative* cache. The number of possible entries is the set-associative *way*. Figure 2.13 illustrates these definitions.

Large fully associative caches are not practical, because the detection of a cache hit or miss requires that all tags be checked in the worst case. The linear search can be avoided with the use of *content-addressable memories* (CAMs), also called associative memories. In a CAM, instead of addressing the memory structure as an array (i.e., with an index), the addressing is by matching a key with the contents of (part of) all memory locations in the CAM. All entries can be searched in parallel. A matching entry, if any, will raise a flag indicating its presence. In the case of a fully associative cache, the key is a part of the address generated by the ALU, and the locations searched in parallel are the tags of all cache entries. If there is no match, we have a miss; otherwise, the matching entry (there can be only one in this case) indicates the position of the cache hit.

While conceptually quite attractive, CAMs have for main drawbacks that (i) they are much more hardware-expensive than SRAMs, by a factor of 6 to 1, (ii) they consume more power, and (iii) they are difficult to modify. Although fully associative hardware structures do exist in some cases, e.g., for write buffers as we shall see in this section, for TLBs as we shall see in the next section, and for other hardware data structures as we shall see in forthcoming chapters, they are in general very small, up to 128 entries, and therefore cannot be use for general-purpose caches.

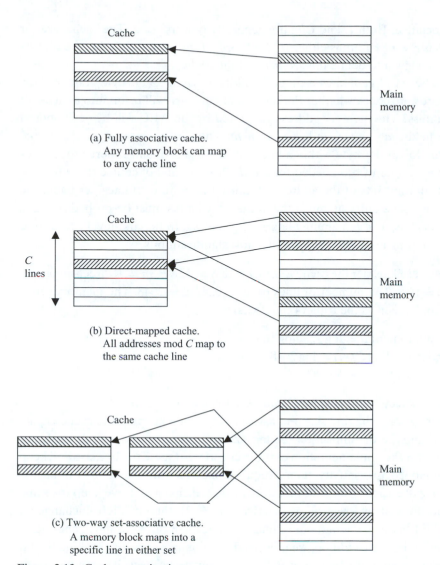

(a) Fully associative cache.
Any memory block can map
to any cache line

Main
memory

C
lines

Cache

(b) Direct-mapped cache.
All addresses mod C map to
the same cache line

Main
memory

Cache

(c) Two-way set-associative cache.
A memory block maps into a
specific line in either set

Main
memory

Figure 2.13. Cache organizations.

In the case of direct-mapped caches, the memory block will be mapped to a single entry in the cache. This entry is *memory block address mod C*, where C is the number of cache entries. Since in general-purpose microprocessors C is a power of 2, the entry whose tag must be checked is very easy to determine.

In the case of an *m*-way set-associative cache, the cache is divided into *m banks* with C/m lines per bank. A given memory block can be mapped to any of m entries, each of which is at address *memory block address mod C/m* in its bank. Detection of a cache hit or miss will require m comparators so that all comparisons can be performed concurrently.

A cache is therefore completely defined by three parameters: The number of cache lines, C; the line size L; and the associativity m. Note that a direct-mapped cache can be considered as one-way set-associative, and a fully associative cache as

C-way associative. Both *L* and *C*/*m* are generally powers[6] of 2. The cache size, or capacity, *S* is $S = C \times L$: thus either (C,L,m) or (S,L,m), a notation that we slightly prefer, can be given to define the *geometry* of the cache.

When the ALU generates a memory address, say a 32-bit byte address, how does the hardware check whether the (memory) *reference* will result into a cache hit or a cache miss? The memory address generated by the ALU will be decomposed into three fields: *tag*, *index*, and *displacement*. The *displacement d*, or *line offset*, indicates the low-order byte within a line that is addressed. Since there are *L* bytes per line, the number of bits needed for *d* is $d = \log_2 L$, and of course these bits are the least significant bits of the address. Because there are *C*/*m* lines per bank, the *index i* of the cache entry at which the *m* memory banks must be probed requires $i = \log_2(C/m)$ bits. The remaining *t* bits are for the tag. In the first-level caches that we are considering here, the *t* bits are the most significant bits.

> **EXAMPLE 3:** Consider the cache (S,m,L) with $S = 32KB$, $m = 1$(direct-mapped), and $L = 16B$. The number of lines is $32 \times 1024/16 = 2048$. The memory reference can be seen as the triplet (t,i,d), where:
>
> The displacement $d = \log L = \log 16 = 4$.
> The index $i = \log(C/m) = \log 2048 = 11$.
> The tag $t = 32 - 11 - 4 = 17$.

The hit–miss detection process for Example 3 is shown in Figure 2.14.

Let us now vary the line size and associativity while keeping the cache capacity constant and see the impact on the tag size and hence on the overall hardware requirement for the implementation of the cache. If we double the line size and keep the direct-mapped associativity, then *d* requires one more bit; the number of lines is halved, so *i* is decreased by 1; and therefore *t* is left unchanged. If we keep the same line size but look at two-way set associativity ($m = 2$), then *d* is left unchanged, *i* decreases by 1 because the number of lines per set is half of the original, and therefore *t* increases by 1. In addition, we now need two comparators for checking the hit or miss, or more generally one per way for an *m*-way cache, as well as a multiplexer to drive the data out of the right bank. Note that if we were to make the cache fully associative, the index bits would disappear, because $i = \log(C/C) = \log 1 = 0$.

From our original four questions, one remains, namely: What happens if on a cache miss all cache entries to which the missing memory block maps are already occupied? For example, assume a direct-mapped cache. Memory blocks *a* and *b* have addresses that are a multiple of *C* blocks apart, and *a* is already cached. Upon a reference to *b*, we have a cache miss. Block *b* should therefore be brought into the cache, but the cache entry where it should go is already occupied by block *a*. Following the principle of locality, which can be interpreted as favoring the most recent references over older ones, block *b* becomes cached and block *a* is evicted.

---

[6] *m* is not necessarily a power of 2. In that case, if *m'* is the smallest power of 2 larger than *m*, then there are *m* banks of *C*/*m'* lines.

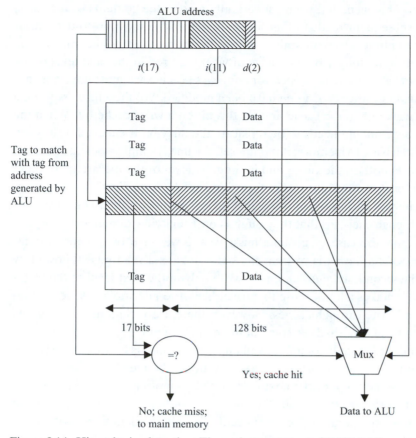

Figure 2.14. Hit and miss detection. The cache geometry is (32 KB,1,16).

In the case of an *m*-way set-associative cache, if all *m* cache entries with the same mapping as the block for which there is a miss are occupied, then a *victim* to be evicted must be selected. The victim is chosen according to a *replacement algorithm*. Following again the principle of locality, a good choice is to replace the line that has been not been accessed for the longest time, that is, the *least-recently used* (LRU). LRU replacement is easy to implement when the associativity *m* is small, for example *m* ≤ 4. For the larger associativities that can happen in second- or third-level caches, approximations to LRU can be used (Chapter 6). As long as the (maybe two) most recently used (MRU) lines are not replaced, the influence of the replacement algorithm on cache performance is minimal. This will not be the case for the paging systems that we discuss in the next section.

Write Strategies
In our answers to the top-level questions we have assumed that the memory references corresponded to reads. When the reference is for a write, (i.e., a consequence of a store instruction), we are faced with additional choices. Of course, the steps taken to detect whether there is a cache hit or a cache miss remain the same.

In the case of a cache hit, we must certainly modify the contents of the cache line, because subsequent reads to that line must return the most up-to-date information. A first option is to write only in the cache. Consequently, the information in the cache might no longer be the image of what is stored in the next level of the memory hierarchy. In these *writeback* (or *copyback*) caches we must have a means to indicate that the contents of a line have been modified. We therefore associate a *dirty bit* with each line in the cache and set this bit on a write cache hit. When the line becomes a victim and needs to be replaced, the dirty bit is checked. If it is set, the line is written back to memory; if it is not set, the line is simply evicted. A second option is to write both in the cache and in the next level of the hierarchy. In these *write-through* (or *store-through*) caches there is no need for the dirty bit. The advantage of the writeback caches is that they generate less memory traffic. The advantage of the write-through caches is that they offer a consistent view of memory.

Consider now the case of a cache miss. Again, we have two major options. The first one, *write-allocate*, is to treat the write miss as a read miss followed by a write hit. The second, *write-around*, is to write only in the next level of the memory hierarchy. It makes a lot of sense to have either write-allocate writeback caches or write-around write-through caches. However, there are variations on these two implementations, and we shall see some of them in Chapter 6.

One optimization that is common to all implementations is to use a *write buffer*. In a write-through cache the processor has to wait till the memory has stored the data. Because the memory, or the next level of the memory hierarchy, can be tens to hundreds of cycles away, this wait is wasteful in that the processor does not need the result of the store operation. To circumvent this wait, the data to be written and the location where they should be written are stored in one of a set of temporary registers. The set itself, a few registers, constitutes the write buffer. Once the data are in the write buffer, the processor can continue executing instructions. Writes to memory are scheduled as soon as the memory bus is free. If the processor generates writes at a rate such that the write buffer becomes full, then the processor will have to stall. This is an instance of a structural hazard. The same concept can be used for writeback caches. Instead of generating memory writes as soon as a dirty replacement is mandated, the line to be written and its tag can be placed in the write buffer. The write buffer must be checked on every cache miss, because the required information might be in it. We can take advantage of the fact that each entry in the buffer must carry the address of where it will be written in memory, and transform the buffer into a small fully associative extra cache. In particular, information to be written can be coalesced or overwritten if it belongs to a line already in the buffer.

The Three C's

In order to better understand the effect of the geometry parameters on cache performance it is useful to classify the cache misses into three categories, called the three C's:

1. Compulsory (or cold) misses: This type of misses occurs the first time a memory block is referenced.

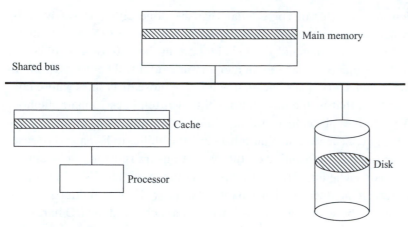

Figure 2.15. Cache coherency and I/O.

2. Conflict misses: This type of misses occurs when more than m blocks vie for the same cache entries in an m-way set-associative cache.
3. Capacity misses: This type of misses occurs when the working set of the program is too large for the given cache size, even under ideal conditions: fully associative cache and optimal replacement algorithm (cf. Section 2.3).

To these three C's one can add a fourth one, *coherence* misses, which are present in multiprocessor systems (cf. Chapter 7). However, even with single processors, maintaining a coherent view of the memory hierarchy is a problem to be dealt with because of I/O.

Caches and I/O

The presence of a cache will affect I/O operations. Consider the system shown in Figure 2.15. A processor and its cache hierarchy are connected to the main memory via a shared processor–memory bus. An I/O device, here a disk, is also connected to that bus. Though this figure is an oversimplified representation of a microprocessor system, it is sufficient for our purposes here. In reality, the main memory and the I/O subsystem would be connected through a bus bridge, and there would be an I/O bus connecting to a variety of I/O controllers.

We have to consider what happens when information is transferred from (to) memory to (from) the disk. Let us look first at the case of an I/O read, that is, some data are transferred from the disk to main memory. If some of the area where the data are going to reside in main memory is already cached (the hatched portion in the cache in the figure), the cached data will not be correct after the transfer. Either the cached data must be marked as invalid, using a *valid bit*, or it has to be overwritten during the transfer so that it is consistent with the new memory contents. In the case of an I/O write (i.e., transfer from main memory to disk), the contents of main memory are always correct if the cache is write-through. However, if the cache is writeback and data to be transferred are in a cached line with its dirty bit set, then the most up-to-date data are in the cache and it is these data that should be written to disk.

Invalidation and transfer of correct data can be done either in software by the O.S. or in hardware. In the software implementation, the O.S. scans entries in the cache. The O.S. will demand the invalidation, in the case of a read, of the cache entries that are mapped to the main memory area that will be overwritten. In the case of a write and a writeback cache, it will *purge* those dirty lines whose contents must be written, that is, the dirty lines will be written back to main memory before the I/O write takes place. In a hardware implementation, a bus *snoopy* protocol will be used, and the cache controller must have the ability to listen and to react to all activities on the bus. Depending on the type of bus transaction, cache entries can be invalidated or cache lines transferred in lieu of memory blocks. Snoopy protocols will be described in much detail in Chapter 7 when we look at multiprocessors. The I/O controller can be seen as a processor without a cache, and the I/O hardware protocol is a simplified version of a general snoopy protocol.

2.2.2 Cache Performance

The basic performance metric for a cache is the *hit ratio h*, defined as

$$h = \frac{\textit{number of memory references that hit in the cache}}{\textit{total number of memory references to the cache}}$$

Since h is most of the time between 0.90 and 0.99, it is often more convenient to talk about the miss ratio $(1 - h)$. It is psychologically more appealing to reduce the miss ratio from 0.05 to 0.04 (a 20% reduction) than to increase the hit ratio from 0.95 to 0.96 (an increase of 1%). Of course, what is important is the overall impact on performance, for example, on *IPC* and execution time.

A metric related to h that takes into account all levels of the memory hierarchy is the *average memory access time*. In the case of a single-level cache, we have

$$Av. \; Mem. \; Access \; Time = hT_{cache} + (1 - h)T_{mem}$$

where T_{cache} is the time to access the cache, (e.g., 1 cycle), and T_{mem} is the main memory latency, (e.g., 50 cycles). In the case of a hierarchy of caches, the formula is expanded the obvious way. For example, with two levels of cache, we have

$$Av. \; Mem. \; Access \; Time = h_1 T_{L1} + (1 - h_1) h_2 \, T_{L2} + (1 - h_1)(1 - h_2)T_{mem}$$

where T_{L1} (respectively, T_{L2}) is the access time to the first-level L1 cache (respectively, second-level L2 cache), h_1 is the hit ratio for L1, and h_2 is the *local hit ratio* for L2, that is, only the references that missed in L1 are counted for determining the hit ratio for L2. In general, h_2 is much lower than h_1.

The goal therefore is to reduce the average memory access time. From the cache design viewpoint, we want to increase h without increasing T_{cache}. Let us look at how the geometry parameters of a cache affect h and T_{cache}. We consider each parameter – capacity, associativity, and line size – in turn, modifying one parameter while leaving the other two unchanged.

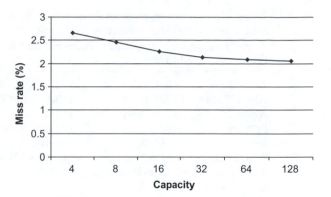

Figure 2.16. Miss rate vs. capacity. The data cache is $(S,2,64)$ with S varying from 4 to 128 KB. The application is 176.gcc from Spec 2000. Data are taken from Cantin and Hill [CH03]. The WWW site http://www.cs.wisc.edu/multifacet/misc/spec2000cache-data/ gives cache performance data for all Spec 2000 benchmarks.

Increasing the capacity S of a cache will certainly result in reducing both capacity and conflict misses. Figure 2.16 shows this effect (we have plotted miss rates because they show the effect more vividly). However, we cannot increase S indefinitely, because at some point the access time T_{cache} will itself increase. For a given clock frequency, the greater access time may result in an extra cycle in accessing the cache, thus wiping out all benefits of an incremental decrease in the miss rate. L1 caches – both I-caches and D-caches – have 64 KB as maximum sizes. For on-chip L2s, the maximum size depends mostly on how much area is left on chip. L3 sizes can be several megabytes.

Similarly, the higher the associativity m, the better the hit rate h (cf. Figure 2.17), because conflict misses will be reduced. For L1 caches there is usually a big drop when moving from direct-mapped to two-way, a smaller drop from two- to four-way, and then no real change. As mentioned previously, the associativity is limited by the number of comparisons that can be performed in parallel and by the need to have their results available without increasing T_{cache}. Most L1s today are two-way set-associative; there are less frequent occurrences of direct-mapped and four-way set associativity. L2s' associativities range from direct-mapped to 16-way.

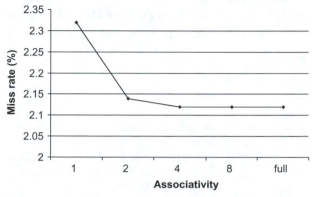

Figure 2.17. Miss rate vs. associativity. The data cache is $(32\ KB, m, 64)$ with the associativity m ranging from direct-mapped (1) to full. The application and the source are the same as in Figure 2.16.

Table 2.1. Geometries of two microprocessor families. Some of these numbers, mostly for L2 caches, may differ depending on implementation

Processor	I-Cache	D-Cache	L2
Alpha 21064	(8 KB, 1, 32)	(8 KB, 1, 32) WT	Off-chip (2 MB,1,64)
Alpha 21164	(8 KB, 1, 32)	(8 KB, 1, 32) WT	(96 KB,3,64) WB
Alpha 21264	(64 KB,2,64)	(64 KB,2,64)	Off-chip (16 MB,1,64)
Pentium	(8 KB,2,32)	(8 KB,2,32) WT/WB	Off-chip up to 8 MB
Pentium II	(16 KB,2,32)	(16 KB,2,32) WB	"Glued" (512 KB,8,32) WB
Pentium III	(16 KB,2,32)	(16 KB,4,32) WB	(512 KB,8,32) WB
Pentium 4	Trace cache 96 KB	(16 KB,4,64) WT	(1MB, 8,128) WB
Core Duo	(32 KB,2,64)	(32 KB,4,64) WB	(4MB,8,128) WB shared

The situation is not as clear-cut for the third parameter, the line size L. As can be seen in Figure 2.18, the best line size depends on the application. On the one hand, a larger L can reduce the number of compulsory misses by implicitly prefetching more data per miss. On the other hand, at equal S and m, longer lines may increase capacity and conflict misses. It all depends on the amount of spatial locality found in the application. For a given application, S, and m, there is an optimal line size. In Figure 2.18, we see a case where longer line sizes are best (application *ijpeg*), one where short lines yield the lowest miss rate (*go*), and one where a middle-size line is best (*gcc*). In practice, L1 I-caches have slightly longer line sizes (64 or 128 bytes) than L1 D-caches (32 or 64 bytes). L2 line sizes are in the 64–512 byte range.

We have already mentioned other design parameters that influence the average access time: the write policy (writeback induces fewer memory writes and thus is preferred), the replacement algorithm (of little importance when $m \leq 4$), and whether the caches are split into I-caches and D-caches (almost necessary for a clean implementation of pipelining) or unified (better for all but L1 caches).

Table 2.1 shows the cache geometries and write policy of two families of microprocessors: the DEC Alpha and the Intel Pentium. For the latter, some of the numbers may have changed over time, depending on the particular Pentium implementation and intended usage. For example, some Xeon Pentium III systems have large L2 caches (1 or even 2 MB). In the case of the Alpha, the 21064 and the 21164

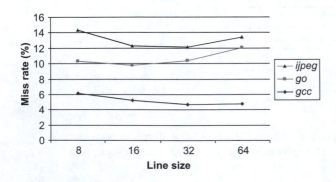

Figure 2.18. Miss rate vs. line size. The data cache is (16 KB,1,L), where L varies from 8 to 64 bytes. The applications are from Spec 95 (from VanVleet et al. [VABBK99]).

have the same microprocessor core. The 21264 has a much more complex execution engine, out-of-order instead of in-order (cf. Chapter 3). Because of this change in instruction execution, the designers felt that longer access times for L2 could be hidden better than in the 21164. Therefore, the chip has larger L1 caches and no L2 cache. In the successor to the 21264 (the 21364, which was never commercially produced because of the demise of DEC), the intent was to keep the 21264 execution model but to return to the cache hierarchy philosophy of the 21164, namely, small L1s and a very large L2 on chip. In the case of the Pentium, the L2 of Pentium II was on a separate chip, but it was "glued" to the processor chip, thus allowing fast access. In the Pentium 4, the I-cache has been replaced by a *trace cache* that has a capacity equivalent to that of an 8 KB I-cache. The design challenges and the advantages brought forth by trace caches will be discussed in Chapter 4.

Finally, we should remember that while we have concentrated our discussion on h and T_{cache}, we have not talked about the parameter T_{mem}, the time to access memory and send the data back to the cache (in case of a cache read miss). T_{mem} can be seen as the sum of two components: the time T_{acc} to access main memory, that is, the time to send the missing line address and the time to read the memory block in the DRAM buffer, plus the time T_{tra} to transfer the memory block from the DRAM to the L1 and L2 caches and the appropriate register. T_{tra} itself is the product of the bus cycle time T_{bus} and the number of bus cycles needed, the latter being L/w, where L is the (L2) line size and w is the bus width. In other words,

$$T_{mem} = T_{acc} + (L/w)T_{bus}$$

EXAMPLE 4 Assume a main memory and bus such that $T_{acc} = 5$, $T_{bus} = 2$, and $w = 64$ bits. For a given application, cache C1 has a hit ratio $h_1 = 0.88$ with a line size $L_1 = 16$ bytes. Cache C2 has a hit ratio $h_2 = 0.92$ with a line size $L_2 = 32$ bytes. The cache access time in both cases is 1 cycle. The average memory access times for the two configurations are

$$Mem1 = 0.88 \times 1 + (1 - 0.88)(5 + 2 \times 2) = 0.88 + 0.12 \times 9 = 1.96$$
$$Mem2 = 0.92 \times 1 + (1 - 0.92)(5 + 4 \times 2) = 0.92 + 0.08 \times 13 = 1.96$$

In this (contrived) example, the two configurations have the same memory access times, although cache C2 would appear to have better performance. Example 4 emphasizes that a metric in isolation, here the hit ratio, is not sufficient to judge the performance of a system component.

2.3 Virtual Memory and Paging

In the previous sections we mostly considered 32-bit architectures, that is, the size of programmable registers was 32 bits. Memory references (which, in general, are generated as the sum of a register and a small constant) were also 32 bits wide. The addressing space was therefore 2^{32} bytes, or 4 GB. Today some servers have main memories approaching that size, and memory capacities for laptops or personal workstations are not far from it. However, many applications have data sets that are larger than 4 GB. It is in order to be able to address these large data sets that we have now 64-bit ISAs, that is, the size of the registers has become 64 bits. The addressing space becomes 2^{64} bytes, a huge number. It is clear that this range of addresses is much too large for main memory capacities.

The disproportion between addressing space and main memory capacity is not new. In the early days of computing, a single program ran on the whole machine. Even so, there was often not enough main memory to hold the program and its data for the whole run. Programs and data were statically partitioned into *overlays* so that parts of the program or data that were not used at the same time could share the same locations in main memory. Soon it became evident that waiting for I/O, a much slower process than in-core computations, was wasteful, and *multiprogramming* became the norm. With multiprogramming, more than one program is resident in main memory at the same time, and when the executing program needs I/O, it relinquishes the CPU to another program. From the memory management viewpoint, multiprogramming poses the following challenges:

- How and where is a program loaded in main memory?
- How does one program ask for more main memory, if needed?
- How is one program protected from another, for example, what prevents one program from accessing another program's data?

The basic answer is that programs are compiled and linked as if they could address the whole addressing space. Therefore, the addresses generated by the CPU are *virtual addresses* that will be translated into *real*, or *physical*, addresses when referencing the physical memory. In early implementations, base and length registers were used, the physical address being the sum of the base register and the virtual address. Programs needed to be in contiguous memory locations, and an exception was raised whenever a physical address was larger than the sum of the base and length registers. In the early 1960s, computer scientists at the University of Manchester introduced the term *virtual memory* and performed the first implementation of a *paging system*. In the next section are presented the salient aspects of paging that influence the architecture of microprocessor systems. Many issues in paging system implementations are in the realm of operating systems and will only be glanced over in this book. All major O.S. textbooks give abundant details on this subject.

2.3.1 Paging Systems

The most common implementation of virtual memory uses paging. The virtual address space is divided into chunks of the same size called (virtual) *pages*. The physical address space, (i.e., the space used to address main memory), is also divided into chunks of the same size, often called physical pages or *frames*. The mapping between pages and frames is fully associative, that is, totally general. In other words, this is a relocation mechanism whereby any page can be stored in any frame and the contiguity restriction enforced by the base and length registers is avoided.

Before proceeding to a more detailed presentation of paging, it is worthwhile to note that the division into equal chunks is totally arbitrary. The chunks could

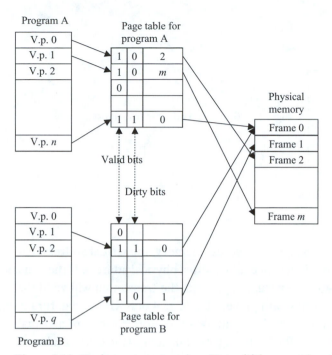

Figure 2.19. Paging system overview. Note: (1) in general n,q are much larger than m; (2) not all of programs A and B are in main memory at a given time, (3) page n of program A and page 1 of program B are shared.

be *segments* of any size. Some early virtual memory systems, such as those present in the Burroughs systems of the late 1960s and 1970s, used segments related to semantic objects: procedures, arrays, and so on. Although this form of segmentation is intellectually more appealing, and even more so now with object-oriented languages, the ease of implementation of paging systems has made them the invariable choice. Today, segments and *segmentation* refer to sets of pages most often grouped by functions, such as code, stack, or *heap* (as in the Intel IA-32 architecture).

Figure 2.19 provides a general view of paging. Two programs A and B are concurrently partially resident in main memory. A mapping device, or *page table* – one per program – indicates which pages of each program are in main memory and gives their corresponding frame numbers. The translation of virtual page number to physical frame number is kept in a *page table entry* (PTE) that, in addition, contains a *valid bit* indicating whether the mapping is current or not, and a *dirty bit* to show whether the page has been modified since it was brought into main memory. The figure shows already four advantages of virtual memory systems:

- The virtual address space can be much larger than the physical memory.
- Not all of the program and its data need to be in main memory at a given time.
- Physical memory can be shared between programs (multiprogramming) without much *fragmentation* (fragmentation is the portion of memory that is allocated and unused because of gaps between allocatable areas).
- Pages can be shared among programs (this aspect of paging is not covered in this book; see a book on operating systems for the issues involved in page sharing).

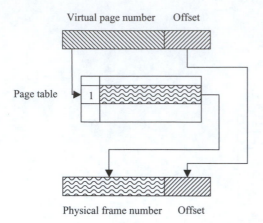

Figure 2.20. Virtual address translation.

When a program executes and needs to access memory, the virtual address that is generated is translated, through the page table, into a physical address. If the valid bit of the PTE corresponding to the virtual page is on, the translation will yield the physical address. Pages sizes are always a power of 2, (e.g., 4 or 8 KB), and naturally physical frames have the same size. A virtual address therefore consists of a virtual page number and an offset, that is, the location within the page (the offset is akin to the displacement in a cache line). Similarly, the physical address will have a physical frame number and the same offset as the virtual address, as illustrated in Figure 2.20. Note that it is not necessary to have virtual and physical addresses be of the same length. Many 64-bit architectures have a 64-bit virtual address but limit the physical address to 40 or 48 bits.

When the PTE corresponding to the virtual page number has its valid bit off, the virtual page is not in main memory. We have a *page fault*, that is, an exception. As we saw in Section 2.1.4, the current program must be suspended and the O.S. will take over. The page fault handler will initiate an I/O read to bring the whole virtual page from disk. Because this I/O read will take several milliseconds, time enough to execute billions of instructions, a *context switch* will occur. After the O.S. saves the process state of the faulting program and initiates the I/O process to handle the page fault, it will give control of the CPU to another program by restoring the process state of the latter.

As presented in Figure 2.20, the virtual address translation requires access to a page table. If that access were to be to main memory, the performance loss would be intolerable: an instruction fetch or a load–store would take tens of cycles. A possible solution would be to cache the PTEs. Although this solution has been implemented in some research machines, the usual and almost universal solution is to have special caches devoted to the translation mechanism with a design tailored for that task. These caches are called *translation look-aside buffers* (TLBs), or sometimes simply translation buffers.

TLBs are organized as caches, so a TLB entry consists of a tag and "data" (in this case a PTE entry). In addition to the valid and dirty bits that we mentioned previously, the PTE contains other bits, related to protection and to recency of access.

Table 2.2. Page sizes and TLB characteristics of two microprocessor families. Recent implementations support more than one page size. In some cases, there are extra TLB entries for a large page size (e.g., 4 MB) used for some scientific or graphic applications

Architecture	Page size	I-TLB	D-TLB
Alpha 21064	8 KB	8 entries (FA)	32 entries (FA)
Alpha 21164	8 KB	48 entries (FA)	64 entries (FA)
Alpha 21264	8 KB	64 entries (FA)	128 entries (FA)
Pentium	4 KB	32 entries (4-way)	64 entries (4-way)
Pentium II	4 KB	32 entries (4-way)	64 entries (4-way)
Pentium III	4 KB	32 entries (4-way)	64 entries (4-way)
Pentium 4	4 KB	64 entries (4-way)	128 entries (4-way)
Core Duo	4 KB	64 entries (FA)	64 entries (FA)

Because TLBs need to cache only a limited number of PTEs, their capacities are much smaller than those of ordinary caches. As a corollary, their associativities can be much greater. Typical TLB sizes and associativities are given in Table 2.2 for the same two families of microprocessors as in Table 2.1. Note that there are distinct TLBs for instruction and data, that the sizes range from 8 to 128 entries with either four-way (Intel) or full associativity (Alpha). Quite often, a fixed set of entries is reserved for the O.S. TLBs are writeback caches: the only information that can change is the setting of the dirty and recency of access bits.

The memory reference process, say for a load instruction, is illustrated in Figure 2.21. After the ALU generates a virtual address, the latter is presented to the TLB.

In the case of a TLB hit with the valid bit of the corresponding PTE on and no protection violation, the physical address is obtained as a concatenation of a field in the PTE and the offset. At the same time, some recency bits in the TLB's copy of the PTE can be modified. In the case of a store, the dirty bit will be turned on. The physical address is now the address seen by the cache, and the remainder of the memory reference process proceeds as explained in Section 2.2. If there is a TLB hit and the valid bit is off, we have a page fault exception. If there is a hit and the valid bit is on but there is a protection violation (e.g., the page that is being read can only be executed), we have an access violation exception, that is, the O.S. will take over.

Figure 2.21. Abstracted view of the memory reference process.

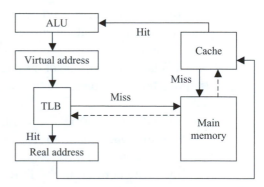

In the case of a TLB miss, the page table stored in main memory must be accessed. Depending on the implementation, this can be done entirely in hardware, or entirely in software, or in a combination of both. For example, in the Alpha family a TLB miss generates the execution of a *Pal* (privileged access library) routine resident in main memory that can load a PTE from a special hardware register into the TLB. In the Intel Pentium architecture, the hardware walks the hierarchically stored page table until the right PTE is found. Replacement algorithms are LRU for the four-way set-associative Intel, and not-most-recently-used for the fully associative TLBs of the Alpha. Once the PTE is in the TLB, after an elapsed time of 100–1000 cycles, we are back to the case of a TLB hit. The rather rapid resolution of a TLB miss does not warrant a context switch (we'll see in Chapter 8 that this may not be the case for multithreaded machines). On the other hand, even with small TLB miss rates, the execution time can be seriously affected. For example, with a TLB miss rate of 0.1 per 1000 instructions and a TLB miss rate resolution time of 1000 cycles, the contribution to *CPI* is 0.1, the same as would arise from an L2 miss rate 10 times higher if the main memory latency were 100 cycles. This time overhead is one of the reasons that many architectures have the capability of several page sizes. When applications require extensive memory, as for example in large scientific applications or in graphics, the possibility of having large page sizes increases the amount of address space mapping that can be stored in the TLB. Of course, this advantage must be weighed against the drawback of memory fragmentation.

In the case of a page fault we have an exception and a context switch. In addition to the actions taken by the O.S. that are briefly outlined below, we must take care of the TLB, for its entries are reflecting the mapping of the process that is relinquishing the processor, not that of the incoming process. One solution is to invalidate the TLB (do not confuse this invalidation with turning off the valid bit in a PTE entry used to indicate whether the corresponding page is in main memory or not). A better solution is to append a *process ID number* (PID) as an extension to the tag in the TLB. The O.S. sets the PID when a program starts executing for the first time or, if it has been swapped out entirely, when it is brought back in. PIDs are recycled when there is an overflow on the count of allowable PIDs. There is a PID register holding the PID of the current executing process, and the detection of a hit or miss in the TLB includes the comparison of the PID in this register with the tag extension. On context switch, the PID of the next-to-execute process is brought into the PID register, and there is no need to invalidate the TLB. When a program terminates or is swapped out, all entries in the TLB corresponding to its PID number are invalidated.

A detailed description of the page fault handler is outside the scope of this book. In broad terms, the handler must (these actions are not listed in order of execution):

- Reserve a frame from a free list maintained by the O.S. for the faulting page.
- Find out where the faulting page resides on disk (this disk address can be an extension to the PTE).
- Invalidate portions of the TLB and maybe of the cache (cf. Section 2.2.1).

- Initiate a read for the faulting page.
- Find the page(s) to replace (using some replacement algorithm) if the list of free pages is not long enough (a tuning parameter of the O.S.). In general, the replacement algorithm is an approximation to LRU.
- Perform cache purges and/or invalidations for cache lines mapping to the page(s) to be replaced.
- Initiate a write to the disk of dirty replaced page(s).

When the faulting page has been read from the disk, an I/O interrupt will be raised. The O.S. will take over and, among other actions, will update the PTE of the page just brought in memory.

Figure 2.21 implies that the TLB access must precede the cache access. Optimizations allow this sequentiality to be relaxed. For example, if the cache access depends uniquely on bits belonging to the page offset, then the cache can be indexed while the TLB access is performed. We shall return to the topic of *virtually indexed* caches in Chapter 6. Note that the larger the page size, the longer the offset and therefore the better the chance of being able to index the cache with bits that do not need to be translated. This observation leads us to consider the design parameters for the selection of a page size.

Most page sizes in contemporary systems are the standard 4 or 8 KB with, as mentioned earlier, the possibility of having several page sizes. This choice is a compromise between various factors, namely, the I/O time to read or write a page from or to disk, main memory fragmentation, and translation overhead.

The time t_x to read (write) a page of size x from (to) disk is certainly smaller than the time t_{2x} to transfer a page of size $2x$, but $t_{2x} < 2t_x$. This is because t_x is the sum of three components, all of which are approximately the same: *seek time*, that is, the time it takes for the disk arm to be positioned on the right track; *rotation time*, that is, the time it takes for the read–write head to be positioned over the right sector; and *transfer time*, that is, the time it takes to transfer the information that is under the read–write head to main memory. The seek time, which ranges from 0 (if the arm is already on the right track) up to 10 ms, is independent of the page size. Similarly, the rotation time, which is on the average half of the time it takes for the disk to perform a complete rotation, is also independent of the page size. Like the seek time, it is of the order of a few milliseconds: 3 ms for a disk rotating at 10,000 rpm. There remains the transfer time, which is proportional to the page size and again can be a few milliseconds. Thus, having large page sizes amortizes the I/O time when several consecutive pages need to be read or written, because although the transfer time increases linearly with page size, the overhead of seek and rotation times is practically independent of the page size.

Another advantage of large page sizes is that page tables will be smaller and TLB entries will map a larger portion of the addressing space. Smaller page tables mean that a greater proportion of PTEs will be in main memory, thus avoiding the double jeopardy of more than one page fault for a given memory reference (see the exercises). Mapping a larger address space into the TLB will reduce the number of

Table 2.3. *Two extremes in the memory hierarchy*

	L1 cache	Paging System
Line or page size	16–64 bytes	4–8 KB
Miss or fault time	5–100 cycles	Millions of cycles
	5–100 ns	3–20 ms
Miss or fault rate	0.1–0.01	0.0001–0.000001
Memory size	4–64 KB	A few gigabytes (physical)
		2^{64} bytes (virtual)
Mapping	Direct-mapped or low associativity	Full generality
Replacement algorithm	Not important	Very important

TLB misses. However, page sizes cannot become too large, because their overall transfer time would become prohibitive and in addition there would be significant memory fragmentation. For example, if, as is the custom, the program's object code, the stack, and the heap each start on page boundaries, then having very large pages can leave a good amount of memory unused.

Cache and TLB geometries as well as the choice of page sizes are arrived at after engineering compromises. The parameters that are used in the design of memory hierarchies are now summarized.

2.3.2 Memory Hierarchy Performance Assessment

We can return now to the four questions we asked at the beginning of Section 2.2.1 regarding cache design and ask them for the three components of the memory hierarchy that we have considered: cache, TLB, and main memory (paging). Although the answers are the same, the implementations of these answers vary widely, as do the physical design properties, as shown in two extremes in Table 2.3. To recap:

1. When do we bring the contents of a missing item into the (cache, TLB, main memory)?

The answer is "on demand." However, in the case of a cache, misses can occur a few times per 100 memory references and the resolution of a cache miss is done entirely in hardware. Miss resolution takes of the order of 5–100 cycles, depending on the level of the memory hierarchy where the missing cache line (8–128 bytes) is found. In the case of a TLB, misses take place two orders of magnitude less often, a few times per 10,000 instructions. TLB miss resolution takes 100–1000 cycles and can be done in either hardware or software. Page faults are much rarer and occur two or three orders of magnitude less often than TLB misses, but page fault resolution takes millions of cycles to resolve. Therefore, page faults will result in context switches.

2. Where do we put the missing item?

In the case of a cache, the mapping is quite restrictive (direct mapping or low set associativity). In the case of a paging system, the mapping is totally general (we shall see some possible exception to this statement when we look at *page coloring* in Chapter 6). For TLBs, we have either full generality or high set associativity.

3. How do we know it's there?

Caches and TLB entries consist of a tag and "data." Comparisons of part of the address with the tag yield the hit or miss knowledge. Page faults are detected by indexing page tables. The organization of page tables (hierarchical, inverted, etc.) is outside the scope of this book.

4. What happens if the place where the missing item is supposed to go is already occupied?

A replacement algorithm is needed. For caches and TLBs, the general rule is (approximation to) LRU with an emphasis on not replacing the most recently used cache line or TLB PTE entry. For paging systems, good replacement algorithms are important, because the page fault rate must be very low. O.S. books have extensive coverage of this important topic. Most operating systems use policies where the number of pages allocated to programs varies according to their working set.

Memory hierarchies have been widely studied because their performance has great influence on the overall execution time of programs. Extensive simulations of paging systems and of cache hierarchies have been done, and numerous results are available. Fortunately, simulations that yield hit rates are much faster than simulations to assess *IPC* or execution times. The speed in simulation is greatly helped by a property of certain replacement algorithms such as LRU, called the *stack property*. A replacement algorithm has the stack property if, for (say) a paging system, the number of page faults for a sequence of memory references for a memory allocation of x pages is greater than or equal to the number of page faults for a memory of size $x + 1$. In other words, the number of page faults is a monotonically nonincreasing function of the amount of main memory. Therefore, one can simulate a whole range of memory sizes in a single simulation pass. For cache simulations, the stack property will hold set by set. Other means of reducing the overall simulation time of cache hierarchies and generalizing the results to other metrics and other geometries include mechanisms such as filtering the reference stream in a preprocessing phase and applying clever algorithms for multiple associativities.

Finally, while LRU is indeed an excellent replacement algorithm, it is not optimal. The optimal algorithm for minimizing the number of page faults (or cache misses on a set by set basis) is due to Belady. Belady's algorithm states that the page to be replaced is the one in the current resident set that will be accessed further in the future. Of course, this optimal algorithm is not realizable in real time, but the optimal number of faults (or misses) can be easily obtained in simulation and thus provide a measure of the goodness of the replacement algorithm under study.

2.4 Summary

Pipelining is the basic architectural principle found in all modern processors. It allows overlapped execution of consecutive instructions. In a simple implementation, a processor pipeline consists of five stages: instruction fetch, instruction decode, execution, memory access, and writeback of results in registers. Stages are separated by buffers or pipeline registers. The state of the processor is modified only during the last stage, thus allowing the treatment of precise exceptions and interrupts.

The theoretical throughput of the pipeline of one instruction per cycle ($IPC = 1$) cannot be achieved, because of data and control hazards. Some data hazards due to read-after-write (RAW) dependencies can be dealt with by forwarding results from pipeline registers to the execution unit. Performance degradation due to control flow instructions can be mitigated using branch prediction techniques.

An *IPC* of one requires that instruction fetches and memory accesses be performed in one cycle. With main memory accesses taking 10–100 cycles, caches are necessary to get close to an ideal *IPC*. Caches are high-speed buffers that contain images of instructions and data stored in memory. The most common cache organization is set-associative, a compromise between the simplest and most restrictive direct-mapped organization and the most complex and totally general fully associative scheme. Caches are characterized by their geometry: capacity, associativity, and line size. The main performance metric associated with caches is the hit rate, that is, the proportion of memory references that are found in the cache.

In general-purpose computer systems, the O.S. supports multiprogramming, whereby several (parts of) programs reside simultaneously in main memory. Virtual memory, and its implementation through paging systems, allows programs to be as large as the address space and provides a means to keep in main (physical) memory a portion of an executing program corresponding to its working set. Pages of virtual space (i.e., fixed-size blocks of the program and its data) are mapped into main memory. The mapping device is a page table. The virtual-to-real address translation is speeded up by the use of special caches, named translation look-aside buffers (TLBs).

2.5 Further Reading and Bibliographical Notes

Textbooks on computer architecture or computer organization such as Patterson and Hennessy's [PH04] and Shen and Lipasti's [SL04] give excellent introductions to pipelining and the memory hierarchy. Instruction pipelining, originally called instruction overlap or instruction lookahead, was first introduced in IBM's Project Stretch [Bu62], a precursor (1962) to the IBM System/360 Model 91. The f-p units of the latter, designed in the mid 1960s, were pipelined [AEDP67]. Kogge's book [K81] is a superb reference on theoretical and practical aspects of pipelining, including the design of dynamic configured pipelines where the pipelines can perform distinct computations. Kogge states that, as of 1980, the distinction between overlap and pipelining had become fuzzy. Today, pipelining is the term of choice.

The five-stage pipeline of Section 2.1 is the one found in the MIPS R3000 and is described in detail in Patterson and Hennessy [PH04]. The alternative design shown in Figure 2.9 was implemented in the original Intel Pentium. A comparison between these two approaches is given in Golden and Mudge [GM94]. A description of a Wallace tree multiplier can be found in Kogge's book.

Caches were first introduced in the IBM System/360 Model 85 [CGP68] in the late 1960s; Wilkes [W65] had defined the concept of "slave" memory a few years earlier. The story of the naming of caches, originally intended to be called high-speed memory buffers or muffers (*sic*), is recounted in the book by Pugh, Johnson, and Palmer [PJP91], which contains fascinating tidbits about the IBM System/360 and 370 models. A. J. Smith [S82] wrote an extensive survey on cache memories (up to the early eighties). A review of the performance of caches was updated a decade later by Przybylski [P90]. The classification of cache misses into three C's is due to Mark Hill [H87]. The data used for Figures 2.16 and 2.17 come from Cantin and Hill [CH03]. Full cache performance data for SPEC 2000 can be found at http://www.cs.wisc.edu/multifacet/misc/spec2000cache-data/. Figure 2.18 uses data from VanVleet et al. [VABBK99].

Virtual memory was first introduced in the Atlas computer designed by Kilburn and his colleagues at the University of Manchester in the early 1960s [KELS62]. The mapping device for the paging system was an associative memory! Denning's survey [D70] is an early (1970) basic reference for virtual memory systems. Any good textbook on operating systems will discuss virtual memory and its implementation via paging or segmentation. There exist many papers on replacement algorithms. Belady's optimal algorithm [Be66] was published in 1966. TLBs were introduced for the IBM System/370 in the early 1970s.

Translation look-aside buffers (TLBs) have also been called translation buffers (TBs) in the DEC VAX, associative memory in the GE-645 Multics implementation, and directory look-aside in the early implementations of IBM System/370. It seems that the first use of the term TLB was in a paper by Case and Padegs [CP78] describing the architecture of System/370. The term "look-aside" comes from an early paper by Lee [L69] describing a fully associative cache that was looked "aside" the main memory, in contrast with the "look-ahead" property of pipelining.

Uhlig and Mudge [UM97] surveyed the state of the art in trace-driven simulation a decade ago. Not much of a conceptual nature has changed since. Mattson et al. [MGST70] first proved the stack property for LRU and Belady's algorithm. Many trace-driven simulators are in the public domain. For example, Dinero developed by Mark Hill and his students is available at http://www.cs.wisc.edu/~markhill/DineroIV/.

EXERCISES

1. (Sections 2.1.2 and 2.1.4) Assume that you want to use only one ALU for the basic five-stage pipeline of Section 2.1.2. A problem arises when you implement branches in that the ALU needs to be used twice: once for branch target computation and once for making the register comparison. Design the data path and control unit with this constraint. What are the performance implications?

2. (Section 2.1.5) In the alternative five-stage pipeline of Figure 2.9, there are already two ALUs. If these two were used respectively for branch target computation and register comparison, what would be the penalties for branch instructions:

(a) In the case where stalling occurs as soon as a branch is recognized?

(b) In the case where a branch-not-taken prediction policy is used?

3. (Section 2.1.4) Some authors have advocated that the target address calculation for a branch and the register comparison be both done in the ID stage, arguing that the comparison can be done very fast (e.g., at the same time as the source registers are copied in the ID/EX register).

(a) What changes are to be made to the forwarding unit and the stalling control unit in order to implement this optimization?

(b) How many cycles will be saved if both registers are available?

4. (Section 2.1.4) Assume that an interrupt is detected at time t. One of the instructions currently in the pipeline at time t generates an exception before its completion. How would you solve this problem?

5. (Sections 2.1.3 and 2.1.5) What modifications are necessary for the pipeline design and forwarding paths of Section 2.1.3 if load–store instructions include auto-increment instructions of the form

$$R_i \leftarrow Mem[R_j + displ], \quad R_j \leftarrow R_j + c$$

(and similarly for stores), where the two operations are considered to be part of the same instruction and c is a constant that depends on the size of the data that are loaded (or stored). Auto-increment loads (and stores) will have their own opcodes.

6. (Section 2.1.6) Consider the addition of two single-precision f-p numbers in the IEEE standard representation. The last step in the addition is the normalization of the result. What is the maximum number of bits that might have to be shifted left in order to get a normalized result? What is the maximum number of bits that might have to be shifted right in order to get a normalized result?

7. (Section 2.1.6) Repeat the previous exercise for the multiplication case.

8. (Section 2.2.1) Which of the following statements concerning the hit rate of a direct-mapped cache is (are) generally true:

(a) The hit rate will increase if we double the cache capacity without changing the line size.

(b) The hit rate will increase if we double the line size without changing the capacity.

(c) The hit rate will increase if we keep the same capacity and line size but the cache is made two-way set-associative.

9. (Section 2.2.1) Arrays A and B contain 1 K (1024) elements each. Each element is 4 bytes. The first element of A ($A[0]$) is stored at physical address 0x0000 4000.

The first element of B ($B[0]$) is stored at physical address 0x0001 0800. A physical address is 32 bits. Assume that only arrays A and B will be cached in the following fragment of code (i.e., the index i will be in a register):

```
for (i = 1023; i >= 0; i--) {
    A[i] = i;
    B[i] = A[i]+i;
    }
```

The cache is a 4 KB direct-mapped cache with line size 16 bytes. The write policy is writeback. Initially, all entries in the cache are marked as invalid.

    (a) How many cache lines are there in the cache?

    (b) What will be the cache contents at the end of the program fragment (i.e., when all 1024 iterations of the loop have completed)?

    (c) How many read misses and write misses did occur? Would the number of read and write misses have been different if the 4 KB cache had been two-way set-associative (keeping the same 4 KB capacity and 16 byte line size)?

    (d) How many bytes were written back to memory?

10. (Section 2.2.1) Repeat the previous exercise for a write-through cache.

11. (Section 2.2.1) As a designer you are asked to evaluate three possible options for an on-chip write-through data cache. Some of the design options (associativity) and performance consequences (miss rate, miss penalty) are described in the table below:

Data cache options	Miss rate	Miss penalty
Cache A: Direct mapped	0.08	4 cycles
Cache B: Two-way set-associative	0.04	6 cycles
Cache C: Four-way set-associative	0.02	8 cycles

    (a) Assume that load instructions have a *CPI* of 1.2 if they hit in the cache and a *CPI* of 1.2 + (miss penalty) otherwise. All other instructions have a *CPI* of 1.2. The instruction mix is such that 20% of instructions are loads. What is the *CPI* for each configuration (you'll need to keep three decimal digits, i.e., compute the *CPI* as x.xxx)? Which cache would you choose if *CPI* is the determining factor?

    (b) Assume now that if the direct-mapped cache is used, the cycle time is 20 ns. If the two-way set-associative cache is used, the cycle time is 22 ns. If the four-way is used, the cycle time is 24 ns. What is the average time per instruction? Which cache would you choose if average time per instruction is the determining factor?

    (c) In the case of the two-way set-associative cache, the replacement algorithm is LRU. In the case of the four-way set-associative cache, the replacement algorithm is such that the most recently used (MRU) line is not replaced;

the choice of which of the other three is replaced is random and not part of the logic associated with each line in the cache. Indicate what bits are needed to implement the replacement algorithms for each line.

12. (Sections 2.2 and 2.3) Here is the skeleton of part of a program that simulates the memory hierarchy of a computer system. Only the instruction fetch simulation is outlined:

```
Get_next_tuple (operation,vaddress);
    case: operation = 0/* we have an instruction fetch*/
    Extract_TLB_fields;
    Check_TLB;
    If not TLBhit then Get_PTE_from_Main_Memory;
    Get_physical_address;
    Extract_cache_fields;
    Check_cache;
    If not cachehit then Get_Cache_Block_from_Main_Memory;
    Put instruction in IR;
    case:....
```

From the instruction fetch viewpoint, the hierarchy consists of a four-way set-associative TLB of 64 entries and a two-way 8 KB set-associative cache with 32 byte lines (each instruction is 4 bytes). Both structures use an LRU replacement algorithm.

The computer system runs under an operating system with paging. The page size is 4 KB. Both virtual and physical addresses are 32 bits.

The input to the program is a trace of tuples (operation,addresses). An operation of value 0 indicates an instruction fetch.

(a) The routine "Extract_TLB_fields" takes a 32-bit address, called *vaddress*, as input parameter. It should return two values: *tagtlb* and *indextlb*, which will be used to check the TLB. Indicate in pseudocode how you would get them. An example of pseudocode (with no particular meaning) is:

xyz = abc shifted right by 16;
xyz = xyz and 0x0000 00ff

(b) The routine "Check_TLB" takes *tagtlb* and *indextlb* as input parameters. It returns a Boolean value *TLBhit* indicating whether there is a TLB hit or a TLB miss. In the case of a hit, it returns also a *physical_frame_number* value that indicates the mapping between the virtual page number and the physical frame number. (You can assume that on a TLB hit there is no page fault.) In the worst case, how many comparisons are needed in "Check_TLB" to see whether you have a hit or a miss? What are the theoretical minimum and maximum values of *physical_frame_number*? If the first 16 K of physical memory are reserved for the operating system and I/O and are not pageable, and if the physical memory is 256 MB, what are the real minimum and maximum values of *physical_frame_number*?

(c) In the case of a miss, the routine "Get_PTE_from_Main_Memory" will return *physical_frame_number*. The routine "Get_physical_address" takes *vaddress* and *physical_frame_number* as input parameters and returns a 32-bit *physical_address* value. Write the pseudocode for "Get_physical_address".

(d) The routine "Extract_cache_fields" takes *physical_address* as input parameter and returns two values: *tagcache* and *indexcache*, which will be used to access the cache. Write the pseudocode for this routine.

(e) Assume:
  • No page fault.
  • It takes 1 cycle to obtain *physical_address* in the case of a TLB hit, and 100 cycles in the case of a TLB miss.
  • Once *physical_address* has been obtained, it takes 1 cycle to get the instruction in IF/ID in the case of a cache hit, and 50 cycles in the case of a cache miss.

If the TLB hit rate is 0.995 and the cache hit rate is 0.97, what is the average instruction fetch time?

13. (Section 2.3) Which of the following statements concerning the capacity of a TLB is (are) true?

(a) A larger TLB will reduce the number of cache misses.

(b) A larger TLB will reduce the number of page faults.

14. (Section 2.3) Upon a load instruction, the event "data-TLB hit" followed by "data-cache hit" is the most likely to occur among the four possibilities of the Cartesian product (data-TLB hit, data-TLB miss) × (data-cache hit, data-cache miss). Are the three other events possible? Justify your answers with an example for each possibility or an explanation of the impossibility.

15. (Sections 2.2 and 2.3) Assume that it takes 1 cycle to access and return the information on a data-TLB hit and 1 cycle to access and return the information on a data-cache hit. A data-TLB miss takes 300 cycles to resolve, and a data-cache miss takes 100 cycles to resolve. The data-TLB hit rate is 0.99, and the data-cache hit rate is 0.95. What is the average memory access time for a load data reference? Now the data cache is an L1 D-cache and is backed up by an L2 unified cache. Every data reference that misses in L1 has a 60% chance of hitting in L2. A miss in L1 followed by a hit in L2 has a latency of 10 cycles. What is the average memory access time for a load data reference in this new configuration?

REFERENCES

[AEGP67] S. Anderson, J. Earle, R. Goldschmitt, and D. Powers, "The IBM System/360 Model 91: Floating-point Execution Unit," *IBM Journal of Research and Development*, 11, Jan. 1967, 34–53

[Be66] L. Belady, "A Study of Replacement Algorithms for a Virtual Storage Computer," *IBM Systems Journal*, 5, 1966, 78–101

[Bu62] W. Bucholz (Ed.), *Planning a Computer System: Project Stretch*, McGraw-Hill, New York, 1962

[CGP68] C. Conti, D. Gibson, and S. Pitkowsky, "Structural Aspects of the IBM System 360/85; General Organization," *IBM Systems Journal*, 7, 1968, 2–14

[CH03] J. Cantin and M. Hill, Cache Performance for SPEC CPU2000 Benchmarks, Version 3.0, May 2003, http://www.cs.wisc.edu/multifacet/misc/spec2000cache-data/

[CP78] R. Case and A. Padegs, "The Architecture of the IBM System/370," *Communications of the ACM*, 21, 1, Jan. 1978, 73–96

[D70] P. Denning, "Virtual Memory," *ACM Computing Surveys*, 2, Sep. 1970, 153–189

[GM94] M. Golden and T. Mudge, "A Comparison of Two Pipeline Organizations," *Proc. 27th Int. Symp. on Microarchitecture*, 1994, 153–161

[H87] M. Hill, Aspects of Cache Memory and Instruction Buffer Performance, Ph.D. Dissertation, Univ. of California, Berkeley, Nov. 1987

[K81] P. Kogge, *The Architecture of Pipelined Computers*, McGraw-Hill, New York, 1981

[KELS62] T. Kilburn, D. Edwards, M. Lanigan, and F. Sumner, "One-level Storage System," *IRE Trans. on Electronic Computers*, EC-11, 2, Apr. 1962, 223–235

[L69] J. Lee, "Study of 'Look-Aside' Memory," *IEEE Trans. on Computers*, C-18, 11, Nov. 1969, 1062–1065

[MGST70] R. Mattson, J. Gecsei, D. Slutz, and I. Traiger, "Evaluation Techniques for Storage Hierarchies," *IBM Systems Journal*, 9, 1970, 78–117

[P90] S. Przybylski, *Cache Design: A Performance Directed Approach*, Morgan Kaufman Publishers, San Francisco, 1990

[PH04] D. Patterson and J. Hennessy, *Computer Organization & Design: The Hardware/Software Interface*, Third Edition, Morgan Kaufman Publishers, San Francisco, 2004

[PJP91] E. Pugh, L. Johnson, and J. Palmer, *IBM's 360 and Early 370 Systems*, The MIT Press, Cambridge, MA, 1991

[S82] A. Smith, "Cache Memories," *ACM Computing Surveys*, 14, 3, Sep. 1982, 473–530

[SL04] J. P. Shen and M. Lipasti, *Modern Processor Design Fundamentals of Superscalar Processors*, McGraw-Hill, 2004

[UM97] R. Uhlig and T. Mudge, "Trace-driven Memory Simulation: A Survey," *ACM Computing Surveys*, 29, 2, Jun. 1997, 128–170

[VABBK99] P. VanVleet, E. Anderson, L. Brown, J.-L. Baer, and A. Karlin, "Pursuing the Performance Potential of Dynamic Cache Lines," *Proc. ICCD*, Oct. 1999, 528–537

[W65] M. Wilkes, "Slave Memories and Dynamic Storage Allocation," *IEEE Trans on Electronic Computers*, EC-14, Apr. 1965, 270–271

3 Superscalar Processors

3.1 From Scalar to Superscalar Processors

In the previous chapter we introduced a five-stage pipeline. The basic concept was that the instruction execution cycle could be decomposed into nonoverlapping stages with one instruction passing through each stage at every cycle. This so-called *scalar* processor had an ideal throughput of 1, or in other words, ideally the number of instructions per cycle (*IPC*) was 1.

If we return to the formula giving the execution time, namely,

$$EX_{CPU} = Number\ of\ instructions \times CPI \times cycle\ time$$

we see that in order to reduce EX_{CPU} in a processor with the same ISA – that is, without changing the number of instructions, N – we must either reduce *CPI* (increase *IPC*) or reduce the cycle time, or both. Let us look at the two options.

The only possibility to increase the ideal *IPC* of 1 is to radically modify the structure of the pipeline to allow more than one instruction to be in each stage at a given time. In doing so, we make a transition from a scalar processor to a *superscalar* one. From the microarchitecture viewpoint, we make the pipeline *wider* in the sense that its representation is not linear any longer. The most evident effect is that we shall need several functional units, but, as we shall see, each stage of the pipeline will be affected.

The second option is to reduce the cycle time through an increase in clock frequency. In order to do so, each stage must perform less work. Therefore, a stage must be decomposed into smaller stages, and the overall pipeline becomes *deeper*.

Modern microprocessors are therefore both wider and deeper than the five-stage pipeline of the previous chapter. In order to study the design decisions that are necessary to implement the concurrency caused by the superscalar effect and the consequences of deeper pipelines, it is convenient to distinguish between the *front-end* and the *back-end* of the pipeline. The front-end, which corresponds to the IF and ID stages, now must fetch and decode several instructions at once. The number m of instructions brought (ideally) into the pipeline at each cycle defines the processor as an *m-way* superscalar. The back-end, which corresponds to the

EX, Mem, and WB stages, must execute and write back several instructions concurrently.

Superscalar microprocessors can be divided into two categories. In both cases, instructions proceed in the front-end in program order. In *in-order*, or *static*, superscalar processors, the instructions leave the front-end in strict program order and all data dependencies are resolved before the instructions are passed to the back-end. In *out-of-order*, or *dynamic*, superscalar processors, the instructions can leave the front-end and execute in the back-end before some of their program-order predecessors. In a dynamic superscalar, the WB stage, now called the *commit* stage, must be designed in such a way that the semantics of the program are respected, that is, the results must be stored in the order intended by the source code. Out-of-order processors are arguably more complex to design and to implement than in-order ones. It is estimated that for the same number of functional units, they require 30% more logic, and, naturally, the design complexity translates into longer time to market.

Theoretically, if we have an m-way superscalar with a clock frequency k times that of a scalar one with the same ISA, we should realize an mk speedup. While this theoretical speedup can be approached for small m and k, there are behavioral, design, and technological factors that limit the increase in m and k. We give here a nonexhaustive list of the most salient ones:

- In order to sustain the concurrent execution of many instructions, that is, have a large m, we need to uncover a large amount of *instruction-level parallelism* (ILP). This is especially difficult in an in-order processor, wherein instructions that have (RAW) dependencies cannot leave the front-end until the dependencies are resolved. In an out-of-order processor there is more latitude to find independent instructions, but it is at the cost of increased hardware and design complexity. While some researchers envisioned 8-way and even 16-way dynamic superscalars, there is no current implementation that is more than 6-way, and the trend is not towards increasing m.
- A second factor that limits m is that the back-end requires at least m functional units. Although implementing a large number, say n, of functional units is not limiting with respect to the amount of logic needed, the number of forwarding paths grows as n^2. Some of these paths will necessarily be long, and the wire lengths may prevent forwarding in a single cycle.
- Several factors limit improvements in cycle time. A first constraint, already mentioned, is that power dissipation increases with frequency. A second constraint is that pipeline registers, (i.e., the stable storage between stages, must be written and read at each cycle), thus providing a physical lower bound on the cycle time.
- Deep pipelines, (i.e., those having a large k), have a significant drawback. The resolution of some speculative action, like a branch prediction, will be known only late in the pipeline. In the case of a misspeculation, recovery is delayed and may contribute to a loss in performance (lower *IPC*) compared to a shorter

pipeline. The trend to deep pipes, exemplified by the Pentium 4 with a branch misprediction penalty of 20 cycles (the pipeline was up to 31 stages in the Pentium D) vs. only 10 stages in the Pentium III, was reversed in the Intel Core architecture, which has a 14-stage pipeline.

In-order superscalar microprocessors, the logical successors of the pipeline processors of the previous chapter, were the first in production. When both in-order and out-of-order microprocessors became available, the relative ease of implementation of in-order processors allowed their manufacture with faster clock speed. Until the mid 1990s, the performance of in-order "speed demons" tended to dominate that of the out-of-order "brainiacs," which had slower clock speed but higher *IPC*. After that time frame, the out-of-order processors started to take over, thanks in part to Moore's law, which allowed more functionality and more hardware assists on chip.

Today high-performance single-processor microprocessors are out-of-order ones. The speed advantage of the in-order processors has disappeared since power dissipation has capped the increases in clock frequency. Because of the limit imposed on speed by power dissipation, because of the continuous validity of Moore's law, which allows more logic on a chip, and because the performance that can be attained with a single processor cannot be increased without adding extreme design complexity, the single processor is being replaced by multiprocessors. Whether multiprocessors on a chip (CMP) will consist of simple in-order or complex out-of-order processors, or a mix, is still an open question (cf. Chapters 7 and 8). Thus, it is important to study both types of microarchitectures.

This chapter gives overviews of the instruction pipelines of an in-order processor, the DEC Alpha 21164 (vintage 1994), and of an out-of-order one, the Intel Pentium P6 architecture started in the early 1990s and still in use, as exemplified by the Intel Pentium III (announced in 1999) and the recent Pentium Core. Whereas we can describe the Alpha instruction pipeline with the knowledge that we have so far, the transition from an in-order to an out-of-order processor requires the introduction of new concepts such as *register renaming*, *reorder buffer*, and *reservation stations*. In this chapter, the basic concepts are explained. Detailed and/or alternate implementations, for components of both the front-end (such as branch prediction and register renaming) and the back-end (such as instruction scheduling and load speculation), will be presented in Chapters 4 and 5. Because of their historical importance and because they have strongly influenced the design of current microprocessors, we will also present the scoreboard of the CDC 6600 and Tomasulo's algorithm for the IBM System 360/91.

Because the focus of this book is on microarchitecture, we do not emphasize compiler techniques that can enhance performance. Compiler optimizations are quite important for in-order processors, for they can remove statically some data dependencies. We conclude the chapter with an introduction to the design paradigm of *very long instruction word* (VLIW)/ *explicitly parallel instruction computing* (EPIC). In VLIW/EPIC processors, the compiler is responsible for detecting and scheduling the instruction-level parallelism. The compiler decides which operations can execute in the same cycle under the constraints of the concurrency offered by the functional units and the data flow of the program. We will use the Intel Itanium as the example general-purpose processor. The VLIW technique is also widely used in embedded processors where programs are short and can be hand-tuned.

Finally, the reader may have noticed that so far we have not mentioned the memory hierarchy design and whether memory latencies might be better tolerated in static or dynamic superscalars. Part of the answer is that for long latencies, like those occurring on misses that percolate up to main memory, both architectures will suffer performance degradation. Latencies are of the order of 100 cycles, and it is impossible to schedule statically enough instructions to cover that span of time. In the case of dynamic superscalars, many queuing structures will be full before the memory access is resolved, and the pipeline(s) will be stalled because of structural hazards. Since context switching, which requires saving and restoring states, takes longer than a memory access, this is not a viable solution. An alternative is to implement in hardware several contexts – that is, fast, stable storage units – that can hold the state of a process. Context switching now can be very fast, especially for lightweight processes, or *threads*, that share a common address space. This technique, called *multithreading*, will be discussed in detail in Chapter 8.

3.2 Overview of the Instruction Pipeline of the DEC Alpha 21164

3.2.1 General Organization

The DEC Alpha 21164 (Figure 3.1), introduced in 1994, is a four-way in-order RISC superscalar processor. Its clock frequency was 300 MHz, and there were 9.3 million transistors on chip. The RISC label means that the Alpha ISA is of the load–store type with all instructions being register–register except for those accessing memory. There are 32 64-bit integer registers and 32 floating-point registers, and an additional 8 integer registers used only by the Pal code (recall Section 2.3.1). Since it is four-way, up to four instructions can pass through each stage of the front-end on any given cycle. Its predecessor, the Alpha 21064, was only two-way.

The back-end consists of four functional units. There are two integer pipelines and two floating-point pipelines. Both integer pipelines can perform the simple arithmetic and logical operations, including the address computation for load–store instructions. One integer pipe has a shifter and multiplier associated with it. The multiply operation is partially pipelined, and its latency depends on the size of the data (32 or 64 bits). The other integer pipe handles branches. Integer operations other than multiply, conditional moves, and divide have a latency of 1 cycle. Integer divide is handled in software. One floating-point unit is dedicated to multiplication; the other one handles all other operations, including divide – the only operation that is not pipelined. The latency of all floating-point operations except divide is 4 cycles.

The instruction pipeline is shown in Figure 3.2. As can be seen, the front-end takes 4 cycles. The overall number of stages is seven for the integer pipelines and

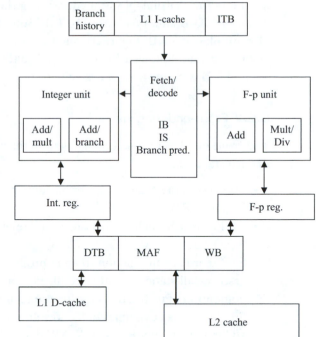

Figure 3.1. Alpha 21164 block diagram (simplified from Bhandarkar's book [B95]).

nine for the floating-point pipelines. Since some of the basic steps of instruction execution take more than one stage, this processor is sometimes referred to as *super-pipelined*. This property is true of all general-purpose microprocessors of that era and thereafter.

The on-chip memory hierarchy main parameters can be found in Tables 2.1 and 2.2 in Chapter 2. To recap, the L1 I-cache and L1 D-cache are 8 KB, direct-mapped and with 32-byte lines. Since the page size is 8 KB or more, the caches can be virtually addressed (cf. Chapter 6.1). The L2 cache is 96 KB, is three-way set-associative, and has 32-byte lines. The L1 D-cache is write-through, and the L2 is writeback. L1 data cache misses to the same line that has not yet been requested from L2 can be merged in a *miss address file* (MAF). Stores can also be merged in

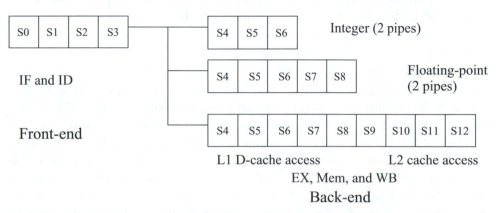

Figure 3.2. The 21164 instruction pipeline (stage S4 of the memory pipe uses an integer pipe).

a write buffer. Virtual–physical address translation is handled by a fully associative 48-entry I-TLB and a 64-entry D-TLB. Both TLBs can handle several page sizes, all multiples of 8 KB. Figure 3.2 shows that the L1 D-cache hit latency is 3 cycles, whereas a miss followed by a hit in L2 takes an extra 6 cycles. Prefetching (see Section 6.2) is performed extensively for the L1 I-cache.

3.2.2 Front-end Pipeline

The front-end has four stages, labeled S0 through S3. In broad terms, the function of each stage is:

- S0: Access the I-cache and bring four instructions into one of two instruction buffers (IBs).
- S1: Perform branch prediction, calculate branch target address, and validate the I-cache access.
- S2: Steer each instruction to an appropriate functional unit. This *slotting* stage resolves all static execution conflicts, that is, structural hazards caused by the contention of instructions for functional units.
- S3: Perform all dynamic conflict resolution: detect and schedule forwarding and stalling due to any RAW or WAW dependencies.

Instructions can move from one stage to another only if all instructions in the subsequent stage have been processed. Note that for integer programs, a maximum of two arithmetic instructions can leave S3 on a given cycle. If there are more than two instructions in S2 that require the use of an integer pipeline, only the first two will pass to S3. Instructions in S0 and S1 will stall, and no new instructions will be fetched. Note that this is not a bubble, for no stage is left empty.

Let us look in slightly more detail at each stage, starting with S0 and S1. In S0, the I-cache and the I-TLB are accessed in parallel. Four instructions (they must be aligned in the same I-cache line; otherwise, only those remaining in the line are considered) are returned and stored in one of two four-entry IBs, assuming that one of these is totally empty. Each instruction is already partially decoded, that is, a 4 byte instruction is supplemented by 5 bits of information that will be used in S1 for branch prediction and in S2 for slotting. Since the I-cache is virtually indexed, the verification of a hit or miss is done in S1. In case of a miss, a request is made to L2, using a stream buffer prefetching technique that will be explained in Chapter 6. Naturally, in the case of a miss the contents of the just-filled instruction buffer are voided. In S1 branch prediction is performed (branch prediction is treated thoroughly in Chapter 4); suffice to say here that the branch predictor of the 21164 is not very sophisticated by today's standard. It uses the 5 predecoded bits to recognize that one of the instructions is a branch and to perform the prediction. The branch target address is also computed in S1, and if the prediction is for branch taken, the PC is modified accordingly. Although it appears that a bubble in the front-end is required for a successful branch-taken prediction, quite often this no-op slot will be amortized because of the stage-to-stage instruction-passing mechanism requiring total emptiness of a stage before it is refilled.

S0 and S1 correspond approximately to the functionality of the IF and part of the ID stage of a scalar processor. S2 and S3 correspond to the reminder of the ID stage plus the functions that are provided by the forwarding and stalling units. Of course, the latter are expanded, because the back-end has multiple functional units. The S2 slotting stage takes the four instructions from the current instruction buffer and places them in its slotting register if the latter is empty. When S3 does not have any more instructions to process, the S2 stage passes to S3, in strict program order, all instructions remaining in the slotting register that can be assigned to one of the four execution and memory pipelines.

EXAMPLE 1: Assume that the four instructions in the slotting register are:

$i1$:   R1 ← R2 + R3   # Use integer pipeline 1
$i2$:   R4 ← R1 − R5   # Use integer pipeline 2. Notice the RAW with $i1$
$i3$:   R7 ← R8 − R9   # Requires an integer pipeline
$i4$:   F0 ← F2 + F4   # Floating-point add

The first two instructions only will be passed to S3 and the two integer pipelines: the third one requires also an integer pipeline, and the fourth one cannot advance, because the third one is blocked. S2 is therefore the stage where structural hazards for functional units are detected.

S3 is the *issue* stage. The main logic apparatus is a *scoreboard* (cf. the Sidebar on the CDC 6600 scoreboard) that monitors the execution of instructions in progress and sends control signals for forwarding and writing in result registers. The status of all registers and the progress of the instructions in the back-end are monitored exactly, because all instructions have fixed latencies except for (i) integer multiplies and floating-point divides, whose latencies can be easily computed by the score-board once the size of the data is known, and (ii) load accesses to the L1 cache, because there can be a hit or a miss. Once an instruction leaves the S3 stage, it will run to completion unless there is a control hazard or it is dependent on a load instruction that resulted in a cache miss (see next section).

Data hazards, (i.e., RAW and WAW dependencies), are resolved during S3. No instruction can leave S3 unless the source registers are available either directly or as a byproduct of forwarding in the next cycle. In the example above, because the integer subtract $i2$ has a RAW dependency with its integer add predecessor $i1$, it would be stalled for one cycle and its successors would have to remain in the S2 stage. While there is certainly a loss in *IPC* due to the RAW dependency, there is no bubble in the overall execution. At least one instruction has progressed. This is the case for the great majority of integer instructions (conditional moves – introduced in Section 3.4 of this chapter – and multiplies are the major exceptions). RAW dependencies in floating-point instructions reaching S3 in the same cycle stall the dependent instruction for 4 cycles (floating-point divide takes longer). WAW dependencies are resolved by preserving the program order for writes. In particular, if two instructions are scheduled to write the same register without an intervening RAW dependency, they are prevented from doing so in the same cycle, and the first one in program order must write the register first. This situation is extremely rare in in-order

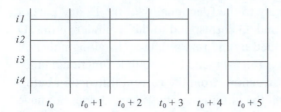

At time t_0 the four instructions are in stage S0.

All four are in S1 at time $t_0 + 1$ and in S2 at $t_0 + 2$. New instructions fill stages S0 and S1.

At time $t_0 + 3$ only $i1$ and $i2$ pass to S3. $i3$ and $i4$ remain in S2. No new instructions are fetched.

At time $t_0 + 4$, $i1$ passes to the back-end. $i2$ remains in S3; $i3$ and $i4$ remain in S2. No new instructions are fetched.

At time $t_0 + 5$, $i2$ passes to the back-end. $i3$ and $i4$ pass to S3. The instructions in S1 and S0 can progress, and new instructions are fetched.

Figure 3.3. Illustration of occupancy of the front-end.

processors, for if it took place the result of the first instruction would never be used (see the exercises). Nonetheless, it needs to be checked for.

Figure 3.3 illustrates the progression in the front-end of the four instructions in Example 1.

3.2.3 Back-end: Memory Operations and Control Hazards

On a load–store instruction, the address computation is performed during stage S4 in either of the integer pipelines. The beginning of the L1 D-cache and D-TLB accesses is also done during S4. During S5, the cache and TLB controllers check whether there is a hit or a miss. In case of a hit, the data are forwarded if needed and written to either the integer or the floating-point register file during S6. Thus, the latency of an L1 hit is 2 cycles, because the data are available at the end of S5. In case of a miss, the L2 cache is accessed starting at stage S5. The data will become available at S12.

Some details are omitted in this description because they are peculiar to the 21164. For example, the result of a floating-point load is available only one cycle later for forwarding purposes. Let us simply note that several L1 misses can be pending and that stores are written first in a write buffer. These two hardware assists allow concurrency in memory operations but do not prevent totally the possibility of structural hazards, because the buffers (MAF and write buffer) can become full. The designs and uses of these buffers will be treated more fully in Chapter 6.

Since the latency of an L1 hit is 2 cycles, there can be a bona fide stall if the consumer of the load is the instruction following it. The scoreboard prevents the dependent instruction from issuing for the cycle where the load was issued and, as was the case for the scalar pipelines, for the subsequent one. If both the load and its dependent instruction reached S3 in the same cycle, say t, the load will be issued at $t + 1$ and the dependent instruction at $t + 3$. A real bubble occurs during time $t + 2$, because no instruction can move from S2 to S3 (not all instructions in S3 have been issued) and the dependent instruction and its successors cannot move from S3 to S4.

The scoreboard, though, cannot know whether there will be a hit or a miss. It speculatively assumes a hit, because that is the common case; the guess will be right over 90% of the time. If it guessed wrong – and this will be known at stage S5 – instruction issue can still go on until an instruction dependent on the load wants to issue. If such an instruction had already been issued, and the scoreboard knows that, it will be aborted and reissued when the L2 access is over.

The resolution of control hazards is also dependent on information kept by the scoreboard. In the case of branches, once the branch is issued in stage S3, it does not matter whether it was predicted to be taken or not taken. The only difference is that a branch predicted to be taken might have forced a bubble because of the need for a target address computation. Branch resolution occurs in stage S5. On a misprediction, all instructions that were issued after the branch, including those issued during the same cycle but posterior in program order, must be aborted. The PC is reset to the correct value, and the pipeline starts refilling. The penalty of misprediction is 6 cycles, but it can translate into a more damaging impact on *IPC* when one considers the number of instruction issues (a maximum of four per cycle) that have been missed. In the case of precise exceptions, the instructions following the one causing the exception are aborted. Once the pipeline has been completely drained, because further precise exceptions for instructions preceding in program order the first one has been detected may occur (cf. Section 2.1.4), the Pal code will take over. Floating-point arithmetic instructions are imprecise. Interrupts will force a complete pipeline drain.

It is interesting to note that the branch misprediction penalty is more severe, by 1 cycle, in the 21164 than in its predecessor, the two-way 21064 processor. On the other hand, the load latency in the 21164 is 1 cycle less than in the 21064. We can surmise that, faced with the choice of optimizing the hardware to decrease either the load latency or the branch misprediction penalty, the designers preferred the former, perhaps because they were more confident in the accuracy of their improved branch predictor.

We implied that all structural hazards were detected in stage S2. This is not completely correct, as mentioned previously, because of the limited capacity of some buffers associated with the D-cache. When such a buffer is full and some new instruction wishes to store an entry in it, all following instructions are aborted and the pipeline is refilled, starting at stage S0 with the PC pointing to the instruction that could not proceed.

3.2.4 Performance Assessment

It is difficult to quantify exactly the improvements in execution time brought about by the Alpha 21164 multiple-issue[1] processor and by its deep pipeline compared to that of a single-issue five-stage processor like the MIPS 3000 of the previous

---

[1] We will sometime use "multiple-issue" instead of "*m*-way." In the Alpha 21164 the maximum number of instructions that can be fetched at S0 (i.e., four) is the same as the maximum number of instructions that can be issued at stage S3. That is not necessarily true of all superscalars.

chapter. Architectural enhancements such as a more extensive memory hierarchy, overlapping of memory accesses, and better branch prediction techniques cloud the picture. These effects weigh still heavily, albeit to a lesser extent, when the 21164 is compared with its two-issue predecessor, the 21064, which has only one integer and one floating-point pipeline. Nonetheless, the following measurements are of interest:

- When running SPECfp92 and SPECint92, the average *IPC* is less than 1. It almost reaches 2 on two of the Specfp92 programs. On floating-point programs, the *IPC* is almost double that of the 21064, and on integer programs it is almost 50% better.
- Because the clock frequencies of the two processors are in a 3:2 ratio, the improvements in execution time are more dramatic (ratios of 3:1 and more than 2:1).
- On commercial workloads, the *IPC* of the Alpha 21164 plummets to less than 0.3, the main reason being cache misses percolating through the whole memory hierarchy. The 21164's *IPC* is marginally better than that of the 21064 (less than 0.25). However, the execution time on the 21164 is faster by a factor of 60% because of the differences in clock frequency.
- The ratio of instances when more than one instruction is issued in a given cycle to the total number of instructions varies from about 50% to 70% (double the ratio for the 21064), depending on the programs. In commercial and integer programs, two instructions are issued in almost half of the issuing cycles (we differentiate between issuing cycles and total cycles: in the latter, the pipeline might be stalled because, mainly, of the occurrence of L2 cache misses). More than one instruction is issued in floating-point programs in more than half of the issuing cycles, and in more than 20% of the issuing cycles three or four instructions are issued.

Finally, the importance of compiler optimizations is far from being negligible.

EXAMPLE 2: Consider the following code sequence:

i1	R1 ← Mem[R2]	# Load in R1
i2	R4 ← R1 + R3	# RAW with instruction *i1*
i3	R5 ← R1 + R6	# RAW with instruction *i1*
i4	R7 ← R4 + R5	# RAW with instructions *i2* and *i3*

Assume all instructions were in the slotting register (stage S2) at time *t*. At time *t* + 1 instructions *i1* and *i2* can advance to S3. Instruction *i3* cannot, because of structural hazards (only two integer pipes exist; and recall that load–store instructions use one integer pipe for address computation). The only action that occurs at time *t* + 2 is the issuing of the load instruction. Instruction *i2* cannot issue because of the RAW dependency. Only instruction *i1* progresses at time *t* + 3, because loads have a 2-cycle latency. Instruction *i2* issues at time *t* + 4, and during that cycle instructions *i3* and *i4* advance to the S3 stage. At time $t + 5$, *i3* will issue, but *i4* won't because of the RAW dependency and will do so only at time $t + 6$.

The reader can verify that if an integer no-op were inserted between instructions *i1* and *i2*, instructions *i2* and *i3* would be advancing together to S3 at time $t + 2$. They would both issue at time $t + 4$, and instruction *i4* would issue at time $t + 5$, that is, one cycle earlier than in the original code.

3.2.5 Recap

In this section, we have presented an in-order four-way superscalar, the Alpha 21164. The major advances over a single-issue five-stage scalar processor are:

- A wider pipeline: four functional units and access to the D-cache in the back-end.
- A deeper pipeline: the front-end has four stages and the back-end from three to five, depending on the function.
- A scoreboard monitoring all instructions in flight in the back-end, so that for-warding and stalling can be implemented (this replaces the forwarding-and-stalling unit of the five-stage pipe).

In the description of what might be called a second generation superscalar (the Alpha 20164 being a first generation one), we have seen the importance of branch prediction in that a misprediction causes a 6-cycle penalty that translates into 24 lost issue slots. Similarly, speculation is needed when accessing the cache, at the cost, on a misspeculation, of replaying some of the instructions that are in flight.

Still, there is some room for improvement. For example, with more logic, in-structions could proceed through the front-end even if a successor stage were not completely empty. Nonetheless, this processor has reached one of the goals of a superscalar: many programs can have an *IPC* greater than 1.

Sidebar: The Scoreboard of the CDC 6600

The CDC 6600, introduced in 1964, was a major step forward in the design of pow-erful computers. There are four features that at that time were advances in the state of the art:

- Separate functional units (not pipelined; pipelining came about with the CDC 7600 a few years later), which could operate concurrently under the supervision of a scoreboard (i.e., a control unit).
- Interleaving of main memory modules.
- Relocation registers for multiprogramming.
- Multithreading of I/O peripheral processors.

Here, we present only the first feature and take some liberties with the actual ISA of the CDC 6600, mostly in not differentiating the specific roles of the three sets of registers: floating-point, long integer, and address integer.

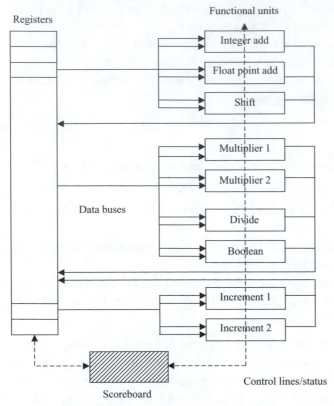

Registers

Functional units

Data buses

Control lines/status

Scoreboard

Figure 3.4. The CDC 6600 back-end.

A simplified block diagram of the layout of the functional units is shown in Figure 3.4. The CDC 6600 had 10 functional units divided physically into four groups:

- Group I with a long-integer adder, a floating-point adder, and a shifter.
- Group II with two floating-point multipliers.
- Group III (which shared its data buses with group II) with a floating-point divider and a logical unit (Boolean).
- Group IV with two incrementers for address calculations.

The astute reader will have noticed that we have listed only nine units. The tenth one is a branch unit that works in cooperation with a partner unit to modify the PC, if necessary. The same reader will also have noticed that there is no integer multiplier or integer divider. Integer multiplication can be performed through the floating-point multiplier without conversion of the numbers (using the double precision mantissa), and integer division requires either software or conversion to floating-point numbers.

Once an instruction has been fetched and decoded, it will follow four steps under the control of the scoreboard:

1. *Issue*: If there is a free functional unit for the instruction and if there is no WAW hazard, the instruction is said to be *issued*. If either of these conditions is

Table 3.1. Conditions and actions in the CDC 6600 scoreboard

Condition checking	Scoreboard setting
Issue step: Unit free $U_a = 0$ and no WAW ($P_i = 0$)	*Issue step:* Unit busy $U_a = 1$; record F_i, F_j, F_k Record Q_j, Q_k and R_j, R_k (e.g., $R_j = 1$ if $P_j = 0$ else if $P_j = b$ then $R_j = 0$ and $Q_j = b$) Record $P_i = U_a$
Dispatch: Source registers ready: R_j and $R_k = 1$	*Dispatch:* Send F_j and F_k to unit a
Execute: At end, ask for permission to write	*Execute:*
Write result: If some issued but not dispatched instruction before this instruction in program order is such that either its Q_j or $Q_k = a$, then stall	*Write result:* Set $U_a = 0$ and $P_i = 0$

false, the instruction, and its successors, is stalled until both conditions become true.

2. *Dispatch:* When the instruction is issued, the execution unit is reserved (becomes *busy*). Operands are read in the execution unit when they are both *ready* (i.e., are not results of still-executing instructions). This prevents RAW hazards.

3. *Execution:* One or more cycles, depending on functional unit's latency. When execution completes, the unit notifies the scoreboard that it is ready to write the result.

4. *Write result:* Before writing, the scoreboard checks for WAR hazards. If one exists, the unit is stalled until all WAR hazards are cleared (note that an instruction in progress, i.e., whose operands have been read, won't cause a WAR).

Of course, there are opportunities for optimization such as buffering and forwarding (see the exercises), and also there are occurrences of extra stalls, for example, when two units in the same group want to store results in the same cycle.

In order to control the four steps in the back-end, the scoreboard needs to know:

- For each functional unit, whether it is free or busy: flag U_a for unit a.
- For each instruction in flight, including the one that wishes to issue:
  ○ The names of the result F_i and source F_j, F_k registers.
  ○ The names Q_j, Q_k of the units (if any) producing values for F_j, F_k.
  ○ Flags R_j, R_k indicating whether the source registers are ready.
  ○ Its status, that is, whether it is issued, dispatched, executing, or ready to write.
- For each result register F_i, the name of the unit, if any, that will produce its results, say P_i (this is slightly redundant, but facilitates the hardware check).

Then, the scoreboard functions as in Table 3.1. Note that the write result step requires an associative search.

Table 3.2. Snapshot of the scoreboard

Unit	Inst. status	U	F_i	F_j	F_k	R_j	R_j	Q_j	Q_k
Mul1	Exec	1	4	0	2	1	1		
Mul2	Issue	1	6	4	8	0	1	Mul1	
Add	Exec	1	8	2	12	0	0		
Reg.	0	2	4	6	8	10	12	14	16
Unit			Mul1	Mul2	Add				

EXAMPLE 3: Assume that the two multipliers have a latency of 6 cycles and the adder has a latency of 1 cycle. Only registers with even numbers are shown in the following table, because it is assumed that these are floating-point operations using pairs of registers for operands. Assume all registers and units are free to start with:

$i1$:	R4 ← R0 * R2	# will use multiplier 1
$i2$:	R6 ← R4 * R8	# will use multiplier 2; RAW with $i1$
$i3$:	R8 ← R2 + R12	# will use adder; WAR with $i2$
$i4$:	R4 ← R14 + R16	# will use adder; WAW with $i1$

The progression of the instruction through the first few cycles is elaborated on below. Table 3.2 is a snapshot of the scoreboard after cycle 6.

- Cycle 1: $i1$ is issued, and the first row of the scoreboard is as shown in Table 3.2 except that the instruction status is issue. Note that the contents (i.e., the P_i) of register 4 indicate the Mul1 unit.
- Cycle 2: The status of $i1$ becomes dispatch, and instruction $i2$ is issued. This is indicated by the second row of the table and the contents of register 6.
- Cycle 3: Instruction $i1$ is in execute mode, but $i2$ cannot be dispatched, because of the RAW dependency ($R_j = 0$). Instruction $i3$ can issue, though, as shown in the third row and the contents of register 8.
- Cycle 4: Instruction $i3$ can dispatch, but $i4$ cannot issue, for two reasons: the adder is busy, and there is a WAW dependency with $i1$ (this latter condition is easily checked by looking at the contents of register 4).
- Cycle 6 (no change in the scoreboard during cycle 5): Instruction $i1$ is still executing, instruction $i2$ is still in the issue stage, and instruction $i3$ asks for permission to write. The permission will be refused because of the WAR dependency with instruction $i2$.
- The situation will remain the same until instruction $i1$ asks for permission to write, at cycle 8, which is granted immediately.
- At the next cycle, (i.e., cycle 9), instruction $i2$ will be dispatched and instruction $i3$ will be able to write, allowing instruction $i4$ to issue, and so on.

Note that despite all these restrictions, most notably the requirements that instructions issue in order, instructions can complete out of order.

3.3 Introducing Register Renaming, Reorder Buffer, and Reservation Stations

The fetch and decode stages of in-order and out-of-order processors need not be different. Front-end tasks such as multiple instruction fetch, branch prediction, and decoding are independent of how the back-end will execute the stream of instructions. The differences between the two types of superscalar microprocessors start with the decision of when instructions leave the front-end and how they are processed by the back-end.

In an in-order processor, instructions must leave the front-end in program order. Instructions may be prevented from issuing because of RAW and WAW dependencies. In an out-of-order processor, WAR and WAW dependencies will be avoided by *register renaming*. Because instructions can complete out of program order, means to impose the program order are necessary, and this will be the function of the *reorder buffer*. Moreover, instructions may leave the front-end and not be ready to execute yet because of either RAW dependencies or structural hazards such as busy functional units. These instructions will have to wait in *reservation stations*, or equivalently, remain in an *instruction window*.

3.3.1 Register Renaming

Whereas RAW dependencies are algorithm-dependent, WAR and WAW are present because of a scarcity of resources, namely registers. Instead of being true dependencies, they are *name* dependencies. WAW and WAR dependencies can be avoided with register renaming. To illustrate the concepts of register renaming, consider the following example.

> **EXAMPLE 4.A:** Assume all registers are available at the beginning of the following sequence of instructions and that three instructions can issue per cycle:
>
> | | | |
> |---|---|---|
> | *i1:* | R1 ← R2/R3 | # division takes a long time to complete |
> | *i2:* | R4 ← R1 + R5 | # RAW dependency with *i1* |
> | *i3:* | R5 ← R6 + R7 | # WAR dependency with *i2* |
> | *i4:* | R1 ← R8 + R9 | # WAW dependency with *i1* |

In an in-order processor such as the Alpha 21164, only the first instruction would be issued, because of the RAW dependency between *i2* and *i1*. Instruction *i2* would be issued when the divide was in its last cycle of execution, and instructions *i3* and *i4* would be issued at the same time as *i2*, or maybe at the next cycle, depending on the rules of issue for the particular processor. The WAR and WAW dependencies would disappear as soon as the RAW dependency was removed.

In an out-of-order processor, the RAW dependency will of course be enforced. But its presence should not prevent instructions following the dependent one to start their execution if they do not need the results that have not yet been generated. The WAR and WAW dependencies are avoided by providing extra register, or register-like, storage.

In this first pass at explaining register renaming, we simply give a high-level view without paying attention to the number of physical registers, how they are obtained, and how they are released. Let us call the ISA-defined registers the *logical* or *architectural* registers, and the total register storage the *physical* registers. The logical registers of an instruction will be renamed, or mapped, to physical registers when an instruction reaches the last stage of the front-end. The source operands' names are replaced by the physical registers to which they map, and the destination register is given a new physical register name. In other words, if $R_i \leftarrow R_j \; op \; R_k$ is the (next) instruction whose registers must be renamed, $Rename(R_a)$ is the current mapping table, and *Freelist* is a list of physical registers that have not been allocated with *first* pointing to the next one available, then register renaming proceeds as follows:

Renaming Stage. $Inst_m$: $R_i \leftarrow R_j \; op \; R_k$ becomes $R_a \leftarrow R_b \; op \; R_c$, where
$R_b = Rename(R_j)$;
$R_c = Rename(R_k)$;
$R_a = freelist(first)$;
$Rename(R_i)= freelist(first)$;
$first \leftarrow next(first)$.

EXAMPLE 4.B: Continuing Example 4.a, let us assume that at the beginning of the sequence all logical registers are renamed to their own name. *Freelist* contains, in numerical order, physical registers R32, R33, and so on. When instructions *i1, i2,* and *i3* reach the renaming stage together under our three-way assumption, then:

- For instruction *i1*, the source registers R2 and R3 retain their names. The destination register R1 is renamed R32.
- For instruction *i2*, the source register R1 has become R32 and the source register R5 retains its name. The destination register R4 is renamed R33.
- For instruction *i3*, the source registers R6 and R7 retain their names. The destination register R5 is renamed R34.

After the first cycle, the sequence is now:

i1:	R32 ← R2/R3	# Division takes a long time to complete
i2:	R33 ← R32 + R5	# Still a RAW dependency with *i1*
i3:	R34 ← R6 + R7	# No WAR dependency with *i2* anymore
i4:	R1 ← R8 + R9	# Unchanged yet

At the next cycle both instructions *i1* and *i3* can start executing (not *i2*, because of the RAW dependency), and register renaming can be done for *i4*. R1 will be renamed R35, and instruction *i4* becomes:

i4:	R35 ← R8 + R9	# No WAW dependency with *i1* anymore

Note that R1 has been renamed twice. It is clear that instructions following *i4* and using R1 as a source operand expect the result of *i4* as the correct one, and register renaming must enforce the latest mapping.

3.3.2 Reorder Buffer

Let us continue with Example 4.b. It is very likely that instructions *i3* and *i4* will compute their results before *i1* and *i2*. We must prevent the results stored in R34 and R35 from being put in their corresponding logical registers (R5 and R1) before the contents of R32 and R33 are stored in R1 and R2, respectively. Otherwise, when *i1* stores its results in R1, it would overwrite the value already stored in R1 as a result of instruction *i4*. As another possibility, if *i1* generated an exception, (e.g., a divide by zero), we would not want the value computed by *i3* to be part of the process state.

Storing the results in program order is achieved with the help of a *reorder buffer* (ROB). Conceptually, the ROB is a FIFO queue where each entry is a tuple (flag, value, result register name, instruction type) with the following meanings for the tuple components (we restrict ourselves to arithmetic instructions for the time being):

- The flag indicates whether the instruction has completed execution.
- The value is the value computed by the instruction.
- The result register name is the name of the logical register where the results must be stored.
- The instruction type shows the type of instruction such as arithmetic, load, store, branch, and so on.

When an instruction is in the renaming stage, an entry corresponding to it is inserted at the tail of the ROB with the flag *false* indicating that the result has not been computed yet. That is, we have the following additional steps in the renaming stage:

Renaming stage (additional steps)
```
ROB(tail) = (false, NA, Rᵢ, op);
tail ← next(tail)
```

When the execution of the instruction is completed, the value is put in the corresponding entry in the ROB, and the flag indicates that the result can be stored in the result register.[2] However, this last action, called *commit*, will be performed only when the instruction is at the head of the ROB. That is:

Commit stage
```
if ((ROB(head) = Instₘ) and flag(ROB(head)))
                    then begin Rᵢ = value; head ← next(head) end
                    else repeat same test next cycle
```

Note that either an instruction must carry the index of the ROB entry or some equivalent scheme must be provided so that instructions and corresponding ROB entries are identifiable when the instruction completes the execution stage.

---

[2] Putting the value in the ROB is one possible implementation. We shall see another scheme in Chapter 4.

Table 3.3. Snapshots of the reorder buffer (ROB)

	Flag	Value	Reg. name	Type	
(a) After renaming of the first three instructions					
i1	Not ready	None	R1	Arit	Head
i2	Not ready	None	R4	Arit	
i3	Not ready	None	R5	Arit	
					Tail
(b) After completion of execution of i3 and i4					
i1	Not ready	None	R1	Arit	Head
i2	Not ready	None	R4	Arit	
i3	Ready	Some	R5	Arit	
i4	Ready	Some	R1	Arit	
					Tail
(c) After commit of i1					
i1	Ready	Some	R1	Arit	
i2	Not ready	None	R4	Arit	Head
i3	Ready	Some	R5	Arit	
i4	Ready	Some	R1	Arit	
					Tail

EXAMPLE 4.C: Let us continue our example, and let us assume that the ROB is empty when instruction *i1* reaches the register renaming stage.

After the renaming of the first three instructions, the ROB looks like the one depicted in Table 3.3(a). The three instructions that are having their destination registers renamed are entered in the ROB in program order. In the next cycle, instruction *i4*, and the following two not shown in the example, will be entered at the tail of the ROB.

Some cycles later, instructions *i3* and *i4* will have computed their results before *i1* has completed its own. These results will be entered in the ROB, as shown in Table 3.3(b), with the flags of the respective entries indicating that results are ready to be stored. However, the results will not be stored in the logical result registers, because these instructions are not at the head of the ROB.

When instruction *i1* completes, identical actions are performed. Now, at the next cycle, the result from *i1* can be written in logical register R1, because *i1* is at the head of the ROB. This commit operation, performed by a *retire unit*, can be considered as the last stage of the instruction pipeline. The ROB contents now look like Table 3.3(c).

After the cycle in which instruction *i2* terminates, the remaining three instructions are ready to commit. In general it is a good idea to balance the number of instructions able to commit in the same cycle with the number of instructions that can be entered in the ROB at the renaming stage, so in a three-way processor, all three instructions *i2*, *i3*, and *i4* would commit in the same cycle. In the same way as register renaming must identify the last renaming instance of a register, instruction committing must ensure that the youngest entry in the ROB can overwrite older entries. If, for example, *i2* and *i4* were to try to write in the same cycle in the same logical register, only *i4* would be allowed to do so.

3.3.3 Reservation Stations and/or Instruction Window

In the preceding sections, we have identified actions that must be performed by the front-end, namely, register renaming and inserting instructions in program order in the ROB. We have also shown how the results of computations are stored in logical registers in program order via the commit operation. However, besides implementation considerations, we have skipped over important parts of the process, such as where instructions wait before being executed and how an instruction knows that it is ready to be executed.

After the front-end has renamed the registers of an instruction and entered its corresponding tuple in the ROB, it will *dispatch*[3] the instruction to a *reservation station*. A reservation station is a holding place for an instruction and must contain, in one form or another:

- The operation to be performed.
- The values of the source operands or their physical names (a flag should indicate whether there is a value or a name).
- The physical name of the result register.
- The entry in the ROB where the result should be stored.

Reservation stations can be grouped in a centralized queue, sometimes called an *instruction window*, or can be associated with (sets of) functional units according to their opcodes. Independently of whether the instructions queues are centralized or not, when more than one instruction is ready in a given cycle for a functional unit, there is contention for that functional unit and a *scheduling* decision must be taken. Quite often, the oldest instruction, that is, the first one in program order, will be the one issued first. Other possibilities, such as issuing first those instructions identified as *critical*, are possible (see Chapter 5).

The last task that we have to describe is the detection of the readiness of an instruction to *issue*. This will occur when both its source operands are values. The operands will be the inputs to a functional unit that will execute the operation. In order to know when to issue, we can associate a *ready bit* with each physical register to indicate whether the result for that register has been computed or not. When

---

[3] Academic authors and industry manuals show no consistency in the distinction between *dispatch* and *issue*. We will say that a *dispatch* is a front-end task (filling a reservation station) and an *issue* is a back-end task (sending the ready instruction to a functional unit). Note that we are guilty of some inconsistency in that, for historical reasons, we have shown the issue step before the dispatch step for the CDC 6600 scoreboard.

the destination register of an instruction is mapped, during the renaming stage, we turn its ready bit off. When an instruction is dispatched, if the ready bit of a source register is on, we pass to the reservation station the contents of the register and set the corresponding flag to *true* (ready). If the ready bit of a source register is off, we pass the name of the register and set the corresponding flag to *false*. The instruction will be issued when both flags are true. Thus:

Dispatch Stage. For instruction I_m : R_a ← R_b op R_c, where the registers are physical registers:

```
    If all reservation stations for op are full
            then stall and repeat next cycle;
    fill (next) reservation station for op with the tuple
    {  operator = op,
      if Ready(Rb) then (value[Rb],true) else (Rb, false),
      if Ready(Rc) then (value[Rc],true) else (Rc, false),
      Ra,
      pointer to ROB entry
    }
```

and:

Issue Stage

```
If (flag(Rb) and flag(Rc))
        then send (value[Rb], value[Rc]) to functional unit
        else repeat next cycle
```

When an instruction completes, it broadcasts the name of the physical register and its contents to all the reservation stations. Each reservation station that has the name of this physical register as one of its source registers will grab the contents and set the corresponding flag to true. At the same time, the contents are stored in the physical destination register with its ready bit turned on. The results are also stored in the ROB if the latter is the resource for physical registers.

EXAMPLE 4.D: We have assumed that all registers were available. More precisely, we assumed that the contents of the logical registers were committed and that all other physical registers were free. When R1 is renamed R32 (instruction *i1*), the ready bit of R32 is turned off. When *i2* is dispatched, the name "R32" is sent to the reservation station holding *i2* and the corresponding flag is turned off. Therefore, *i2* is not ready to be issued. When *i1* completes its execution, it broadcasts the name "R32" along with the result of the operation it performed. The reservation station holding *i2* recognizes the name, grabs the result, and turns the corresponding flag on, allowing *i2* to be issued at the next cycle.

The sidebar on the IBM System 360/91 and Tomasulo's algorithm gives one specific implementation of renaming, ROB, and instruction issuing. As we shall see in the next section, the implementation of the Pentium P6 architecture follows

Table 3.4. Instruction flow and resources involved in an out-of-order processor

	Step	Resources read	Resources written or utilized
Front-end	Fetch	PC Branch predictor I-cache	PC Instruction buffer
	Decode–rename	Instruction buffer Register map	Decode buffer Register map ROB
	Dispatch	Decode buffer Register map Register file (logical and physical)	Reservation stations ROB
Back-end	Issue	Reservation stations	Functional units D-cache
	Execute	Functional units D-cache	Reservation stations ROB Physical register file Branch predictor Store buffer, and so on.
	Commit	ROB Physical register file Store buffer	ROB Logical register file Register map D-cache

Tomasulo's algorithm quite closely. Other mechanisms are described in Chapter 4.

3.3.4 Recap

Table 3.4 summarizes the flow of an instruction in an out-of-order processor. We have chosen to split the decode–rename–dispatch steps into two steps (decode–rename and dispatch) because in many microarchitectures there is a queue of instructions ready to be dispatched that are in an internal representation different from what was stored in the instruction buffer. Similarly, we have split the issue–execute steps into issue and execute although both involve execution in the functional units or the D-cache. Our motivation is that issue removes instructions from the reservation stations whereas execute will, as its last action, modify the reservation stations, the ROB, and the physical register file as well as other data structures, depending on the type of instruction (e.g., the use of store buffers will be explained when we look at memory operations).

Sidebar: The IBM System 360/91 Floating-point Unit and Tomasulo's Algorithm

In the mid 1960s, IBM was looking for a response to the CDC 6600 at the high end of computing power. The Model 91 was introduced in 1967, three years after the 6600, as an answer to the CDC 6800, a projected follow-up to the 6600 that was never delivered. In 1968, the Model 91 was renamed Model 95, with the main improvement a faster core memory. CDC answered in 1969 with the CDC 7600, a pipelined version of the 6600. By that time, the production of Models 91 and 95 was stopped, in part because a cheaper and simpler model, the Model 85, was able to outperform them with the inclusion of a major system component: cache memory.

The IBM System 360/91 has its roots in Project Stretch, a one-of-a-kind super-computer that emphasized pipelining and optimized design of floating-point units. The Model 91 was intended mostly for scientific computations, and great care was taken to have the peak capability of delivering a floating-point result per cycle. In this sidebar, we present only an abstraction of the design of the floating-point unit of the Model 91, which consisted of:

- A pipelined floating-point adder with three reservation stations.
- A pipelined floating-point multiplier–divider with two reservation stations (divisions were implemented by an iterative reciprocal followed by a multiplication).
- A (floating-point) instruction queue.
- A set of floating-point registers.
- Load buffers for loads from main memory.
- Store buffers for stores to main memory.
- A common data bus (CDB) to broadcast results from the adder, multiplier, and load buffers to the reservation stations, the register file, and the store buffers.

In this presentation, load and store buffers are not considered. On the other hand, a reorder buffer (ROB) is included so that instructions can be committed in order, a requirement that did not exist in the original floating-point unit of the Model 91, as well as a register map, which was not strictly necessary either, because the renaming was performed with names of reservation stations rather than with ROB entries (a flag associated with the register file was sufficient to distinguish between names and values). The resulting structure, on which the concepts of register renaming, reservation stations, and ROB are illustrated, is shown in Figure 3.5.

In this implementation, a variant of what has become known as Tomasulo's algorithm, a reservation station entry consists of six fields:

- a bit indicating whether the reservation station is free or not;
- two fields per source operand – a flag and a data field – so that if the flag is on, the datum is a value, and otherwise it is a tag;
- a field that contains a pointer (tag) to the ROB entry where the result of the instruction will be stored.

The basic idea is that the ROB will serve a dual purpose: First, the original one, that is, the structure will ensure that instructions are committed in program order, and, second, it will also implement the set of physical registers. The mapping between logical registers and physical registers will be a table indexed by logical register number. The name of a physical register will be either an index to an ROB

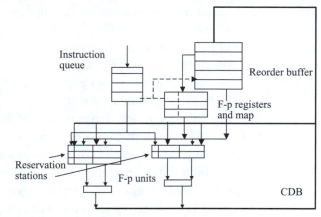

Figure 3.5. Abstracted structure of the IBM System 360/91 floating-point arithmetic unit.

entry, also called a *tag*, or the logical register itself. In our descriptions we will denote by R0, R1,..., Rm the logical registers, and by E0, E1,..., En the ROB entries.

An ROB entry consists of three fields: two fields for the physical register, that is, a flag and data (if the flag is on, a result has been computed by the instruction and stored in the ROB; otherwise, the content of the associated field is a tag), and a field with the name of the logical register where the result should be stored when the entry is at the head of the ROB.

The instructions are in the instruction queue. We can consider that we are at the decode–rename stage. We will only perform one decode–rename per cycle; it is fairly simple to extend the description to a wider machine (see the exercises).

Once the instruction is in the instruction queue, the five steps outlined in Table 3.4 proceed as follows:

1. *Decode–rename.* The decoding will steer the instruction towards one of the two sets of reservation stations (recall that we only consider floating-point operations). If the intended set is full, we have a structural hazard. At the same time, we check if there is a free entry in the reorder buffer (the latter is best implemented as a circular queue). If the ROB is full, we have another instance of a structural hazard. If either form of structural hazard is present, we stall the flow of incoming instructions until all structural hazards are removed. In the absence of structural hazards or once they have been removed, we reserve a reservation station and the tail entry of the ROB for the instruction.

2. *Dispatch.* We fill the reservation station and the tail entry of the ROB. More precisely:
   a. We look at the map for the source operands. For each operand, if the map indicates a logical register, this register contains a valid value. If the map indicates an ROB entry, the flag in the latter is checked to see whether the entry contains a value or a tag. In all cases, the contents of either the logical register or the ROB entry are sent to the reservation station with the ready

> bit set on if the reservation station now contains a value, and off if it contains a tag.
>
> b. We set the map of the result register to the tag (the name of the tail entry of the ROB) and enter the tag in the reservation station. Note that this step must be done *after* the source operands have been looked at, because a register can be both a source and a result.
>
> c. We enter the instruction at the tail of the ROB with the result flag off.

3. *Issue.* When both flags in a reservation station are set to ready (are on), the instruction can be issued to the functional unit to start execution unless all stages of the latter are stalling because the unit is waiting for the CDB to broadcast its result. If more than one reservation station in the same set is ready to issue in the same cycle, some scheduling algorithm will resolve the contention.

4. *Execute.* Execution proceeds normally until the last execution cycle. At that point, the unit asks for ownership of the common data bus (CDB). If there is more than one unit asking for the CDB in the same cycle, some (hardwired) priority scheme will resolve the contention. Once the unit has ownership of the CDB:

> a. It broadcasts the result of its operation and the tag associated with the instruction.
>
> b. The result is stored in the ROB entry identified by the tag, and the flag indicating a result in the ROB entry is set.
>
> c. The result is stored as well in all reservation stations that have the tag as an operand. In such reservation stations, the result replaces the tag, and the corresponding flag (ready bit) is set.

5. *Commit.* At each cycle, the bit indicating a result in the entry at the head of the ROB is checked. If it is on, the result is stored in the logical register indicated by the ROB entry, and the entry is deleted.

To illustrate Tomasulo's algorithm (cf. Table 3.5), we consider the same example as for the CDC 6600 scoreboard, namely, the following sequence of instructions:

i1:   R4 ← R0 * R2   # will use reservation station 1 of multiplier
i2:   R6 ← R4 * R8   # will use reservation station 2 of multiplier; RAW with *i1*
i3:   R8 ← R2 + R12   # will use reservation station 1 of adder; WAR with *i2*
i4:   R4 ← R14 + R16   # will use reservation station 2 of adder; WAW with *i1*

The adder and multiplier are pipelined with latencies of 1 and 4 cycles, respectively.

  If there were no dependencies, a multiplication (respectively, addition) being decoded at time t_0 would be dispatched at time $t_0 + 1$, be issued at time $t_0 + 2$, start executing at time $t_0 + 2$, finish executing at time $t_0 + 5$ (respectively, at time $t_0 + 2$), broadcast at time $t_0 + 6$ (respectively, at time $t_0 + 3$), and commit if it were at the head of the ROB at time $t_0 + 7$ (respectively, at time $t_0 + 4$).

Table 3.5. Illustration of Tomasulo's algorithm

Flag	Data	Logical register	
0	E1	R4	Head
0	E2	R6	
			Tail

ROB

Index	...	4	5	6	7	8
Map		E1		E2		

Register Map

Free	Flag1	Oper1	Flag2	Oper2	Tag
0					
0					
0					

Adder Reservation Stations

Free	Flag1	Oper1	Flag2	Oper2	Tag
0					
1	0	E1	1	(R8)	E2

Multiplier Reservation Stations

(a) At cycle $t_0 + 2$. Reservation station 1 of the multiplier is now free.

Flag	Data	Logical register	
0	E1	R4	Head
0	E2	R6	
0	E3	R8	
0	E4	R4	
			Tail

ROB

Index	...	4	5	6	7	8
Map		E4		E2		E3

Register Map

Free	Flag1	Oper1	Flag2	Oper2	Tag
0					
1	1	(R14)	1	(R16)	E4
0					

Adder Reservation Stations

Free	Flag1	Oper1	Flag2	Oper2	Tag
1	0	E1	1	(R8)	E2

Multiplier Reservation Stations

(b) Cycle $t_0 + 4$. Reservation station 1 of the adder has become free. Note the change in the register map for R4.

Flag	Data	Logical register	
0	E1	R4	Head
0	E2	R6	
1	(*i3*)	R8	
0	E4	R4	
			Tail

ROB

Index	...	4	5	6	7	8
Map		E4		E2		E3

Register Map

Free	Flag1	Oper1	Flag2	Oper2	Tag
0					
0					
0					

Adder Reservation Stations

Free	Flag1	Oper1	Flag2	Oper2	tag
0					
1	0	E1	1	(R8)	E2

Multiplier Reservation Stations

(c) Cycle $t_0 + 5$. The first addition has stored its result in ROB.

Flag	Data	Logical register	
1	(*i1*)	R4	Head
0	E2	R6	
1	(*i3*)	R8	
1	(*i4*)	R4	
			Tail

ROB

Index	...	4	5	6	7	8
Map		E4		E2		E3

Register Map

Free	Flag1	Oper1	Flag2	Oper2	Tag
0					
0					
0					

Adder Reservation Stations

Free	Flag1	Oper1	Flag2	Oper2	Tag
0					
1	1	(i1)	1	(R8)	E2

Multiplier Reservation Stations
(d) Cycle $t_0 + 7$. The second multiplication is ready to issue, and
    instruction $i1$ is ready to commit.

Flag	Data	Logical register	
0	E2	R6	Head
1	(i3)	R8	
1	(i4)	R4	
			Tail

ROB

Index	...	4	5	6	7	8
Map		E4		E2		E3

Register Map

Free	Flag1	Oper1	Flag2	Oper2	Tag
0					
0					
0					

Adder Reservation Stations

Free	Flag1	Oper1	Flag2	Oper2	Tag
0					
0					

Multiplier Reservation Stations
(e) Cycle $t_0 + 8$. Instruction $i1$ has committed. The only instruction in
execution is $i2$.

Table 3.5 shows snapshots of the reservation stations, register map, and ROB at important junctures.

- At cycle $t_0 + 2$ (see Table 3.5(a)) instruction *i1* has started to execute. Instruction *i2* has been dispatched and is in reservation station 2 of the multiplier, waiting for the result broadcast of instruction *i1*. Instructions *i3* and *i4* are still in the instruction queue.
- At cycle $t_0 + 4$, that is, 2 cycles later (Table 3.5(b)), instruction *i3* is now ready to broadcast and *i4* has been dispatched. Note that register R4, which was renamed as ROB entry E1 and tagged as such in reservation station Mult2, is now mapped to ROB entry E4.
- At cycle $t_0 + 5$ (Table 3.5(c)) *i3* broadcasts its result, which is stored in the ROB entry E3. Both the adder (instruction *i4*) and the multiplier (instruction *i1*) are ready to broadcast. Let us assume the adder has priority.
- At cycle $t_0 + 6$, the adder broadcasts its result.
- At cycle $t_0 + 7$ (Table 3.5(d)), the multiplier can finally broadcast its result, which is picked up by reservation station Mult2 and the head of the ROB.
- At cycle $t_0 + 8$ (Table 3.5(e)), instruction *i1* can commit. Instruction *i2* has issued and is in its execute stage.

Tomasulo's algorithm, or a variant of it, is the basis of the design of out-of-order microprocessors.

3.4 Overview of the Pentium P6 Microarchitecture

3.4.1 General Organization

The Intel family of Pentium processors is by far the most prevalent general-purpose microprocessor architecture today. The first Pentium, introduced in 1993, was a successor to the ×86 series of Intel microprocessors. The Pentium ISA, called IA-32 at Intel, has been extended with the introduction of MMX (for "multimedia extensions") instructions for the Pentium II and SSE instructions for the Pentium III. The implementation of MMX instructions was intended to improve the performance of multimedia communications and numeric-intensive applications by using limited single-instruction multiple-data (SIMD; see Chapter 7) features. SSE (for "streaming SIMD extension") instructions extend MMX for streaming in both the floating-point units and the memory subsystem. However, all Pentium processors, including the Pentium 4 and the Core architecture, are binary-compatible with their predecessors. While the compatibility is certainly a boon for application designers, the inherent constraints of an antiquated ISA, such as the paucity of programmable registers and the CISC instruction set, have presented the designers with additional challenges. Intel engineers – and their counterparts at AMD, which uses the same ISA for its processors – have responded brilliantly.

Figure 3.6. A high-level view of the P6 microarchitecture. The fetch–decode unit is the front-end; the dispatch–execute unit is the back-end: the retire unit restores program order in instruction completion. (Adapted from http://www.x86.org/ftp/manuals/686/p6tour.pdf.)

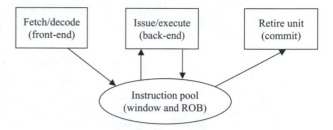

The original Pentium was an in-order two-issue superscalar. The two integer pipelines shared their IF and ID stages and had the structure of the five-stage pipeline described in Section 2.1.5. Floating-point instructions were also pipelined in a floating-point unit. RAW and WAW dependencies were checked at the ID stage. With the introduction of the Pentium Pro in 1995, Intel followed a radically different implementation approach, called the P6 microarchitecture. The Pentium II, a renaming of the Pentium Pro; the Pentium III (circa 1999); the Pentium 4 (circa 2001), which has significant implementation differences from the Pentium III; the Pentium M (circa 2004); and the Core Architecture (circa 2005) are based on the out-of-order P6 model, with the microarchitectures of the latter two models resembling more the Pentium III's than the Pentium 4's.

A high-level view of the instruction flow in the P6 microarchitecture is shown in Figure 3.6. To recast it in terms we have introduced before, the fetch–decode unit will implement the front-end of the pipeline. It will fetch, decode, rename, and dispatch instructions in the centralized reservation station (the instruction window), which is part of the *instruction pool* in the figure. Instructions from the pool will be issued to the dispatch–execute unit, that is, the functional units and cache hierarchy. The results will be returned to the reservation station and the reorder buffer, the latter being also part of the instruction pool. Finally, the instructions will be committed by the retire unit, which will write results in registers and the storage hierarchy.

Before describing the instruction pipeline of the P6, it is worth noting that the number of transistors needed for the implementation of the Pentium Pro (not including caches) was twice that of the Alpha 21164 (more than 4 million vs. less than 2 million). The Pentium Pro pipelines are about twice as deep as those of the Pentium, thus allowing fewer logic gates per stage and leading to the possibility of higher clock frequencies. For integer benchmarks, such as SPECint95, that hardly exercise the memory hierarchy, the Pentium Pro running at 200 MHz had almost the same performance as the Alpha 21164 at 333 MHz (both processors were announced in the first quarter of 1996). On floating-point applications, the Alpha had a clear advantage, in part due to its much larger on-chip caches (recall Table 2.1).

The CISC instruction set of the IA-32 architecture requires a more complex decoding than that of a RISC processor. Several stages of the front-end will be devoted to it. Part of the decoding will consist in transforming the variable-length IA-32 instructions into RISC-like sequence of operations, called μops. Depending

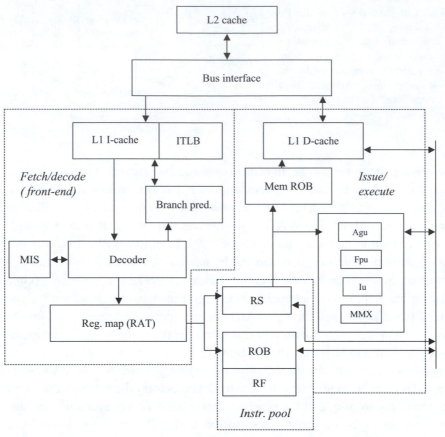

Figure 3.7. Block diagram of the P6 microarchitecture. Some liberties have been taken with the number of functional units, the memory interface unit, and so on. The fetch–decode unit of Figure 3.6 is at left: I-cache, ITLB, branch prediction, decoder, and register map. The execution unit, D-cache, and associated MOB are at the right. The instruction pool consists of the reservation stations (RS) and the ROB. The register file (RF) is close to the ROB.

on the implementation, three to six μops at a time can pass from the front-end to the instruction pool for the back-end. In the following, a P6 implementation with a maximum of three μops per cycle that can pass from the front-end to the back-end, that is, a three-way superscalar (although, since five μops can be issued from the instruction pool to the execution units, one could call it a five-way superscalar) is described. The CISC ISA also constrains the retire unit. All the μops that constitute an instruction must be retired in the same cycle, because instructions must be committed atomically.

A somewhat simplified block diagram of the P6 microarchitecture, as implemented for example in the Pentium III and fairly similar to what is present in the Core architecture, is shown in Figure 3.7. The descriptions that follow are mostly based on the Pentium III implementation. In several instances in later chapters, we will mention features of the Pentium 4. Multicores will be presented in Chapters 7 and 8.

3.4.2 Front-end

Following the nomenclature given in Table 3.4, the front-end consists of instruction fetch (IF plus branch prediction done in four stages), decode (ID in two stages), rename (two stages), and dispatch (one stage).

The first four stages of the front-end bring (part of) an I-cache line, that is, a variable number of instructions in an instruction buffer (IB) along with marks that show the boundaries of the individual variable-length instructions. The first stage is used to select the source of the PC value – either the address of the next instruction in the sequence, or a predicted target address for a branch, or a corrected branch address if the prediction was wrong. Branch prediction is also performed during this first stage. It implies not only guessing the branch direction, but also predicting (and not computing) the target address. The hardware structure to perform this task is a *branch target buffer* (BTB; cf. Chapter 4). The BTB is organized as a cache indexed by the PC, and it takes 2 cycles to access it and deliver the target address back to the first stage. Therefore, a bubble must be inserted in the pipeline when a branch is predicted to be taken. As was the case for the Alpha 21164, and even more so here because of the large number of instructions in the pool, it is almost certain that the bubble will be absorbed long before instructions slowed by it are ready to retire. If there is no branch, or rather no branch predicted to be taken, the I-cache and I-TLB are accessed during stages 2, 3, and 4 and, assuming no cache or TLB miss, deliver marked instructions in the instruction buffer if the latter is empty. In case the IB is not empty, stalling in the fetch mechanism will occur.

Decoding, that is, translating IA-32 instructions into μops, takes two stages. First, three instructions are taken from the IB and are sent, in order, to three decoders that will operate in parallel. Because of the instructions' variable lengths, the 16 byte IB can hold between 1 and 16 instructions (the average is between 5 and 6), so in general there will be work to do in the next stage for the three decoders. However, there are several conditions that prevent full usage of the three decoders. For example, only the first decoder can decode *complex* instructions, that is, those that require the microinstruction sequencer (MIS in Figure 3.7), and only one branch at a time can be decoded. If the branch is predicted to be taken, and this fact was marked by the BTB when the instructions reached the IB, the target address is computed and verification of the predicted branch address is performed in the next stage. In case of a difference, we have a *misfetch* (see Chapter 4): the front-end is flushed and restarted at stage 1 with the new address (the BTB is updated correspondingly). The same actions take place if the branch was unconditional and not detected by the BTB. If the flow of instructions was correct, up to six μops are stored in a six-entry μop queue.

The next two stages of the front-end will take three μops at a time from the μop queue, rename the registers they use, allocate them in the reorder buffer and, if need be, in load–store buffers, and dispatch them in reservation stations. Register renaming follows the scheme presented in the previous section, that is, ROB entries are used as physical registers.

The register map, called the *register alias table* (RAT) in Intel parlance, indicates by setting an appropriate bit whether a register is mapped to a logical register (e.g., the EAX, EBX, etc., integer registers) or to one of the 40 ROB entries, with the ROB implemented as a circular queue. The mapping is not as straightforward as one would expect, because of the intricacies of the IA-32 ISA, such as integer registers that can be partially read or written and floating-point registers that are organized in a stack fashion. We refer the reader to Intel manuals for these details. In order to rename three μops at a time, the RAT is six-ported to read the names of the six source operands. An allocator checks that there are three ROB entries available. If this is not the case (structural hazard), the renaming stalls until this availability condition is fulfilled. The names of the ROB entries become the names of the destination registers. However, the RAT renaming of source operands must be overridden in two cases, namely: (i) if some μop(s) commits in the same cycle and its ROB name corresponds to one of the renamed source operands, then the latter must be changed to refer to the logical register that is committed; and (ii) name dependencies within the three currently renamed μops must be resolved as indicated in the example in the previous section.

Once the μops have been through the renaming process, they are dispatched[4] in the next cycle to reservation stations that are organized in a centralized instruction window. The allocator must check that there are three available reservation stations. This checking is slightly more complex than the one for the ROB, because reservation stations are not cleared in order. A bit map is used to indicate which reservation stations are free.

Finally, some extra work is needed for load–store instructions. We shall study the actions that need to be taken when we look at memory operations in the next section.

3.4.3 Back-end

The structure of individual reservation stations and of entries in the ROB follows what has been described in the previous section. The number of entries in the single instruction window depends on the particular model, for example, 20 reservation stations in the Pentium III, but over 120 in the Pentium 4 (cf. Table 5.1). The number of functional units also depends on the model. In the Pentium III, because three μops are inserted in the register window in a cycle, the window is three-ported for the *control part* of the reservation stations (ready flags and result tag) and six-ported for the two operands with three ports for sources from the register file and three from the ROB. Issuing of μops to the functional units or the cache hierarchy proceeds as in Tomasulo's algorithm with the further optimization of forwarding, that is, results can become inputs to functional units in the same cycle as they are written in in the ROB. Up to five μops can be issued per cycle, but this number

---

[4] We keep the terminology of the preceding section. Intel's literature uses *dispatch* for what we call *issue*.

is constrained by the readiness of the µops, as well as by the type of functional unit they require and the availability of the result bus when the operation completes. For example, in some implementations the floating-point units and one of the integer units share the same port out of the instruction window; therefore only one floating-point instruction and one integer unit, using another port, can be issued concurrently. When several µops are ready in the same cycle, scheduling gives priority to instructions that have waited longest in the window. Once a µop has been issued, its reservation station is freed and becomes available for another µop. Scheduling and issuing occupy each one stage.

The latencies of individual functional units depend on the operation being performed and the particular Pentium model. For example, an integer unit has a latency of one cycle, that is, the back-end pipeline (not including the retire step) has three stages. Upon completion of execution of a µop in a functional unit, the result is broadcast (unless there is contention for a result bus) and stored in the ROB as in Tomasulo's algorithm. It is at this point that control hazards, branch misprediction, and exceptions are resolved. When a branch has been mispredicted, the following actions take place:

- The front-end is flushed, and new instructions are fetched at the correct PC. The front-end processes these new instructions up to the renaming stage.
- The back-end continues to execute until all µops have written their results. µops that were ahead of the branch in the ROB commit.
- When the back-end is drained and all µops ahead of the branch have committed, the µops behind the branch in the ROB are discarded, and all mapping in the RAT for ROB entries is discarded. The mispredicted branch is retired, and normal operation can continue, that is if the front-end was stalled at the renaming stage it can now proceed.

When an instruction (more specifically a µop) has raised an exception, the result carries a flag that identifies that condition. When the µop reaches the head of the ROB and is ready to be committed, the whole processor is cleared of all µops and fetching of new instructions is prevented. Since all µops before the faulting one were retired, (i.e., the results stored in the register file), the processor is in a valid architectural state and the exception handler can be activated. Interrupts are treated in a similar fashion.

Branch misprediction is quite detrimental to performance. In the best case for the implementation we have discussed (viz., the branch has been scheduled and issued without delay), 12 cycles have elapsed since the branch was predicted when the prediction has been found erroneous: 9 cycles in the front-end, and 3 cycles (scheduling, issue, execute) in the back-end. In case of a misprediction, a significant number of µops could be in the pipeline, either in the front-end, in the back-end, or already in the ROB. As pipelines get deeper, the importance of a sophisticated branch predictor becomes crucial.

Out-of-order processing adds a new twist to memory operations.

EXAMPLE 5: Consider the following sequence of loads and stores that are separated by nonmemory operations that we do not show:

i1:   ld   R1, memory address 1

       . . .

i2:   st   R2, memory address 2

       . . .

i3:   ld   R3, memory address 3

If the three memory addresses are different, the three instructions can access the memory hierarchy in any order, subject of course to potential dependencies with nonmemory operations. If memory addresses for instructions *i2* and *i3* are the same, the only correct access order for these two instructions is the program order. Renaming would not help if instruction *i3* were to put its result in the ROB before instruction *i2* had completed, for we have restricted renaming to registers and it has no influence on memory addresses. On the other hand, because such address conflicts are not the common case, there can be significant gains in allowing loads to be executed before previous stores. Therefore, there needs to be a mechanism for such occurrences of *load speculation*. We shall return to this subject in detail in Chapter 5. At this point, we just give an overview of a rather conservative scheme that will nonetheless explain the presence of the memory order buffer (MOB) in Figure 3.7.

The main idea is that a load is checked against all previous (in program order) stores and that stores are committed to the memory hierarchy in program order. In the case of a load, the load can proceed:

- If all previous stores have been committed to the memory hierarchy.
- If all previous stores have computed the memory addresses they will access and they differ from the memory address accessed by the load.
- If some previous store accesses the same address as the load and the data to be stored are ready; in that case the load can proceed with the ready data without accessing the memory hierarchy.

However, the load must wait:

- If some previous store has its memory address not computed yet, or if some previous store has the same address as the load and the data to be stored are not ready.

Moreover, as can be expected from an out-of-order processor, a cache miss for a load should not prevent instructions not depending on this load from proceeding. In particular, other loads and stores should be able to access the cache, and thus the cache hierarchy must be *lockup-free* (also called *nonblocking*; cf. Chapter 6), that is, more than one memory request should be able to be in progress at any given time.

The conditions for load speculation require that loads[5] and stores be buffered not only in the ROB but also in a structure connected to the cache hierarchy interface. This structure is the MOB. In the P6 microarchitecture, loads are executed as a single μop, whereas stores are a sequence of two μops, one for the data and one for the address. The MOB has a 16-entry load buffer (LB) and a 12-entry store buffer (SB); an entry in the SB has room for an address and data. Both LB and SB are circular buffers.

When, in the last stage of the front-end, μops are entered in reservation stations and in the ROB, load μops are entered in the LB and store μop pairs are entered in the SB. Their positions in the buffer are their identifications (MBIDs). An LB entry will contain the MBID of the previous store, thus allowing the checking against stores described in the paragraph before last. In fact, this checking, performed when the load address is ready, is done on only the bits used to index the L1 D-cache (12 bits). This partial checking may lead to some false positives, but it simplifies the MOB logic and allows concurrency between the checking and cache access. If the load is allowed to proceed per the conditions stated above, the LB entry will be vacated when the data are returned. If the data are not ready or in case of a false positive, the load remains in the LB until the constraining condition is removed. Stores are committed to the memory hierarchy in order. That is, stores remain in SB until they are at the head of the queue, both the address and data have been computed, and their corresponding entries in the ROB have been committed.

The most common occurrence is for a load to hit in the L1 D-cache with a small latency (in general 2 cycles). If there is a miss, the load remains in the LB until the data come back from the next level in the memory hierarchy. We shall see how to deal with the impact of this miss in forthcoming chapters.

The last event that takes place for an instruction is its retirement or commitment. Note that we are talking about instructions and not μops, for the IA-32 ISA expects instructions to be atomic. To that effect, μops are marked in the ROB as being the first or the last (or both, or neither) of an instruction. All μops constituent of the same instruction retire together, although not necessarily in the same cycle. Therefore, during a multicycle retirement, interrupts are not handled, in order to preserve the atomicity of the instruction and a valid architectural state. Retirement is a 2 cycle operation: read the contents of the ROB and write the register file. These two actions can themselves be pipelined.

3.4.4 Recap; P6 Microarchitecture Evolution

The P6 microarchitecture, and its first implementation the Pentium Pro, were radically different from those of the ×86's and Pentium processors. Besides the out-of-order paradigm – by far the most striking novelty in the P6 – other factors were:

---

[5] The IA-32 ISA allows operations with memory operands. For example, an add can have an operand source register, and a second source operand can be the content of a memory address. Such an operation would be decoded into a load μop followed by an add μop.

much deeper pipelines in the front-end and the back-end, more functional units and thus a better chance at exploiting instruction-level parallelism, and a nonblocking memory hierarchy that could alleviate the load latency penalties. Granted, the increased depth of the instruction pipeline was needed because of the extra work to be done, such as renaming in the front-end and scheduling and issuing in the back-end, but nonetheless each stage had less to do, and therefore the clock frequency could be increased. The downside of deeper pipelines and higher clock frequencies was longer penalties due to branch misprediction and cache misses.

When the Pentium Pro was introduced in 1995, it ran at 200 MHz vs. 60 MHz for the 1993 Pentium and had 5.5 million transistors vs. 3.1. Four years later the clock frequency was 500 MHz and the die had 8.2 million transistors, the increase resulting mostly from the addition of MMX instructions and extra registers to facilitate their execution. An important jump in the number of transistors occurred when the L2 cache was put on chip. The 1999 Pentium III Xeon with a 256 KB L2 cache required 28 million transistors and ran at 700 MHz.

In 2000, the Pentium 4 was introduced. Its microarchitecture, relabeled Netburst, presented several new features (whether they generate performance improvements or not depends on the application). In particular the front-end used a *trace cache* instead of an L1 I-cache (cf. Chapter 4) that allowed shortcuts in decoding of instructions into μops, and the back-end used ALUs that could compute at twice the clock rate of other parts of the instruction pipeline (in other words, some single-stage parts of the front-end now took two stages). The first Pentium 4 ran at 1.5 GHz – that is, the ALUs ran at 3 GHz – and had 42 million transistors. In 2002, the first *hyperthreaded* Pentium 4 was introduced (hyperthreading is a limited version of *simultaneous multithreading* (SMT) that will be discussed in Chapter 8) and was clocked at slightly over 3 GHz with 55 million transistors.

Newer implementations ran at faster clock speeds until 2003 and, as a consequence of Moore's law, had more transistors on chip. The increased availability of transistors on chip has mainly been translated into increases in the amount of on-chip cache memory. However, other structures also grew (larger queues, larger ROB, more reservation stations, etc.), and more sophisticated algorithms could be implemented for, say, branch prediction and cache access. It is also around this time that the 32-bit architecture was extended to a 64-bit architecture. While the raw speed improved, the penalties of wrong predictions became more costly (>20 cycles for a branch misprediction in the Pentium 4, vs. >10 in the Pentium III), and it took more cycles to access some structures such as caches and branch target buffers. Most importantly, though, the combination of increased speed and increased number of transistors put the power problem at the forefront (recall Figure 1.4).

Reducing power dissipation and the ever-increasing importance of the mobile computing market led Intel to the design of the Pentium-M, introduced in 2003 and specifically targeted for laptops and hand-held devices. The Pentium-M microarchitecture resembles that of the Pentium III with a slightly deeper pipeline, enhancements in the cache hierarchy, and more sophisticated branch prediction and load speculation.

The confluence of Moore's law still being valid and of speed limitations imposed by power issues has motivated the introduction of a new computing paradigm: *chip multiprocessing* (CMP, an on-chip implementation of *symmetric multiprocessing* (SMP)), which will be discussed in Chapters 7 and 8. Intel processors on CMPs run at clock speeds between 2 and 3 GHz. In 2006, Intel announced a four-processor CMP following its two-processor chip introduced in 2004. Each processor follows the Intel Core microarchitecture design, which looks like an improved Pentium III or Pentium M with enhancements such as μops fusion (i.e., replacing two μops by a single one) and great attention to power consumption control (cf. Chapter 9).

3.5 VLIW/EPIC Processors

3.5.1 The VLIW/EPIC Design Philosophy

In Chapter 2, where we presented a simple pipelined processor, we did not elaborate on how its control unit was implemented. Today, most often the control unit is built as an array of AND–OR gates (or equivalent), called a PAL (for "programmable array logic"). When transistors were not as plentiful, another method, called *microprogramming*, was used. Even today, both array logic and microprogrammed control units can coexist with the microprogramming used for those instructions in the ISA that are deemed to be too complex for PALs. A case in point is the implementation of string instructions in the P6 architecture (recall the MIS associated with the decoder in Figure 3.7).

As we saw in the previous chapter, the execution of an instruction can be broken into a series of elementary steps such as incrementing the program counter, a register-to-register transfer, an add for the ALU, and so on. In the microprogramming context, each elementary operation is called a *microoperation*. A *microprogram* is a sequence of microoperations that interprets the execution of (part of) the instructions in the ISA. If a very limited number of microoperations, say a single one, can be activated in a given cycle, we have a *vertical microprogramming* implementation. If, on the other hand, a large number of them can be activated, say one per possible control point in the processor, we have *horizontal microprogramming*.

Our point here is not to discuss microprogramming but to note that the VLIW concept descends directly from horizontal microprogramming. In a VLIW processor, a *long instruction* specifies multiple operations that can be performed simultaneously, for example, a memory operation (load or store), an integer arithmetic operation, and a floating-point operation. The EPIC philosophy builds on the VLIW concept and embodies three main principles:

- The compiler should play the key role in detecting the instruction-level parallelism (ILP).
- The architecture should provide features that assist the compiler in determining the most common ways of exploiting ILP.

- The architecture should provide mechanisms to communicate the parallelism detected by the compiler to the underlying hardware.

A VLIW ISA then would define templates of long instructions, that is, the patterns of those operations that can be performed simultaneously. The compiler would generate code by putting together in a single long instruction operations that can be performed in the same cycle without hazards.

EPIC processors are therefore statically scheduled. Instructions are executed in program order, and it behooves the compiler to find optimizations in detecting instruction level parallelism. However, even if the compiler can detect a large amount of ILP, difficulties remain for static scheduling because of the uncertainties of branch prediction and the various latencies that can arise in memory operations. Extensive software and hardware assists for branch prediction, load speculation, and associated recoveries are therefore the architecture features that must be provided.

In view of the fact that out-of-order processors were found to have better performance, why did designers at Intel and Hewlett-Packard advocate an EPIC approach in the mid 1990s? Their two main arguments were:

- The hardware of in-order statically scheduled processors is much simpler than that of out-of-order processors. There is no need for mechanisms such as register renaming or hardware structures such as reorder buffers. The real estate saved can be used for other structures, and the ease in logic should allow for faster clock cycles. Time has shown that the speed-related claim did not hold true, in part because of the ingenuity of out-of-order processor designers and in part because the limitation in clock speed stems not only from logic complexity but also from factors, such as power dissipation, that hinder performance in similar fashion for both types of processors.
- Compiler-based exploitation of ILP should be favorable in that the compiler can look at the whole program rather than the comparatively small instruction window. Because in addition the compiler is aware of the availability of functional units at each cycle, it should be able to create multiple operation instructions more effectively than a purely dynamic scheme. Moreover, the knowledge of operation latencies should allow alleviating the advantage that renaming registers gives to out-of-order processors for preventing WAR and WAW dependencies. Consider, for example, the following two instructions with the WAR dependency on R3:

R1 ← R2 + R3
R3 ← R4 * R5

The multiplication could start up to $m - 2$ cycles before the addition if multiplication takes m cycles and addition takes 1.

Predication

Nevertheless, the problems due to branch prediction and memory latencies need to be addressed. The number of branches to be executed can be reduced by using *predication.* Predicated instructions are tagged with the *name* of a predicate, (i.e., a Boolean value), typically generated by the result of the computation of the conditional expression following an "if" statement. If the predicate is true the instruction is executed otherwise it is not. The simplest form of a predicated instruction is a *conditional move*, such as the one found for example in the ISA of the DEC Alpha. As an illustration, the sequence of two instructions corresponding to the high-level statement "if $A = = 0$ then $B = C$" with the values of A, B, and C being respectively in registers R1, R2, R3 would be translated into an ISA without conditional moves as

```
bnez    R1,Label /* branch if R1 ≠ 0*/
move    R2, R3 /* R2 ← R3 */
Label: add R4, R5, R2
```

With the availability of a conditional move, the first two instructions can be replaced by a single instruction as in

```
cmovz R2,R3,R1 /* R2 ← R3 if R1 = 0*/
add R4, R5, R2 /* no need for label*/
```

Predication can be very useful to avoid branches in the case of if–then–else statements. An *if-conversion* is shown for the "diamond" example of Figure 3.8, corresponding to the high-level language statement "If (conditional expression) then S1 else S2." On the left is the usual code: The conditional expression is evaluated. It is then tested: if true, the branch is taken and the sequence of statements S1 is executed; if false, the sequence of statements S2 is executed. Note that we need an unconditional branch after the last statement in S2. With predication the conditional expression is computed and yields a predicate. All statements in S1 and S2 are predicated with the name of the predicate. The statements in S1 are to be executed if the predicate is true, and those in S2 are to be executed if the predicate is false. Note that the value of the predicate is needed only when the results have to be committed, so if, for example, S1 is a single statement with long latency, it can be started before the value of the predicate is known. Also, statements in S1 and S2 can be executed concurrently. The example shows that two transfer-of-control instructions, one of which needs to be predicted, have been avoided. As shown in this example, predication is quite attractive if the number of instructions in S1 and S2 is rather small and the branch is highly unpredictable.

However, predication has some drawbacks. First, there must be resources, namely, registers, dedicated to storing predicates, because several branches can be performed concurrently. Granted, predicated registers are only 1 bit wide, and this will not much affect the amount of processor state. However, the names of these registers are the tags used for the predicated instructions. In the example in Figure 3.8, the value of the predicate would be stored in a register and the name of the register would be part of the instructions in S1 and S2. Thus, each predicated instruction needs a field as wide as the logarithm of the number of predicate

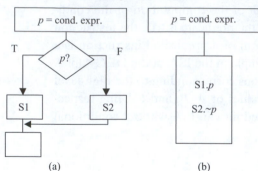

Figure 3.8. Example of if-conversion: (a) usual code, (b) predicated code.

registers. This might increase substantially the length of instructions and/or result in awkward instruction formats. Second, predicated instructions that will not commit still use resources until the last pipeline stage. There might be means to abort the instructions as soon as it is discovered that the predicate is false, but it would add complexity to the design, something that EPIC designers would frown upon in view of their first argument listed. In any case, the predicated instructions must be fetched from the I-cache, thus potentially decreasing the bandwidth from the latter. Whether predication enhances performance or not is still a subject of debate.

Control Speculation

In addition to predication, EPIC designers advocate the use of control speculation. This means hoisting a basic block of instructions above a branch. These instructions become *speculative.* Of course, speculative instructions cannot be committed until the branch condition is known. The advantages of this speculation are that resources can be better utilized in portions of programs that exhibit low ILP, the heights of long dependence chains can be lowered, and instructions with long latency can be started earlier, as was the case for predication. In addition, however, to the fact that results of speculative instructions must be buffered until the branch condition has been resolved, another problem that may arise is that of exceptions. An exception raised by a speculative instruction, or a predicated instruction, should not be handled if the speculative instruction is not to be executed. A way to avoid this problem is to append a 1-bit tag, often called a *poison bit*, to the result register of a speculative instruction that has raised an exception. The poison bit percolates through to result registers of instructions that use a register with a poison bit as a source operand. If the speculation was correct, then the exception must be handled (and hence a mechanism must be provided to let the hardware know where the exception occurred); otherwise it can be ignored.

Finally, the prediction of the latency of load operations is quite difficult. We already have seen that in both in-order and out-of-order superscalars, some guessing and subsequent repair work was needed. The same will be true for EPIC processors. Statically managing the cache hierarchy by software prefetching (cf. Section 6.2.1), and specifying in which member of the cache hierarchy a particular datum should be stored, are attempts at solving this difficult problem.

3.5.2 A Brief Overview of the Intel Itanium

Until Intel and Hewlett-Packard announced their intention to build an EPIC processor, there had been two VLIW general-purpose commercial systems: Multiflow and Cydra-5, both built in the mid 1980s. Although these machines showed some promising performance, they were never successful commercially. They used compilers based on *trace scheduling*, a technique whose description is outside the scope of this book. The main idea is to allow the scheduling of concurrent operations across basic blocks. It involves detecting or guessing the execution frequencies of basic blocks and scheduling first those on the critical path. The remainder of the program is then filled in, taking advantage of long instructions to schedule concurrent operations.

The VLIW approach has been used successfully in a number of embedded processors. Because the code for a given application is fixed and generally quite short, a lot of time can be devoted to compiler or manual optimizations to find the right patterns to put in long instructions. Many of the difficulties presented in the previous section can therefore be avoided, for generality is not of concern.

In 2000, Intel and Hewlett-Packard announced the Itanium (originally called Project Merced). The first generation ran at 800 MHz, and the second generation of these processors is now available. The Itanium 2 processors released after 2004 have a 1.6 GHz clock. There is also a CMP with two hyperthreaded Itanium 2 processors per chip. In the following, we give a brief introduction to the Itanium architecture. The reader interested in the compiler and microarchitecture implementations should consult the references given at the end of the chapter.

General Organization

The Itanium is a realization of Intel's IA-64 architecture. As the name implies, this is a 64-bit ISA. Contrary to the IA-32, which has a paucity of programmer-visible registers, the Itanium realization of IA-64 is register-rich (some will say excessively so), but of course, because visible registers are meant to be statically scheduled, they cannot be augmented by physically renamed registers. Although the Itanium literature mentions renamed (rotated or stacked) registers, these are a subset of the registers mentioned here and are used for procedure call–return protocols and for software pipelining. More specifically, there are:

- 128 65-bit general registers, where the 65th bit is a poison bit as explained previously (an NaT – i.e., "not a thing" – bit in Itanium parlance); 96 of these registers can be rotated in software pipelined portions of code and can also be used in the call–return stacking scheme.
- 128 82-bit floating-point registers, of which 96 can be rotated.
- 64 1-bit predicate registers, of which 48 can be rotated.
- 8 64-bit registers for function calls and returns.

Instructions are packaged in *bundles* of three with a *template* indicating the types of the three instructions. An example of a typical template is MMI, that is, the first two instructions are memory operations and the third one is an integer operation.

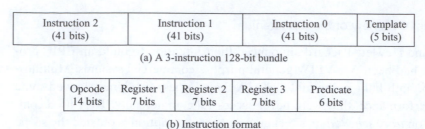

Instruction 2 (41 bits)	Instruction 1 (41 bits)	Instruction 0 (41 bits)	Template (5 bits)

(a) A 3-instruction 128-bit bundle

Opcode 14 bits	Register 1 7 bits	Register 2 7 bits	Register 3 7 bits	Predicate 6 bits

(b) Instruction format

Figure 3.9. Bundle and instruction formats in the Itanium.

There is also the possibility of indicating with a *stop* that some of the operations must be completed before the following ones can go on. In the preceding example, a stop might be necessary between the two M operations (think of a pointer reference followed by a load of a given field). The stop might also be needed at the end of a bundle. Because not all combinations of possible types are possible, the compiler might have to insert no-ops (early studies of code generated for the Itanium found that the number of generated no-ops was nonnegligible). As shown in Figure 3.9, each instruction is 41 bits long and consists of an opcode and room for three registers (7 bits each, because there can be as many as 128 registers of a given type) and for a predicate register. Three instructions plus a 5-bit template form a 128-bit bundle.

A block diagram of the Itanium is shown in Figure 3.10. The pipeline is 10 stages deep, with three stages for the front-end and seven for the back-end. There is a buffer in between the front-end and the back-end that can store up to eight bundles. The buffer allows instruction fetches to continue in case the back-end stalls, and, conversely, the buffer can feed the back-end in case of instruction cache misses or erroneous branch prediction. The back-end consists of four integer units (six in the Itanium 2), four multimedia units (six in the Itanium 2), three branch units, two single-precision floating-point units and another two for extended precision, and two load–store units. The ALAT structure is a fully associative buffer used for load speculation.

The on-chip cache hierarchy is extensive and even more imposing in the Itanium 2. To wit, it consists of:

- 16 KB, four-way set-associative L1 I-cache and L1 D-cache with 32-byte lines. The D-cache is write-through dual-ported, physically addressed and tagged, and has a load latency of 2 cycles. In Itanium 2, the latency has been reduced to 1 cycle even though it has a faster clock.
- L2 is 96 KB, six-way set-associative, uses 64-byte lines, and has a 12 cycle latency.
- L3 is off chip. Its is 4 MB, four-way set-associative, and has 64-byte lines. The latency is 20 cycles.

The dual-processor Itanium 2 running at 1.6 GHz is quoted as having 2.5 MB of L2 and 24 MB of L3 on chip with, for the latter, a latency of 14 cycles.

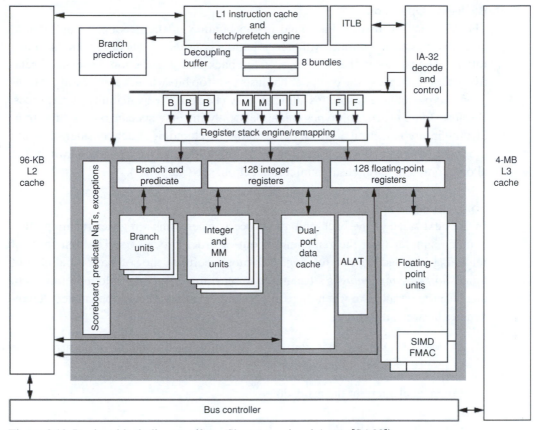

Figure 3.10 Itanium block diagram (from Sharangpani and Arora [SA00]).

The goal of the implementation is to execute two bundles, that is, six instructions, per cycle. To that effect, compiler and hardware need to cooperate more closely than in a purely dynamic scheme.

Front-end Operation

The front-end performs fetching of instructions and branch prediction. A sophisticated two-level branch predictor (see Chapter 4) is enhanced in several ways. First, because of the presence of predicated and speculative instructions, several basic blocks can collapse at the end of the same bundle, and this gives rise to multiway branches. A multiway branch prediction table and associated target address table (in a sense an extension of a branch target buffer) are added to the two-level predictor. Second, four registers can be set programmatically by the compiler for keeping the target addresses of highly predictable branches such as end of loops. Taken branches, the usual case, are resolved in a single cycle, and there is no bubble in the pipeline. Branch instructions can also contain hints for the prefetching of instructions from the L2 cache into an instruction buffer. Of course, these prefetches are not performed if the instructions are already in the L1 I-cache. The third stage of the front-end inserts the bundles into the decoupling buffer.

Back-end Operation

The dispersal of instructions found in the bundles in the decoupling buffer – at most two bundles at a time, with a new bundle considered whenever one has been totally exhausted – is the first stage of the back-end. Instruction dispersal is relatively simple, because the compiler has inserted stop bits whenever necessary. Moreover, the per-bundle templates allow an easy check of the availability of resources. Because some instruction types can appear only in some specific parts of the bundle, the interconnection network between the two bundles under consideration and the functional units does not need to be a complete crossbar (an *n*-by-*n* switch that allows complete parallelism in interconnection; see Chapter 7).

Software Pipelining

In the next stage of the back-end, the processor performs a register renaming that is much simpler than the renaming of out-of-order processors. The first form of renaming is called *register rotation*. It is most useful in the software pipelining of loops. *Software pipelining* is a technique to rearrange the body of loop iterations to increase the parallelism when there are resource constraints or loop-carried dependencies between iterations.

> **EXAMPLE 6:** Assume that you want to double each element of an array. The sequence of instructions will be:
>
> For each element of the array do
> $i1$:   R1   ← A[i]
> $i2$:   R1   ← R1 + R1
> i3:   A[i]   ← R1

If there were no resource constraint except that only one load can proceed at a time, we could start iteration at each cycle as shown on the left in Figure 3.11. In software pipelining, statements from consecutive iterations are brought into the same iteration of the new code by taking "horizontal" slices of the old code as shown on the left of the figure. In a VLIW implementation, the "store, use, load" of consecutive iterations can be done in the same VLIW instruction if the "use" is a single operation as shown in Figure 3.12. Even if the "use" is not a single instruction, the load and store latencies can be hidden with a short "use" basic block.

Whereas traditional architectures suffer from overhead in the unrolling of loops, such as the renaming of registers and the prologue and epilogue at the start and at the end of the iterations, software pipelining circumvents many of these problems, especially if the register renaming can be automated in a simple fashion. In Figure 3.12, we see how the sequential code, possibly unrolled, looks in a straightforward implementation and with software pipelining. The Itanium implementation helps by having some of the registers hold loop counts and pipeline lengths used in the epilogue. Moreover, the register numbers for integer, floating-point, and predicate registers used in the body of the loop are incremented

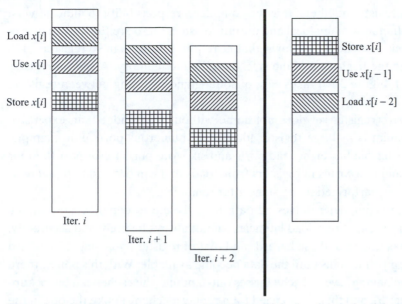

Figure 3.11. Software pipelining. On the left the original code; on the right, the new code.

modulo the number of available registers of a given type that can be rotated at every iteration if the opcode so indicates.

Register Stacking

The second form of renaming has to do with implementation of the stack. The register model is such that the first 32 registers of the 128 general registers are used as they would be in a conventional RISC processor. The others can be used to implement stack frames in procedure call–return protocols. For example, if a procedure A called from the main program uses four local registers, they can be allocated to registers 32 to 35. If procedure A calls another procedure, say procedure B with three parameters, the parameters will be passed to *output* registers 36 through 38. When this second procedure starts executing, the local registers of the caller are hidden and the output registers of the caller become the first local registers of the callee. Their renamed identities start at 32. In this example, the additional local registers will then be from 35 on. During the renaming stage, a simple adder is sufficient to

Figure 3.12. Executions of (a) sequential loop and (b) the same loop software pipelined in a VLIW machine.

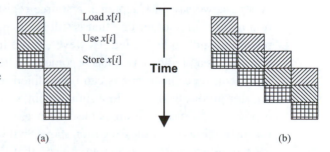

(a)

(b)

get to the right register numbers. It is the compiler's responsibility to indicate via a specific instruction how many local and output registers there are for a given procedure. If the stack so created overflows, that is, requires more than 96 registers (128 − 32 = 96), then the beginning of the stack is spilled in memory. A special register stack engine (cf. Figure 3.10) takes care of spilling and restoring between registers and memory.

The extensive register set does not come without cost. Indeed, an expensive part of the Itanium is its large register file and its numerous ports. For example, the integer register file has eight read ports and six write ports to support the four integer ALUs and two writes in registers from loads that can occur simultaneously. Register reads are performed in the stage after renaming.

Although the compiler resolves all data hazards due to dependencies among arithmetic–logical operations, load latencies cannot always be predicted accurately. A scoreboard takes care of these hazards and that of register bypassing. If a hazard is detected, the pipeline stalls until the data become available. With this policy, there is no problem in having several cache misses outstanding (the caches can be lockup-free; see Chapter 6), and there is no need for a replay mechanism like the one in the DEC Alpha 21124. Moreover, the scoreboard can take advantage of predication to nullify a stall if either the producer or the consumer of a stalled operation has a predicate that is false. These actions take place in the pipeline stage following the register reads, and some might be deferred till the next stage (the execution stage) by preventing the reading of operands that were to be bypassed.

The last three stages of the pipeline are execution, exception detection, and writeback of registers. The instruction set is rich and well supported by the functional units and the register file ports. Of course, it is during these stages, or earlier if possible, that care must be taken of predication, speculation, and exceptions. Control speculation is handled with poison bits as explained previously. The only type of data speculation that can occur is the one due to the inaccuracy of load latency prediction. The ALAT mentioned previously plays the roles of load and store buffers, as will be explained in Chapter 5. Recovery is necessary for both control and data misspeculation, as well as in the case of a mispredicted branch. Because Itanium is an in-order processor, the steps to be followed are simpler than in an out-of-order superscalar.

Predicate registers are most often set during a compare operation. The values of predicate registers are used in bypassing, instruction nullification, and branching. When, as we saw in Chapter 2, a source register of an instruction is the destination register of another one that is still in the pipeline, bypassing is necessary if the pipeline is not to be stalled. However, if the instruction involving the destination register has a predicate that has become false, the forwarding should not take place. Thus, consumer instructions can be nullified in the read register stage if a source register predicate is false. In a similar vein, some data hazards can be removed if a producer's predicate becomes false. Hence, the predicates must be available when the instructions enter the execution stage. So if we make an inventory of where predicate registers must be available, we see that they are needed for the two bundles (six instructions) in the read register stage and six instructions in the execution stage. In addition, three branches can be resolved in the exception detection stage, involving another three predicate registers. All together, 15 read ports must be available for the predicate register file. A similar analysis indicates that 11 write ports are necessary for the generation of the predicates from various compare instructions. Although 15 read ports and 11 write ports for a register file appears to be a huge investment, recall that predicate registers are only 1 bit long and therefore the reading and writing of the predicate register file can be implemented using multiplexers and decoders.

Predicate values might have to be forwarded to the above points of consumption before they are stored in the predicate register file. Because bypass logic for these predicates would be very expensive, a speculative predicate register file is implemented instead, and a register (a single bit) in that file is written as soon as its value has been computed. It is this speculative register file that is used as a source for predicates. The predicate register that is used to keep the state of the program is written only during the writeback register stage.

Although the hardware support for predication, speculation, and exception handling is nonnegligible, it is much less than what is required for an out-of-order processor. The proof of the pudding, though, is in the performance that can be attained by an EPIC processor. Is the combination of (relative) hardware simplicity and compiler assists sufficient to outweigh the benefits of out-of-order execution? At this point in time (say, Itanium 2 vs. Pentium 4 or Core architecture), the jury would say that it really depends on the type of applications.

3.6 Summary

Superscalar processors were introduced in the late 1980s and early 1990s. They allow the simultaneous execution of several instructions in each stage of the pipeline. To that effect, pipelines are wider than the simple ones presented in the previous chapter, and, to accommodate the added complexity of the operations to be performed at each stage and the decreases in cycle time, they are also deeper.

Although all instructions proceed in program order in the front-end (fetch, branch prediction, and decode) of the pipeline, a major distinction exists in the ordering of execution in the back-end (execution and writeback). In in-order processors, exemplified in this book by the Dec Alpha 21164, all data dependencies are checked in the last stage of the front-end. Instructions leave the front-end in program order, and once they leave the front-end they will complete without delay (except, of course, if there are branch mispredictions or cache misses). Control of the interface between the front-end and the back-end and monitoring of the execution in the back-end are performed with a scoreboard. The scoreboard idea was originated in the Control Data 6600.

In out-of-order processors, instructions can leave the front-end in any order. This implies that WAR and WAW dependencies must be resolved, that instructions that have passed through the front-end but are not ready to be executed must be queued, and that some mechanism must be implemented in order to store the results in a semantically correct way, that is, in program order. These functions are realized respectively through register renaming, reservation stations (instruction window), and the reorder buffer. A classical way to integrate these mechanisms is through Tomasulo's algorithm, first implemented in the floating-point unit of the IBM System 360/91.

The first out-of-order microprocessor was Intel's Pentium Pro. Since then, the Intel P6 microarchitecture, whose basic implementation follows closely Tomasulo's algorithm, has given birth to numerous Intel microprocessors, each new model showing definite microarchitectural improvements. During the period where speed was able to increase at the same rate as Moore's law, the tendency was to have deeper pipelines, the Pentium 4 being the flagship of this trend. However, with power limitations, with the difficulty of exploiting more instruction-level parallelism because of the design complexity of adding more features to barely increase performance, and with the increased penalties with pipeline depth due to misspeculation, we are now seeing slightly less deep pipelines, as in the Core architecture, which are the building blocks of Intel chip multiprocessors.

By the beginning of the century, it was clear that out-of-order processors would perform better than in-order superscalars. However, the emergence of chip multiprocessors reopens the question of whether at equal chip area the performance of a larger group of simple processors might surpass that of a smaller number of complex processors.

Finally, we can make the hardware simpler by passing the complexity to the software, namely, the compiler, which can be made to schedule and allow the parallel execution of instructions. This is the basic idea behind the VLIW/EPIC model, represented in general-purpose processors by the Intel Itanium family. Though there are success stories for VLIW processors for embedded systems, and though they reportedly consume less power, it is not clear the concept will lead to improved performance and reduced cost in the general-purpose area.

3.7 Further Reading and Bibliographical Notes

The study of superscalar processors is a staple of modern computer architecture texts. An excellent early survey is by Smith and Sohi [SS95]. Gwennap first introduced the characterization of "speed demons" versus "brainiacs" in a 1993 *Microprocessor Report Newsletter* editorial. Six years later, Gwennap in his farewell editorial [G99] noted that "brainiacs" had all but disappeared since out-of-order processors, even with CISC ISAs, had joined the camp of the speed demons thanks to advances in microarchitecture implementation.

It is interesting to note that the earliest processors that allowed multiple instruction issue were of the VLIW type, thus relying mainly on compiler sophistication. This is not to say that the potential of exploitation of instruction-level parallelism was not studied. Already in the 1960s Bernstein had formalized in a more general form what we now call RAW, WAR, and WAW dependencies [B66]. Two early interesting studies among many are those in the early 1970s by Tjaden and Flynn [TF70] that showed that parallelism within basic blocks was severely limited, and by Riseman and Foster [RF70] that demonstrated that this parallelism was much more prevalent if one could avoid control hazards – a nice motivation for branch prediction that really came into full bloom only a decade later. Taking a slightly different tack, Kuck and his group at Illinois [ABKMNW69] showed that a substantial amount of parallelism could be exploited in scientific programs if one were to perform loop transformations and remove some conditional hazards with the use of what we call now predication. Nonetheless, it took almost two decades before production superscalar processors started to be commercially successful.

The DEC Alpha architecture and its first two implementations, the 21064 and 21164, are described in the book by Bhandarkar [B95]. See also Edmonson et al. [ERPR95] for further details on the 21164. The measurements reported in Section 3.2.4 are extracted from Cvetanovic and Bhandarkar [CB96]. Seymour Cray and James E. Thornton designed the CDC 6600. Thornton's book is a classic [T70]. A very readable introduction to the CDC 6600 by the same author [T64] can be found in Bell and Newell's anthology.

Reservation stations and the register renaming concept were first implemented in the IBM System/360 Model 91. A whole issue (January 1967) of the *IBM Journal of Research and Development* is devoted to this machine. The most germane paper for this chapter is Tomasulo's paper [T67], but the paper by Anderson et al. [AST67] is also worth reading in that it discusses also pipelining, branch handling, and memory interleaving. In Tomasulo's original scheme, reservation stations were the renamed physical registers. A more general renaming scheme was presented in Keller's survey [K75] that will be elaborated on it Chapter 4. Because imprecise interrupts were allowed in the Model 91, there was no need for a reorder buffer (ROB). Smith and Pleszkun [SP88], while studying precise interrupts, were the first to introduce the ROB as a means to squash instructions following the one that generated the interrupt. Sohi [S90] generalized the concept and was the first to suggest that the ROB could also be used as the physical medium for renamed registers. At approximately the same time, Hwu and Patt [HP86] used an instruction window to combine (centralized) reservation stations and ROB.

The Intel P6 microarchitecture was introduced in 1995. A brief general tour can be found in an Intel publication [I95]. Descriptions of the implementation of the various concepts, as found in the Pentium Pro, the Pentium II, and the Pentium III, are given in the papers by Colwell et al. [CPHFG05], Papworth [P96], and Keshava and Pentkovski [KP99]. The Pentium 4 is described in Hinton et al. [HSUBCKR01] and in Boggs et al. [BBHMMRSTV04]. The Pentium M and its power-saving facilities are described in Gochman et al. [GRABKNSSV03]. The same group designed the Core architecture.

Fisher, the chief designer of Multiflow, and Rau, the principal architect of Cydra-5, have been the main advocates for EPIC. The design philosophy is laid out in Schlansker and Rau [SR00]. The IA-64 architecture and Itanium micro-architecture are presented in Huck et al. [HMRKMZ00] and Sharangpani and Arora [SA00], respectively. McNairy and Soltis [MS03] describe the Itanium 2 enhancements. Hwu and his group have developed IMPACT, a highly sophisticated compiler for EPIC architectures; see for example [ACMSCCEOH98]. Software pipelining and its application to VLIW processors were introduced by Lam [L88]. Register stacking resembles the register windows originally found in Berkeley's RISC [PS81] and then later commercialized in the Sun SPARC architecture.

EXERCISES

1. (Sections 3.2.2 and 3.2.3) The Alpha 21124 is called "in order." However, instructions can complete out of order. Give two examples of such an occurrence.

2. (Section 3.2.2) There is no check for a WAR dependency in an in-order Alpha 21164 processor. Why?

3. (Section 3.2.2) Give an example of a WAW dependency that could happen in an Alpha 21164. This is also called a producer–producer problem and does not make much sense, but it can occur when programs have been patched too often.

4. (Sections 2.2 and 2.3) What does the scoreboard of an Alpha 21164 entail? Is it more or less complicated than the CDC scoreboard?

5. (Section 3.2.3) In the Alpha 21164, interrupt handling requires draining the whole pipeline. Could the back-end only be drained and instructions restarted with the first instruction in stage S3? Justify your answer.

6. (Section 3.2.3) On a TLB miss (either instruction or data) in the Alpha 21164, PAL code is called upon to retrieve the missing information and bring it to the TLB. During that time, interrupts are disabled. Why?

7. (Section 3.2, Sidebar) In Figure 3.3, several functional units with various latencies (e.g., the integer adder, the floating-point multipliers, and the shifter) share the same buses to transmit results to registers. How could the scoreboard control the start of computation on these units so that buses will be free when a result has to be written back? (Hint: Think of a clever way to maintain a busy–idle structure that shifts at every cycle.)

8. (Section 3.2, Sidebar) Consider a CDC 6600-like processor with the following latencies:

- 4 units for an add.
- 10 units for a multiply.
- 20 units for a divide.

Suppose the segment of program with the three instructions (all registers are free at the onset) is

  i1:   R2 ← R3/R5
  i2:   R1 ← R2 + R4
  i3:   R4 ← R6 * R6

If *i1* is issued at t_0, at what time will each instruction complete?

9. (Section 3.2, Sidebar) Repeat Exercise 8, but now assume that each functional unit has buffers to hold input values from registers.

10. (Section 3.2, Sidebar) The CDC 6600 had a successor, the CDC 7600, which had input buffers and *pipelined* functional units. What major differences between the CDC 6600 and CDC 7600 scoreboards can you think of?

11. (Section 3.3) Consider a three-way out-of-order processor. In the renaming stage, three instructions have to be renamed simultaneously. If there is one (or more) RAW dependency between these instructions, the correct renaming cannot be done solely by table lookup. Show the logic – that is, a diagram with comparators, priority encoders, and multiplexers – necessary to perform a correct renaming. (Hint: If you are stuck on this problem, consult, e.g., [SBP00] referenced in Chapter 5.)

12. (Section 3.3) In Exercise 11, we have considered a three-way processor. Consider now the more general case of an *m*-way processor. How do the number of comparators and the number of priority encoders grow with *m*?

13. (Section 3.3) There is some fuzziness in the definitions of *dispatch* and of *issue*. In Table 3.4, we have put dispatch as part of the front-end and issue as part of the back-end. Does this mean that dispatch should be done in order and that issue can be done out of order? Justify your answers.

14. (Section 3.3, Sidebar) Repeat Exercise 9 for Tomasulo's algorithm. Is there any major difference in your results? Give an example sequence where Tomasulo's algorithm would certainly do better than a CDC 7600 scoreboard scheme.

15. (Section 3.3, Sidebar) In the sidebar, we illustrated Tomasulo's algorithm with a single-issue processor. What are the minimal hardware additions that are needed if we want to issue two instructions per cycle?

16. (Section 3.3, Sidebar) In its original implementation, Tomasulo's algorithm was restricted to the floating-point unit of the IBM System 360/91. Floating-point registers were used instead of the ROB. Now that you have seen an implementation of the algorithm for a more complete processor (the P6 microarchitecture), state why it was not necessary to have an ROB in the floating-point unit of the System 360/91.

17. (Sections 3 and 4) Entries in the ROB must be able to store integers as well as floating-point numbers. What would be the advantages and the drawbacks of splitting the ROB into two parts, one for the integer results and one for the floating-point ones? Be sure to consider topics such as register allocation and branch misprediction recovery.

18. (Section 3.4) In the P6 microarchitecture, instructions of the form R1 ← R2 + Mem[R3] are translated into two μops at decode time: one for the load with a temporary register as result, and one for the addition. AMD processors with the same ISA consider the instruction as a single *macro-op* that is issued twice, once to a load unit and once to an integer unit. Are there some advantages to the AMD implementation? If so, what are they?

19. (Section 3.4) In the recent Intel Core architecture, instructions of the form R1 ← R2 + Mem[R3] are *fused* into a single μop. Is this consistent with the RISC philosophy? What are the advantages of fusion?

20. (Section 3.5) Consider the following fragment of code:

```
If a < 0 then
        {b = 1;
          c =2}
else {d = 3;
        e = 4};
```

(a) Recode this fragment using predication.

(b) How many static instructions will be generated if the original code is used? Assume a RISC architecture that can test registers for equal, greater than, or less than in one instruction.

(c) How many static instructions will be generated using the modified predicated code? You can assume full predication.

(d) How many instructions will be executed in the original code if there is a 0.4 probability that $a < 0$? How many instructions if the probability is 0.6?

(e) Repeat (d) for the predicated code. Is predication a good choice if the branch is very unbalanced, that is, the probability of branching one particular way is very high? (You can assume that the programmer knows which way the branch is likely to go, e.g., for a break from a loop.)

REFERENCES

[ABKMNW69] N. Abel, D. Budnick, D. Kuck, Y. Muraoka, R. Northcote, and R. Wilhelmson, "TRANQUIL: A Language for an Array Processing Computer," *Proc. AFIPS SJCC*, 1969, 57–73

[ACMSCCEOH98] D. August, D. Connors, S. Mahlke, J. Sias, K. Crozier, B. Cheng, P. Eaton, Q. Olaniran, and W-m. Hwu, "Integrated Predicated and Speculative Execution in the IMPACT EPIC Architecture," *Proc. 25th Int. Symp. on Computer Architecture*, 1998, 227–237

[AST67] D. Anderson, F. Sparacio, and R. Tomasulo, "Machine Philosophy and Instruction Handling," *IBM Journal of Research and Development*, 11, 1, Jan. 1967, 8–24

[B66] A. Bernstein, "Analysis of Programs for Parallel Processing," *IEEE Trans. on Elec. Computers*, EC-15, Oct. 1966, 746–757

[B95] D. Bhandarkar, *Alpha Implementations and Architecture. Complete Reference and Guide*, Digital Press, Boston, 1995

[BBHMMRSTV04] D. Boggs, A. Baktha, J. Hawkins, D. Marr, J. Miller, P. Roussel, R. Singhal, B. Toll, and K. Venkatraman, "The Microarchitecture of the Pentium 4 Processor on 90nm Technology," *Intel Tech. Journal*, 8, 1, Feb. 2004, 1–17

[CB96] Z. Cvetanovic and D. Bhandarkar, "Performance Characterization of the Alpha 21164 Microprocessor Using TP and SPEC Workloads," *Proc. 2nd Int. Symp. on High-Performance Computer Architecture*, 1996, 270–280

[CPHFG05] R. Colwell, D. Papworth, G. Hinton, M. Fetterman, and A. Glew, "Intel's P6 Microarchitecture," Chapter 7 in J. P. Shen and M. Lipasti, Eds., *Modern Processor Design*, 2005, 329–367

[ERPR95] J. Edmondson, P. Rubinfeld, R. Preston, and V. Rajagopalan, "Superscalar Instruction Execution in the 21164 Alpha Microprocessor," *IEEE Micro*, 15, 2, Apr. 1995, 33–43

[G99] L. Gwennap, "Brainiacs, Speed Demons, and Farewell," *Microprocessor Report Newsletter*, 13, 7, Dec. 1999

[GRABKNSSV03] S. Gochman, R. Ronen, I. Anati, R. Berkovits, T. Kurts, A. Naveh, A. Saeed, Z. Sperber, and R. Valentine, "The Intel Pentium M Processor: Microarchitecture and Performance," *Intel Tech. Journal*, 07, 2, May 2003, 21–39

[HMRKMZ00] J. Huck, D. Morris, J. Ross, A. Knies, H. Mulder, and R. Zahir, "Introducing the IA-64 Architecture," *IEEE Micro*, 20, 5, Sep. 2000, 12–23

[HP86] W.-m. Hwu and Y. Patt, "HPSm, A High-Performance Restricted Data Flow Architecture Having Minimal Functionality," *Proc. 13th Int. Symp. on Computer Architecture*, 1986, 297–307

[HSUBCKR01] G. Hinton, D. Sager, M. Upton, D. Boggs, D. Carmean, A. Kyker, and P. Roussel, "The Microarchitecture of the Pentium4 Processor," *Intel Tech. Journal*, 1, Feb. 2001

[I95] Intel Corp, "A Tour of the P6 Microarchitecture," 1995, http://www.x86.org/ftp/manuals/686/p6tour.pdf

[K75] R. Keller, "Look-ahead Processors," *ACM Computing Surveys*, 7, 4, Dec. 1975, 177–195

[KP99] J. Keshava and V. Pentkovski, "Pentium III Processor Implementation Tradeoffs," *Intel Tech. Journal*, 2, May 1999

[L88] M. Lam, "Software Pipelining: An Effective Scheduling Technique for VLIW Machines," *Proc. ACM SIGPLAN Conf. on Programming Language Design and Implementation*, SIGPLAN Notices, 23, 7, Jul. 1988, 318–328

[MS03] C. McNairy and D. Soltis, "Itanium 2 Processor Microarchitecture," *IEEE Micro*, 23, 2, Mar. 2003, 44–55

[P96] D. Papworth, "Tuning the Pentium Pro Microarchitecture," *IEEE Micro*, 16, 2, Mar. 1996, 8–15

[PS81] D. Patterson and C. Séquin, "RISC I: A Reduced Instruction Set VLSI Computer," *Proc. 8th Int. Symp. on Computer Architecture*, 1981, 443–457

[RF70] E. Riseman and C. Foster, "The Inhibition of Potential Parallelism by Conditional Jumps," *IEEE Trans. on Computers*, C-21, 12, Dec. 1972, 1405–1411

[S90] G. Sohi, "Instruction Issue Logic for High-Performance, Interruptible, Multiple Functional Unit, Pipelined Computers," *IEEE Trans. on Computers*, C-39, 3, Mar. 1990, 349–359 (an earlier version with coauthor S. Vajapeyam was published in *Proc. 14th Int. Symp. on Computer Architecture*, 1987)

[SA00] H. Sharangpani and K. Arora, "Itanium Processor Microarchitecture," *IEEE Micro*, 20, 5, Sep. 2000, 24–43

[SP88] J. Smith and A. Pleszkun, "Implementation of Precise Interrupts in Pipelined Processors," *IEEE Trans. on Computers*, C-37, 5, May 1988, 562–573 (an earlier version was published in *Proc. 12th Int. Symp. on Computer Architecture*, 1985)

[SR00] M. Schlansker and B. Rau, "EPIC: Explicitly Parallel Instruction Computing," *IEEE Computer*, 33, 2, Feb. 2000, 37–45

[SS95] J. Smith and G. Sohi, "The Microarchitecture of Superscalar Processors," *Proc. IEEE*, 83, 12, Dec. 1995, 1609–1624

[T64] J. Thornton, "Parallel Operation in the Control Data 6600," *AFIPS Proc. FJCC*, pt. 2, vol. 26, 1964, 33–40 (reprinted as Chapter 39 of C. Bell and A. Newell, *Computer Structures: Readings and Examples*, McGraw-Hill, New York, 1971, and Chapter 43 of D. Siewiorek, C. Bell, and A. Newell, *Computer Structures: Principles and Examples*, McGraw-Hill, New York, 1982)

[T67] R. Tomasulo, "An Efficient Algorithm for Exploiting Multiple Arithmetic Units," *IBM Journal of Research and Development*, 11, 1, Jan. 1967, 25–33

[T70] J. Thornton, *Design of a Computer: The Control Data 6600*, Scott, Foresman and Co., Glenview, IL, 1970

[TF70] G. Tjaden and M. Flynn, "Detection and Parallel Execution of Independent Instructions," *IEEE Trans. on Computers*, C-19, 10, Oct. 1970, 889–895

4 Front-End: Branch Prediction, Instruction Fetching, and Register Renaming

In this chapter, we revisit the actions that are taken during the front-end of the instruction pipeline: instruction fetch, instruction decode, and, for out-of-order processors, register renaming.

A large part of this chapter will be devoted to branch prediction, which in turn governs instruction fetch. We have already seen in previous chapters the importance of branch prediction in that (i) branch instructions, or more generally transfer of control flow instructions, occur very often (once every five instructions on average), and (ii) branch mispredictions are extremely costly in lost instruction issue slots. The performance penalty of misprediction increases with the depth and the width of the pipelines. In other words, the faster the processor (the greater the depth) and the more it can exploit instruction-level parallelism (the greater the width), the more important it is to have accurate branch predictors.

We shall start our study of branch prediction by examining the anatomy of a branch predictor, an instance of a general prediction model. This model will highlight the decision points: when we predict, what we predict, how we predict, and how to provide feedback to the predictor. For the two types of prediction, branch direction and branch target address, the emphasis will first be on the "how." Because there have been hundreds of papers devoted to branch direction prediction, the highlight will be on what may be considered to be the most important schemes, historically and performancewise. We shall look only briefly at branch statistics and static prediction schemes, and concentrate on dynamic schemes using branch prediction buffers (BPBs), starting with the simplest ones, the pattern history tables (PHTs), which can have accuracies of over 80%, and moving on up to the most complex schemes, which can have accuracies of over 95%. In the case of target address prediction, we shall examine branch target buffers (BTBs) and their interactions with BPBs. We shall then integrate these buffers within the structure of the front-end of the instruction pipeline. The placement of the BTB will motivate us to introduce trace caches, a form of instruction cache that has been mentioned in connection with the Pentium 4.

In the remainder of this chapter, we shall look very briefly at the decoding stage, which is not simple for processors that run an instruction set based on the Intel

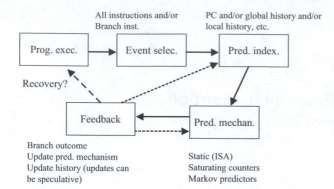

Figure 4.1. Anatomy of a branch predictor.

IA-32 ISA. Then we shall revisit the register renaming stage. In Chapter 3, we saw how the reorder buffer (ROB) could be used as an extension to the logical registers. We shall examine another way of providing register renaming, namely, using an extension of the ISA-defined register file with a physical file of extra registers. The pros and cons of each method will be presented.

4.1 Branch Prediction

4.1.1 Anatomy of a Branch Predictor

A general predictor model consists of an event source, an information predictor, and, most often, a feedback mechanism. In the case of branch prediction, we have (Figure 4.1):

- *Event source:* The source of events, that is, branches, is the program dynamic execution. It might contain some predictive information. The information can be expressed explicitly if the ISA allows it, for example, by having a bit in the opcode indicating the most likely outcome of the branch. Or it can be deduced implicitly: For example, a predictor of the branch's outcome could be linked to whether the branch is forward or backward. Input from a feedback mechanism, such as profiling, can improve on the prediction at that level.

- *Event selection:* The events on which predictions will be made are the transfer of control (branch, return from functions) instructions, but, as we shall see, we can attempt predictions on all instructions and never use the predictions for nonbranch instructions. These extraneous predictions are similar in spirit to the computation of branch target addresses in the decode stage of the five-stage pipeline in Section 2.1.4. If the instruction was not a branch, the result of the target address calculation was discarded.

- *Predictor indexing:* Prediction schemes access one (or more) table(s), sometimes organized in a cachelike fashion. Indexing of these tables can use (parts of): the program counter (PC) pointing to the branch instruction on which prediction is performed, the global history of the outcomes of previous branches, the local history of the outcomes of previous branches with the same PC, the history of the path leading to the current instruction, or a combination of some or all of these selectors.

Table 4.1. Control flow instruction statistics (data from Lee et al. [LCBAB98])

Application	% Control flow	% Cond. branches (% those taken)	% Uncond. (% direct)	% Calls	% Returns
SPEC95int	20.4	14.9 (46)	1.1 (77)	2.2	2.1
Desktop	18.7	13 (39)	1.1 (92)	2.4	2.1

- *Predictor mechanism:* This can be a static scheme (in which case the predictor indexing step does not exist), or a dynamic scheme such as a finite-state machine (saturating counters) or a Markov (correlation) predictor.
- *Feedback and recovery:* The real outcome of the predicted branch is known a few cycles after the prediction. If the prediction was correct, the feedback mechanism should reinforce the predictor's confidence. If the prediction was erroneous, not only should the predictor state be changed, but also a recovery process has to take place. Note that the feedback can influence the index (past history) as well as the mechanism (actual prediction) itself.

About 20% of executed instructions are control flow instructions: conditional and unconditional branches, function calls, and returns. Table 4.1 lists some of the characteristics of these control flow instructions for the averages of five SPEC95 integer benchmarks and five desktop applications. Although the data are over 10 years old, they are still representative of integer programs, desktop applications, and commercial database queries, with the exception that the percentage of indirect branches in unconditional branches has slightly increased in applications programmed with object-oriented languages.

Conditional branch instructions in these types of programs occur, on the average, every six or seven instructions. In scientific programs, branches occur slightly less often and are more predictable, because many of the branches are of the end-of-loop variety.

To put these statistics in perspective, consider a four-way superscalar. The frequencies of branches shown in Table 4.1 mean that a branch will have to be predicted, on the average, every other cycle. Figure 4.2 shows the interbranch latencies between prediction requests in a (simulated) four-way out-of-order processor. As

Figure 4.2. Histogram of interbranch latencies. The data (from Jiménez et al. [JKL00]) are for the SPEC2000int suite simulated on a four-way out-of-order microprocessor.

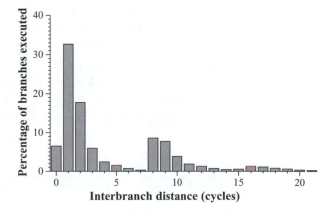

can be seen, 40% of the time there is no or only one cycle separating predictions. Since branch resolution might take of the order of 10 cycles, about five branches will be in flight in a predicted state. When one of these predictions turns up to be erroneous, up to 40 (four-way × 10 stages) instructions will have been issued on the "wrong path." If there was any doubt in the mind of the reader of the importance of accurate and fast branch prediction, these statistics should be convincing enough.

4.1.2 Static Prediction Schemes

Early branch prediction schemes were of the *static* type, that is, a branch was predicted to be taken or not taken once for all its executions. The strategy followed most often was to predict that the branch was to be taken. Although the data in Table 4.1 do not seem to support this choice, early studies included both conditional and unconditional transfers of control, and quite often the evidence was gathered on traces of scientific programs where taken branches were more prevalent. In the most comprehensive study of the early 1980s on this topic, it was reported that about two-thirds of branches were taken, but 30% of all branches were unconditional transfers, including function calls[1] and returns, which are of course taken. These figures are consistent with those of Table 4.1: for conditional branches, there is no clear indication of the dominance of one direction over the other. Variations on the branch-taken strategy included (i) taking advantage of the opcode and (ii) observing that most backward branches (e.g., ends of "for" loops) are taken, whereas forward branches are not taken as often, because a nonnegligible proportion of them are included to take care of unusual cases in the computation (e.g., termination of a linked list traversal). However, improvements in accuracy with these changes were barely noticeable. Slightly better results were obtained via profiling, but clearly this methodology can only be applied to production programs.

The other side of the coin is that implementing a branch-not-taken strategy, in the context of pipelined processors, has no associated cost (recall Section 2.1.4). Naturally, such a strategy by itself is not conceivable today, because the penalties of misprediction are so high.

4.1.3 Simple Dynamic Schemes

The need for accurate branch prediction schemes was recognized as soon as pipelined machines became the norm. The increase in branch misprediction penalties fueled the quest for more and more accurate *dynamic* predictors that are probed on each branch instance. Schemes evolved from simple finite-state machines encoding the state of a few previous instances of a branch to predict the next outcome, to more complex predictors that rely on the history not only of the branch but also of other, correlated parts of the program. Investigations for improved branch predictors have

---

[1] In the IBM ISA, the instruction "Branch and Link Register" used for function calls is sometimes a not-taken branch if used solely for setting the register.

been a staple of microprocessor implementation and microarchitecture research for the past 25 years.

In the static strategies, the prediction is done at decode time when it is recognized that the instruction is a branch. In dynamic schemes the "when to predict" can be advanced to the instruction fetch stage. If the "what to predict" is only whether the branch will be taken or not, the earlier prediction stage is not important. Of course, the situation will be totally different when we wish to also predict the branch target address. For the time being, though, we restrict ourselves to the branch direction.

The two problems we have to solve to predict the direction for a given branch are (i) where to find the prediction and (ii) how to encode the prediction. Let us start with the second of these problems.

As in many other aspects of speculation in computer systems, the most educated way we can guess the future is to look at recent past behavior. For a conditional branch, the simplest most recent past fact of interest is the direction it took the last time it executed. So if the branch was taken at its ith execution, chances are that it will be taken at its $(i + 1)$th one (and vice versa for "not taken"). Therefore we can associate with each branch a single bit that is set at resolution time and indicates whether the branch was taken or not. The next time this same branch is fetched, or decoded, the setting of the bit will yield the prediction.

This very simple scheme can be improved by providing a little hysteresis and requiring two wrong predictions in a row before changing the prediction. Of course, we have to extend the recent past to include a record of the last two resolutions of the branch. The main motivation for this modification lies in the prediction of branches at the end of loops. In the case where the prediction is simply the direction that the branch took last, the prediction for the branch terminating the loop, (i.e., being taken), will be correct until it is time to exit the loop, when the prediction will become wrong. There is nothing much that one can do about that exit misprediction if the number n of loop iterations is large, for the $n - 1$ previous instances of the branch will indicate that it was taken. When the loop is executed anew – for example, if it is an inner loop in nested loops or in a function called several times – the first prediction for the end of the loop will be "not taken," because that is what happened the last time that branch was executed. Of course, the prediction is incorrect. We can eliminate this wrong prediction by enforcing that two wrong predictions in a row are necessary for a change in the prediction.

The mechanism to record the directions of the last two branches is called a *2-bit saturating counter*. This is a four-state finite-state machine with the following states:

- *Strong taken:* The last two instances of the branch were taken (encoding 11).
- *Weak taken:* The last instance was not taken, but the previous one was taken (encoding 10).
- *Weak not-taken:* The last instance was taken, but the previous one was not taken (this is also the initial state, i.e., a default not-taken strategy) (encoding 01).

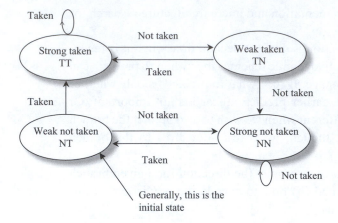

Figure 4.3. A two-bit saturating counter for branch prediction. The TT, TN, and so on, within the states indicate the outcomes of the last two executions of the branch.

- *Strong not-taken:* The last two instances of the branch were not taken (encoding 00).

The state diagram is shown in Figure 4.3. The encodings are arbitrary but have been chosen here so that the highest bit of the encoding yields the direction (1 for taken, 0 for not taken) and the counter uses a Gray code (only one bit changes per transition). The "saturating" part comes in when the counter is in a strong state and the prediction is correct. The state is therefore left unchanged.

Getting back to our motivating example, consider the following fragment of code where m and n are large:

EXAMPLE 1:

```
for (i = 0; i < m; i++)
        for (j = 0; j < n; j++)
        begin S₁; S₂; ...; Sₖ end;
```

It is easy to see that there will be two mispredictions per instance of the outer loop, that is, $2m$, in the single-bit scheme. In the 2-bit saturating counter scheme, the loop-ending branch will be in the strong taken state after two iterations of the inner loop. When the last instance of the loop is executed, there is a misprediction and the state becomes weak taken. At the first iteration of the new execution of the loop, the prediction of the loop-ending branch that is in the weak taken state will be correct, and the state will become strong taken again. The saturating counter scheme mispredicts $1 + m$ times if there are m instances of the outer loop, that is, half as much as the single-bit scheme. Of course, one can find examples where the single-bit scheme would perform better (see the exercises), but they do not correspond as well to common programming patterns.

We should note also that the transitions between states are open to more choices. As long as the strong states are saturating and are reached from all other states in at most two transitions – that is, strong taken (respectively, strong not-taken) reached when two consecutive executions of the branch yield a "taken"

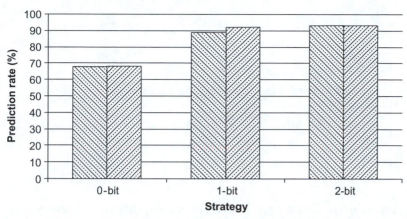

Figure 4.4. Accuracy (inflated) of simple dynamic branch prediction schemes. The bars at the left are averages for 26 traces (IBM System/370, DEC PDP-11, CDC 6400) as reported in Lee and Smith [LS84]. The bars at the right are for 32 traces (MIPS R2000, Sun SPARC, DEC VAX, Motorola 68000) as reported in Perleberg and Smith [PS93].

(respectively, "not taken") outcome – the intent of the method is respected. Experiments have shown that the state diagram of Figure 4.3 gives marginally the best performance, but there can be instances of applications where a different four-state finite-state machine with or without saturating states would yield higher accuracy.

What is important, though, is to see the improvements of the 2-bit saturating counter over static schemes and single-bit history. Figure 4.4 gives an idea of how much improvement can be expected. The prediction accuracies are inflated for two reasons: (i) unconditional branches are included (for 20% of unconditional branches and a 0.92 prediction rate, this inflates the result by about 2%), and (ii) prediction bits are associated with each possible branch after its first execution, a feature that is unrealistic, as we soon shall see. A "not taken" policy is followed on the first encounter of the branch.

The 0-bit strategy is one where the branch prediction is determined once and for all by the direction taken by the first execution of the branch. It yields the same prediction accuracy as a static strategy based on opcodes. There is a significant improvement when we use a 1-bit strategy. The improvement of the 2-bit saturating counter over the 1-bit is small but not negligible (between 1.3% and 4.3% in prediction accuracy, but more encouragingly we can say that it is a decrease in mispredictions by 15% to 35%).

Why stop at 2-bit counters? Why not have 3-bit saturating counters with eight states? The prediction could be the dominant direction: For example, if the last three executions of a branch were taken, not taken, taken (a state TNT), the prediction would be "taken." Experiments have shown that the additional number of states yielded minimal improvements that, most of the time, were not worth the extra storage cost.

Now we return to the first problem we mentioned, namely, how the predictions are stored and accessed. The data in Figure 4.4 were obtained by assuming that

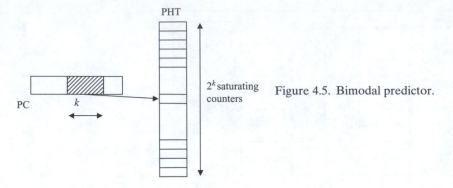

Figure 4.5. Bimodal predictor.

prediction bits are associated with each individual branch, that is, with every possible address. This is of course unrealizable practically; it would involve a table of the order of 2^{30} entries for a 32-bit addressing space, assuming that each instruction takes 4 bytes. Storing the prediction with the instruction is not an option either, for it would imply modifying code every 5 instructions on the average. Taking our cue from memory hierarchy studies, we could organize the prediction table, or BPB, as a cache. This would be quite wasteful of space, because the tags would be much more costly in storage than the "data," that is, the prediction bits. Nonetheless, it is interesting to see what the degradation in accuracy would be. If the "infinite" BPB were replaced by a four-way set associative cache of 1024 entries, the accuracy for the 2-bit saturating counter scheme in the second set of traces in Figure 4.4 would drop by 2% or 3%. If the cache had only 256 entries, then the drop would be 7% or 8%. So, clearly, the size of the BPB is important.

One way to circumvent the cost of tags is to suppress them. We can have then a BPB with a large number of entries, since each of them is only 2 bits. The table, called a *pattern history table* (PHT), is indexed by selected bits of the PC or some hashing function thereof (cf. Figure 4.5). From time to time, with a frequency that decreases with increasing PHT size, two different branches are assigned the same 2-bit counter when the PC bits that are used result in the same index for the two branch addresses. This *aliasing* degrades the performance slightly compared to the cache approach, but it is more than compensated by the fact that at equal storage cost, the PHTs can have an order of magnitude more entries.

Figure 4.6 shows the accuracy of a PHT-based predictor, often called a *bimodal* predictor, as a function of the size of the PHT. In this particular experiment, the average accuracy of conditional branches in the first 10 million instructions of 10 SPEC89 traces reached 93.5% for a bimodal predictor with a PHT of 2 KB (8 K counters).

Bimodal predictors were present in many microprocessors of the early 1990s. Sometimes, the predictor is embedded in the instruction cache. There can be one counter per instruction (Alpha 21264, i.e., 2 K counters), or two counters per cache line (one for every two instructions in the Sun UltraSPARC, also 2 K counters), or one counter per cache line (1 K counters in the AMD K5, which has the same ISA as the Intel IA-32 and therefore can have a variable number of instructions per cache line). In other cases, the predictor uses a separate PHT, as in the Sun SPARC 64

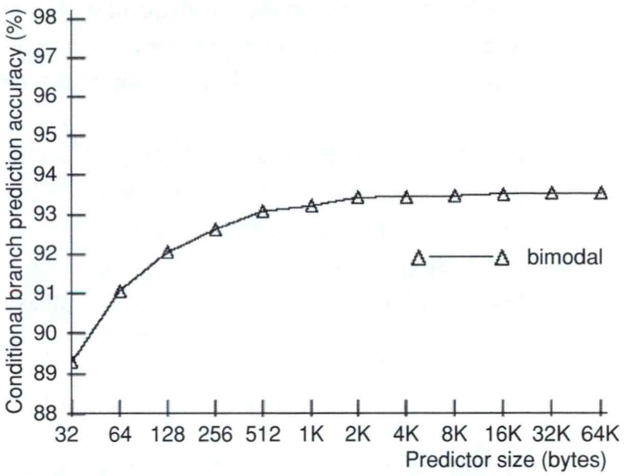

Figure 4.6. Accuracy of a bimodal predictor as a function of its PHT size (data from McFarling [M93]).

(1 K counters), the MIPS R10000 (512 counters), or the IBM PowerPC 620 (2 K counters). In the Pentium, the predictor is integrated with the target address prediction mechanism (BTB), and therefore the cache model is needed (cf. Section 4.1.7). The combined PHT–BTB has 512 entries.

Returning to our model of Section 4.1.1, we have discussed the timing of the predictions and the predictor structure. What remains to be described is the last box of the diagram, namely, feedback and recovery. For the bimodal predictor that we have considered, the only feedback needed is an update of the 2-bit counter corresponding to the branch that is executing. Accessing the predictor for the update is done in a similar fashion to the access for prediction. However, there is a choice for the timing of the prediction. It can be done:

- when the actual direction of the branch has been found in the execute stage, or
- when the branch commits, or
- speculatively when the prediction is performed.

In the case of a bimodal predictor, the last choice does not make much sense (it can only reinforce the decision), but, as we shall see in the next section, it needs to be considered for more complex predictors. Updating either in the execute stage or at commit time has the inconvenience that several predictions of the same branch might have occurred already, (e.g., in tight loops), because of the depth of the pipeline and the multiple-instruction issue. Though updating in the execute stage will occur earlier than in the commit stage, it has the disadvantage that, because of out-of-order execution, some branches that are on the wrong path of a previous branch might have their predictors modified. Overall, though, studies have shown that in the case of bimodal predictors the update timing has practically no effect on the prediction accuracy and therefore can be done at commit time.

We have seen in Chapter 3 how branch misprediction recovery was handled in the case of in-order processors, where all information is stored in a scoreboardlike fashion, and in the case of out-of-order processors, using a reorder buffer as the renaming register file. In Section 4.4 of this chapter, we shall address the recovery problem for other renaming schemes.

To close this section on the first dynamic predictor, we examine the specific actions related to branch prediction, branch execution, PHT updating, and potential misprediction recovery that are taken at various stages of the pipeline.

BIMODAL BRANCH PREDICTOR. (PC_{subset} are the bits of the PC used in indexing the PHT; a "taken" prediction will have the value "true"; a "not taken" the value "false"; $PC+$ points to the instruction after the branch.)

Fetch Stage. Access PHT; $pred \leftarrow higherbit[PHT[PC_{subset}]]$

Decode Stage. compute $taken\_branch\_address$;

```
    case:
    ...
    Conditional branch: if pred then PC ← taken_branch_address;
    ...
```

Rename Stage. When the branch instruction is entered in the ROB, $taken\_branch\_address$ will be part of the ROB entry.[2]

Execute Stage. The branch condition $brcd$ is evaluated and set to "true" if the branch was to be taken, and to "false" otherwise.

Commit Stage.

```
if (pred = brcd) then PHT[PC_subset] ← (PHT[PC_subset].pred) /*state transition*/
        else begin PHT[PC_subset] ←(PHT[PC_subset].not pred); /*update*/
                flush ROB;
                    if pred then PC ← PC+ else PC ←taken_branch_address;
                end;
```

4.1.4 Correlated Branch Prediction

The bimodal dynamic strategy is a tremendous improvement over any static scheme, but still is not sufficiently powerful for modern microprocessors. One of the weaknesses of the 2-bit method is that it only takes into account a small amount of the past history of the branch that is predicted. In contrast with this *local* approach, a number of *global* schemes use the history of the outcomes of other branches whose executions directly precede that of the branch being predicted. A well-known example that motivates the global schemes is the segment of code from the SPEC program *eqntott* shown in Example 2.

EXAMPLE 2:

```
if (aa==2)        /*b₁ */
        aa=0;
if (bb==2)        /*b₂ */
        bb=0;
if (aa!=bb){      /*b₃ */
    .....
}
```

---

[2] Recall that every instruction "carries" its PC in order to implement precise exceptions.

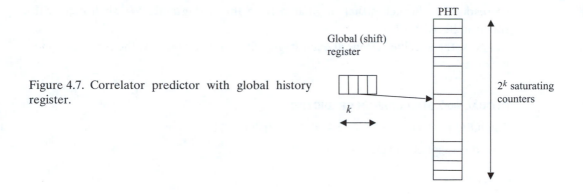

Figure 4.7. Correlator predictor with global history register.

As the reader can easily verify, if both branches b_1 and b_2 are taken, branch b_3 will necessarily be not taken. No local predictor scheme for b_3 can deduce this information. In order to *correlate* the outcomes of b_1 and b_2 with that of b_3 we need to record and use the fact that b_1 and b_2 were taken. The recording can be done by using a *global (shift) register*, also called a *history register*, in which a 1 is inserted (at the right) whenever a branch is taken, and a 0 is inserted when a branch is not taken. Bits that are shifted out at the left are lost. Now, instead of selected bits of the PC to index the PHT, we use the global register (Figure 4.7). This type of predictor is often called *two-level*, the first level being the global register (and its extensions, as we shall see below) and the second level being the table of counters.

Now we need to address the update problem. In the case of the bimodal predictor, only the data structures storing the predictions needed updating, but in the case of two-level predictors, both the index (i.e., the global register) and the table of counters require updates. For the same reasons as those set forth for the bimodal predictor, the PHT(s) will be updated nonspeculatively. However, such is not the case for the global register.

We have two options for the update of the global register: (i) a nonspeculative update, whereby a bit in the global register will be inserted at (branch) instruction commit, and (ii) a speculative update, whereby a bit is inserted when the branch is predicted at decode time. The mechanism to implement the first strategy is therefore extremely simple. However, it has two major defects. Consider a branch instruction b that is predicted at time t and committed at time $t + \Delta t$. In Example 2, this could be branch b_1. Any branch b' that needs to be predicted during the interval Δt, say in our example b_2 or b_3, will not benefit of the outcome of b even if the latter is very predictable. Moreover, the global register for two consecutive predictions for any branch, say branch b, might include different ancestors of branch b, even if the same path leading to b was repeated, because of effects such as mispredictions or cache misses that alter the timing of branches before b. For these two reasons, correlations like the one presented in Example 2 might be overlooked. The alternative is to speculatively update the global register when the prediction is performed. A bit is inserted according to the prediction. Of course, now we need a repair mechanism when there is a misprediction, because all bits following the mispredicted one correspond to branches that originated from the wrong path. We shall deal with repair in Section 4.1.6.

Now the specific actions at each stage, with no detail on how the repair is done, become:

GLOBAL REGISTER BRANCH PREDICTOR

Fetch Stage. `Access PHT;` $pred \leftarrow higherbit[PHT[GR]]$

Decode stage: `compute` $taken\_branch\_address;$
`case:`
```
        ...
```
`Conditional branch: begin` $GR_{old} \leftarrow GR;$ `GR` $\leftarrow$ `concatenate (`$leftshift(GR,1)$`, pred);`
                        `if` $pred$ `then PC` $\leftarrow taken\_branch\_address;$
                `end;`
```
        ...
```

Rename Stage. `When the branch instruction is entered in the ROB, the` $taken\_branch\_$ $address$ `will be part of the ROB entry.`

Execute Stage. `The branch condition` $brcd$ `is evaluated and set to "true" if the branch was to be taken, and to "false" otherwise.`

Commit Stage.
```
        if (pred = brcd) then PHT[GRold] ← (PHT[GRold],pred)
        else begin PHT[GRold] ← (PHT[GRold],not pred);
                flush ROB; GR ← concatenate(repairedGR, not pred);
                if pred then PC ← PC+ else PC ←taken_branch_address;
        end;
```

Experiments have shown that global predictors do not perform as well as local predictors when the number of counters is small, or equivalently the global register is short. They perform better and their accuracies continue to increase when the number of entries is large, for now the global register pattern can identify more accurately which branch is predicted.

The global scheme just presented has lost an important component that was present in the bimodal predictor, namely, the location within the program of the branch being predicted. Therefore, in order to reduce aliasing we might want to reintroduce the PC, in some form, in the indexing process. One of the simplest ways to do so is to hash (e.g., XOR) bits of the PC and of the global register to form the indexing function for the PHT (cf. Figure 4.8). This particular scheme is called *gshare*. Its predictors follow the performance pattern described in the previous paragraph for the global register scheme. However, their accuracy is consistently better than that of global predictors. Some experiments have shown that a *gshare* predictor with a 14-bit global register and a PHT with 2^{14} counters yielded conditional branch accuracy almost perfect for floating-point benchmarks and accuracies from 0.83 to 0.96 for the SPEC 95 integer benchmarks (the program *go* was an outlier with a

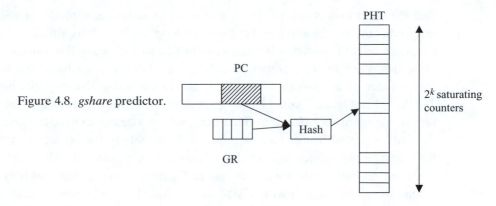

Figure 4.8. *gshare* predictor.

dismal accuracy of 0.65). *gshare* predictors are used in the AMD K6 Altheon, the Sun UltraSPARC III, and the IBM Power4 among others.

The specific actions for *gshare* are similar to those of the correlated predictor, the only difference being in the indexing of the PHT.

gshare BRANCH PREDICTOR

Fetch Stage. Access PHT; $pred \leftarrow higherbit[PHT[hash(GR,PC_{subset})]]$

Decode Stage.

    Compute taken_branch_address;

    case:

    ...

    Conditional branch:

    begin GR_old←GR; GR ← concatenate(leftshift(GR,1), pred);

                    if pred then PC ←taken_branch_address;

            end;

    ...

Rename Stage. When the branch instruction is entered in the ROB, *taken_branch_address* will be part of the ROB entry.

Execute Stage. The branch condition *brcd* is evaluated and set to "true" if the branch was to be taken, and to "false" otherwise.

Commit Stage.

    if (pred = brcd) then

                PHT[hash(GR_old,PC_subset)] ← (PHT[hash(GR_old,PC_subset)],pred]

            else begin PHT[hash(GR_old,PC_subset)] ←

    (PHT[hash(GR_old,PC_subset)], not pred];

            flush ROB; GR ← concatenate(repairedGR, not pred);

                if pred then PC ← PC+ else PC ← taken_branch_address;

                end;

4.1.5 Two-level Branch Predictors

Although *gshare* reintroduces some locality in the indexing process, it is not sufficient for deducing patterns of individual branches. Consider Example 1, and assume that the inner loop is executed only five times ($n = 4$). The bimodal predictor will mispredict the branch at the end of the inner loop one out of five times, and a global predictor might mispredict it from zero to five times, depending on the number of branches and their outcomes inside the loop. On the other hand, if a local history register were associated with the branch at the end of the loop, the pattern of "4 taken, 1 not taken" would be recognized after a training period, and the prediction would be correct after that. Therefore, we can attempt to have the first level of the two-level predictor be more attuned to the locality of the branches and replace the single global register with a table of local history registers (BHT).

If we go back to the global scheme of Figure 4.7, we see that not only can we extend the global register with a BHT as mentioned in the previous paragraph, but we could also have several PHTs, each of them selected by bits of the PC, thus giving a new dimension in which to reintroduce part of the branch address information. At the extreme, we could have a history register per branch address, thus recording the history of each possible branch, and a PHT also for each possible branch address. In summary, the choices could be:

- One global history register and one PHT (cf. Figure 4.7), or Global–global.
- One global history register and several PHTs (cf. Figure 4.9(a)), or Global–set (at the extreme, the "set" is one per branch address). Bits from the PC select the PHTs.
- One BHT (at the extreme, one entry per branch address) of registers (selected by bits of the PC) and one PHT (cf. Figure 4.9(b)), or Set–global.
- One BHT and a set of PHTs (cf. Figure 4.9(c)), or Set–set.

Note that having several PHTs can be quite expensive in storage (see the exercises). In a first approximation, the table of history registers uses fewer bits than one PHT as soon as the number of counters in the PHT is sufficiently large. For example, 32 registers of 8 bits require 32 bytes of storage, and the associated PHT needs 2^8 counters, or 512 bits, that is, twice as much. Introducing a second PHT with the same length for the history registers would make the PHT storage 4 times as much as what is used for the history registers. Therefore, if the Set–set or Global–set scheme is chosen, the number of PHTs will be small.

Experiments have shown that either a Set–global or Set–set configuration performs slightly better than *gshare* for the same PHT size and with a limited number of history registers. The latest Intel microprocessors, from the Pentium III on, use two-level predictors of this type.

The introduction of local history registers allows the detection of patterns but might hide the correlation that was discovered with the global scheme. However, correlations are not that frequent, and in order to achieve the same accuracy, the global register in the Global–global scheme must be significantly longer than the local history registers in the Set–global configuration. For example, a Set–global scheme with 1024 local history registers of 12 bits each and hence a PHT of 2^{12} counters take less storage than a Global–global scheme with a global register of 14 bits and an associated PHT of 2^{14} counters. However, the accuracy of the Global–global

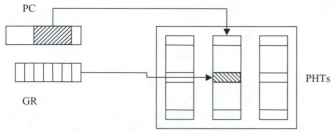

(a) 1 Global register, several PHTs (global–set). Selected bits of the PC point to a PHT; the GR points to a row of the PHTs.

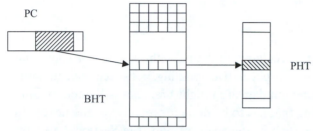

(b) Table of local history registers (BHT) and one PHT (set–global). Selected bits of the PC point to a local history register, which in turn points to a saturating counter in the PHT.

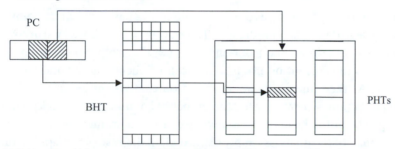

(c) Table of local history registers (BHT) and several PHTs (set–set). Selected bits of the PC point to a local history register, which in turn points to a row in the PHTs. Other bits of the PC select the PHT.

Figure 4.9. Alternatives in two-level predictors.

scheme would be lower on most programs. Arguably, what is needed is a scheme that can predict both the correlations and the patterns. These *hybrid predictors* will be introduced in Section 4.1.8.

The functions to be performed in each stage of the pipeline are similar to those of the global register scheme, which itself is a two-level predictor. Changes occur in the functions to access the BHT if it is present instead of a single global register, and in the choice of the PHT. The repair mechanism is more complex, as we see next.

4.1.6 Repair Mechanisms

Because the repair mechanism introduces some complexity, it is important to know whether there is a benefit to having speculative updating and a repair mechanism.

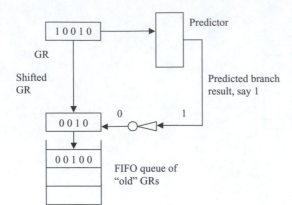

Figure 4.10. Repair mechanism for global register (or *gshare*) predictor. At prediction time, the GR is shifted left. If the prediction is "taken" (bit 1), a 0 is inserted at the right of the GR before inserting it into the FIFO queue. At repair time, the right new GR will be at the head of the queue.

The answer is an emphatic yes: speculative updating without repair is sometimes better and sometimes worse than nonspeculative updating, but speculative updating with repair is always a win. If the number of in-flight branches is limited, because for example of the checkpointing that has to be done for repair (see the next paragraph) and for other structures such as the register map (see Section 4.4 of this chapter), the win is not as great, but still sufficiently important to warrant the repair mechanism.

Repair in the global predictor and *gshare* schemes is based on checkpointing the global history register at each prediction. This is what we indicated earlier with the notation $GR_{old} \leftarrow GR$. Since the front-end does not disturb program order, the global register up to the current bit not included can be checkpointed and entered in a FIFO queue. At the same time, the predicted outcome is shifted in the global register. If the prediction is correct, when the branch is committed its checkpointed global register will be at the head of the queue, because commitment is also in program order. The head of the queue is simply discarded. In the case of a misprediction with repair at commit time, the head of the queue appended with the bit complement of the prediction becomes the new global register, and all other entries are discarded. A simple optimization, shown in Figure 4.10, inserts the corrected GR in the FIFO queue. If repair is to be done at execute time, then as soon as a misprediction has been detected, the global register can be restored similarly, but only the entries in the queue between the one corresponding to the misprediction and the tail are removed. To implement this optimization, each branch must carry a tag indicating the index of its entry in the FIFO queue. Such a scheme is used in the global predictor of the Alpha 21264. It requires little hardware: a FIFO queue where each entry is a pair (tag, history register) and where the number of entries is the maximum number of branches that can be in flight in the back-end at any given time (or some smaller number, if a full queue is a structural hazard). Note that the saved global register, and the PC for *gshare*, are also needed for indexing the PHT for nonspeculative update purposes. Of course, other optimizations are possible (see the exercises).

When a local scheme is used, speculative update with repair is still beneficial, but somewhat less so than in global schemes, because many of the entries in the BHT are not dependent on the mispredicted branch. However, a speculative update without repair does not give good results. On the other hand, a commit-time nonspeculative update yields acceptable performance without the repair complexities. If one were to implement a repair mechanism, checkpointing of the whole BHT would not be acceptable because of the time and space involved as soon as the BHT has more than a few entries. An alternative would be to checkpoint only the predicted local history registers and save them in a FIFO queue as in the global scheme. Whereas checkpointing is fast and easy, repair is more difficult, because not only the mispredicted local register must be repaired, but also all subsequent local registers that were inserted in the queue after it.

A better way, which we only sketch here, is to use a FIFO queue as in the global scheme, with each entry now consisting of the branch address and the speculatively updated local register. The queue will be used during prediction as well as for the repair. When a prediction is to be made, the BHT is indexed as usual and the FIFO queue is searched associatively for the branch address at the same time. If the branch address is found in the queue, the local register of the entry is used to index the access to the PHT in lieu of a local register in the BHT. For each prediction, a new entry is inserted in the queue, independently of whether it comes from the queue already or from the BHT. If the branch at the head of the queue was correctly predicted, and this is known at commit time, the entry in the queue replaces the local history register in the BHT. Upon a misprediction, entries in the queue are discarded as in the global scheme. Because several entries in the queue might correspond to the same branch address, the mispredicted branch must still be uniquely identified (see the exercises).

Before continuing with even more sophisticated predictors, we turn our attention to branch target address prediction.

4.1.7 Branch Target Address Prediction

When a branch is taken, predicting its direction is only part of the task. The other part is to predict the branch target address. Without this latter prediction, the fetching of new instructions has to wait till address computation. In the simple pipelines of Chapter 2, this was not too much of a burden. Address computation was done speculatively during the decode stage, and a single cycle was lost if the branch was correctly predicted. Of course, the full penalty was incurred in the case of a misprediction. With a superscalar the speculative address computations, one per instruction in an m-way machine, cannot all be performed early without adding a definite burden to the front-end, such as m extra adders in the simplest case of a RISC ISA. In the case of an ISA like the IA-32 of the Intel P6 microarchitecture, detecting the beginning of instructions and performing address computations can take several stages, as shown in Chapter 3. Therefore, if we want to avoid target address computation penalties, we need a mechanism to predict target branch addresses. To facilitate the discussion, we consider first the case of a processor that fetches a single instruction at a time. We then extend the concept to the case of superscalars.

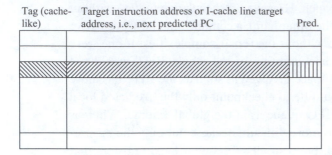

Tag (cache-like)   Target instruction address or I-cache line target address, i.e., next predicted PC   Pred.

Figure 4.11. Organization of an integrated branch target buffer (BTB).

Recall that we can make a prediction on the direction that a branch will take at instruction fetch time, because the indexing in the predictor, say the PHT, depends only on the PC and maybe history registers that are speculatively updated. If the instruction is not a branch, no harm is done: the prediction is simply discarded. Unfortunately, we cannot do the same to predict a target address.

If we were to associate a target address with each 2-bit counter in the PHT, a prediction of branch taken would update the PC to the associated target address even if the instruction were not a branch. Fetching new instructions starting at this *bogus* address is certainly to be avoided. An alternative is to have a cachelike structure, or BTB, that records the addresses of the branches and the target addresses associated with them. At instruction fetch, if there is a hit in the BTB and the branch is predicted to be taken, then the PC is set to the target address stored in the BTB, and an instruction fetch with this new PC can be instantiated.

Figure 4.11 shows an *integrated* BTB–PHT. As can be seen, the amount of storage occupied by the BTB is much larger than that for the PHT. Moreover, the number of entries in the BTB is somewhat limited in that it functions as a cache and needs to be accessed in a single cycle. Two possible other organizations are shown in Figure 4.12 and Figure 4.13.

In the case of a decoupled BTB–PHT (cf. Figure 4.12), accesses to the BTB and the PHT are performed in parallel. If the PHT indicates that the branch is predicted to be taken and there is a BTB hit, then the PC is set to the next address field in the BTB and the next instruction is fetched from this new address. If the PHT indicates that the branch will not be taken or if there is a BTB miss, then the branch instruction proceeds with the PHT prediction as if there were no BTB. In order

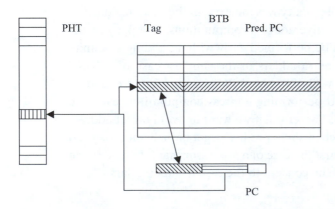

PHT   BTB   Tag   Pred. PC

PC

Figure 4.12. Organization of a decoupled BTB–PHT.

BTB + BHT

Tag   Target address, i.e., next (predicted) PC   Local hist.   PHTs

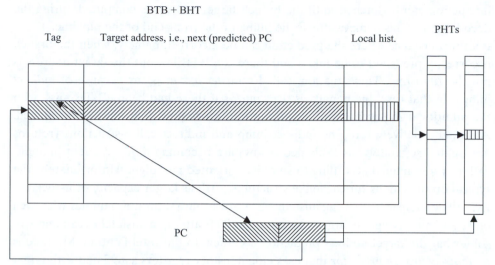

PC

Figure 4.13. Integrating a BTB with a Set–set two-level predictor.

to make the BTB more space-efficient, only taken branches are entered in it, and this filling of the BTB occurs after it has been determined in the back-end that the branch was taken. The BTB is managed as a cache with the usual replacement algorithm if it is set-associative. In some architectures, like the IBM PowerPC 620, the access to the (256-entry, two-way set-associative) BTB is performed in the first cycle, and access to the PHT (2 K counters) in the second. If there is a BTB hit and the PHT indicates a not-taken prediction, the fetching resumes with the old value of the PC. In this case, there is a penalty of one cycle, but it is not as important as the penalty due to a misprediction.

So far, we have considered only a PHT predictor for the branch direction. Of course, we could have a two-level predictor in the decoupled case. Another alternative is to integrate the BTB with the BHT. The combined BTB–BHT (Figure 4.13) has the same structure as the original BTB, but now the local history register associated with the branch replaces the field in the entry devoted to the 2-bit counter. The second level of the predictor, (i.e., one or several PHTs), is the same as in Set–global or Set–set predictors. Note that we need to enter both taken and not taken branches in the BTB, because we need their histories independently of their outcome. A scheme of that sort is implemented in the P6 microarchitecture with 4-bit-wide local registers and 512 entries in the BTB (the number of distinct PHTs is never specified in the Intel literature). On a BTB miss, a static prediction "backward taken, forward not taken" is performed.

When we consider predictions of both the branch direction and the target address, we see two instances where we can have mispredictions. The first one, the more costly, is when the direction of the branch is mispredicted. In that case, all instructions fetched after the branch must be nullified, and there can be a large number of them, because recovery happens only when the mispredicted branch is at the head of the reorder buffer. The second is when a branch is correctly predicted to be taken but there is a BTB miss. In that case the penalty is that no new instruction can be fetched until the branch target address is computed during the decode stage. This penalty affects the filling of the front-end of the pipeline. There is a third instance where the prediction can be incorrect, namely, when the branch is correctly predicted to be taken and there is a BTB hit, but the target address is not the right one. This situation, called a *misfetch,* can occur because of *indirect* jumps. In that case, the penalty is the same as if there had been a BTB miss, with the additional requirement of squashing the instructions that have been fetched. Although relatively rare, the indirect jump and indirect call instructions (returns are treated separately, as explained below) are becoming more frequent in applications programmed according to an object-oriented paradigm. Unfortunately, the typical optimizations for cachelike structures, such as larger capacity or associativity, will not help in decreasing misfetches. Associating a saturating counter with each entry and modifying the target address in the BTB after two misfetches can improve somewhat the target address prediction accuracy. In the Intel Pentium M, there is an *indirect branch predictor* that uses global history registers associated with target addresses and that helps in decreasing the number of misfetches.

We examine in the following the main changes with respect to a bimodal predictor in the branch prediction mechanism in the case of an integrated BTB with a bimodal predictor (see the exercises for the other BTB organizations).

INTEGRATED BTB WITH BIMODAL BRANCH PREDICTOR. (In addition to its own PC, the branch will carry the index of its BTB hit.)

Fetch Stage. Access BTB:
```
    if BTBhit then /*returns the index to the entry with the hit*/
            begin pred ←higherbit[BTB[Pred[index]]];
                if pred then
                        begin predPC← BTB[Target[index]];
                              PC ← predPC
                        end
            end
    else pred ←false;    /*BTB miss*/
```

Decode Stage.
```
compute taken_branch_address;
    case:
    ...
    Conditional branch: if pred then
                    if predPC ≠ taken_branch_address/*misfetch*/
                        then begin
                            squash instructions in fetch stage;
                            BTB[Target[index]] ←taken_branch_address;
                            PC ← taken_branch_address
                        end;
    ...
```

Execute Stage. The branch condition *brcd* is evaluated and set to
"true" if the branch was to be taken, and to "false" otherwise.
Commit Stage.
```
if (pred = brcd) then
                   if pred then BTB[Pred[index]] ← (BTB[Pred[index]], pred);
                   else begin
                   if brcd then createBTBentry(PCbranch,
                                        taken_branch_address,WT);
                          /* This is a cachelike replacement*/
                          flush ROB;
                          if pred then PC ← PC+
                          else PC←taken_branch_address;
                   end;
```

Table 4.2, where m_{pred} is the penalty for a mispredict and m_{fetch} the one for
a misfetch, summarizes the possible situations. We assume that the BTB and the
branch direction predictor (PHT or two-level) are accessed in the same cycle and
that the direction predictor's outcome has the highest priority.

The metric for m_{fetch} and for m_{pred} can be a number of cycles or, in the case
of a superscalar, the number of instruction issue slots that have been lost. With
$Miss_f$ and $Miss_p$ the percentages of branches that are misfetched and mispredicted,
respectively (some branches can be both, as shown in two rows of Table 4.2), the
contribution to the CPI due to branch execution, or the branch execution penalty
bep expressed as a number of cycles, can be written in a first approximation (see the
exercises) as

$$bep = Miss_f \times m_{fetch} + Miss_p \times m_{pred}$$

Which of the decoupled and the integrated BTB predictor yields the smaller
bep? For the same number of entries in the BTB and roughly the same amount of
storage in both designs for the BHT and PHTs in one case, and for a Global–set
or Global–global predictor in the other, there is no clear winner. The integrated

Table 4.2. Penalties for BTB and predictor (mis)predictions

BTB	Dir. Pred.	Target Pred.	Outcome	Penalty
Hit	Taken	Correct	Taken	0
Hit	Taken	Wrong	Taken	m_{fetch}
Hit	Taken	Correct	Not taken	m_{pred}
Hit	Taken	Wrong	Not taken	$m_{fetch} + m_{pred}$
Hit	Not taken	Don't care	Taken	m_{pred}
Hit	Not taken	Don't care	Not taken	0
Miss	Taken	None	Taken	m_{fetch}
Miss	Taken	None	Not taken	$m_{fetch} + m_{pred}$
Miss	Not taken	None	Taken	m_{pred}
Miss	Not taken	None	Not taken	0

BTB will store fewer predicted target addresses, because both taken and not taken branches are entered. In a first approximation, we can say that its $Miss_f$ is double that of the decoupled design. On the other hand, its prediction accuracy is generally slightly better, and this is more than enough to compensate, for m_{pred} is at least three times more than m_{fetch} in current microprocessors. However, it is cheaper in storage to improve the accuracy of the decoupled scheme by extending the length of the global register than to increase the capacity of the BTB in the integrated case. On the other hand, the integrated scheme does not require communication between two different hardware structures, and this could be the determining factor in case the prediction is on the critical path.

Until now, we have avoided the slight complexity brought upon by the fact that several instructions can be fetched together. However, the only BTB hit of importance is for the first one in program order whose address is equal to or greater than the *PC*. We can therefore design the BTB with tag comparators that implement this operation. An alternative is to use partial tags with the possibility of having bogus hits. Since the latter will be extremely infrequent and checked at address verification time in the decoder, as is done for all branch-taken predictions, the additional penalties are minimal.

We close this subsection with three optimizations. In each case, we cannot mask completely the misfetch or mispredict penalties, but we can save a few cycles.

Call–Return Mechanisms

A procedure call is an unconditional branch to a target address that will remain the same during program execution. So it is a prime candidate for an entry in the BTB. If the call is indirect, there is no easy remedy for a misfetch. A return from a procedure is implemented either as an instruction of its own or as an indirect jump to the contents of a specific register that has been loaded by the procedure call. In contrast with calls that select the same target address, returns transfer control to many different addresses, depending on the location of the call. A typical example is the use of a print routine: its call address remains the same during execution of a program, but because it is called from various parts of the program, the returns will be to different locations. Entering the return address in the BTB will lead to frequent misfetches. These misfetches can be almost all avoided in one of two ways. When an instruction call is recognized, the corresponding return address is pushed on the top of a *return address stack.* In the first approach, when a return is recognized, the stack is popped and the BTB miss corresponding to the taken prediction associated with the return will be squashed. Instead, new instructions will be fetched from the PC set to the popped address. Note that this scheme requires waiting until a return is recognized (decode stage), and therefore only a portion of the misfetch penalty is recovered. If instead the address of the return instruction and its target address are entered on the stack, then this partial penalty can be avoided if the branch prediction mechanism checks the BTB and the return stack in parallel. The downside of this second approach is that one has to wait for the first return instruction to be decoded and for its target address to be computed. If each time the procedure is called it is from a different location, there will be no gain.

Misfetches can still occur if the stack overflows. Generally, the stack is implemented as a circular queue, so that in case of overflow the most recent entries can overwrite the oldest ones. Note also that the stack must be repaired in case of call–returns on a misspeculated path. Saving the pointer to the top of the stack register at branch prediction time and restoring it when the mispredicted branch reaches the head of the reorder buffer is sufficient for this purpose. Most microprocessors today use a return stack with a few entries: from 1 in the MIPS R10000 to 12 in the Alpha 21164 and 16 in the Intel Pentium III and successors.

Resume Buffers

The roots of the second optimization lie in the dual-path implementation found in older machines such as the IBM System 360/91. The main idea is that when a branch is decoded, both the fall-through instructions and those following the target address are fetched, decoded, and enqueued in separate buffers. At branch resolution time, one of the buffers becomes the execution path and the other is discarded. The same idea can be applied in a restricted fashion for processors that cannot predict a target address and modify the PC on a BTB hit in a single cycle (the Intel P6 microarchitecture and the MIPS R10000 are two such examples). On a BTB hit and "taken" prediction, the fall-through instructions in the same cache line as the branch and in the following cache line are kept in a *resume buffer*. If the prediction was incorrect, the correct path is in this resume buffer. One or two cycles may be saved that way at a very low implementation cost.

Loop Detector and Count Predictor

When a given branch shows a repeated pattern of many taken followed by a single not taken, one can assume that an end-of-loop branch has been encountered. Since the number of iterations can be much larger than the length of a history register, a special *loop predictor* can be useful. It is easy to set up and requires a counter for each recognized loop that contains the predicted recorded count. Such an additional predictor can be found in the Intel Pentium M.

4.1.8 More Sophisticated and Hybrid Predictors

There are at least two sources of potential inaccuracy in the predictors we have seen so far. The first one, common to all structures that cannot contain information for all possible cases, is due to the limited capacity of the predictors. Because storing and updating information for all possible dynamic executions of all branches is not possible, either the information may not be present or there is a possibility of aliasing. The second one, mentioned previously, is that there is a tension between prediction for branch correlation, (i.e., global information), and particular patterns for each branch (i.e., local information).

The first source of inaccuracy can be viewed as similar to what happens in cache accesses. The equivalents for branch predictions to the three C's types of misses (cold, capacity, and conflict) are:

- The first prediction for a branch (cold miss) is the default prediction, (i.e., "not taken"), in the case of an integrated BTB–PHT. In the case of a decoupled BTB–PHT, either the initialized prediction in the PHT or the prediction for an aliased branch will be the result.
- The limited size of the PHT implies that not all distinct branches can have their prediction stored at the same time (capacity miss).
- Predictions for two branches can map to the same PHT entry (conflict miss).

In all cases except that of an integrated BTB–PHT, what is needed are means to reduce the effects of aliasing. This is not necessarily an argument in favor of the integrated BTB–PHT, for the latter is likely to have the largest number of capacity misses. It has been observed that in global prediction schemes (those of main interest here), branch prediction aliasing due to lack of associativity occurs more often than aliasing brought about by limited capacity. In decoupled BTB–PHTs, associativity cannot be provided in a straightforward manner, because PHTs do not carry tags. An alternative is to use several PHTs, with some discriminatory factor in choosing which one to use for a particular branch.

Aliasing is not always detrimental. When two branches are biased the same way, either most often taken or most often not taken, there is no harm if they share the same PHT entry. We have a case of *neutral aliasing*. On the other hand, if their biases are opposite to each other, or if one is easily predictable while the other fluctuates between taken and not taken, we have *destructive aliasing*.

Because most branches are often heavily biased, it is possible to associate this information with the branch address, for example in the BTB. One possibility is to record a potential branch outcome as a *bias bit* in the BTB entry when the branch is first entered or when entered upon a replacement. This bias bit can be determined by the compiler or can be based on whether the branch is forward or backward. The PHT, which in this scheme should be addressed differently than the BTB, is again a table of 2-bit saturating counters, but instead of predicting whether the branch should be taken or not, it predicts whether the branch direction should *agree* with the bias bit. Only the PHT entry is updated when the branch outcome is known, that is, the counter is incremented if agreement held, and decremented otherwise.

In other words, the following action for branch direction prediction should be taken in the fetch stage:

AGREE PREDICTOR. (Only a sketch for the branch direction prediction is given; it requires a decoupled BTB–PHT.)

Fetch Stage. Access BTB:

```
    If BTBhit then /*returns index*/
        begin bias ← BTB[Biasarray [index]];
             Access PHT; agreebit ←higherbit[PHT[PCsubset]]
             pred ← XNOR(bias,agreebit);
        end
    else pred ← false;
...
```

Commit Stage.

```
if index is valid    /* we had a BTB hit*/
                then if brcd = bias then PHT[PCsubset] ← (PHT[PCsubset],bias)
        /*reinforce*/
                                        else PHT[PCsubset] ← (PHT[PCsubset],not bias)
```

Now, two branches that alias in the PHT and are both strongly biased, but possibly in different directions, will not destroy each other. Of course, the scheme does not help if one branch is strongly biased and the other one is not.

A related design is to associate not only a bias bit with each BTB entry, but also a saturating counter that indicates the confidence that can be given to the bias bit. If the counter is saturated, then the prediction is that of the bias bit, and the PHT is neither consulted nor updated. Otherwise, the PHT is consulted and updated upon knowledge of the branch outcome, as in the agree scheme. The advantage of this scheme is that biased branches will be predicted with their entries' saturating counters and will not access the PHT. The latter is used only for less predictable branches. Thus, the amount of aliasing is reduced by the *filter* imposed on very predictable branches, because they do not influence the PHT contents.

We can mitigate the effects of destructive aliasing by replicating the PHT. One possible design is to have two PHTs, accessed similarly, for example in a *gshare* fashion, where one of the PHTs is intended for branches biased towards "taken" and the other for branches biased towards "not taken." A third PHT, a *choice* PHT accessed through the branch address only, will decide which of the two *direction* PHTs' predictions should be chosen for that particular branch. In this *bi-mode* predictor, updating is done only for the PHT that was chosen to give the direction. The choice PHT is also updated unless its prediction was not the branch outcome but the direction PHT was correct. In other words, if for example the choice PHT said to consult the "taken" PHT and the latter correctly predicted "not taken," the choice PHT is left unchanged. In this design, aliasing of branches that are mostly taken (or mostly not taken) is not destructive. Of course, destructive aliasing still occurs in the case of one branch outcome agreeing with the choice while the other does not.

A second possible design is the *skewed* predictor, whereby three different hashing functions index three PHTs. A majority vote indicates the predicted direction. By use of the skewing functions, the probability of aliasing in more than one of the PHTs is made quite small. In some sense, the skewing provides associativity (the

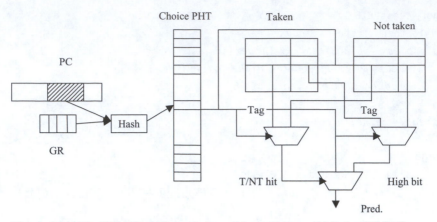

Figure 4.14. The YAGS predictor (adapted from Eden and Mudge [EM98]).

same reasoning has been applied as a proposal to decrease conflict misses in caches; see Chapter 6). If the prediction is wrong, the three PHTs are updated; if it is correct only those that are correct are updated. The rationale for the partial updating is that the PHT that had the incorrect prediction must be holding the correct prediction for another branch.

The bias bits and confidence counters added to a BTB entry represent a small additional investment for a design that is already expensive in storage. On the other hand, having three PHTs instead of one in the replicated PHT designs can be overly taxing. What might be best in designs that either have no BTB or use a decoupled BTB–PHT organization is to take advantage of the bias that exists from most branches as in the bi-mode predictor and to limit the aliasing of those less predictable branches as in the skewed case. At the same time, we do not want to expand storage unduly. A proposal along these lines is the YAGS ("yet another global scheme"), shown in Figure 4.14.

As in the bi-mode predictor, YAGS has a choice PHT that is indexed by the branch address and directs the prediction to one of two predictors. However, because the choice predictor already indicates a bias towards "taken" or "not taken" and therefore takes care of neutral aliasing, what would be useful is to discover instances where the bias is not followed consistently. So we can replace the bi-mode direction PHTs by structures that indicate exceptions to the direction predicted by the choice PHT. More precisely, when the choice PHT indicates "taken" and the outcome is "not taken," the branch address is entered, via a *gshare*-like indexing, in a "not taken" cache (NT cache in the figure). The T cache is filled in the same way for a "not taken" choice and a "taken" outcome. An entry in these caches consists of a (partial) tag and a 2-bit saturating counter. Now, when a prediction is to be made, the choice PHT and the caches are accessed concurrently. If the choice PHT indicates "taken" (respectively, "not taken") and there is a miss in the NT cache (respectively, T cache), the prediction is "taken" (respectively "not taken"). If there is a hit, the prediction is what is given by the 2-bit counter in the NT cache (respectively, T cache). This is the function of the three muxes in Figure 4.14, summarized in another format in Table 4.3.

Table 4.3. Decision process for the prediction in the YAGS predictor

Choice PHT	"Taken" cache	"Not taken" cache	Prediction
T	N/A	Miss	T
T	N/A	Hit	*Higherbit*[NT2BC[*index*]]
NT	Miss	N/A	NT
NT	Hit	N/A	*Higherbit*[T2BC[*index*]]

Updating of a cache occurs if the cache was used. A new entry in a cache is created, eventually replacing an old one, if the choice PHT made the wrong decision. Because the caches record exceptions, their number of entries does not have to be as large as the number of counters in the choice PHT. It has been shown that at equal storage, the accuracy of a YAGS predictor with 6-bit tags was slightly better than that of the bi-mode predictor, which in turn was better than *gshare*. Of course, as soon as the PHTs' capacities are sufficient to almost nullify the effect of the lack of associativity, the schemes perform similarly.

In the bi-mode and YAGS predictors there is a choice PHT that selects other PHTs, or similar tables, to yield the prediction. The design can be generalized in such a way that the choice PHT now selects one of two complete predictors, for example, a global *gshare*-like predictor on one hand and a local predictor driven by a BHT on the other hand. The choice PHT can be a *tournament* predictor (P_T) with transitions for individual entries as shown in Figure 4.15, which, in fact, is nothing more than a variation on the saturating counters PHT. The overall scheme, called a *combining* or *hybrid* predictor, is shown in Figure 4.16. When a branch needs to be predicted, the tournament predictor P_T indicates which of the two predictors P_1 or P_2 should be followed (cf. the dashed arrows in Figure 4.16). Since P_1 and P_2 operate independently accesses to individual entries in each of the predictors can use different indexing functions. Updating of P_1 and P_2 can be done either speculatively

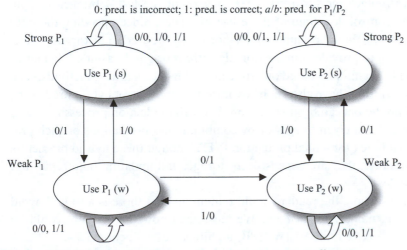

Figure 4.15. State diagram for an entry in a tournament predictor.

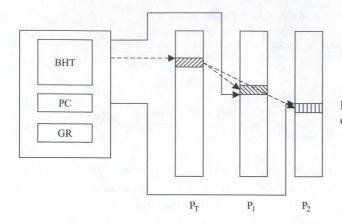

Figure 4.16. Schematic of a hybrid (or combining) predictor.

P_T P_1 P_2

or when the branch is known depending on the predictor's type. Updating of P_T follows the state transitions of Figure 4.15, that is, no modification is made if P_1 and P_2 were in agreement (both right or both wrong, indicated in the figure by 0/0 and 1/1). In the other cases, it depends on the previous states. By analogy with Figure 4.3, we have labeled the two states at the top of the figure as "strong" and those at the bottom as "weak." For example, it takes two incorrect predictions from P_1 along with two correct predictions from P_2 to move from a strong P_1 choice to a weak P_2 one, with the possibility of both P_1 and P_2 being correct or incorrect simultaneously in between these two incorrect (correct) predictions from P_1 (from P_2). A hybrid predictor is used in the Alpha 21264 (see the sidebar at the end of this section).

There exist many other types of sophisticated branch predictors, and the intention here is not to give a complete survey. The few examples that are given now are just a sample of what is still a vigorous area of research.

As a follow-up on the *gshare* philosophy, indexing of the PHT can be performed by using bits of a single global history register and bits of a PC-selected local history register, thus attempting to rely on both global and local information. Other schemes aim to replace the history Boolean vector of the last n branches by an encoding of the control flow *path* of these last branches. Since encoding the path takes many more bits than the simple taken–not-taken bit used in history registers, care must be taken to provide compression algorithms or good hashing schemes to index in the PHT. Techniques based on artificial intelligence learning methods, such as the use of *perceptrons*, have also been advocated. In the case of hybrid predictors, the number of predictors can be greater than two with a selection process based on past performance for a given branch or by combining the predictions of each predictor to form an index for a final prediction PHT. Though these hybrid predictors can be quite accurate, they are expensive in storage, and updating (and repairing) them is not simple.

To close this section, the reader should remember that there is a way to avoid branch prediction, namely *predication*. We have seen how this concept could be applied when we looked at the VLIW/EPIC architectures in Section 3.5.4.

4.1.9 Recap

Branch prediction is a performance requirement for pipelined processors, and the need for accuracy increases with the depth and the width of the pipeline. In an m-way superscalar with a span between the recognition that an instruction is a branch and its resolution of c cycles, the misprediction penalty is of mc instruction issue slots. Since typical numbers for m and c are 4 and 10, respectively, it is no surprise that an enormous amount of effort has been expended to build accurate branch predictors. Today, sophisticated branch predictors have accuracies of over 95% for integer programs and 97% for scientific workloads.

The basic building block of branch predictors is the 2-bit saturating counter that predicts the direction of the next instance of a branch. Because PHTs, (i.e., tables of 2-bit counters), have limited capacity, aliasing occurs for their access. In modern branch predictors, both local information and global information are used to access the PHTs. The local information includes as one of its indexing components the branch address and consists of one or more PHTs. The global information is related to the history of previous branches on the path to the current one and consists of one or more history registers. These two-level branch predictors can be classified according to the number of history registers (one or several) and the number of PHTs (again, one or several). The most sophisticated branch predictors use a tournament predictor, based on the same idea as that of saturating counters, to choose which of the two predictors (say, one mostly based on local information and one based on global information) will be used for predicting the branch direction. Because of the distance between a branch prediction and its execution, history registers are most often updated speculatively. Repairing the history is not a simple task if the number of registers is large.

Branch predictors can also predict the target of the branch. BTBs, organized as caches, are used to that effect. In performance assessment one must distinguish between a misprediction (wrong direction; will be known at execution time) and the less costly misfetch (wrong target address; will be known at decode time).

Sidebar: The DEC Alpha 21264 Branch Predictor

Although the DEC Alpha 21264, introduced in 1998, has the same ISA as the in-order four-way Alpha 21164 presented in Section 3.1, its microarchitecture is quite different in that it is a four-way out-of-order superscalar processor. Its pipeline is also longer, so that a branch misprediction results in a loss of 7 cycles vs. the 6 cycles of the 21164; this small difference is more important than it appears, for the out-of-order execution will allow more in-flight instructions.

The branch predictor of the Alpha 21264 consists of three components (cf. Figure 4.17):

- A tournament predictor of 4 K entries. Indexing is done via a 12-bit global register that records the outcomes of the last 12 branches.

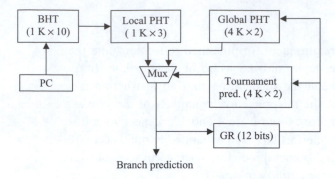

Branch prediction

Figure 4.17. The Alpha 21264 branch predictor (adapted from Kessler [K99]).

- A Global–global predictor PHT of 2-bit counters. It has 4 K entries and is accessed via the same 12-bit global register used for the tournament predictor.
- A Set–global predictor using a BHT of 1 K local registers. The local registers in the BHT are 10 bits long and are used to access a single 1 K PHT of 3-bit saturating counters. Selection of the local registers is performed via bits of the PC.

The global register is updated speculatively, whereas the local, global, and tournament predictors are updated when the branch commits and retires.

The accuracy of this branch predictor shows definite improvements over the simple bimodal predictor of the Alpha 21164, which has a single PHT with 2 K entries (twice the size of the local PHT of the 21264). In the SPEC95 floating-point benchmarks, the misprediction rate is now almost negligible except in one case (*su2cor*). In the integer benchmarks, the misprediction rate is often cut in half. However, when a transaction-processing workload is considered, the simple bimodal predictor is slightly superior. The reason may be that the number of branches is quite large and they don't correlate with each other. Therefore, the larger predictor of the 21164 performs slightly better.

The reader might have noticed that we have not described target address prediction. In the Alpha 21264, a form of BTB is embedded in the I-cache and will be described in Section 4.3 in connection with line-and-way prediction.

4.2 Instruction Fetching

4.2.1 Impediments in Instruction Fetch Bandwidth

In an m-way superscalar, the goal of the fetching unit, (i.e., the part of the front-end that feeds instructions to the decoder), is to deliver m instructions every cycle. Three factors contribute to make this goal of fetching m instructions difficult to achieve:

- The determination of the next address from which the instructions should be fetched: This is taken care of by branch prediction – with, of course, the possibility of misprediction.

- The instruction cache bandwidth: If the m instructions are in two different cache lines, then it is most likely than only the first line can be fetched in a given cycle. Of course, if there is an I-cache miss, the delay will be much greater.
- Break in the control flow (taken branches): This last factor has two components. First, the fetched address can be such that it starts in the middle of a cache line and therefore the instructions in the cache line before it must be discarded, and second, only a subset of the m instructions may be useful if a branch that is taken is not the last of the m instructions.

The fact that fewer than m instructions might be passed on to the decode stage in a given cycle does not necessarily imply that the overall IPC will be significantly reduced. As we have already seen, true data dependencies (i.e., lack of instruction-level parallelism) and structural hazards (i.e., lack of resources) play an important role in limiting IPC. Moreover, depending on the mix of instructions, not all m instructions can always be decoded in one cycle (see the next section). Furthermore, buffering of fetched instructions, as present in the two processors that we have studied in Chapter 3, smoothes over the limitations introduced by the lack of a perfect instruction fetch bandwidth. Nonetheless, attempting to have m instructions ready for the decode stage(s) at each cycle is certainly worthwhile.

Having dealt at length with branch prediction in the previous section, we consider here only the two other bulleted factors, starting with the effect of the instruction cache bandwidth. Reducing I-cache misses through optimized code placement is a topic we shall touch upon in Chapter 6. Having longer I-cache lines will increase the probability that the m instructions are in the same line at the expense of possibly more I-cache misses. So there is certainly a limiting line size; going beyond it would be detrimental (recall Table 2.1; I-cache line sizes are generally 32 or 64 bytes, i.e., between 8 and 16 instructions). If the hardware senses that the remainder of the current line will not hold m instructions, a possibility is to prefetch the "next" line in the instruction buffer.[3] The prefetch can be done in the same cycle in a direct-mapped I-cache if the cache is organized in banks so that consecutive lines are in different banks. However, the concept of "next" becomes muddy when the cache is set-associative, the current trend as per Table 2.1. The savings due to a higher hit ratio brought about by the set associativity generally outweigh those resulting from this limited form of prefetch. Even in the case of a direct-mapped cache, the prefetch can also cause a misfetch if the next line does not correspond to the next sequence of code, for example because of a replacement. Thus, address checking, and eventually repair, are necessary even if there is no transfer of flow of control. The situation is somewhat similar to what we encountered in the data cache access in the Alpha 21164 (recall Section 3.1.3) where on a load–store operation it was optimistically assumed that there was an L1 hit in a first cycle, but this decision could be overridden in the next cycle when a miss was detected.

---

[3] The "next" prefetch in the instruction buffer is not to be confused with *nextline* prefetching in the I-cache, which will be covered in Chapter 6.

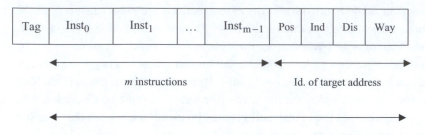

Will be repeated $k = l/m$ times, where l is the I-cache line size

Figure 4.18. Line-and-way prediction in an I-cache.

When the m instructions do not start at the beginning of a cache line or when they straddle two cache lines (either through the prefetch just discussed or because the target instruction of a taken branch can be fetched in the same cycle), they have to be aligned in the instruction buffer. This merging can be done in a *collapsing buffer* that sits in front of the instruction buffer. If such a scheme is implemented, the front-end requires an extra pipeline stage and hence the misfetch penalty is increased by 1 cycle.

Fetching in the same cycle both the sequential code via access to the I-cache and the target instruction plus some of its followers is quite demanding, for the latter implies a BTB lookup plus an I-cache access in the case of a hit. Even if the sequential code and the target address are in different banks, this is too much to ask, especially if the cache is set-associative. To assess the difficulty, recall that in the P6 microarchitecture even a BTB hit resulted in a 1-cycle bubble. This extra cycle can be eliminated in many instances if the BTB is integrated within the I-cache. A possible design is as follows (Figure 4.18).

A cache line contains k sublines of m instructions each. Associated with each subline is a pair (*position, next*) that indicates the position within the current line of the first branch predicted to be taken and the target address in the I-cache for where the next block of m instructions should be fetched. The next field is itself a triple (*index, displacement, way*) wherein *index* points to the line where the next block of instructions reside, *displacement* is the number of bytes since the beginning of the target address line, and *way* is the bank in case the I-cache is set-associative. During the fetch cycle, the branch direction predictor is consulted. If it indicates that a branch is going to be taken, a *line-and-way* prediction is used to fetch the next block of instructions. Line and way fields are set when there is a cache miss and a new line is brought in. Line-and-way predictions are trained like BTB entries, with the possibility of having saturating counters to provide hysteresis. The advantages of the integrated I-cache–BTB are that (i) both the instruction TLB and the tag comparison (for access, not for checking later) can be bypassed and that instructions can be fetched on consecutive cycles in case of taken branches, and (ii) there is a significant savings in space (see the exercises). The drawback is that the information is not quite as precise as in a BTB because the contents of a target line might have been replaced. Thus, there is a slight increase in misfetches of bogus addresses.

BTB-like designs integrated with the I-cache, similar to the one just described, have been implemented in the AMD Athlon K5 and successors as well as in the Alpha 21264.

4.2.2 Trace Caches

The impediments to fetching instructions that we have described in the previous subsection show that if the instruction fetch unit is limited to one branch prediction per cycle (which is the general case, as we shall see in the next section), then at most one basic block or m instructions, whichever is smaller, can be fetched per cycle. If we were willing to lengthen the front-end part of the pipeline and incur more costly misprediction penalties, the single-basic-block constraint could be lessened to the straddling of two basic blocks. If we were to allow multiple branch predictions per cycle, for example, with a multibanked BTB, then contiguous basic blocks, (i.e., basic blocks linked by branches that are not taken), could be fetched. A better scheme would be one that would allow the fetching of multiple basic blocks, whether they are contiguous or not. *Trace caches* are an attempt to achieve this goal.

The basic idea behind trace caches is to supplement, or even replace, the instruction cache with a cache that contains sequences of instructions recorded in the order in which they were decoded (or committed). Such sequences are called *traces*. Instead of the PC indexing into the I-cache, it indexes into the trace cache. Assuming all predictions are correct, the whole trace can be fetched in one cycle, and all instructions within the trace will be executed. Naturally, there are restrictions on the length and composition of traces, choices of how to design the trace cache, and issues of how and when traces are to be built and subsequently fetched.

Figure 4.19(a) gives an abstracted view of a conventional instruction fetch unit using an I-cache, and Figure 4.19(b) shows the same unit when a trace cache is present. We describe the new components in this latter part of the figure.

As in any cache, a trace cache entry consists of a tag and data. Here the data constitute a trace as defined above. A trace is limited in length primarily by its total number of instructions, a constraint stemming from the physical implementation of the trace cache. Other trace selection criteria may be: (i) the number of conditional branches in the traces because of the number of consecutive predictions that can be assumed to be correct is limited, (ii) the fact that merging the next block would result in a trace longer than the trace line (i.e., no partial blocks), and (iii) the last instruction is a procedure call–return or an indirect jump. The tag is primarily the address of the first instruction in the trace, but this alone may not be sufficient.

To illustrate this last point, consider, for example, the diamond-shape portion of code shown in Figure 4.20, corresponding to a basic block B1 starting at address L1 followed by an if–then–else construct (basic blocks B2 and B3) and another basic block B4 that finishes with a branch instruction.

Let us assume that a trace is at most 16 instructions and that it cannot contain partial blocks. There are two possible traces in the code of Figure 4.20 that start at address L1. The first one, corresponding to the "then" path, consists of B1, B2,

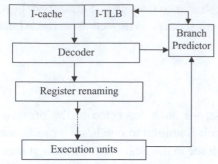

(a) Instruction fetch unit using an I-cache

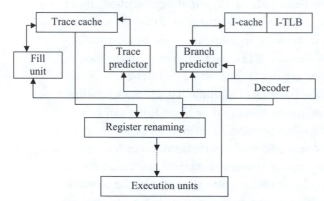

(b) Instruction fetch unit using a trace cache

Figure 4.19. Block diagrams of two possible instruction fetch units.

and B4, for a total of 16 instructions. The second, corresponding to the "else" path, consists of B1, B3, and B4, a total of 15 instructions; merging in the next block would overflow the 16-instruction limit. If we want to store both traces in the trace cache – that is, obtain *path associativity* – the tag needs more information than address L1. One possibility is to record the number of branches and their predicted outcomes. There could be more information stored in an entry if more flexibility is desired: for example, target addresses of not-taken branches could be added so that if the branch is indeed taken, fetching of the next trace could be done rapidly.

Continuing with the building blocks of Figure 4.19(b), we see that the contents of a trace are fed to the register renaming stage in the front-end of the pipelining, bypassing the decode stage. This is not always necessarily so – that is, the instruction sequence of a trace need not be fully decoded – but it is a big advantage for

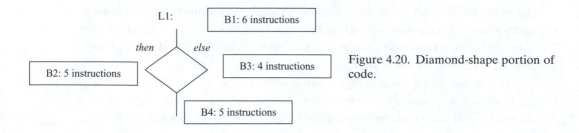

Figure 4.20. Diamond-shape portion of code.

processors with CISC ISAs such as Intel's IA-32, because the trace can consist of μops rather than full instructions.

In a conventional fetch unit, static images of the object code are used to fill the I-cache lines. In contrast, the trace cache lines must be built dynamically. As in the I-cache, new traces will be inserted when there is a trace cache miss. The sequences of instructions that are used to build the traces can come either from the decoder (the Intel Pentium 4 solution, as shown in Figure 4.19(b)) or from the reorder buffer when instructions commit. The drawback of filling from the decoder is that traces corresponding to wrong path predictions might be in the trace cache; but they may be useful later, so this is not much of a nuisance. The disadvantage of filling from the reorder buffer is a longer latency in building the traces. Experiments have shown that there is no significant difference in performance between these two options.

On a trace cache miss, a fill unit that can hold a trace cache line collects (decoded) instructions fetched from the I-cache until the selection criteria stop the filling. At that point, the new trace is inserted in the trace cache, with (naturally) a possible replacement. On a trace cache hit, it is not sure that all instructions in the trace will be executed, for some of them are dependent on branch outcomes that may differ from one execution to the next. Therefore, the trace is dispatched both to the next stage in the pipeline and to the fill unit. If all instructions of the trace are executed, no supplementary action is needed. If some branch in the trace has an outcome different from the one that was used to build the trace, the partial trace in the fill unit can be completed by instructions coming from the I-cache, and this newly formed trace can be inserted in the trace cache.

Branch prediction is of fundamental importance for the performance of a conventional fetch unit. In the same vein, an accurate next trace predictor is needed. There are many possible variations. Part of the prediction can be in the trace line, namely, the starting address of the next trace. An expanded BTB that can make several predictions at a time, say all those that need to be done for a given trace start address, can furnish the remaining information to identify the next trace. An alternate way is to have a predictor basing its information on a path history of past traces and selecting bits from the tags of previous traces to index in the trace predictor table.

In the Intel Pentium 4, the data part of the trace cache entries contains μops. Each line can have up to six μops (recall that the decoder in this processor can decode three μops per cycle). The Pentium 4 trace cache has room for 12 K μops, which, according to Intel designers, means a hit rate equal to that of an 8 to 16 KB I-cache. In fact, the Pentium 4 does not have an I-cache, and on a trace cache miss, the instructions are fetched from L2. The trace cache has its own BTB of 512 entries that is independent of the 4 K entry BTB used when instructions are fetched from L2. With the same hit rate for the I-cache and the trace cache, the two advantages of an increased fetch bandwidth and of bypassing the decoder seem to be good reasons for a trace cache in an *m*-way processor with large *m* and a CISC ISA. Of course, the trace cache requires more real estate on the chip (see the exercises).

Although the Pentium 4 is the only industrial microprocessor that has replaced its I-cache by a trace cache, newer implementations of the P6 microarchitecture use toned-down versions of it. In the Intel Core2, there exists an 18-instruction buffer between the fetch and decode stages that is associated with the loop detector and predictor. If the detected loop is straight code, (i.e., we are in *loop stream* mode), and short enough, then its instructions can be stored in the buffer, thus bypassing the instruction fetch and branch prediction stages. In a more recent version of Core, the buffer is now full of μops, like a Pentium 4 trace, and therefore can be accessed after the decode stage.

4.3 Decoding

In the case of a single-issue pipeline and RISC processor ISA, decoding is straight-forward. Recall, however, that it is during decoding that branch address calculation takes place.

When we increase the width of the pipeline so that now *m* instructions pass concurrently from stage to stage in the front-end, not only does the number of needed decoders grow from 1 to *m*, but also, if we were to follow the branch address calculation speculation for each instruction, we would need *m* adders. Even in the case of RISC instructions, the decoders are not hardware-cheap. For an opcode of 8 bits, this is one-out-of-256 decoding hardware for each of the *m* instructions. Moreover, performing branch address calculation for every possible instruction is overkill. When the ISA is for a CISC computer, there is the additional problem of detecting the start and the end of the variable-length instructions.

Several techniques and limitations have been used to alleviate some of these complexities, namely:

- Restrict the number of branch instructions decoded to one per cycle. If the resolution of the branch is *c* cycles away, this still allows *c* branches in flight, which is more than sufficient when *c* is the order of 10.
- Use *predecoded bits* appended to the instruction, or to each individual byte, during an instruction cache miss transfer from L2 to the I-cache.
- In the case of CISC ISAs, reduce the number of complex instructions that can be decoded in a single cycle. For example, the P6 microarchitecture implementation presented in Chapter 3 has three decoders: two for simple instructions, (i.e., instructions that are translated into a single μop), and one for complex ones. In the more recent Intel Core architecture, there are now three simple decoders. In the AMD Athlon, which has the same IA-32 ISA (albeit with 64-bit registers), there are three decoders, which can translate instructions into one or two *macro-ops* (the equivalent of μops) and a microprogrammed *vector decoder* for more complex instructions. In the AMD processor, the decodes can proceed concurrently, for instructions are steered to the correct decoder in parallel thanks to the predecoded bits.
- Have an extra decoding stage for, for example, steering instructions towards instruction queues, or perform optimizations such as *fusion* (recall Section 3.4.4).

Predecoded bits can be used to facilitate the decoding, dispatch, and issue stages. For example, in the MIPS R10000, 4 bits are appended to each instruction to designate its class (integer, floating-point, branch, load–store, etc.) and the execution unit queue to which it should be dispatched. The partial decoding is done when the instruction cache line is loaded into the I-cache. In the AMD Athlon, each individual byte is predecoded as if it were the beginning of an instruction. In the AMD K7, a 3-bit field (it used to be 5 in the AMD K5) is logically appended to each byte. It indicates how many bytes away is the start of the instruction following the one starting on the given byte. These 3-bit fields are stored in a *predecode cache* that is accessed in parallel with the I-cache. A clear advantage of this technique is that detection of instruction boundaries is performed only once, when the instruction is loaded into the I-cache, and not at every one of its executions. This saves work (and thus power dissipation). On the other hand, the size of the I-cache is almost doubled.

The Intel designers have taken a different approach. In the Core architecture, the latest P6 microarchitecture instantiation, one stage of the pipeline is dedicated to bringing instructions into an instruction buffer (more like a queue), where their boundaries are determined. They are then steered toward either a simple decoder or the complex decoder. It is during this stage that fusion possibilities are recognized (the typical example is compare-and-test followed by a branch instruction), and if possible the two instructions together are sent to a single simple decoder.

Although decoding might not be considered an area where there exist great intellectual challenges, the sheer amount of hardware and work that is needed during that stage is one of the roadblocks to increasing the width of superscalar processors.

4.4 Register Renaming (a Second Look)

We have seen in Chapter 3 that register renaming was a common technique to avoid WAR and WAW dependencies in out-of-order processors. We saw in Section 3.2 one possible register renaming scheme using the reorder buffer as an extension to the register file. The idea is based on Tomasulo's algorithm (Section 3.2 sidebar), and a variation of it is implemented in some instantiations of the Intel P6 microarchitecture (Section 3.3.2) among others. We now undertake a more complete coverage of register renaming. We avoid unnecessary repetition of what was covered in Chapter 3; in particular, we do not expand on the motivation for having a register renaming mechanism.

There are basically three ways to implement the register renaming concept, namely:

1. Use the reorder buffer (ROB) as presented earlier.
2. Have a *monolithic* physical register file where any register can represent at any given time the committed value of an architectural register.
3. *Extend* the architectural register file with a physical register file. Committed values are found in the original architectural register file (as in the reorder buffer implementation).

Each of these implementations has its own advantages and drawbacks, and each of them can be found in some recent microprocessor.

When implementing a register renaming scheme, decisions have to be taken on:

- Where and when to allocate and release physical registers.
- What to do on a branch misprediction.
- What to do on an exception.

In all three implementation schemes, allocations occur in a front-end stage following decoding. There have been proposals for "virtual registers" where allocation is delayed until it is known that the instruction is on a correctly speculated path, but we shall not consider them here. In the postdecoding stage, every architectural result register is renamed to a free physical register, and a map of these renamings is updated. In the case of the ROB, the physical register is (part of) the next ROB entry. In the other two schemes, a list of free registers is maintained, and renamed registers are taken from this list.

Releasing a physical register is easy in the case of the ROB. When renaming occurs, the ROB entry contains the name of the register where the result should be stored. When the instruction commits, the ROB entry is released and the register file is written. In the other two schemes, the releasing decision is more complex.

Let us return to the example at the beginning of Section 3.2.

EXAMPLE 3: Consider the segment of code:

```
i1:   R1 ←R2 / R3      # division takes a long time to complete
i2:   R4 ← R1 + R5     # RAW dependency with i1
i3:   R5 ← R6 + R7     # WAR dependency with i2
i4:   R1 ← R8 + R9     # WAW dependency with i1
```

and the renaming:

```
i1:   R32 ← R2 / R3    # division takes a long time to complete
i2:   R33 ← R32 + R5   # still a RAW dependency with i1
i3:   R34 ← R6 + R7    # no WAR dependency with i2 anymore
i4:   R35 ← R8 + R9    # second renaming of R1
```

Because instruction $i1$ takes a long time to execute, instruction $i2$ will not be issued when register R1 is renamed for a second time in instruction $i4$. Therefore the value of register R32 must be kept, because it is an input operand for $i2$. Note also that it is quite probable that register R35 will contain its result before register R32 obtains its own, but the commitment of instruction $i4$ must follow that of instruction $i1$ to protect program order. This latter property is enforced by the reorder buffer (sometimes called an *activity list* when the ROB is not used as an extension of the register file), independently of the register renaming scheme.

In the *monolithic register scheme* there is no real distinction between the architectural registers and the physical registers. The register map contains the latest

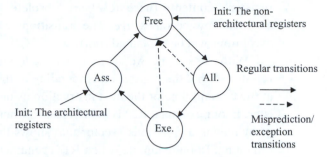

Figure 4.21. State diagram for the state of a register in the monolithic scheme (adapted from Liptay [L92]).

mapping of architectural registers to physical registers. In the above example, after the renaming stage of instruction *i4*, architectural register R1 is mapped to physical register R35. We shall see the consequences of this mechanism when we look at recovery of mispredicted paths and exceptions. For the time being, we concentrate on the register release mechanism.

Consider register R32. As soon as all readings of R32 have been done (i.e., in our example, after instruction *i2* has been issued and the architectural register it had been renamed for is renamed again, here at instruction *i4*), R32 can be put on the free list of registers. A possible way to implement this is to use a counter per renamed register that would be incremented every time the register is referenced as a source operand (e.g., the counter for register R32 would be incremented during the renaming stage of instruction *i2*) and decremented when the instruction using the renamed register is issued. Then the renamed register could be released when the architectural register mapped to it is had been renamed anew (at instruction *i4* in our example) and the value of the counter was null (after instruction *i2* had been issued).

However, maintaining counters along with registers and having the test depend on two conditions – null counter and renaming of the architectural register – is too cumbersome. A slightly more conservative approach, in the sense that registers are released later than in the counter scheme, is to release a renamed register once the instruction with a new instance of its renaming is committing. In the previous example this would mean that register R32 would be released when instruction *i4* commits.

If we follow this last releasing condition, a physical register passes through four states as shown in Figure 4.21. Initially, the architectural registers are in the state *assigned* and the remaining registers in the state *free*. When a free register is used as a result register, it becomes *allocated*, for example, R32 at the renaming stage of instruction *i1*. When the result value is generated, at the end of the execution of the instruction, its state becomes *executed*, that is, its contents are available for following instructions that could not issue because of RAW dependencies depending on it. This happens at the end of execution of instruction *i2* for R32. When the instruction for which it was a result register commits, the state becomes *assigned*, that is, in essence, this register becomes an architectural register. When the release condition of the previous paragraph happens, at commit of instruction *i4*, the register's contents (here R32) are obsolete, and its state that was necessarily *assigned* now becomes *free*. The transitions corresponding to mispredictions and exceptions will be explained shortly.

With this scheme, we see that we need to know the previous mapping of a result register so that the register corresponding to the previous mapping can be released at the commit time of the next instruction using the same (architectural) result register. In our example, R32 is to be released when *i4* commits. This can be taken care of by having a "previous" vector that shows the previous instance of the physical renaming. In our example, when R1 is renamed in *i4*, the "previous" field for R35 will be R32.

The monolithic scheme and where it influences the various stages in the pipeline are therefore as follows:

MONOLITHIC RENAMING

Renaming Stage. $Inst_m$: $R_i \leftarrow R_j$ op R_k becomes $R_a \leftarrow R_b$ op R_c, where
$R_b = Rename(R_j)$; $R_c = Rename(R_k)$;
$R_a = freelist(first)$; $Prev(R_a) = Rename(R_i)$; $State(R_a) = allocated$;
$Rename(R_i) = R_a$; $first \leftarrow next(first)$;
$ROB(tail) = (false, NA, R_a, op)$; $tail \leftarrow next(tail)$;

Issue Stage. ...if $((State(R_b) = (executed$ or $assigned))$ and $(State(R_c) = (executed$ or $assigned)))$ then issue $Inst_m$.

Execute Stage (End). $State(R_a) = executed$;

Commit stage.
if$((ROB(head) = Inst_m)$ and $flag(ROB(head)))$
           then begin $R_a = value$; $State(R_a) = assigned$;
           $State(Prev(R_a)) = free$; $head \leftarrow next(head)$ end
                    else repeat same test next cycle

In the *extended register* file case, only physical registers can be in the *free* state, and the state diagram for these registers needs to be modified (see the exercises). When an instruction commits, the result must be stored in the architectural register mapped to the physical register. This implies that either the map has the capability of being associatively searched for the physical register yielding the architectural register, or a field with the name of the resulting architectural register must be present in each ROB entry, that is, the ROB entry is a five-tuple (*flag*, *value*, *arch*, *reg*, *phys*, *reg*, *op*).

We now turn our attention to repair mechanisms when a branch has been mispredicted. We have already seen that no harm is done in the case of an ROB-based renaming. When the branch instruction percolates to the head of the ROB, all instructions after the branch are canceled, and since the ROB entries implicitly carry the mapping of physical registers, the only action to be taken, from the register-renaming viewpoint, is to invalidate all mappings from architectural to physical registers, that is, ROB entries. A valid bit is present to that effect in the mapping table. A similar solution is possible for the extended register file when the ROB entries carry the architectural result register name.

However, that method will not work in the monolithic scheme, because the mapping cannot be deduced directly from the ROB. Instead, at each branch prediction, the mapping table and its associated state and previous fields need to be saved. When the branch reaches the head of the ROB, if the prediction was successful, then the saved map can be discarded; otherwise, the saved copy is used when computation restarts on the corrected path. Because several branch predictions can be in flight, several copies of the map may need to be saved. Saving them in a circular queue with head and tail pointers indicating the earliest and latest maps is a possible implementation. Note that when there is a misprediction, all registers that were not in the assigned state become free. This is shown by the dashed transitions in Figure 4.21.

In the ROB and extended register schemes, when an exception occurs, the repair mechanism used for branch mispredictions is sufficient. This is not true for the monolithic scheme, because maps are not saved at every instruction. The only recourse is to undo the mappings from the last instruction renamed up to the instruction that caused the exception. This may take several cycles, but fortunately, this is at the time when the exception must be handled, which in itself will take hundreds if not thousands of cycles; therefore, the overhead is not important.

From a functional viewpoint, the ROB-based implementation seems the most natural and elegant. Register renaming repair is easy for branch mispredictions and exceptions. There is no need for map saving. However, there are major drawbacks in comparison with the monolithic scheme (we leave it as an exercise to find advantages and drawbacks of the extended register implementation). First, space is wasted in the ROB-based scheme in that each entry must have fields for register renaming purposes, even if the instruction does not generate any result. Of course, there is no need to save maps, so some of the monolithic scheme's space advantage disappears. Second, at commit time, the need to store a result in an architectural register implies that the commit will take 2 cycles. However, retiring the instruction and writing in the register file can be pipelined. Third, and in the author's view the most important factor, the ROB serves many purposes: physical register file for both integer and floating-point values, and holder of in-flight instructions. Thus, it must be designed so that it can supply operands to all integer and floating-point functional units as well as values to the register file at commit time. The number of read ports necessary is much greater than in the case of the monolithic scheme, where register files for integer and floating-point units can be split and where there is no need to transfer values at commit time. The same analysis holds true for write ports. Because read and write ports are expensive in space and power, the current trend would appear to be for implementations with a monolithic scheme, but the simplicity of the ROB scheme still seems to be compelling.

As said earlier, each of the three schemes can be found in modern microprocessors. The P6 microarchitecture is ROB-based with an ROB that can hold 40 μops for the Intel Pentium III and Pentium M and more than double that in the Intel Core. In contrast, the Intel Pentium 4 uses a monolithic scheme with 128 physical registers. The MIPS R10000 and the Alpha 21264 also use a monolithic register file. The 21164 has 41 extra integer and 41 extra floating-point registers. The ROB has 80 entries. The IBM PowerPC uses an extended register file mechanism.

4.5 Summary

The front-end of an m-way superscalar should deliver m decoded instructions per cycle waiting to be issued to the execution units. This ideal situation presents numerous challenges that necessitate a steady flow of more than m instructions until its last stage.

Feeding the pipeline with the instructions on the correct path of execution cannot wait until control flow decisions are made deep in the back-end. Accurate branch prediction is a necessity. We have shown how branch direction prediction has evolved from a table of simple four-state counters to two-level and tournament predictors that rely on the local history of a branch as well as the global history of branches that precede it in the dynamic execution. These direction predictors are often supplemented by target address predictors, either as standalone structures or embedded in the I-cache. Repair mechanisms needed when mispredictions and exceptions occur add to the complexity of branch prediction schemes.

The instructions fetched from the I-cache, or in some instances a trace of already decoded instructions, are kept in buffers or queues before being sent to the decode stage. For processors with complex ISAs the decode stage must also determine the boundaries of instructions. This process can be helped by the use of a predecoder inserted between the L2 cache and the L1 I-cache.

In the case of out-of-order processors, the decoded instructions are passed to the rename stage so that WAR and WAW dependencies can be eliminated. We have seen in Chapter 3 how the reorder buffer, needed to enforce the program order semantics, can be used to implement this renaming and provide the processor with extra registers. In this chapter, we have shown two schemes that extend the architectural register file by providing an extra set of physical registers. We have given the mechanisms needed to allocate and free these extra registers as well as for restoring the correct register state after mispredictions and exceptions.

4.6 Further Reading and Bibliographical Notes

The anatomy of a predictor has its roots in a paper by Cheng et al. [CCM96] and in the literature of feedback control. Many studies, such as Lee et al. [LCBAB98], have reported the frequencies of branch occurrences, and others, such as Jiménez et al. [JKL00], also give the interbranch distances.

There have been hundreds of papers on branch prediction mechanisms. For a recent substantial bibliography, see Loh [L05]. Jim Smith published the seminal study that introduced the two-bit saturating counter scheme in 1981 [S81]. Alan

Smith and his students (Lee and Smith [LS84], Perleberg and Smith [PS93]) performed early studies of its efficiency. The *gshare* predictor and the first mention of a hybrid predictor can be found in McFarling's 1993 report [M93]. Two-level and/or correlator predictors were introduced concurrently by Pan et al. [PSR92] and Yeh and Patt [YP92b]. Patt and his students have published extensively on the topic, and their taxonomy of two-level predictors is widely used [YP92a]. Calder and Grunwald [CG94], as well as Hao et al. [HCP94], have shown the performance advantages of speculative updating of global prediction schemes. The paper by Eden and Mudge [EM98] introducing the YAGS predictor also reviews alternatives that lead to hybrid branch predictors. Early design options for BTBs can be found in Perleberg and Smith [PS93] and later in Fagin and Russell [FR95]. The first return-stack mechanism evaluation can be found in Kaeli and Emma [KE91]. Repair mechanisms for global and local predictors are investigated and evaluated by Jourdan et al. [JSHP97] and Skadron et al. [SMC00].

Conte et al. [CMMP95] investigated instruction fetch mechanisms for high bandwidth. The original line-and-way prediction is found in Calder and Grunwald [CG95]. Trace caches were first introduced in a patent by Peleg and Weiser [PW94]. Rotenberg et al. [RBS96] and Patel et al. [PFP99] have investigated and evaluated several trace cache design options. Performance limitations of trace caches are found in Postiff et al. [PTM99] and might give a clue to why further implementations of the P6 microarchitecture have reverted to conventional I-caches. The "look behind" mechanism of the CDC 6600 [T70] can be considered as an early version of the loop buffers found in the Intel Core.

The register renaming techniques described in this chapter can be found in Smith and Sohi's paper [SS95]. Sima [S00] surveys register renaming techniques. The detail of one possible implementation of the monolithic scheme, as done in the IBM System/9000, is described by Liptay [L92]. The reader should refer to the bibliography of Chapter 3 for sources on the ROB-based design.

Kessler [K99] is a good source for the Alpha 21264 microarchitecture. Cvetanovic and Kessler [CK00] report on its performance. The Intel Pentium 4 is summarily described in Hinton et al. [HSUBCKR01], and the Intel Pentium M in Gochman et al. [GRABKNSSV03]. Christie [C96] describes the AMD K5 architecture.

EXERCISES

1. (Section 4.1.3) The outcomes of branch execution for a given branch can be seen as a string of bits, 1 for taken and 0 for not taken. For example, the string for the end of loop branch looks like "111…1110111…1110.…111…1110".

  (a) Consider a diamond structure, that is, code of the form "if *condition* then *S1* else *S2*." What are the prediction accuracies of a 1-bit scheme and of a 2-bit scheme when the conditional expression's value alternates between *true* and *false*?

(b) Find a string where the prediction accuracy for a single-bit scheme is 50% and that of a saturating counter scheme as depicted in Figure 4.3 is zero in steady state. Can you think of a programming pattern that fits this type of string?

(c) Can you modify the state diagram of Figure 4.3 so that the string you found in part (b) yields a 50% prediction accuracy? If so, find another string for this new state diagram that yields zero accuracy in steady state. Does it correspond to a more likely programming pattern?

2. (Section 4.1.3) Show a state diagram for a scheme where the 2-bit counter is replaced by a 3-bit shift register keeping track of the last three executions of the branch and predicting according to the majority decision of these three executions. Is this a reasonable alternative to a 2-bit saturating counter in terms of performance and cost?

3. (Section 4.1.4) Assume a 3-bit global register (initialized to all 0's) and a two-level Global–global scheme.

(a) How many entries are there in the PHT?

(b) Show the contents of the global register and of the PHT (where each entry is initialized to the weak not-taken case and follows the state diagram of Figure 4.3), after the following sequence of branch executions has taken place: 1 taken (T) branch, 3 not-taken (NT) branches, 1 T branch, 3 NT branches, 1 T branch. With *pred* being the prediction and *act* the actual outcome as per the given string, show your results for each branch, for example, in the form (GR) (*pred*) (*Updated* GR) (*act*) (PHT). Assume a speculative update for GR and a nonspeculative one for the PHT that occurs before the next branch prediction. Two typical entries could be

(i) $(000)(0)(000)(1)(01, 01, 01, 01, 01, 01, 01, 11)$ or

(ii) $(000)(0)(000)(1)(01, 01, 01, 01, 01, 01, 01, 11)$;
    misprediction, restore GPR to (001).

4. (Section 4.1.5) Assume that the global register is k bits long and that m bits of the PC are used to select among PHTs.

(a) How many bits are used to implement the Global–global scheme?

(b) How many bits are used to implement the Global–set scheme?

5. (Section 4.1.5) Assume that k bits of the PC are used to access the BHT, that the local history registers are p bits long, and that m bits of the PC are used to select among PHTs.

(a) How many bits are used to implement the Set–global scheme?

(b) How many bits are used to implement the Set–set scheme?

6. (Section 4.1.5) The question that microarchitects usually face in the context of a two-level branch predictor is: "If I have a certain amount of chip area that I can devote to branch prediction, how should I divide it among the various branch prediction data structures?" Answer this question assuming a budget of 8 K bits plus a few extra bits, say less than 100. Of course, you should come up with more than one possible design.

7. (Section 4.1.6) In the repair mechanism for a Global–global scheme, a FIFO queue of global registers is accessed at three different times:

- When the branch prediction is made (insertion at end of the queue).
- When the branch prediction is correct and the instruction is committed (deletion from the front of the queue).
- When the branch prediction is incorrect at the end of the execute stage (deletion of several consecutive entries in the FIFO queue).
    (a) What extra hardware (tags, pointers, etc.) must be added so that recovery is possible? If there is a maximum of m branches in flight, can the FIFO queue be less than m entries? If so, what are the consequences?
    (b) A suggestion is to have each FIFO entry tagged with the PC of the branch it corresponds to. Then the branch would not have to carry a tag. Why is this not possible?

8. (Section 4.1.6) [JSHP97] In the global repair scheme, one can avoid the FIFO queue of saved global registers by using a longer global register. Indicate how long the global register should be, and describe the implementation structures and the steps necessary for each of the three bulleted points of the previous exercise.

9. (Section 4.1.7) In the equation giving the branch execution penalty bep of a processor with a BTB and a PHT, we approximated the term $Miss_f \times m_{fetch}$. Give a better formulation, following the entries in Table 4.2.

10. (Section 4.1.7) Show that when a special call–return stack is implemented, returns corresponding to calls from various locations can be predicted as soon as the return instruction is fetched if the return address is flagged appropriately in the BTB.

11. (Section 4.1.8) There are several possibilities in updating policies for a tournament predictor. Indicate which ones you would recommend when the local predictor is a bimodal one and the global predictor is of the *gshare* type.

12. (Section 4.2.1) Consider an I-cache of 16 KB, two-way set-associative with line size of 32 bytes. Assume a RISC machine with each instruction being 4 bytes. How much real estate (i.e., how many bits) is needed to implement the line-and-way prediction depicted in Figure 4.18 when branch prediction fields are available every four instructions? How large a direct-mapped BTB could be implemented using the same number of bits?

13. (Section 4.2.2) [PTM99] In addition to the conventional hit rate, other metrics have been identified for the evaluation of trace caches, namely fragmentation, duplication, and indexability. Give your own definitions of these metrics. If one defines the efficiency as the ratio (unique instructions)/(total instruction slots), how do fragmentation and duplication relate to efficiency?

14. (Section 4.4) In Example 3, why can't register R32 become free in the monolithic scheme as soon as instruction *i4* finishes executing?

15. (Section 4.4) Draw a state diagram for the extended register file's physical registers similar in spirit to that of Figure 4.21 for the monolithic case.

16. (Section 4.4) State advantages and drawbacks of the extended register file implementation for register renaming vs. the monolithic and the ROB-based implementations.

Programming Projects

1. (Section 4.1.3) Using a simulator (which you might have to modify slightly), instrument a number of applications to test the accuracy of a bimodal branch predictor and of a *gshare* predictor when the PHT is 8 K bits.

2. (Section 4.1.5) Implement your solutions to Exercise 6 in a simulator, and test which solution gives the best accuracy for a sample of applications on a suitable benchmark (e.g., a selection of parts of SPEC2006 integer programs). Do not draw any general conclusion from this experiment.

3. (Section 4.1.8) Using a simulator, implement a hybrid branch predictor of your choice, assuming that you have a budget of 6 K bits plus a few more bits if necessary for some history register(s). Record the accuracy of your predictor on the same benchmarks as in the previous programming project, and compare your results.

REFERENCES

[C96] D. Christie, "Developing the AMD-K5 Architecture," *IEEE Micro*, 16, 2, Mar. 1996, 16–27

[CCM96] I-C. Cheng, J. Coffey, and T. Mudge, "Analysis of Branch Prediction via Data Compression," *Proc. 7th Int. Conf. on Architectural Support for Programming Languages and Operating Systems*, Oct. 1996, 128–137

[CG94] B. Calder and D. Grunwald, "Fast & Accurate Instruction Fetch and Branch Prediction," *Proc. 21st Int. Symp. on Computer Architecture*, 1994, 2–11

[CG95] B. Calder and D. Grunwald, "Next Cache Line and Set Prediction," *Proc. 22nd Int. Symp. on Computer Architecture*, 1995, 287–296

[CK00] Z. Cvetanovic and R. Kessler, "Performance Analysis of the Alpha 21264-based Compaq ES40 System," *Proc. 27th Int. Symp. on Computer Architecture*, 2000, 192–202

[CMMP95] T. Conte, K. Memezes, P. Mills, and B. Patel, "Optimization of Instruction Fetch Mechanisms for High Issue Rates," *Proc. 22nd Int. Symp. on Computer Architecture*, 1995, 333–344

[EM98] A. Eden and T. Mudge, "The YAGS Branch Prediction Scheme," *Proc. 31st Int. Symp. on Microarchitecture*, 1998, 69–77

[FR95] B. Fagin and K. Russell, "Partial Resolution in Branch Target Buffers," *Proc. 28th Int. Symp. on Microarchitecture*, 1995, 193–198

[GRABKNSSV03] S. Gochman, R. Ronen, I. Anati, R. Berkovits, T. Kurts, A. Naveh, A. Saeed, Z. Sperber, and R. Valentine, "The Intel Pentium M Processor: Microarchitecture and Performance," *Intel Tech. Journal*, 07, 2, May 2003, 21–39

[HCP94] E. Hao, P.-Y. Chang, and Y. Patt, "The Effect of Speculatively Updating Branch History on Branch Prediction Accuracy, Revisited," *Proc. 27th Int. Symp. on Microarchitecture*, 1994, 228–232

[HSUBCKR01] G. Hinton, D. Sager, M. Upton, D. Boggs, D. Carmean, A. Kyker, and P. Roussel, "The Microarchitecture of the Pentium 4 Processor," *Intel Tech. Journal*, Feb. 2001, 1–12

[JKL00] D. Jiménez, S. Keckler, and C. Lin, "The Impact of Delay on the Design of Branch Predictors," *Proc. 33rd Int. Symp. on Microarchitecture*, 2000, 67–76

[JSHP97] S. Jourdan, J. Stark, T.-H. Hsing, and Y. Patt, "Recovery Requirements of Branch Prediction Storage Structures in the Presence of Mispredicted-path Execution," *International Journal of Parallel Programming*, 25, Oct. 1997, 363–383

[K99] R. Kessler, "The Alpha 21264 Microprocessor," *IEEE Micro*, 19, 2, Mar. 1999, 24–36

[KE91] D. Kaeli and P. Emma, "Branch History Table Prediction of Moving Target Branches Due to Subroutine Returns," *Proc. 18th Int. Symp. on Computer Architecture*, 1991, 34–42

[L92] J. Liptay, "Design of the IBM Enterprise System/9000 High-end Processor," *IBM Journal of Research and Development*, 36, 4, Jul. 1992, 713–731

[L05] G. Loh, "Advanced Instruction Flow Techniques," Chapter 9 in J. P. Shen and M. Lipasti, Eds., *Modern Processor Design*, 2005, 453–518

[LCBAB98] D. Lee, P. Crowley, J.-L. Baer, T. Anderson, and B. Bershad, "Execution Characteristics of Desktop Applications on Windows NT," *Proc. 25th Int. Symp. on Computer Architecture*, 1998, 27–38

[LS84] J. Lee and A. Smith, "Branch Prediction Strategies and Branch Target Buffer Design," *IEEE Computer*, 17, 1, Jan. 1984, 6–22

[M93] S. McFarling, "Combining Branch Predictors," *WRL Tech. Note*, TN-36, Jun. 1993

[PFP99] S. Patel, D. Friendly, and Y. Patt, "Evaluation of Design Options for the Trace Cache Fetch Mechanism," *IEEE Trans. on Computers*, 48, 2, Feb. 1999, 193–204

[PS93] C. Perleberg and A. Smith, "Branch Target Buffer Design and Optimization," *IEEE Trans. on Computers*, 42, 4 Apr. 1993, 396–412

[PSR92] S. Pan, K. So, and J. Rahmey, "Improving the Accuracy of Dynamic Branch Prediction Using Branch Correlation," *Proc. 5th Int. Conf. on Architectural Support for Programming Languages and Operating Systems*, Oct. 1992, 76–84

[PTM99] M. Postiff, G. Tyson, and T. Mudge, "Performance Limits of Trace Caches," *Journal of Instruction-Level Parallelism*, 1, Sep. 1999, 1–17

[PW94] A. Peleg and U. Weiser, "Dynamic Flow Instruction Cache Memory Organized Around Trace Segments Independent of Virtual Address Line," U.S. Patent Number 5,381,533, 1994

[RBS96] E. Rotenberg, S. Bennett, and J. Smith, "Trace Cache: A Low Latency Approach to High Bandwidth Instruction Fetching," *Proc. 29th Int. Symp. on Microarchitecture*, 1996, 24–34

[S81] J. Smith, "A Study of Branch Prediction Strategies," *Proc. 8th Int. Symp. on Computer Architecture*, 1981, 135–148

[S00] D. Sima, "The Design Space of Register Renaming Techniques," *IEEE Micro*, 20, 5, Sep. 2000, 70–83

[SMC00] K. Skadron, M. Martonosi, and D. Clark, "Speculative Updates of Local and Global Branch History: A Quantitative Analysis," *Journal of Instruction-Level Parallelism*, 2, 2000, 1–23

[SS95] J. Smith and G. Sohi, "The Microarchitecture of Superscalar Processors," *Proc. IEEE*, 83, 12, Dec. 1995, 1609–1624

[T70] J. Thornton, *Design of a Computer: The Control Data 6600*, Scott, Foresman and Co., Glenview, IL, 1970

[YP92a] T.-Y. Yeh and Y. Patt, "Alternative Implementations of Two-Level Adaptive Branch Prediction," *Proc. 19th Int. Symp. on Computer Architecture*, 1992, 124–134

[YP92b] T.-Y. Yeh and Y. Patt, "A Comprehensive Instruction Fetch Mechanism for a Processor Supporting Speculative Execution," *Proc. 25th Int. Symp. on Microarchitecture*, 1992, 129–139

5 Back-End: Instruction Scheduling, Memory Access Instructions, and Clusters

When an instruction has passed through all stages of the front-end of an out-of-order superscalar, it will either be residing in an instruction window or be dispatched to a reservation station. In this chapter, we first examine several schemes for holding an instruction before it is issued to one of the functional units. We do not consider the design of the latter; hence, this chapter will be relatively short. Some less common features related to multimedia instructions will be described in Chapter 7.

In a given cycle, several instructions awaiting the result of a preceding instruction will become ready to be issued. The detection of readiness is the *wakeup* step. Hopefully there will be as many as *m* instructions in an *m*-way superscalar, but maybe more, that have been woken up in this or previous cycles. Since several of them might vie for the same functional unit, some scheduling algorithm must be applied. Most scheduling algorithms are a variation of first-come–first-served (FCFS or FIFO). Determination of which instructions should proceed takes place during the *select* step. Once an instruction has been selected for a given functional unit, input operands must be provided. Forwarding, also called *bypassing*, must be implemented, as already shown in the simple pipelines of Chapter 2 and the examples of Chapter 3.

One particular instruction type that is often found to be on the critical path is the *load* instruction. As we have seen before, load dependencies are a bottleneck even in the simplest processors. Moreover, load latency is variable, because it depends on cache accesses. To add to this variability, it is often not known at compile time if a given load is conflicting with a previous store, because the analyses of some indexing functions are practically intractable. As was the case with flow of control, speculation can be performed, and we shall consider several schemes for load speculation and their repair mechanisms.

In the last section of this chapter we present briefly some back-end optimizations. The treatment is not exhaustive. Many more schemes have been proposed to increase performance or to reduce power consumption with as little effect as possible on execution time. For example, we introduce yet another form of speculation called *value prediction*. As another example, because windows are large, it is quite possible that FIFO, or oldest instruction first, may not be the best scheduling strategy. We shall discuss the detection of *critical* instructions and see how the recognition of critical instructions can influence scheduling. Finally, because of the larger number of functional units and the concomitant lengthening of the wires used to connect them, forwarding such that a result becomes available in the cycle following the cycle where it was generated may not be possible. We shall look at the concept of *clustered microarchitectures*, which deal explicitly with the forwarding and scheduling problems.

The last stage of instruction execution is commitment. We have introduced the reorder buffer previously and considered its role in repair mechanisms for branch mispredictions and exceptions. We shall not return to it explicitly in this chapter.

5.1 Instruction Issue and Scheduling (Wakeup and Select)

5.1.1 Centralized Instruction Window and Decentralized Reservation Stations

Instructions leaving the register rename stage, the last stage of the front-end, may not be ready to execute right away because of RAW dependencies or structural hazards such as the lack of a free functional unit. As we saw in Chapter 3, in-order processors would put these stalled instructions in a FIFO queue and instructions would be removed from it in program order, that is, the order in which they were put in. However, in an out-of-order processor, a queue is not a good design choice, because instructions following a stalled one in program order are allowed to start their execution as soon as the right conditions – such as readiness of operands and availability of the right functional unit – are met. In Chapter 3, we found two solutions for storing stalled instructions. These solutions are at opposite ends of the spectrum of possibilities. In the case where the implementation strictly follows Tomasulo's original algorithm, reservation stations sitting in front of their associated functional unit hold the stalled instructions and the ready flags and names for their operands. This decentralized design is followed, for example, in the IBM PowerPC series. At the other end of the design options, the instructions, again with the ready flags and names of their operands, are added to an instruction window, which can be seen as a centralized reservation station for all functional units. The Intel P6 microarchitecture follows this scheme.

Naturally, nothing prevents a hybrid solution between these extremes. Reservation stations can be shared among groups of functional units. For example, in the MIPS R10000 there are three sets of reservation stations of 16 entries: a set each for the integer and address calculation functional units, the floating-point units, and the load–store units. Table 5.1 gives the number of reservations station windows and their sizes as well as the numbers of functional units they serve for a few recent microprocessors. The numbers and types of functional units are not quite accurate: we have blended together address generation units and what are commonly called load–store units, that is, those units that hold the resolved addresses for pending

Table 5.1. Numbers of reservations stations and functional units (integer, |, and floating-point) in selected microprocessors. See text for notes

Processor	RS type	Number of res. stations	Functional units: int.	l/s	fp
IBM PowerPC 620	Distributed	15	$4^{(1)}$	1	1
IBM Power4	Distributed	31	$4^{(2)}$	2	2
Intel P6 (Pentium III)	Centralized	20	$3^{(3)}$	2	$4^{(4)}$
Intel Pentium 4	Hybrid (1 for mem. op., 1 for rest)	126 (72,54)	$5^{(5)}$	2	$2^{(6)}$
Intel Core	Centralized	32	$4^{(3)}$	$3^{(7)}$	$7^{(8)}$
AMD K6	Centralized	72	3	3	3
AMD Opteron	Distributed	60	3	3	3
MIPS R10000	Hybrid (1 for int., 1 for mem., 1 for fp)	48 (16,16,16)	2	1	2
Alpha 21264	Hybrid (1 for int/mem, 1 for fp)	35 (20,15)	2	2	2
UltraSPARC III	In-order queue	20	2	1	$3^{(9)}$

(1) The branch unit is included in this count.
(2) The branch unit and a unit for manipulating condition registers are included in this count.
(3) A jump unit is included in this count.
(4) Two multimedia (MMX) units and a catch-all unit are included in this count.
(5) Two pairs of integer units run at double speed.
(6) These units are for MMX and floating point.
(7) Store address and store data are distinct units, to allow fusion.
(8) There are two floating-point and five MMX–SSE units.
(9) One unit is for MMX-like operations.

memory instructions. We have also included the multimedia units with the floating-point units for the Pentium, AMD, and SPARC architectures. The idea is to give an estimate of the parallelism in the back-end. More often than not, each functional unit is designed for a particular purpose. For example, it would be incorrect to assume that three floating-point multiplications can be issued simultaneously for a processor that is shown as having three floating-point units. In general, only one floating-point multiplier is present (although it can be pipelined as indicated in Section 2.1.6).

Independently of whether the instruction window is centralized, hybrid, or distributed, each instruction slot in the instruction window(s) (or reservation stations) will contain tags (names), flags for each of its operands, and some bit(s) indicating the state of the instruction (e.g., waiting to be issued or already issued). The tags identify the renamed registers that will provide the source operands, and the flags indicate whether the operands are ready or not. Instruction issue then will consist of two steps, which we elaborate on below: *wakeup* and *select*.

The variety of options shown in Table 5.1 indicates that there are a number of compromises that must be considered while choosing between centralized, hybrid, and distributed instruction windows. From a strict resource allocation viewpoint, at equal number of entries a single large window is better than several windows based on instruction type, for it is well known that static partitioning of resources yields worse performance than dynamic allocation (as the study of virtual memory systems has taught us in a definite fashion). However, as the windows become larger, other considerations, related to efficiency and power, come into play. Let us elaborate on some of them, starting with a discussion of the wakeup step.

5.1.2 Wakeup Step

The wakeup step corresponds to the "dispatch" in Tomasulo's algorithm. When a result is generated, the tag identifying it is broadcast to the reservations stations (in the following we consider a centralized instruction window as a unique set of reservation stations). An associative lookup is performed in the reservation stations, and for each match the corresponding flag is set to ready. When all flags of a reservation station are set to ready, the instruction is woken up and, potentially, can be issued. However, because there could be more than one instruction ready to issue competing for the same functional unit, a selection, or scheduling, process is needed (see next section).

In a back-end that has f functional units, up to f results can be generated in a cycle. This implies that f buses must carry the results and that f comparators must be associated with each operand entry in the instruction window. Because there are two operands per instruction, this means that $2fw$ comparators are needed for a window of w entries. The larger f and w are, the longer the lines (wires) carrying the identification tags of the results will be and, of course, the larger the number of buses and comparators. All these factors increase the wakeup–select time and the power requirements. More realistically, we can group functional units so that they share some buses and restrict the number of comparators for each operand per reservation station to be equal to the issue width. Nonetheless we are still confronted by the fact that trying to have more instructions concurrently in the back-end – by either increasing the window size so that we have more instructions candidates for issue on a given cycle, or making the back-end wider to achieve more concurrency in execution, or both – is expensive in both logic and power and might result in wakeup and select times exceeding the intended cycle time (or portion thereof if both wakeup and selection must be performed in the same cycle).

In a noncentralized instruction window scheme, the lengths of the tag-carrying lines are shorter, because each distributed window is itself shorter. Moreover, the number of lines is also smaller, for not all functional units can generate results of a given type. As a consequence, the overall number of comparators and the wakeup time are reduced. The risk of missing some instruction ready to issue that would have been present in a centralized window is minimal as long as the distributed windows are not too small.

5.1.3 Select Step

The select step corresponds to the "issue" step in Tomasulo's algorithm. The design advantage of distributed windows is even greater when we consider this scheduling step. After wakeup, a number of instructions are ready to start their execution. Some of them may conflict, that is, ask for the same resource. To solve this problem, instructions woken up in this cycle and the not yet issued entries that were woken

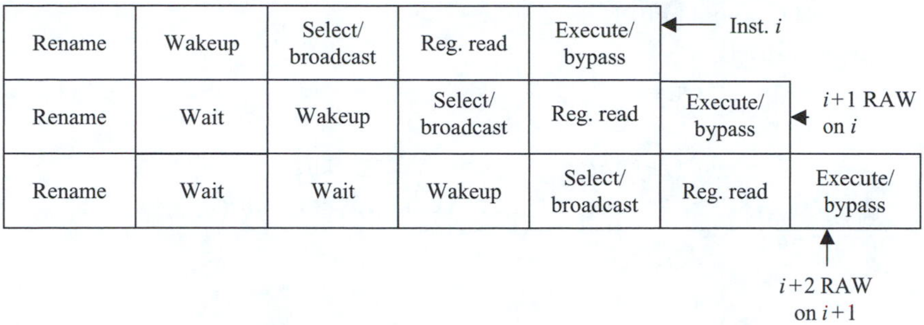

Rename	Wakeup	Select/ broadcast	Reg. read	Execute/ bypass	← Inst. *i*
Rename	Wait	Wakeup	Select/ broadcast	Reg. read	Execute/ bypass	*i*+1 RAW on *i*
Rename	Wait	Wait	Wakeup	Select/ broadcast	Reg. read	Execute/ bypass

i+2 RAW
on *i*+1

Figure 5.1. Pipeline execution for three consecutive dependent instructions. The three instructions were decoded and renamed in the same cycle.

up in previous cycles will send a request signal to a priority encoder. The latter will answer with grant signals to those entries that should move forward in the pipeline in the next cycle. In general, the priority is related to the position in the instruction window, with the older instruction having the highest priority. Each entry can be seen as a leaf of a tree, and requests walk up the tree till its root, the priority encoder. Grants walk back from the root to the leaf entries. As can be readily seen, the depth of the tree will be shorter for smaller instruction windows, although the depth is often shortened for large windows by providing a scheduler per (group of) functional unit(s) of a given type. In that case, the instruction window is closer to the Tomasulo implementation as described in Chapter 3.

Once an instruction has been selected, the tag of the result register can be broadcast. If the latency of execution is one cycle, this will allow a RAW-dependent instruction to be stalled only for 1 cycle, as shown in Figure 5.1.

In summary, the wakeup and select stages are as follows:

WAKEUP–SELECT. (*woken* is a flag associated with the instruction in its reservation station; it is set when the instruction is woken and reset after the instruction has been selected.)

Wakeup Stage
```
if not woken then
        begin
                if any broadcast_result_register_name = tag1
                        then flag1 ← true;
                if any broadcast_result_register_name = tag2
                        then flag2 ← true;
                if (flag1 and flag2) then woken ← true;
        end;
```
Select Stage
```
if woken then
        begin
                top ← check(priority);
                        /*returns true if instruction is top priority*/
```

```
                if top then
                begin
                     issue;
                     woken ← false;
                     if latency_execution = 1 then
                         broadcast_result_register_name;
                end
         end;
```

5.1.4 Implementation Considerations and Optimizations

The question facing designers is at which point a centralized window scheme should be abandoned in favor of a distributed or hybrid one. The main criterion for the choice is whether the wakeup–select steps are on the critical path. If this happens to be the case, an alternative solution is worth investigating. Windows of 64 entries in a 4-wide superscalar with a clock in the gigahertz range are close to the decision point. As can be seen in Table 5.1, the multigigahertz Intel Pentium 4 has two (large) windows with two schedulers each, whereas its slower predecessor and successor, the Intel Pentium III and Intel core, have a smaller centralized window. Similarly, the AMD Opteron, also a multigigahertz processor, has four sets of reservation stations, a departure from the microarchitecture of the 500 MHz AMD Athlon with its centralized window.

An alternative, or a requirement when the wakeup–select time is more than the intended 2 cycles even with hybrid or distributed windows, is to introduce a third pipeline stage for, for example, broadcast. Simulations at the circuit level have shown that wakeup is more time-consuming than selection, but the times for the two steps are of the same order of magnitude. However, a problem can occur for two instructions with a RAW dependency as in the following example.

EXAMPLE 1:

i: $R_{51} \leftarrow R_{22} + R_{33}$
$i + 1$: $R_{43} \leftarrow R_{27} - R_{51}$

If wakeup–select is done as shown in Figure 5.1, then after instruction i has been selected, it is safe to wake up and select instruction $i + 1$ in the next cycle. However, if wakeup–selects are in two consecutive stages and broadcast in a third one, then the wakeup for instruction $i + 1$ has to wait till it is sure that instruction i has been selected; that is, the two instructions cannot be executed in the back-end on consecutive cycles. In the example above, if instruction i was not selected and then at the next cycle instruction $i + 1$ was, then the wrong value of R_{51} would be an operand of the subtraction. A possible palliative is to speculate that the woken-up instruction will be selected and allow the second instruction to proceed. Measurements have shown that more than 90% of the time, an instruction that has been selected will subsequently wake up either no or one instruction; thus, the probability of being wrong is small. Nonetheless, the cost of such a solution is that some checkup and abort logic is required in case the guess was erroneous. Moreover, increasing the depth of the front-end of the pipeline in order to provide more concurrency in the back-end is not without an associated increased performance penalty when branches are mispredicted. For example, in the Pentium 4, which has one wake-up stage followed by three scheduling stages, the branch misprediction penalty is 20 cycles, vs. 10 cycles in the simpler Pentium III with a single scheduling stage. Of course, the addition of these specific scheduling stages is only part of the reason for a doubling of the penalty in terms of loss of instruction issue slots. Though the introduction of the trace cache (cf. Section 4.2.2) saves decoding steps, many other stages of the front-end that were performed in a single cycle in the Pentium III now take 2 cycles in the twice as fast Pentium 4.

The two-instruction sequence in Example 1 highlights the fact that the name given to the result of the selected instruction (in this case R_{51} for instruction i) must be broadcast as soon as the selection is performed if its forthcoming execution has a single-cycle latency, because instruction $i+1$ depends on the broadcast tag to be woken up. If one waited until the end, or even the start, of execution, one or more cycles later, it would be too late. For longer-latency operations, delays are inserted before the broadcast. Once again, this broadcast can be speculative, for in one instance, a load operation, it is not certain that the predicted latency, that of a first-level cache hit, will be correct. In case of a cache miss, all instructions dependent on the load that have been woken up and possibly selected must be aborted, and their ready bit corresponding to the result of the load must be reset.

The speculative wakeup and the cache miss possibility imply that an instruction must remain in its reservation station after it has been scheduled, for it might have been selected erroneously. Because instructions should not be reselected unless there was some misspeculation, each entry in the window will have a bit indicating that the selection has been done. This bit will be reset in the same way as a ready bit. A reservation station will be freed only once it is ascertained that its corresponding instruction has not been speculatively selected. Of course, the removal can also be a consequence of aborted instructions due to branch misprediction. In order to keep a scheduling policy approximating "oldest instruction first," a window can be compacted when instructions are leaving it, or some circular queue scheme can be implemented. At any rate, we can understand now why the windows appear to be so large compared to the number of functional units and the issue width: there can be many instructions in flight past the stage where they are decoded and inserted in a window.

Once an instruction has been selected, the opcode and the operands must be sent to a functional unit. In schemes that follow closely Tomasulo's reservation station implementation, the opcode and operands that were already computed will come from the reservation stations or from the ROB. In the case of an integrated register file, the instruction window (opcode) and the physical register file supply these items. In both cases, though, one of the operands might be the result of the instruction whose result allowed the wakeup. In Example 1, instruction $i+1$ requires the result R_{51} of instruction i. This result must be forwarded from the stage in the integer unit where it was computed to the input of the integer unit (the same one or another) that will use it as an operand, bypassing the store in, say, the physical register file at commit time. Although conceptually this is as simple as forwarding in the five-stage pipeline of Chapter 2, the scale at which it must be done makes it challenging. The number of required forwarding buses is the product of the number of stages that can be the producers of the forwarding (it can be more than one per functional unit if the latter implements several opcodes with different latencies) and the issue width. Trying to improve performance by increasing the number of functional units and the issue width is translated into a quadratic increase in the number of wires as well as an increase in their overall length. In multigigahertz processors, this might imply that forwarding cannot be done in a single cycle. In the last section of this chapter, we shall introduce clustered processors, which are a possible answer to the challenge.

5.2 Memory-Accessing Instructions

Instructions transmitting data to and from registers, namely the load and store instructions, present challenges that are not raised by arithmetic–logical instructions. Load instructions are of particular importance in that many subsequent instructions are dependent on their outcome.

An important feature that distinguishes memory-accessing instructions from the other instruction types is that they require two computing stages in the back-end, namely address computation and memory hierarchy access. The presence of these two separate stages led to irresolvable RAW dependencies in the simple five-stage pipelines of Chapter 2. In the first design that we presented, a bubble had to be inserted between a load and a subsequent instruction, depending on the value of the load; in the second design a bubble needed to be introduced when the RAW dependency was between an arithmetic–logical instruction and the address generation step of a load–store instruction.

In superscalar implementations, the address generation is either done in one of the integer units (cf. the Alpha 21164 in Section 3.1.3) or done in a separate pipeline that is interfaced directly with the data cache (the most common alternative in current designs; see, for example, the AGU in the Intel P6 microarchitecture of Section 3.3.3). In in-order processors, like the Alpha 21164, RAW dependencies between a load and a subsequent instruction decoded in the same cycle will delay the dependent instruction, and therefore all following instructions, by 1 cycle. As mentioned in Chapter 3, the check for such an occurrence is done in the last stage of the front-end, using a scoreboard technique that keeps track of all instructions in flight. In out-of-order processors, in a similar fashion, the wakeup of instructions depending on the load is delayed by the latency of the data cache access. A number of compiler techniques have been devised to alleviate the load dependency delays, and the reader is referred to compiler technology books for more information.

In contrast with the simple pipelines of Chapter 2, where we assumed that the Mem stage always took 1 cycle, real implementations dealing with caches need to "guess" the latency of the load operation. As we saw in Chapter 3 in the case of the in-order Alpha, the guess was the common case, namely, a first-level data cache hit. In case of a miss, instructions dependent on the load cannot be issued, and if one of them has already been issued, it is aborted. We also saw in the first section of this chapter that the wakeup stage in out-of-order processors was speculative because of the possibility of cache misses. A consequence was that instructions had to remain in their windows or reservation stations until it was certain that they were no longer subject to speculation (i.e., committed or aborted due to branch mispre-diction), because they might be woken up again if they were dependent on a load operation that resulted in a cache miss.

As already mentioned in Section 3.3.3 when giving an overview of the Intel P6 microarchitecture, out-of-order processors add another opportunity for optimiza-tion, namely *load speculation*. There are two circumstances wherein a load cannot proceed without speculation: (i) the operands needed to form the memory address are not yet available, and (ii) the contents of the memory location that will be addressed are still to be updated. Speculation on the load address is mostly used in conjunction with *data prefetching*. We will return to the topic of address prediction when we discuss prefetching in Chapter 6. In this section, we present some tech-niques for the second type of speculation, generally called *memory dependence pre-diction* because the dependencies are between load and preceding store instructions.

5.2.1 Store Instructions and the Store Buffer

Let us first elaborate on the way store instructions are handled. There are two possi-ble situations once the memory address has been generated (whether address trans-lation via a TLB is needed or not is irrelevant to this discussion): either the result to be stored is known, or it still has to be computed by a preceding instruction. How-ever, even in the first case, the result cannot be stored in the data cache until it is known that the store instruction will be committed. Therefore, store results and, naturally, their associated store addresses need to be stored in a *store buffer*. The store buffer is organized as a circular queue with allocation of an entry at decode time and removal at commit time. Because the store result might be written in the cache later than the time at which it is known (because instructions are committed in order), status bits for each entry in the store buffer will indicate whether:

- The entry is available (bit AV).
- The store has been woken up and the store address has been computed and entered in the store buffer, but the result is not yet available in the store buffer (state AD).
- The store address and the result are in the store buffer, but the store instruction has not been committed (state RE).
- The store instruction has been committed (state CO).

When the store instruction has been committed (head of the ROB and head of the store buffer), the result will be written to the cache as soon as possible, and

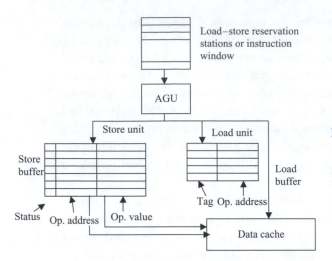

Figure 5.2. Load–store unit.

the corresponding entry in the store buffer will then become available. In case of a branch misprediction, all stores preceding the mispredicted branch will be in entries with state CO, showing that they are committed when the branch reaches the head of the ROB. As part of the misprediction recovery process, all other entries in the store buffer will become available. In the case of an exception, the process is similar except that entries in state CO must be written in the cache before handling the exception. An abstracted view of the load–store unit with a store buffer is shown in Figure 5.2. The presence of the load buffer will be explained in the forthcoming paragraphs.

Actions that are specific to stores in various stages are summarized below:

STORE-INSTRUCTION-SPECIFIC ACTIONS. (These result from instructions of the form *Mem[op.address]* ← R_i. We do not show actions such as inserting the instruction in the ROB or committing the instruction. Each entry in the Store buffer consists of the tuple {AV bit, state, address, name or value}.)

Dispatch Stage

```
if store buffer full then stall for 1 cycle;/* structural hazard*/
    else begin
        reserve entry at tail (AV off, st. unknown, ad. unknown, Rᵢ.name);
    end;
```

Memory Address Computation Stage (End)

```
                entry ← (AV off, AD, op.address, Rᵢ.name);
                    if Rᵢ has been computed then
                    entry ← (AV off, RE, op.address, Rᵢ.value)
                    else wait for broadcast of Rᵢ name to modify entry
```

Commit Stage

```
    entry ← (AV off, CO, op.address, Rᵢ.value);
    /*some cycles later the value will be stored in the memory hierarchy AV
    will be turned on*/
```

5.2.2 Load Instructions and Load Speculation

Let us consider now how load instructions will proceed. While keeping the basic framework of an out-of-order processor, we start by imposing restrictions on the order in which loads and stores can interact and then relax some of these constraints with the goal of improving performance by increasing potential concurrency. Of course, implementation cost and complexities grow when we introduce predictors and concomitant recovery mechanisms.

In order to simplify the presentation, we will assume that the load and store instructions share a dedicated instruction window. It is not difficult to generalize to the case of a single centralized window.

In the most restricted implementation, the load–store window is a FIFO queue. Load and store instructions are inserted in program order (this will always be true, as the front-end processes instructions in program order), and they are removed in the same order, at most one instruction per cycle. Moreover, a load can be issued only when the store buffer is empty. Clearly, all memory dependences are resolved at that point, and the load will find the correct value in the memory hierarchy.

This solution does not take advantage at all of the information that can be found in the store buffer. A more natural scheme is to compare the address of the load operand with all store addresses in the store buffer. If there is no match, the load can proceed. This mechanism is often called *load bypassing*. Note that it requires an associative search of the address portion of the store buffer, and one must also be careful that the operand address of the last store, which could be an instruction issued in the cycle just preceding that of the load, is already stored in the buffer or available for comparison. However, if there is a match and the matching address store has not yet committed, (i.e., is not in state CO), then the load cannot proceed or, more precisely, the cache will not be accessed. In case of multiple matches, the last store in program order is the one considered to be the match, and we assume in the following discussion that "match" is synonym with "last match in program order." The load will be reissued when the corresponding store has left the store buffer.

The result information contained in the store buffer is not used in the load bypassing scheme. In the case of a match between the load address and a store address in the store buffer, if the latter has a result associated with it (state RE or state CO), this result can be sent directly to the result register of the load. We have now what is called *load forwarding*, and the load instruction has completed (but not committed, for it is not at the head of the ROB). If the match is for an entry that is waiting for its result (state AD), then the load will wait until the store entry reaches the state RE. Forwarding and load completion will then occur simultaneously.

In summary:

LOAD BYPASSING AND FORWARDING. (Instruction of the form $R_i \leftarrow Mem[op.address]$; in case of a match, *storebuffer.field* are the components of the most recent matching entry in the store buffer.)

Address Generation (Execute) Stage

```
if (op.address = storebuffer.address) then
   begin abort cache access;
      if (storebuffer.state = RE or storebuffer.state = CO)
              then begin Rᵢ; ← storebuffer.value;
                          broadcast (Rᵢ.name, Rᵢ)
              end;
   else repeat test at next cycle;
   end
```

We now return to the full generality of out-of-order processors, except that we restrict the stores to issue in program order. It has been shown that there is no impact on performance by doing so, and it makes the detection of the last store to match slightly easier. The store buffer is still needed to process the store instructions, but it is not sufficient for checking dependencies between stores and loads. Loads can be issued speculatively in advance of stores preceding them in program order – with, of course, the need for recovery in case of a RAW memory dependence between the load and a not yet completed store. Issuing loads as early as possible has performance advantages in that very often loads are on the critical path of the computation.

Three approaches are possible to solve the *dynamic memory disambiguation* problem:

- Pessimistic: wait until it is certain that the load can proceed with the right operand value. This is very close to the *load bypassing and forwarding* scheme.
- Optimistic: always speculate, that is, continue with load execution immediately. In this case, we need to remember such speculative loads in the load buffer (i.e., a tag identifying the load and its operand address) and implement recovery mechanisms in case there was a dependence with an in-program-order preceding store.
- Dependence prediction: use some predictor to see whether the load should proceed or not. As in the optimistic case, remembering speculated loads and recovery mechanisms are needed, but the intent is to have fewer time-consuming recoveries while allowing the majority of safe loads to proceed immediately.

To illustrate these policies, consider the following example:

EXAMPLE 2: Prior to this instruction, all stores have been committed:

i1: st R1, memadd1

. . . .

i2: st R2, memadd2

. . . .

i3: ld R3, memadd3

. . . .

i4: ld R4, memadd4

All instructions are in the instruction window. We assume that the two load instructions are ready to issue and that there exists a true memory dependency between instructions *i2* and *i3*.

In the pessimistic approach, neither of the load instructions will issue until the stores have issued and computed their addresses. At this point instruction *i3* will wait till instruction *i2* has computed its result (or is in state RE in the store buffer). Instruction *i4* will proceed as soon as the two stores have reached state AD.

In the optimistic scheme, both load instructions will issue as soon as possible, and load buffer entries will be created for each of them. When a store instruction reaches the state CO, its operand address is (associatively) compared with those in the load buffer. If there is no match, as is the case for instruction *i1*, nothing happens. However, when instruction *i2* reaches state CO, its memory address, memadd2, will match the address memadd3 entered for instruction *i3*. The load instruction *i3* will have to be reissued, as well as all instructions in program order after it, including instruction *i4*, although in some implementations the reissuing of instructions can be limited to those dependent on *i3*.

If dependence prediction is used and predicts correctly that instruction *i3* depends on instruction *i2* and that instruction *i4* has no memory dependence, then instruction *i3* will have to wait until instruction *i2* passes to state CO, while instruction *i4* can proceed.

We now look at implementation considerations. In the pessimistic approach, we proceed as in the case of load bypassing and forwarding, with the additional check that there is no store in the instruction window that precedes the load in program order and that has not been issued yet. Because instructions are entered in the window in program order and because, as we saw in the previous section, there is a bit in each reservation station indicating whether the instruction has been issued or not, this additional check is conceptually easy. It is even easier if there is a dedicated instruction window devoted to memory operations. This is basically the solution used in the Intel P6 microarchitecture prior to the launching of the Core architecture.

At the other end of the spectrum, in the optimistic approach all loads are considered speculative, that is, all loads proceed unhampered by possible conflicts after they have computed their operand address. However, the store buffer is checked so that if there is a match with an entry in state CO, the result is forwarded and the cache access is aborted. Regardless of whether this match occurs or not, the load and its associated address are entered in the load buffer. Subsequently each store entry that passes from any other state to the state CO will check entries in the load buffer. If there is a match between the store and a load in the load buffer, the load was misspeculated and must be aborted, as well as all instructions following it in program order (we discuss recovery mechanisms in the following). On the other hand, if the load reaches the head of the ROB, then the speculation was right and the load entry is removed from the load buffer.

The optimistic scheme is based on experiments that have shown that memory dependences are rare, significantly less than 10% of the time for most programs and for implementations with large load–store instruction windows. Nonetheless, load misspeculations are expensive and can be reduced by using dependence predictors. These cautious optimistic approaches require a load buffer as in the optimistic approach. On the other hand, not all loads are speculated. We describe three schemes, from the simplest to the most complex.

SCHEME 1: SINGLE CHANGE. Because memory dependencies are infrequent, a first strategy is to predict that all loads can be speculated as in the optimistic solution. When a load misspeculation occurs, subsequent instances of the misspeculated load will be forced to wait, as in the pessimistic scheme. The change from speculated to nonspeculated will occur only once for a given load instruction. A single bit, appended to the instruction in the instruction cache, is sufficient to indicate the course to follow. Because the bit can be checked at decode time, there is no extra effort required for the issuing of speculated load instructions. When a cache line is replaced and then brought back on a cache miss, the appended bit will be reinitialized to indicate that the load is to be speculated even if prior instances predict the opposite. Because, in general, tens or hundreds of thousands of cycles separate the cache replacement and subsequent miss, the potential change in prediction may in fact be correct. This is basically the scheme used in the DEC Alpha 21264.

SCHEME 2: LOAD PREDICTOR TABLE. The next step in sophistication is to keep a predictor structure that records recent loads and whether they should be speculated or not. A particular implementation could be as follows. The predictor is a set of hash tables indexed by bits of the PC and containing saturating counters with states of the form "strong speculate", "weak nospeculate" and so on. A load buffer entry will be a 4-tuple (*tag, op.address, spec.bit, update.bit*). The *spec.bit* indicates whether we have a speculative load, and the *update.bit*, which is set by store instructions, dictates whether the predictor should be updated at commit or abort time. Each load instruction also carries a *loadspec* bit. Now for a load:

Load Decode Stage. Access the predictor, and set *loadspec* according to the value of the counter associated with the load PC.

After the Operand Address of the Load Has Been Computed. We have the following cases:

- There are no uncommitted younger stores in either the store buffer or the instruction window. Enter (*tag, op.address, off, off*) in the load buffer, and issue the cache access.
- There are younger unresolved stores, and *loadspec* is off. Enter (*tag, op.address, off, off*) in the load buffer, and wait as in the pessimistic solution.
- There are younger unresolved stores, and *loadspec* is on. Enter (*tag, op.address, on, off*) in the load buffer, and issue the cache access.

Before dealing with what happens at commit, we need to consider the actions at a store commit.

Store Commit Stage

```
if no match in load buffer do nothing;
For all matches with spec.bit off set update.bit on;
/* it was correct not to speculate, and no speculation is to be kept*/
For all matches with spec.bit on proceed to load abort;
```

Now we can return to the load commit and the abort process, which takes place before the commit for those loads that were misspeculated.

Load Commit Stage

```
if spec.bit off then
        if update.bit on then reset saturating counter predictor
        entry to "strong nospeculate"
        else increment saturating counter /* would like to speculate
        in the future*/
else increment saturating counter /*speculating was correct*/
```

Load Abort

```
reset saturating counter predictor entry to "strong nospeculate";
recover from the misspeculated load as in the case of an exception
/*or a branch misprediction, depending on the register renaming scheme*/
```

The saturating counter should be initialized so that it takes a few nonspeculative execution instances for a load that would have been correctly speculated before it is indeed speculated. If the register renaming scheme uses the ROB, the recovery is similar to the one after a branch misprediction. Otherwise, because register maps are not saved at every load instruction, the recovery is similar to what happens after an exception and is more expensive. A scheme resembling this one is implemented in the Intel Core architecture.

Let us now envision what an ideal predictor would do, namely, keep all pairs (load, store) that will conflict. Assuming this was possible, the first time a conflict is recorded, the (load, store) pair is entered in an associative table. Since a store (i.e., a writer) can have several loads (i.e., readers) dependent on it, there can be multiple pairs with the same load entry. Similarly, there can be multiple pairs with the same store entry – for example, as a consequence of writing the same variable in both branches of an if–then–else construct and reading that variable after the join of the branches. Now, when a load is speculated, the table is searched. If there are one or more matches on the load address, a check is made to see if the associated store(s) has(ve) been recently fetched and has(ve) not yet reached the CO state in the store buffer. If so, the load is stalled until the store(s) has(ve) reached the CO state. Because keeping large associative tables is impractical, we are going to restrict this scheme by using *store sets*.

SCHEME 3: STORE SETS. A store set is a structure that associates stores with individual loads. Instead of keeping (load, store) pairs, we associate a set of stores with each load. The store sets are initially empty and build up on failed optimistic speculations.

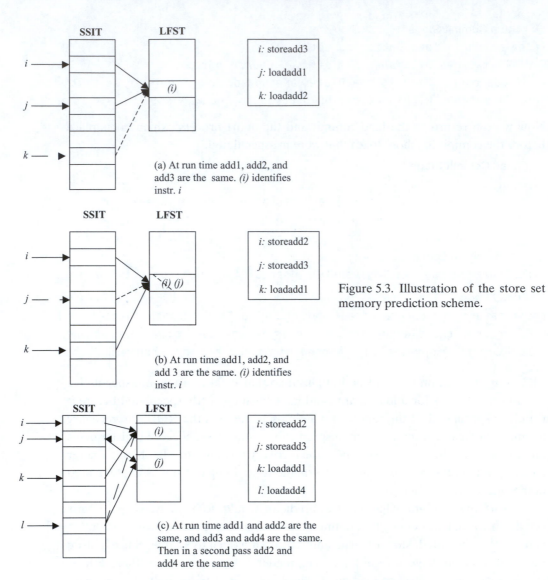

(a) At run time add1, add2, and add3 are the same. (i) identifies instr. i

(b) At run time add1, add2, and add 3 are the same. (i) identifies instr. i

Figure 5.3. Illustration of the store set memory prediction scheme.

(c) At run time add1 and add2 are the same, and add3 and add4 are the same. Then in a second pass add2 and add4 are the same

However, with regard to implementation we have not made much progress, for sets are not easily represented in hardware. A saving feature is that we still restrict stores to issue in program order, so for each load we will keep only the pair with the last fetched store. So we are going to restrict store sets to contain only one store, the most recently fetched. However, this is not quite sufficient, as we are going to see below.

In the store set scheme, two tables, initially empty, are used (cf. Figure 5.3): the store set ID table (SSIT) and the last fetched store table (LFST). The SSIT, indexed by the address of the load–store instructions (PC), contains set ID numbers for each load and store instruction involved in misspeculation. A set ID number is a pointer to an entry in the LFST that keeps track of the last store in each store set, if any, that has been decoded and has not yet reached the state CO. This store is identified by some tag that allows retrieving its position in the store buffer or the instruction window.

Before showing how these tables are filled and updated, let us see how they are used. When a load is decoded, the SSIT is accessed. If the entry is valid and points to a valid LFST entry, then this indicates that a recently fetched store is not yet in state CO in the store buffer; as in the other schemes presented previously, the load cannot proceed until the conflicting store reaches the state CO in the store buffer. If the LFST entry is invalid, then it indicates that the store has already reached the state CO or has committed and the load can proceed with forwarding if possible.

When a store is decoded, it accesses the SSIT. If there is a corresponding LFST entry, then that entry is replaced by the identification of the just-decoded store. When a store reaches the state CO, it must remove itself from the LFST by making itself invalid if it is still there.

When a speculative load is found to have been mispredicted, both the load and the store instruction on which it depends must be entered in the SSIT. There are four possible cases:

- Neither the load nor the store has a store set ID. A new one is created and assigned to both instructions.
- The load has been assigned a store set, but the store has not. The store is assigned the load's store set and becomes the LFST entry (this takes care of multiple stores for the same load if it happens only once).
- The store has been assigned a store set, but the load has not. The load is assigned the store's store set. This takes care of multiple loads for the same store. However, it might create false dependencies with other stores already in the set; the alternative would be to have a store belong to multiple store sets and would complicate the dependence checking.
- Both the load and the store have (distinct) store sets. One of them is declared the winner, and the pointer to the LFST of the loser points to that of the winner. Choosing the winner with the smaller index in the SSIT allows convergence of the process. However, false dependencies may occur.

These four cases are illustrated in Figure 5.3. In Figure 5.3(a), in a first pass over the code, the load at instruction j was mispredicted, for it is in conflict with the store at instruction i. SSIT entries for both instructions are created pointing to an entry in the LFST that identifies instruction i. In a second pass over the code, the load at instruction k is mispredicted. An entry in the SSIT is created, pointing to the already existing LFST entry that contains the identification of the conflicting store (this is shown with the dashed line).

In Figure 5.3(b), in a first pass the store at address i and the mispredicted load are in conflict. In a second pass, it is the store at address j and the load that are in conflict. Both stores point to the same entry in LFST, but because only one of them will be decoded in a given pass over the code (representative of an if–then– else pattern), the identification in the LFST entry will be correct and the load will always be stalled after each branch has been taken once; that is, there are only two possible mispredictions.

In Figure 5.3(c), we illustrate the merging process. In a first pass over the code, each load–store pair contributes one entry in the LFST. In a second pass, the load at instruction l conflicts with the store at instruction j. The SSIT entry at instruction l now points to the LFST entry. If there is a new misprediction (j, l), the entry corresponding to the store at instruction j will point to the same entry as that of the store at instruction i, and the process is stabilized. However, this might create false positives, for example, if the pair (j,k) has no conflict.

Both the limited size of the SSIT table and several of the options mentioned above create false dependencies. These can be alleviated with confidence counters (2-bit saturated) or periodic invalidations of the store sets through valid bits.

When the processor is in recovery mode from some prediction, be it from a branch prediction or a load–store prediction, there is no need to modify the SSIT. In the case of the LFST, it is sufficient to treat the aborted stores as if they had committed, that is, make their entries invalid.

5.2.3 Load Speculation Evaluation

Performance benefits from load speculation depend on the availability of speculation, the miss rate of the speculation, and the cost of misspeculation recovery. These factors are all dependent on the size of the instruction window (store instructions that are in the store buffer in states other than CO remain in the instruction window as per the requirements stated in Section 5.1).

Let us adopt the following terminology. We will say that a load is *conflicting* if at the time it is ready to be issued (i.e., have its operand address computed) there is a previous store in the instruction window whose operand address is unknown. A conflicting load is *colliding* if it is dependent on one of the stores with which it conflicts. What is important to know for a given instruction window size is the number of nonconflicting loads (these will be issued correctly by all policies) and, among the conflicting loads, those that are noncolliding (these can be speculated successfully) and those that are actually colliding (these should not be speculated; if they are, they will result in some recovery penalty). Measurements have shown that in a typical 32-entry load–store queue there will be approximately 25% of nonconflicting loads, and among the remaining 75% of conflicting ones, only 10% actually collide with previous stores. With larger window sizes, the percentage of nonconflicting loads decreases and the percentage of colliding ones increases. Thus, intelligent predicting policies become more important with larger instruction windows, because the performance of both the pessimistic policy (favorable when there is a large percentage of nonconflicting loads) and the optimistic policy (favorable when there is a small percentage of colliding ones) will suffer.

In the same sense that branch prediction accuracy gives a feel for the goodness of a particular predictor, the percentage of predicted loads and the outcomes of these predictions give some idea of the benefits that could be achieved for memory dependence predictors. In scheme 1 of the previous section, an important metric is the percentage of predicted loads, for after a misprediction the load will not be speculated. However, false dependencies may then result, thus preventing some loads from being speculated successfully. Simulations have shown that for the SPEC95 integer programs, from 68% to 95% (average 85%) of loads were speculated. For a couple of floating-point programs the average was 95%. Although these simulations were reported for a very aggressive and unrealistic 16-wide superscalar with a 256-entry load–store instruction window and a 64 K I-cache, they should not be very different for a more realistic processor. Unfortunately, there are no data on false dependencies.

In the case of the store set scheme, the sizes of the instruction window and of the SSIT and LFST is more pertinent to the coverage (number of loads predicted) and accuracy of the predictions. With sufficiently large SSITs, the misprediction rate is negligible, but the number of false dependencies cannot be overlooked. False dependencies can be almost completely removed by introducing confidence (2-bit saturating) counters, with each store entry in the SSIT indicating whether there is a high probability of a real conflict or not.

Again, in the same vein as for branch prediction, what is essential is not the coverage and accuracy of the predictor, but the performance gains that one hopes to achieve. Recall that a misprediction can be costly in that the state has to be recovered and instructions have to be reissued and executed anew. The range of potential gain can be assessed by simulating a policy with no speculation and one with perfect speculation. Simulations for a processor quite similar to the Alpha 21264 showed a potential for a 300% speedup for the perfect case; some performance degradation could, albeit rarely, occur for the optimistic implementation.

The same simulations showed that a store set scheme with sufficiently large SSIT (say, over 4 K entries) and LFST (over 256 entries) approaches the performance of perfect prediction. Confidence counters are not necessary, for the number of false dependencies is rather small, and periodic clearing (cycling policy) of the tables is sufficient to obtain the same level of performance.

5.3 Back-End Optimizations

In this chapter and in the previous one we have examined three optimizations based on speculation, which we can rank in order of importance as:

1. Branch prediction.
2. Load-bypassing stores.
3. Prediction of load latency.

Clearly, branch prediction is a must. It is present, quite often in very sophisticated ways, in all standard microprocessors. Without it, most of the performance advantages of deeply pipelined superscalar processors would evaporate. Load speculation is also important in that loads are often producers of values for subsequent instructions and delaying their execution might be quite detrimental to overall performance. However, not all loads are of equal importance, as we shall see further in Section 5.3.2. Most high-performance microprocessors today have some form of load speculation. Finally, guessing that the load latency will be that of a first-level cache hit is common for the wakeup and select operations. We shall see in the next chapter ways to tolerate or hide load latency in the cache hierarchy.

In this section, we briefly present some optimizations that have been proposed as means to increase performance or to reduce power consumption, goals that are often conflicting. Although none of these optimizations are standard fare, they might be useful in future microprocessor generations. Inasmuch as none of them have been implemented in silicon except in a restricted fashion for the last one, we only briefly present the concepts, assess potential benefits, and point to implementation difficulties.

5.3.1 Value Prediction

As we saw as early as Chapter 2, three types of hazards can slow down pipelined processors:

- *Structural hazards*, such as a paucity of functional units to exploit fully instruction-level parallelism, or limited capacity for structures such as instruction windows, reorder buffer, or physical registers. The increase in capacity is not always an answer, and we discuss this further in Section 5.3.3.
- *Control hazards*, such as those induced by transfer of control instructions. Branch prediction is the main mechanism by which the effect of these hazards is minimized.
- *Data hazards*, such as data dependencies and memory dependencies. Out-of-order processors remove non-RAW dependencies with the use of register renaming. Forwarding and bypassing take care of interdependent instructions that can be scheduled sufficiently far apart without creating bubbles in the pipeline. Load speculation permits one to lessen the number of situations where false memory dependencies could slow down the flow of instructions.

However, we have not been able to deal with true data dependencies whereby a RAW dependency cannot be hidden because there is not enough work for the processor to do before the dependent instruction needs to execute. In the first simple pipeline of Chapter 2, this happened when a load was followed by an instruction requiring the result of the load. In more complex processors, this particular example, along with simple generalizations of such a producer–consumer paradigm, is still a source of performance (*IPC*) degradation. A possible remedy for this true dependence is to predict the value of the result that is needed.

How realistic is it to envision such *value prediction*? If we follow the model of a branch predictor (cf. Figure 4.1) and apply it to value prediction, we have to define the event for which prediction will occur – its *scope* – as well as the predictor's structure and feedback mechanism. Again, as in other forms of prediction, our only way to predict the future is to rely on the recent past. It is therefore necessary to assess

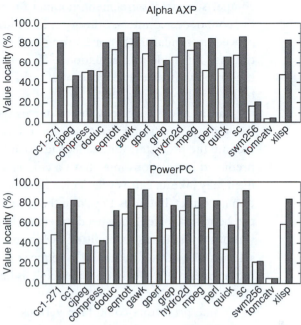

Figure 5.4. Value locality for load instructions. The white bars are strict last values; the black bars are for the recurrence of one of the last 16 values (data from Lipasti and Shen [LS96]).

if (parts of) programs exhibit some *value locality*, for example, the repeated occurrence of a previously seen value in a storage location, or the repetition of a known pattern such as consecutive values that differ from each other by a common stride. Clearly, looking at the whole addressing space is not practical, and realistically value locality must be limited to the architectural registers and the instructions that write into these registers. Figure 5.4 shows the value locality for a variety of benchmarks when the scope is limited to load instructions and the value locality is defined as the fraction of the time the value written in a register was the same as the last one (left bars) or the same as one of the last 16 instances (right bars). As can be seen, in some benchmarks the value locality is quite high, over 40% even with a strict last value, whereas in the remaining three it is quite low (see for example the next to last benchmark *tomcatv*). If the same experiment is repeated for all instructions (that is, unlimited scope), the value locality diminishes significantly.

Leaving aside for a moment how values are predicted, let us assume a predictor structure that holds predicted values for some selected instructions. The hardware structure for the predictor can take forms similar to those for branch prediction, including a confidence counter for whether the prediction should be taken or not. The value predictor can be checked in some stage of the front-end. If there is a predicted value, say for instruction i, it can be stored in the renamed result register, and for subsequent instructions, it looks as if instruction i had executed normally.

Now of course, not only does the value-predicted instruction i need to be executed to be sure that the prediction is correct, but the result of instruction i must be compared with the predicted value. A suggested implementation is to store the prediction in the reservation station when the instruction is issued. At the end of execution of instruction i, its result is compared with the predicted value. If the comparison yields agreement, nothing further needs to be done except to update the confidence counters; otherwise, in addition to the predictor update, a recovery procedure similar to that of a wrong load speculation has to be performed. As was the case for the load speculation, either all instructions following the mispredicted one or only those that depend on it need to be reexecuted, the former alternative being simpler to implement.

Let us assess succinctly the resources required for value prediction in addition to the predictor itself. First, reservation stations have to be wider in order to accommodate the predicted values. Second, each functional unit that generates results for predicted instructions must have a comparator associated with it. The comparison itself may take an extra cycle. This additional time is of no consequence if the prediction is correct, but adds 1 cycle to the recovery penalty. Third, because instructions can be mispredicted, they need to remain in their instruction window or reservation stations until they are committed – which may not be an extra burden if the wakeup–select is speculative, because that requirement is satisfied in that case. Some of these requirements are alleviated if the scope is limited, for example, to load instructions, and if there is a separate load–store instruction queue.

Value predictors could take various forms: last value, stride, context (several past values are recorded and one of them chosen, depending on past patterns), or some hybrid combination of those. Performance evaluation of value prediction according to these schemes is difficult to assess because of the large number of parameters, such as the number of instructions that can be predicted in a single cycle, the penalty for recovery, and the size of the instruction window. Simulations have shown that the context predictors may not be worth the expense. On the other hand, simpler predictors that could potentially increase *IPC* by 5–10% are far from reaching perfect prediction. The gap is due to both the limited coverage of instructions that can be predicted with confidence by simple predictors and the significant penalty incurred on mispredictions. To date, no commercial implementation of value prediction has been proposed, because the performance gains seem too tenuous to be worth the supplemental logic and power that are needed.

5.3.2 Critical Instructions

There are several instances where back-end optimizations should only be performed for instructions whose executions greatly influence the time of execution. These instructions lie on the critical path or, if delayed too much, would become part of the critical path. As potential applications of the identification of these *critical* instructions, the latter could be woken up and selected in priority, or they could be the only ones to which some speculation would be applied. Other possible applications of the detection of critical or noncritical instructions would be the scheduling of instructions in clustered microarchitectures (cf. Section 5.3.3) or steering noncritical instructions towards slower functional units that dissipate less power. In this section, we focus on how to detect critical instructions.

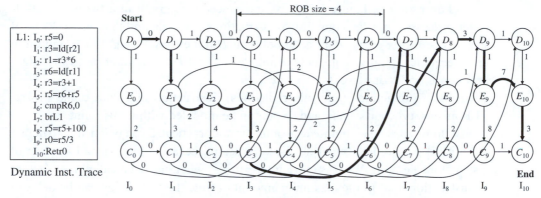

Figure 5.5. Program execution represented as a PERT chart. The critical path is in bold. It is assumed that the branch at instruction I_7 has been mispredicted (from Fields et al. [FBH02]).

The execution of a program can be seen as a weighted acyclic directed graph where nodes represent instructions and arcs represent the dependencies between instructions with weights indicating the interinstruction latency. Such a graph is called a PERT chart or CPM[1] graph in operations research and is used very often for representing and scheduling large projects. Those instructions that lie on the critical path(s) of the PERT chart should have priority, for delaying any one of them would increase the execution time. Scheduling according to the execution of the whole program is of course unrealizable in real time, because the future is not known. So we shall need approximations obtained by looking at segments of programs, the more natural ones being the contents of the instruction window.

Program dependencies are not the only constraints in the program's execution. The limitation on hardware resources brings other dependences (structural hazards). For example, only a limited number of instructions can be concurrent in each stage of the front-end, and similarly, only a limited number of them can be committed in a single cycle. Moreover, the number of execution units that can accommodate instructions of the same type is also restricted. To represent these precedence relations, each instruction can be decomposed as a front-end node, followed by an execution node and ending with a commit node. Such a graph is shown in Figure 5.5, where the front-end nodes are denoted by D (for dispatch, the last stage in the front-end), the execution nodes by E, and the commit nodes by C. Data dependencies and functional unit contention are modeled by edges between E nodes. Limitations on the front-end are modeled by edges between D nodes. To show concurrency in an m-way superscalar, $m-1$ consecutive edges between D nodes will have a weight of 0. The same holds for edges between C nodes for commit limitations. In addition, the size of the reorder buffer (ROB) limits the number of instructions that can be dispatched, and therefore there are edges between some C nodes and some D nodes.

---

[1] PERT stands for the program evaluation review technique, which was used for the first time by the U.S. Navy in the 1950s to monitor the Polaris submarine missile project. CPM stands for the critical path method, which was developed at approximately the same time.

As an example, Figure 5.5 shows the precedence graph in a two-way out-of-order processor that can commit two instructions per cycle and that has an ROB of size 4. Therefore, every other edge between D nodes has a weight of 1, and there are precedence relationships between nodes C_i and D_{i+4} in addition to the edges between E nodes due to data dependencies.

Branch predictions (and mispredictions), instruction and data cache misses, TLB misses, procedure calls, and so on, can be modeled within this framework.

Building such an elaborate tool online is not practical. Even being able to detect the critical path online might not be very useful, because only a small fraction of instructions lie on it. What is more interesting is what has been called the *slack* of an instruction, that is, the maximum amount of time the instruction can be delayed without affecting the overall execution time. However, the computation of the slack of instructions in real time is not any simpler than identifying the critical path. The saving grace is that an approximation of the slack is often sufficient for practical purposes. For example, if the approximation to the slack is above a certain threshold, say 5 cycles, then the instruction can be considered as noncritical. Compiler techniques might be able to yield this approximation. For example, in the code of Figure 5.5, it is pretty clear that instructions I_4 and I_5 do not lie on the critical path and could be computed on a slower integer unit, if one existed, for power-saving purposes.

An interesting approximation, implementable in hardware while the program executes, is to inject a token in an instruction and delay that instruction by a given threshold. The token, represented by a bit passed along during the wakeup select stage, is propagated to the immediate successors of the instruction, but it is removed if it was not on the last arriving edge, that is, the condition that can trigger the issuing of the instruction. After a few instructions (maybe hundreds), the hardware checks whether the token is still alive. If so, the originating instruction was critical with high probability; otherwise, it certainly was not.

A criticality predictor could have a general structure identical to those of the predictors we have already encountered: a table with entries having at least a tag to check whether the instruction should be predicted, and a confidence counter indicating the prediction. An important feature of a criticality predictor is that it does not require a recovery procedure in case of a misprediction. The predictor table can be filled using heuristics such as the following, in order of increasing implementation complexity:

- At each cycle make critical (or increase the confidence counter of) the oldest instruction in the instruction window or in the ROB.
- At each cycle make critical (or increase the confidence counter of) the instruction in the instruction window that has the largest number of immediate dependent instructions, as long as this number is over a certain threshold.
- Use the preceding token heuristic.

Note that these heuristics can be quite conservative. For example, it has been shown via simulation that although in many programs over 80% of the instructions have a slack of over 5 cycles, approximations using only local knowledge yielded only 20% of instructions that were classified as noncritical.

How important is criticality? It is somewhat unclear at this point for the type of processors that we have been looking at. For example, it has been shown that it is not beneficial to try to manage the cache hierarchy by looking at criticality of load instructions rather than locality of data. However, detection of criticality becomes more important for the types of processors introduced in the following.

5.3.3 Clustered Microarchitectures

The width of an out-of-order processor, (i.e., the parameter m in an m-way super-scalar), is limited by a number of factors. Some of these factors are associated with functions performed in the front-end, such as limitations on the instruction fetch bandwidth and on the number of decoders. There are also limitations that become apparent in the back-end, in particular:

- The size of the instruction window(s). In order to find m instructions to be woken up each cycle, the instruction window must be large (and consequently the ROB must be large also). However, large instruction windows are expensive, both in hardware expended and in power dissipated, mainly because of the associative logic needed at each entry.
- In order to increase m, the number of functional units must become larger. This expansion affects forwarding, because the number of point-to-point paths increases proportionally to the square of the number of units. Moreover, with a larger number of functional units, the wires connecting them become longer, and forwarding from any unit to any other unit in a single cycle may not be feasible.
- Finally, the demands on centralized resources will necessarily increase. One particular instance where this is true is in the additional number of read and write ports for the centralized register file.

Each of these drawbacks could be dealt with in isolation. For example, there have been proposals to split the instruction window into a small and fast one for critical instructions (with "critical" defined as in the previous section) and a larger, slower one for noncritical instructions. However, the most promising approach is a clustered microarchitecture.

In the context of microarchitectures, a *cluster* can be defined as a set of functional units, an associated register file, and an instruction window (or reservation stations). Various implementations are possible, depending on whether the register files are completely duplicated or partitioned among the clusters. A generic view of clustered microarchitectures is shown in Figure 5.6.

Let us assume for the time being that each cluster has its own copy of the whole register file. In the case of fully replicated register files, the number of clusters must be small, because the file takes a significant amount of real estate and power; therefore, a crossbar switch for the interconnection network is feasible. Though the

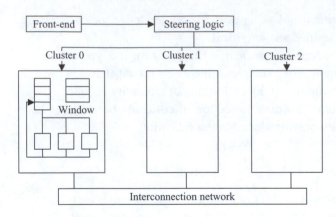

Figure 5.6. Generic clustered micro-architecture. Each cluster has its own register file and instruction window.

register replication may appear costly, it facilitates significantly the operations of the back-end. It is the solution chosen by the designers of the Alpha 21264, where the integer execution unit consists of two clusters, each of them having a full copy of the 80 physical registers.

In a clustered microarchitecture, the front-end needs to perform one more task than in a conventional monolithic out-of-order processor, namely, steering instructions towards the instruction window of one of the clusters. The back-end cluster operations are slightly more complex in that first the results must be copied into the register files of the other clusters, and second the wakeup and select operations have to take into account the latencies caused by intercluster transmissions.

Instruction steering can be done either statically, that is, at compile time, or dynamically by the hardware. The selection of the cluster in which the instruction will execute has a significant influence on performance. Compared to a hypothetical monolithic processor with the same number of functional units and the same issue width, the clustered architecture suffers from two performance effects: (i) some results from one cluster are forwarded to functional units of another cluster with some latency penalty, and (ii) the limitation of resources (functional units) in each cluster requires that the workload be well balanced amongst all clusters.

Instruction steering policies must take into account these two effects, which can sometimes point to conflicting assignments. For example, consider an instruction, most likely a load instruction, whose result is needed by several instructions. From (i) above, steering should be such that the instruction producing a result and the instructions that consume it will be in the same cluster. Furthermore, the instructions that depend on the results from the previous consumers should also be in the same cluster, and so on. Clearly, this will soon violate the requirements for load balancing indicated in (ii). Nonetheless, the general philosophy is to try and assign dependent instructions in the same cluster. However, the number of clusters and the type of interconnect, (i.e., the intercluster latency), play important roles in the steering strategy. A heuristic that works well for a small number of clusters is to assign an instruction to the cluster that will produce the majority of its source operands unless a load imbalance threshold is exceeded. In particular, because memory operations (load–store) are often on the critical path, all instructions that are needed to compute the operand address for the memory operation should be on the same cluster as the memory operation. For a larger number of clusters, a first-fit policy – whereby the instruction window of a cluster is filled by successive instructions and, when it is full, the next cluster's window is filled up, and so on – is a simple method that is good enough.

Back-end operations become more complex when the register file is distributed among clusters. Steering is performed in conjunction with renaming. The decision of which cluster, say cluster c_i, will execute the instruction precedes renaming, and it will be a free register from c_i that will be used as the result register. Its name and c_i are entered in the global renaming map. If a source operand is generated in another cluster, say c_j, the hardware inserts a *copy* instruction that copies the source operand to another free register in c_i. The copy instruction is issued in c_j and follows logically the instruction that generates the contents of the source operand. The copy instruction is also inserted in the ROB so that free registers can be reclaimed. Mapping of the copied register is kept in the renaming table so that if another instruction in c_i needs it, it does not have to be recopied. Note that this requires that the renaming map contain fields for each cluster.

One can assess the performance of a clustered microarchitecture by comparing it with that of a monolithic processor of the same width. Parameters of importance are the number of clusters and the intercluster latency. Designers of the Alpha 21264 report a loss of a few percent or less for their two integer clusters with an intercluster latency of 1 cycle. Simulations using a criticality-based steering policy report average losses of 5% for two-cluster, 10% for three-cluster, and 20% for four-cluster processors when the intercluster latency is 2 cycles and the monolithic processor is 8 wide. These results are certainly encouraging: with a wider processor, the instruction mix that can be issued in a cycle becomes more restricted.

Clustered microarchitectures are an evolutionary path toward getting around the limitations of wide-issue monolithic processors. Important advantages of clusters are that the design of each cluster can be easily replicated and that the programming model is not affected. As we shall see in Chapters 7 and 8, multiprocessing and multithreading are more powerful approaches to increase the parallelism on chip, but they come with more complex designs and with required software modifications.

5.4 Summary

The challenges in sustaining a throughput of m instructions per cycle for an m-way superscalar are also present in the back-end of the pipeline. We have shown the steps that must be taken in the dispatch–issue stages, also known as the wakeup–select process, in order to meet that goal. The larger the designer wants m to be, the more costly it becomes to achieve m issues per cycle, because (i) the instruction window must be larger so that there are enough instructions ready to be executed, and (ii) the number of functional units must also increase. Expanding the instruction window, or equivalently the number of reservation stations, in turn requires more associative logic, thus consuming real estate and power. Having more functional units leads to a quadratic growth in the number of wires for forwarding.

Large instruction windows might potentially create more instructions ready to issue than there are functional units of a certain type. Scheduling of these instructions is generally performed on a "longest in the instruction window" priority, but we saw that there are means to detect the critical instructions, that is, those most likely to reside on the critical path of the computation. A possible solution to the wire problem when there are many functional units is to use clustered microarchitectures.

Among the critical instructions, loads are those most often encountered. Waiting for all stores preceding a load in program order to be completed before issuing the load can significantly impair performance. The use of a store buffer allows issuing of a load once it can check that there is no memory operand conflict with any preceding store. Issuing a load before all memory operands of the preceding stores are known is a speculative mechanism that can be implemented in a variety of ways. The more aggressive solutions to this dynamic memory disambiguation problem require the use of a load buffer and a load–store conflict predictor, and the implementation of a recovery mechanism.

5.5 Further Reading and Bibliographical Notes

Details on the design and implementations of microprocessors cited in this chapter can be found in Keshava and Pentkovski [KP99] for the Intel Pentium III, Hinton et al. [HSUBCRP01] for the Intel Pentium 4, Gochman et al. [GRABKNSSV03] for the Intel Pentium M, Weschler [W06] for the Intel Core microarchitecture, Kessler [K99] for the DEC Alpha 21264, Tendler et al. [TDFLS02] for the IBM Power 4, Keltcher et al. [KMAC03] for the AMD Opteron, and Yeager [Y96] for the MIPS R10000.

Palacharla et al. [PJS97] discuss a number of issues relative to the timing of several stages in the pipeline, in particular, wakeup, select, and forwarding. They also propose a clustered microarchitecture slightly different from the one presented in the text. Stark et al. [SBP00] propose several optimizations for the wakeup and select stages.

Load speculation has been studied thoroughly. Franklin and Sohi [FS96] and subsequently Moshovos et al. [MBVS97] gave comprehensive descriptions of the problem and presented solutions of which the store set scheme, described and evaluated in detail in Chryzos and Emer [CE98], is a direct descendant. (As an aside, [CE98] is a good illustration of how a limit study should be conducted.) Calder and Reinmann [CR00] simulated various load speculation schemes as well as value prediction. Yoaz et al. [YERJ99] investigate the relationships between load speculation and instruction scheduling. Srinivasan et al. [SJLW01] show that locality is more important than criticality when it comes to the management of a first-level cache.

A comprehensive review of value prediction can be found in Shen and Lipasti's book [SL04]; these two authors were early investigators and proponents of the scheme. One of their main publications on the topic is [LS96]. Fields et al. [FBH02] have studied the detection of critical instruction using slack. Applications of criticality to value prediction are used in Tune et al. [TLTC01].

Studies of clustered microarchitectures have been concentrating on the instruction steering mechanisms. Canal et al. [CPG00] studied instruction assignment for a small number of clusters, and Aggarwal and Franklin [AF05] for a larger number. Salverda and Zilles [SZ05] performed a limit study showing where performance losses occur in comparison with an ideal monolithic processor.

It should be mentioned that compiler analysis can be very helpful in scheduling instructions, whether for variable load latencies (e.g., Kerns and Eggers [KE93]), for clustered microarchitectures (e.g., Ozer et al. [OBC98]), or for other aspects of static scheduling. As we saw in Chapter 3, compiler analysis is crucial for VLIW processors.

EXERCISES

1. (Sections 5.1.3 and 5.1.4) Consider a four-way out-of-order superscalar with two integer add–subtract units and one integer multiply unit. At time t there are four instructions in the rename stage:

```
R1 ← R2 + R3    /*latency of add is 1*/
R4 ← R1 − R5    /*latency of sub is 1*/
R6 ← R4 * R7    /*latency of mul is 4*/
R8 ← R2 + R9    /*latency of add is 1*/
```

  (a) Show the instruction sequence after renaming.
  (b) Show a timing diagram of execution, assuming that selection and tag broadcast can be done in a single cycle as in Figure 5.1.
  (c) Repeat part (b), assuming only one integer add–subtract unit. Does it modify the overall execution time?

2. (Section 5.1.4) In the discussion of the wakeup–select steps we have assumed that the execution units have a latency of 1 so that a result tag could be broadcast in the same cycle as the selection. How would you modify the entries in the reservation stations so that other latencies can be considered? You can assume that the latency of a given operation is known during the decode stage.

3. (Section 5.2.2) We have noted that the store buffer is implemented as a circular queue. Should the load buffer also be a circular queue?

4. (Section 5.2.2) In the optimistic load speculation approach, a speculative load must be entered in the load buffer even if a match was found in an entry in the store buffer in state CO. Why?

5. (Section 5.2.2) In the store set scheme, when merging was necessary, we chose to merge in the store set of the instruction with smallest index. Show what would happen if we chose to always merge in the store set of the store instruction (start with the example of Figure 5.3(c), and add a conflict to show instability). Repeat, but choose the store set of the load instruction.

6. (Section 5.2.2) What is the performance effect of aliasing in the SSIT table in the store set scheme? Discuss the cases for store aliasing and for load aliasing.

Programming Project

1. (Section 5.2.2) Using a simulator, perform limit studies on the performance gains that can be attained with the load speculation schemes of Section 5.2.2. You will have to assume a penalty for misprediction recovery commensurate with the other parameters of the simulator.
    (a) For scheme 1, assume an infinite L1 instruction cache.
    (b) For scheme 2, assume an infinite load table predictor.
    (c) For scheme 3, assume infinite SSIT and LFST tables.

REFERENCES

[AF05] A. Aggarwal and M. Franklin, "Scalability Aspects of Instruction Distribution Algorithms for Clustered Processors," *IEEE Trans. on Parallel and Distributed Systems*, 16, 10, Oct. 2005, 944–955

[CE98] G. Chryzos and J. Emer, "Memory Dependence Prediction Using Store Sets," *Proc. 25th Int. Symp. on Computer Architecture*, 1998, 142–153

[CPG00] R. Canal, J. M. Parcerisa, and A. Gonzales, "Dynamic Cluster Assignment Mechanisms," *Proc. 6th Int. Symp. on High-Performance Computer Architecture*, 2000, 133–141

[CR00] B. Calder and G. Reinmann, "A Comparative Survey of Load Speculation Architectures," *Journal of Instruction-Level Parallelism*, 1, 2000, 1–39

[FBH02] B. Fields, R. Bodik, and M. Hill, "Slack: Maximizing Performance under Technological Constraints," *Proc. 29th Int. Symp. on Computer Architecture*, 2002, 47–58

[FS96] M. Franklin and G. Sohi, "A Hardware Mechanism for Dynamic Reordering of Memory References," *IEEE Trans. on Computers*, 45, 6, Jun. 1996, 552–571

[GRABKNSSV03] S. Gochman, R. Ronen, I. Anati, R. Berkovits, T. Kurts, A. Naveh, A. Saeed, Z. Sperber, and R. Valentine, "The Intel Pentium M Processor: Microarchitecture and Performance," *Intel Tech. Journal*, 07, 2, May 2003, 21–39

[HSUBCKR01] G. Hinton, D. Sager, M. Upton, D. Boggs, D. Carmean, A. Kyker, and P. Roussel, "The Microarchitecture of the Pentium 4 Processor," *Intel Tech. Journal*, Feb. 2001, 1–12

[K99] R. Kessler, "The Alpha 21264 Microprocessor," *IEEE Micro*, 19, 2, Apr. 1999, 24–36

[KE93] D. Kerns and S. Eggers, "Balanced Scheduling: Instruction Scheduling when Memory Latency is Uncertain," *Proc. ACM SIGPLAN Conf. on Programming Language Design and Implementation, SIGPLAN Notices*, 28, 6, Jun. 1993, 278–289.

[KMAC03] C. Keltcher, J. McGrath, A. Ahmed, and P. Conway, "The AMD Opteron for Multiprocessor Servers," *IEEE Micro*, 23, 2, Apr. 2003, 66–76

[KP99] J. Keshava and V. Pentkovski, "Pentium III Processor Implementation Tradeoffs," *Intel Tech. Journal*, 2, May 1999

[LS96] M. Lipasti and J. Shen, "Exceeding the Dataflow Limit with Value Prediction," *Proc. 29th Int. Symp. on Microarchitecture*, 1996, 226–237

[MBVS97] A. Moshovos, S. Breach, T. Vijaykumar, and G. Sohi, "Dynamic Speculation and Synchronization of Data Dependences," *Proc. 24th Int. Symp. on Computer Architecture*, 1997, 181–193

[OBC98] E. Ozer, S. Banerjia, and T. Conte, "Unified Assign and Schedule: A New Approach to Scheduling for Clustered Register File Microarchitectures," *Proc. 31st Int. Symp. on Microarchitecture*, 1998, 308–315

[PJS97] S. Palacharla, N. Jouppi, and J. Smith, "Complexity-Effective Superscalar Processors," *Proc. 24th Int. Symp. on Computer Architecture*, 1997, 206–218

[SBP00] J. Stark, M. Brown, and Y. Patt, "On Pipelining Dynamic Instruction Scheduling Logic," *Proc. 34th Int. Symp. on Microarchitecture*, 2000, 57–66

[SJLW01] S. Srinivasan, D.-C. Ju, A. Lebeck, and C. Wilkerson, "Locality vs. Criticality," *Proc. 28th Int. Symp. on Computer Architecture*, 2001, 132–143

[SL04] J. P. Shen and M. Lipasti, *Modern Processor Design Fundamentals of Superscalar Processors*, McGraw-Hill, 2004

[SZ05] P. Salverda and C. Zilles, "A Criticality Analysis of Clustering in Superscalar Processors," *Proc. 38th Int. Symp. on Microarchitecture*, 2005, 55–66

[TDFLS02] J. Tendler, J. Dodson, J. Fields, Jr., H. Le, and B. Sinharoy, "POWER 4 System Microarchitecture," *IBM Journal of Research and Development*, 46, 1, Jan. 2002, 5–25

[TLTC01] E. Tune, D. Liang, D. Tullsen, and B. Calder, "Dynamic Prediction of Critical Path Instructions," *Proc. 7th Int. Symp. on High-Performance Computer Architecture*, 2001, 185–195

[W06] O. Weschler, "Inside Intel Core Microarchitecture," Intel White Paper, 2006, http://download.intel.com/technology/architecture/new_architecture_06.pdf

[Y96] K. Yeager, "The MIPS R10000 Superscalar Microprocessor," *IEEE Micro*, 16, 2, Apr. 1996, 28–41

[YERJ99] A. Yoaz, M. Erez, R. Ronen, and S. Jourdan, "Speculation Techniques for Improving Load Related Instruction Scheduling," *Proc. 26th Int. Symp. on Computer Architecture*, 1999, 42–53

6 The Cache Hierarchy

We reviewed the basics of caches in Chapter 2. In subsequent chapters, when we looked at instruction fetch in the front-end and data load–store operations in the back-end, we assumed most of the time that we had cache hits in the respective first-level instruction and data caches. It is time now to look at the memory hierarchy in a more realistic fashion. In this chapter, our focus is principally on the cache hierarchy.

The challenge for an effective memory hierarchy can be summarized by two technological constraints:

- With processors running at a few gigahertz, main memory latencies are now of the order of several hundred cycles.
- In order to access first-level caches in 1 or 2 cycles, their size and associativity must be severely limited.

These two facts point to a hierarchy of caches: relatively small-size and small-associativity first-level instruction and data caches (L1 caches); a large second-level on-chip cache with access an order of magnitude slower than L1 accesses (L2 cache generally unified, i.e., holding both instructions and data); often in high-performance servers a third-level cache (L3) off chip, with latencies approaching 100 cycles; and then main memory, with latencies of a few hundred cycles. The goal of the design of a cache hierarchy is to keep a latency of one or two cycles for L1 caches and to hide as much as possible the latencies of higher cache levels and of main memory. At the same time, techniques that will improve the hit ratio at any of the cache levels are sought for. In essence, the wall in the *memory wall* (cf. Section 2.2) is replaced by a series of hurdles.

Starting with the L1 caches, we will first look at how to achieve fast access, taking into account that the address generated by the processor is a virtual address (recall Section 2.3.1, Figure 2.20). We will then present means to improve on the L1 hit ratios by hardware and software techniques such as implicitly increasing associativity with *victim caches* or column-associative caches, code placement in instruction caches, and way prediction for set-associative caches.

We will then study means to hide latency, mostly between L2 and the next level in the hierarchy. The main technique is *prefetching*, either via hardware mechanisms or with compiler help or both. Although not exactly in the same vein, allowing more than one cache miss to be in progress is also a way to hide latency. Because out-of-order processors can feed the back-end with instructions following stalled ones, an L1 data cache miss should not prevent other memory instructions from accessing the memory hierarchy. The caches must become *lockup-free*.

We then look at interactions between the cache levels, and notably into shielding of L1 from unnecessary checks required for cache consistency during I/O transfers and actions from other processors in a multiprocessing environment (the full treatment of cache coherency in multiprocessor environments will be done in Chapter 7). We define the *multilevel inclusion property* and show how it can be enforced. We also look at possible trends in the design of large on-chip caches, notably high associativity and the concomitant problem of replacement algorithms, as well as the fact that with large caches wire lengths may impose different access times for parts of the same cache, giving rise to nonuniform cache architectures (NUCAs).

We shall conclude this chapter by looking at advances in main memory design. Buffering to improve latency, high-bandwidth channels, and intelligent memory controllers will be discussed.

6.1 Improving Access to L1 Caches

6.1.1 Physical and Virtual Indexing

In Chapter 2 we looked at caches that were indexed with physical (or real) addresses and with tags that contained the high-order bits of physical addresses. Therefore, access to the cache had to be performed after a TLB access (with a hit in the best case) for the virtual-to-physical address translation. Although it appears that this translation requires an additional pipeline step when fetching an instruction, recall that instructions are often fetched sequentially within the same cache line, from a branch target buffer that contains the next instructions' physical addresses, or from computation on real addresses. Therefore, the translation, when needed, can easily be performed in parallel with the delivery of previous instructions.

In the case of data access, there are three possible organizational choices to access the cache and check for a hit or a miss, namely, use:

- Physical index and physical tags (the organization that we have seen so far).
- Virtual index and virtual tags.
- Virtual index and physical tags.

We discuss each of these in turn, using load operations as the primary example (it is left it to the reader to see that using a physical index and virtual tags makes no sense). We also assume a TLB hit. If there is a TLB miss, it must be resolved before continuing.

Physical Index and Physical Tags
In the discussion that follows, let 2^k be the page size; then the last k bits of the virtual and physical addresses are the same. If the cache can be accessed using only

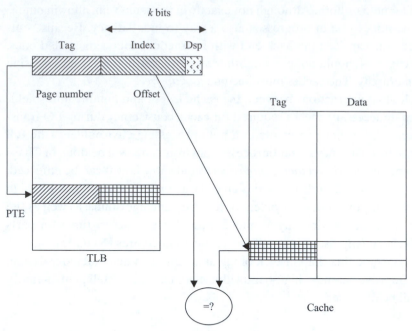

Figure 6.1. Accessing the TLB and the (direct-mapped) cache in parallel.

these k bits, then the first and third organizations above are identical. Assuming a
direct-mapped cache of size 2^k or less, TLB and cache accesses can occur in parallel as shown in Figure 6.1. The low-order $k - d$ bits of the virtual address are used
to access the cache (2^d is the line size), and the remaining high-order bits are used
to access the TLB and check whether there is a TLB hit or a TLB miss. Thus in a
first pipeline stage the TLB and the cache are accessed in parallel. At the end of
that stage, data are forwarded to the register (in case of a load) unless there is a
TLB miss. During the second stage, the tag in the cache is compared with the physical address in the TLB entry. If there is a mismatch, the data in the register are
voided and a replay mechanism is initiated, because we have a cache miss. Otherwise, the execution proceeds normally. In essence, a pipeline stage has been saved
in the common case of a TLB hit followed by a cache hit.

In the case of a direct-mapped cache, the comparison involves a single tag. This
good news is not sufficient to overcome the fact that an L1 cache of size 4 or 8 KB,
the usual page sizes, is too small. Therefore, assuming that the page size cannot
be changed, two solutions are possible: increase the associativity, or increase the
number of bits that won't be translated.

Increasing associativity is limited by the time it takes to perform the comparison step and the levels of multiplexing necessary to latch the correct data into the
register. A possibility is to have large associativity and to predict the set that is being
referenced. This *way prediction* can be extremely simple, like the MRU policy that
predicts the most recently used set as the next one to be referenced. In case of a misprediction, the other tags accessed with the same index need to be checked. Such a

mechanism can be used for an L2 or an off-chip cache, but its accuracy is not good enough for an L1 data cache. Moreover, there is a need to access the information giving the MRU set, which may lengthen the comparison step, because there is a predictive structure to be accessed and this access cannot take place until the cache index has been determined. An alternative is to have a predictor that can be accessed using an XOR combination of bits from the PC of the load and from the index register used in computing the effective address. Both are known long before the actual cache access needs to take place, and therefore the technique is adequate for L1 caches.

Instead of increasing associativity so that TLB and cache can be accessed in parallel, we can increase the number of bits that are the same in the physical and virtual addresses. One way to do this is to restrict the mapping of virtual pages to physical frames so that l additional bits are common in the physical and virtual addresses. Now the direct-mapped cache that can be accessed concurrently with the TLB has a capacity of 2^{k+l} bytes. In this *page coloring* technique, the mapping for the paging system is slightly more restrictive, and a number of heuristics can be devised to mitigate the effects of potential increase in the page fault rate. An alternative to page coloring is to once again use prediction, that is, have a structure that predicts the l extra bits. The prediction can be similar to the way prediction described in the previous paragraph or can use the low-order bits of the virtual address, as in the *TLB-slice* mechanism used in the MIPS R6000.

Virtual Index and Virtual Tags

Why not use the virtual address both for indexing and for tags? At first glance this scheme, that we call *virtual cache*, is attractive in that the TLB would have to be accessed only on a cache miss. However, there are a number of drawbacks that make this solution more complex than it seems.

First, the TLB contains information about page protection and recency of use that must be checked or updated on each cache reference. So the TLB has to be accessed. (However, in the case of virtual addressing that can be done in parallel with the cache access without difficulty.) Second, at each context switch a new virtual address space is activated and therefore the contents of the cache are stale. Either the cache must be flushed on each context switch, or a PID (recall Section 2.3) must be appended to the tag. Still, flushing part of the cache is required when PIDs are recycled back. Third, and most importantly, is what has been called the *synonym* problem.

The synonym problem arises when two virtual addresses correspond to the same physical address. Such synonyms occur when some segment of code or data is shared among processes and their positions in their respective address spaces are not the same (the general case). In a virtual cache, two synonyms might be cached simultaneously. If one of them is modified, the second one becomes inconsistent. Synonyms can be avoided by a variant of page coloring: for a direct-mapped cache indexed with k bits (or equivalently an m-way set-associative cache indexed with $k - \log m$ bits), the software requires that these k bits be the same for synonyms. Of course, this requires that the software know about potential synonyms, which is easier for instruction caches than for data caches (hence the virtual instruction cache in the Sun UltraSPARC systems running under Unix). A hardware solution is to prevent synonyms from being loaded in the cache. On a cache miss, all lines in the cache that could contain a synonym are checked. This requires that the tags of these lines be translated and checked against the physical address of the missing item. If there is a match, the in-cache synonym is invalidated and its contents are stored in the line that the missing item maps to.

> **EXAMPLE 1:** We have an 8 K direct-mapped virtual D-cache with a 16 byte line size; hence, there are 512 lines. The page size is 4 KB. Page 4 of process A and page 17 of process B map to the same physical page, say physical page 14. As can readily be seen (cf. Figure 6.1), from the paging system viewpoint the page offset is 12 bits long and the virtual page number is 20 bits (we have a 32-bit architecture). From the cache viewpoint, the displacement is 4 bits and the index is $13 - 4 = 9$ bits. Therefore, the lowest bit of the page number is part of the index.

Assume that the cache is initially empty and process A reads line 8 of its page 4, that is, line 8 of physical page 14. It will be stored in cache line 8. Now process B reads line 8 of its page 17, again line 8 of physical page 14. Without further checking, it will be stored in line 264 $(256 + 8)$. Now process B writes its line 8, a write hit, resulting in two inconsistent values of line 8 of physical page 14 in the cache, that is, an instance of the synonym problem. It will be avoided if on a cache miss two checks are made: (i) the first one, performed on virtual tags to ensure that there is a miss (this would be the tag at line 264), and (ii) a comparison between the physical page number of the missing item (here page 14) and the physical tag(s) of all other locations in the cache that could potentially be synonyms (here the physical page number corresponding to the virtual tag of line 8).

In the case of a cache hierarchy where the L2 is physically addressed and tagged (always the case), the tag in L2 can be augmented with the identifications of the L1 lines (there may be more than one if the L2 line size is a multiple of the L1 line size) that contain the same memory image as the L2 line. On a miss, checking is done at the L2 level, so that synonyms in L1 are avoided.

Another drawback of the virtual cache is that I/O addresses are physical. As we shall see, the mechanisms used in the interaction between I/O devices and the memory subsystem, as well as those providing cache coherency in multiprocessor systems, are handled using physical addresses.

In sum, the disadvantages of virtual data caches are sufficiently severe so that they are practically not used.

Virtual Index and Physical Tags

This last scheme is a combination of the preceding two. If page coloring is not implemented or not sufficient to ensure that the virtual bits used in the indexing will remain unchanged after the translation, we still have the possibility of synonyms.

The hardware or software methods just described can be used to avoid them. In a memory system with a cache hierarchy, the L2 scheme is preferred because it meshes well with the I/O and multiprocessor coherency requirements that will be seen in Chapter 7. An alternative, implemented in the IBM PowerPC 620, is to have a large associativity while limiting the mapping in a way similar to page coloring but applied to the cache. For example for an m-way set-associative cache of capacity $m \cdot 2^k$, we can enforce that each line in the set has a pattern of l virtual bits ($l < m$) above the lower k bits that is different from those of all other lines. On a reference to the cache, the set is determined by the k untranslated bits, and a prediction is made in a fully associative way on the m patterns of the l virtual bits. Of course, complete tag matching is done in the TLB at the same time. The prediction, that is, the match on l bits, is quite accurate. The drawback of the method is a small potential loss in the number of data that can be stored because lines mapping to the same set with the same l-bit pattern cannot be in cache simultaneously.

6.1.2 "Faking" Associativity

Checking for a hit or miss is one component of the time it takes to access the cache. The second component of prime importance for cache performance is the miss ratio. As we showed in Chapter 2 (Figure 2.17), there is a significant drop in the miss ratio when a direct-mapped cache is replaced by a two-way set-associative one with the same capacity and same line size. In the case of L1 caches, the drop is less significant when one passes from two-way to four-way set associativity, but it is still not negligible.

Providing more associativity to a direct-mapped cache can be done in one of two ways: (i) use the same cache structure, but slightly modify the tagging system so that two lines that would conflict in a direct-mapped structure can be present concurrently, or (ii) add a small buffer that can contain recently replaced lines from the direct-mapped cache.

One instance of the first scheme is the *column-associative* cache. The basic idea is to consider a direct-mapped cache as two independent halves. On a memory reference, say a load, the cache is accessed using the usual index. On a hit, we are done. On a miss, the address is rehashed and a second access takes place. On a hit in this second access, the entries for the first miss and the hit are swapped at the same time as data are forwarded to the register. The swapping is to ensure an LRU ordering for the two entries. Note, however, that it took one or maybe two more cycles to perform the whole operation. On a miss on the second access, we have a bona fide cache miss. The missing line is loaded in the location of the second miss and then swapped with the line in the first half, again to ensure LRU ordering. If we want to limit the second access to a single extra cycle, the rehash must be simple. In the column-associative cache, the rehash is simply to flip the high-order bit of the index. As a consequence, this bit must be also part of the tag.

However, we are not quite finished. Consider the string of references $a, b, c, b, c, b, c, \ldots$ where a and b index in the same location and c indexes in the bit-flipped location from *a* and *b*. In a regular two-way set-associative cache with LRU replacement, we would have misses on the first references to *a*, *b*, and *c* and then a series of hits, because *b* and *c* would be resident in the cache from there on. In the column-associative cache as we have presented it so far, we would first have a miss on *a*, then a miss on *b* with now *b* in the first half and *a* in the second. The reference to *c* accesses the location where *a* is currently stored first, because *c*'s high-order index bit is the opposite of *a* and *b*'s. Since the reference is a miss, a second access is performed at the location where *b* is stored. On this second miss, *b* is ejected; *c* takes its place and then is swapped with *a*, which itself is returned to its original location. But the next access to *b* will first check the location where *a* is now, and the reader can see that *c* will be ejected, and so on. In effect we have a miss at every reference as would happen with a direct-mapped cache. The fix is to append a *rehash bit* that indicates, when it is on, that the entry is not in its original correct location (the case for *a* in the above example after it has been swapped with *b*). When a cache access is performed (in our example, the reference *c*) and there is a miss on the first access to an entry with the rehash bit on (in our example, *a*), we know that there will be a miss in the second access (here, to the location containing *b*) and that the LRU entry is the one just accessed (in our case, *a*). Therefore, we can eject the LRU entry and replace it with the line for which there was a miss. The rehash bit for the latter is set to off. The reader can verify that the only misses are the initial ones to *a*, *b*, and *c*.

COLUMN-ASSOCIATIVE CACHE ALGORITHM. An entry in the cache consists of the tuple {tag, rehash_bit, data}. An entry has an index, and a new entry at line *index* in the cache is filled by the command enter(*index*, *tag*, *rehash_bit*, data). A cache access is decomposed into its *index* and *tag_ref*:

```
if tag(index) = tag_ref then begin hit; exit end; /*hit on first access */
if rehash_bit(index) then begin miss;                /*miss since rehash on*/
                           enter(index, tag_ref, false, data); exit
                 end;
index1 = fliphighbit(index);
if tag(index1) = tag_ref then begin hit;             /*hit on second access*/
                           swap [entry(index1), entry(index)];
                           rehash_bit (index1) ← true; exit
                 end;
enter(index1, tag(ref), true, data);    /*miss on second access*/
swap [entry(index1), entry(index)];
rehash_bit (index1) ← true;
```

The miss ratio for a column-associative cache is smaller than that of a direct-mapped cache of same capacity and line size. On the other hand, the access time to

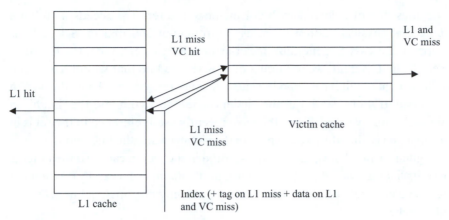

Figure 6.2. Operation of a victim cache.

the second half of the cache is longer. How these two opposing factors influence the average access time to the cache, and the memory subsystem in general, depends on the relative hit ratios and the latency to the next level of the memory hierarchy. As for a comparison with a two-way set-associative cache with the same capacity and line size, the miss ratio of the column-associative cache approaches that of a two-way cache (in fact, in some pathological situations it can be smaller; see the exercises). If a column-associative cache were selected over a two-way cache it would be because the processor cycle time would have to be lengthened if the two-way cache were chosen instead of a direct-mapped cache. This does not appear to be the case anymore in modern microprocessors, but the technique could be applied to other cachelike structures such as TLBs or branch predictors with tags.

Column-associative caches could be expanded to higher associativity, but the rehash bit scheme would not carry over. A proposal to improve the hit ratio of two-way set-associative caches is to use different hashing functions for each of the two banks. In a *skewed-associative* cache, one bank is accessed using the usual index bits while the other is accessed through some XOR combinations of PC bits. The advantage is that conflict misses that would occur in the standard version of set associativity have a low probability of happening in the skewed version because of interbank dispersion (i.e., the hashing function would yield a different set in the second bank) and local dispersion (i.e., lines with consecutive addresses might be placed more randomly). Experiments have shown that miss ratios of two-way skewed associative caches were similar to those of four-way standard set-associative caches, but longer access times and the complexity of the hashing have discouraged industrial implementations.

The second option that we mentioned was to add a small buffer that will contain recently replaced lines from the L1 cache. Such a buffer is called a *victim cache*. The victim cache is a small fully associative cache that will be accessed after there is a miss in the L1 cache (Figure 6.2). The victim cache is behind the L1 cache and before the next level in the memory hierarchy, that is, generally the L2 cache.

In the presence of a victim cache, a memory reference proceeds as follows (we assume that physical addresses are used throughout and that the L1 cache is direct-mapped; it is easy to generalize to set-associative caches). First, the L1 cache is accessed. If there is a hit, we are done; otherwise, the line that would have been replaced in a regular direct-mapped cache becomes the victim. Then the victim cache is probed. If there is a hit in the victim cache, the victim and the line hit in the victim cache are swapped. Thus, the most recently used reference in the set is in the direct-mapped cache. If there is a miss in the victim cache, the line that is evicted from the regular cache, that is, the victim, is stored in the victim cache (if the latter is full, one of its lines is evicted to the next level in the memory hierarchy). When the miss is resolved in a higher level of the memory hierarchy, the missing line is sent to the regular cache.

VICTIM CACHE. An L1 cache access is decomposed into its *index* and *tag_ref*. A victim cache (*VC*) access is an associative search of all tags in *VC* (array *VC.tag*)

L1 Access

```
if tag(index) = tag_ref then begin hit; exit end/*hit in L1*/
```

VC Access

```
victim ← line(index)  /*index is concatenated with the tag of the victim */
          if (one of VC.tag[*] = concat(tag_ref,index), say i then
             begin swap (victim, VC[i]); /*hit in VC*/
             modify_LRU(VC); exit
             end
```

Miss

```
Select LRU line in VC, say j;
     Writeback(VC[j]);
         VC[j] ← victim;
```

Because the victim cache is fully associative, the tag of a victim cache entry consists of the whole physical address except for the d least significant bits, which are used for the displacement within a line. On a swap, the tag of the victim line in the cache will be concatenated with its index, and the index will be stripped from the line in the victim cache when replacing a line in the cache. In general, accessing (swapping) the victim cache takes one extra cycle, but it is worth it if misses can be substantially reduced. Experiments show that small victim caches (say four to eight entries) are often quite effective in removing conflict misses for small (say less than 32 K) direct-mapped caches. The first victim cache was implemented for the HP 7100. In its successor, the HP 7200, the victim cache has 64 entries and can be accessed as fast as a large off-chip L1 data cache of 1 MB (this is 1995 vintage with both the processor and the cache clocked at 120 MHz).

Larger victim caches have been proposed to assist L2 caches. However, a related concept, *exclusive caching,* is preferred. We shall return to the topic in Section 6.3.

6.1.3 Code and Data Reordering

In an out-of-order processor, data cache read misses might be tolerated if there are enough instructions not dependent on the data being read that can still proceed. On an instruction cache miss, though, the front-end has to stall until the instructions can be retrieved, hopefully from the next level in the memory hierarchy. Thus implementing techniques to reduce as much as possible the number of I-cache misses would be very useful. In this section, we present one such technique, a software-based approach called *code reordering*, whose primary goal from the I-cache viewpoint is to reduce the number of potential conflict misses.

The basic idea in code reordering for improving cache performance, and also for reducing branch misprediction penalties, is to reorder procedures and basic blocks within procedures rather than letting the original compiler order be the default. The reordering is based on statistics gathered through profiling. Therefore, the method can only be used for production programs; but this is not much of a deterrent, for production programs are those for which the best performance is needed.

Procedure reordering attempts to place code that is commonly used together close in space, thus reducing the number of conflict misses. For example, in the very simple case where procedure P is the only one to call procedure Q, it would be beneficial to have P and Q occupy consecutive portions of the I-cache. The input to the procedure reordering algorithm is a *call graph*, an undirected graph where the nodes represent the procedures and the weighted edges are the frequencies of calls between the procedures. The most common algorithm is "closest is best," using a greedy approach to do the placement. At each step of the algorithm, the two nodes connected by the edge of highest weight are merged. A merged node consists of an ordered list of all the procedures that compose it. Remaining edges that leave the merged node are coalesced. Procedures, or sets of procedures, say A and B, that are selected are merged, taking into account which of the four possible orderings AB, $A_{reverse}B$, $AB_{reverse}$, $A_{reverse}B_{reverse}$ yields the heaviest connection between the procedures at the boundaries of the two sets.

Basic block reordering is nothing more than trying to maximize the number of fall-through branches. From the cache viewpoint, its advantage is that increasing the length of uninterrupted code sequences allows a more efficient prefetching of lines from the cache into the instruction buffer as well as prefetching between the cache and the next level in the memory hierarchy (see Section 6.2.1). Additionally, because only taken branches are stored in the BTB, the latter can be better utilized. Finally, as we saw in Chapter 4, the correct prediction of taken branches requires an extra cycle in most deeply pipelined microarchitectures, a penalty that is not present for successfully predicted not-taken branches.

Basic block reordering within a procedure proceeds in a manner similar to that of procedure reordering, except that now the call graph is a directed graph, that is, the positions of blocks within a merged node are dictated by the original control flow. Further refinements, using techniques similar to page coloring but applied to the line level, can modify the resulting order so that blocks in concurrently executing procedures are put in nonconflicting positions.

The more refined algorithms give significant improvements in the hit rate of small direct-mapped I-caches. Because most I-caches today are larger than those used in the experiments and because many I-caches are two-way set-associative, the improvements in hit rate might be marginal in modern microprocessors. However, code sequentiality is important for the front-end, as we saw in Section 4.2.1 when considering the impediments in instruction fetch bandwidth.

Cache-conscious data placement is more complex. Algorithms must be devised for the heap, the stack, and global variables. Profiling becomes more of an issue. Consider a compiler like GCC. It performs its operations in roughly the same order for all programs; therefore, code reordering should be beneficial. On the other hand, the data that it uses, such as symbol tables, can be of wildly different sizes; thus data reordering might work for some compilations and not for others. In general, in order to optimize the D-cache performance, knowledge of the type of program by the programmer or the compiler is often required. For example, in linear algebra programs, changes in the code allow traversals of arrays that result in less cache misses. In addition to these transformations, other compiler optimizations can be used, such as *cache tiling*, which divides the loop iteration space into smaller blocks (tiles) and ensures better reuse of array elements within each tile. Another example is the design of sorting algorithms taking into account the cache hierarchy capacity and organization. In both the linear algebra and sorting programs, not only has the cache become exposed to the user (compiler) as a feature of the architecture, but in addition the cache geometries are now inputs to the programs.

6.2 Hiding Memory Latencies

In the previous section, we looked at ways to reduce cache access time and to increase hit ratios in small L1 caches. We now turn our attention to techniques to hide latency.

6.2.1 Prefetching

Until now we have considered only on-demand caching, that is, a cache miss had to be detected before filling in a cache line. *Prefetching* is a predictive technique that attempts to bring data or instructions into their respective caches before their use, so they can be accessed without delay. Prefetching can be implemented with either software instructions or hardware assists. It can be applied to both instructions and data. Prefetching can be performed between any levels of the memory hierarchy, including paging between main memory and disk. However, in this chapter we restrict ourselves to the cache hierarchy in a single-processor environment. Prefetching mechanisms have also been developed in the context of multiprocessors. We shall return to this subject in Chapters 7 and 8.

Because prefetching is predictive, we could try and apply the predictor model that we presented in Section 4.1.1 for branch prediction, but tailoring it now to prefetching. However, there are fundamental differences between the two predictors that prevent the use of the same model. First, the events on which prefetching will be activated are dependent on the technique that is used. For example, as we shall see, prefetching can be done subsequent to a cache miss, or on the occurrence of specific instructions, or on scanning the contents of some cache line. This is in contrast with branch prediction, where the predictor is looked up every time new instructions are fetched. Second, and maybe most importantly, a misprediction in prefetching impacts performance only. The correctness of the program is not at stake. There is no need for a recovery procedure. Of course, we know that this is not the case for branch prediction. As a third difference, success or failure of the prefetch prediction may be known only thousands of cycles after the event, not within a few cycles as in branch prediction, and therefore a feedback mechanism is much harder to implement. Furthermore, the prefetching predictors (from now on abbreviated as prefetchers) do not have a structure that can easily take advantage of such feedback.

Prefetchers can be assessed on three criteria:

- *Accuracy*. This is the ratio

$$\frac{useful\ prefetches}{number\ of\ prefetches\ generated}$$

- *Coverage*. This is the ratio

$$\frac{useful\ prefetches}{number\ of\ misses\ when\ prefetching\ is\ turned\ off}$$

- *Timeliness*. This criterion involves whether the prefetch was too early, thus displacing some useful data in the cache that have to be reloaded before using the prefetched data (this double jeopardy situation is called *cache pollution*), or too late because the data were not yet there when they were needed (such cycles are called *hit–wait* cycles). However, even in the presence of hit–wait cycles, the prefetch is useful.

Note that we can trade off accuracy for coverage and vice versa. At the end, though, what counts is the performance advantage incurred by the prefetcher that was used.

The goal of prefetching is to hide memory latency by increasing the hit ratio in a timely manner. This responds to the "why" of prefetching; we should also answer, or show the alternatives for, the "what," "when," and "where" before showing some of the "how." Ideally, *what* we would like to prefetch is a semantic object, as in the true segmented schemes of virtual memory (recall Section 2.3.1). However, in practice one or more cache lines will be the units of prefetching. The "when" question is twofold: the first part refers to timeliness as just defined (prefetching should ideally occur in such a way that the item being prefetched is in the cache just before its use), and the second part deals with the event that triggers the prefetch. As mentioned earlier, there are many possible such events. *Where* the prefetch item should be stored refers not only to which level of the cache hierarchy should be the recipient of the prefetched item, but also to whether there should be special prefetch buffers that can (exclusively) receive the prefetched information.

Before proceeding to describe a number of prefetching schemes, it is important to warn about some potential disadvantages of prefetching. Independently of the type of prefetcher, prefetch events will compete for resources that are used for regular memory operations. For example, before prefetching a line, one must be sure that it is not already in the cache. In order not to penalize regular memory operations, this might require an extra port to access the cache tags. As another example, prefetches will contend for the memory bus with regular load and store instructions. Priority must be given to the latter, and moreover, as much concurrency as possible should be allowed in transfers between memory levels. The caches therefore must be lockup-free (cf. Section 6.2.2 in this chapter).

Software Prefetching

All powerful microprocessors today have a prefetch instruction in their ISA in one form or another. The simplest one, for example in the Alpha architecture, is a load instruction with the result register being hardwired to 0. This load is called *non-binding*, in contrast with loads to other registers that result in a binding change to the processor state. The line that contains the word being addressed is fetched from the level in the memory hierarchy where it currently resides and is percolated down to the lowest level in the L1 D-cache. More sophisticated prefetch instructions, with various names such as "fetch" and "touch," perform the same operation with the possibility of designating the level in the cache hierarchy where the prefetch should stop, as for example in the Intel Itanium. Some prefetch instructions, associated with the subset of ISA instructions related to multimedia (SSE for Intel, VIS for Sun), work on streams of data (cf. the stream buffers discussed later in this section).

The challenge in software prefetching is related to timeliness. Where should the compiler or programmer insert the instructions so that the data arrive in time? Loops in programs that traverse arrays are prime locations where the prefetch instructions can be used. A simple example is shown in Figure 6.3. Since a prefetch instruction brings a line that will in general contain several elements of the array, often the prefetches should be prevented from occurring every iteration, as would happen in the naive prefetching of Figure 6.3. Thus, either the control structure of the program must be modified with a test (predicate) preceding the prefetch instruction, or the loops must be unrolled as many times as there are array elements in a cache line. Attempts have also been made to generate prefetches in pointer-based structures. The difficulty is that most often loops are quite tight in programs that use linked data structures, and there is very little leeway to generate prefetches unless the algorithms are rewritten with prefetching in mind.

Performancewise, some of the gains that can be incurred via software prefetching must be balanced against the overhead – namely, the number of additional instructions that need to be executed – and register pressure. At the very least, prefetch instructions themselves are now part of the computational load, and some register must be used as a component of the prefetch address. If other instructions are used as a predicate surrounding the prefetch, instructions to compute the predicate become part of the overhead. This can become quite costly, as in the example in

Figure 6.3, where the predicate involves an expensive modulo operation. If loops are unrolled to minimize the number of extra instructions as in the last segment in Figure 6.3, the code is expanded and may lead to more instruction cache misses. Moreover, in loop unrolling, registers are at a premium, and the extra registers needed for the prefetch may lead to structural hazards. As a result, in order to achieve timeliness and low overhead, software prefetchers will tend to have low coverage and hopefully high accuracy.

Original program without prefetching:

```
for (i = 0; i< n; i++)
        inner = inner + a[i]*b[i];
```

Naive prefetch:

```
for (i = 0; i< n; i++) (
        prefetch (&a[i+1]);
        /* might generate an exception on last iteration*/
        prefetch (&b[i+1]);
        inner = inner + a[i]*b[i];
    )
```

Naive prefetch with predicate:

```
for (i = 0; i< n; i++) (
        if (i ≠ n−1 and i mod 4 = 0) then (
        prefetch (&a[i+1]);
        prefetch (&b[i+1]);
        )
        inner = inner + a[i]*b[i];
    )
```

With loop unrolling:

```
        prefetch (&a[0]);
        prefetch (&b[0]);
    for (i = 0; i< n−4; i+=4) (
        prefetch (&a[i+4]);
        prefetch (&b[i+4]);
        inner = inner + a[i]*b[i];
        inner = inner + a[i+1]*b[i+1];
        inner = inner + a[i+2]*b[i+2];
        inner = inner + a[i+3]*b[i+3];
    )
    for (; i<n; i++)
        inner = inner + a[i]*b[i];
```

Figure 6.3. A program to compute an inner product using software prefetching. It is assumed that a cache line contains four array elements. (Adapted from Vanderwiel and Lilja VL00.)

Implementing prefetching instructions asks more of the microarchitecture than just taking care of an extra opcode. As we mentioned above, the caches must be lockup-free, but this is now the norm in modern microprocessors. In addition, as mentioned already, some priority schemes must be embedded in the hardware to give priority to regular memory operations over prefetches. Also, if the prefetch instruction generates an exception, such as a page fault or a protection violation, the instruction should not proceed and the exception should be ignored. Of course, all these needs are also mandatory for hardware prefetchers, and software prefetching implementation costs are low compared to those of hardware prefetchers.

Sequential Prefetching and Stream Buffers

Sequential prefetching, (i.e., the prefetch of a line adjacent to one that has just been referenced), also called *one-block lookahead* (OBL) or *nextline*, is a means to exploit spatial locality of code and data. As we saw before (cf. Figure 2.18) the best line size for a D-cache depends on the application. Sequential prefetching allows making the line size look larger. For I-caches, sequential prefetching will favor programs that have long sequences of code without branches or with branches that will most likely fall through, a goal of the code-reordering algorithms that we have just presented.

There are several variations on OBL, depending on when to initiate the prefetch. Upon referencing line i, a prefetch to line $i + 1$ if it is not in the cache can either (i) be always done, or (ii) be done only if there is a miss on line i, (i.e., *prefetch on miss*), or (iii) be more selective. The always-prefetch strategy will result in high coverage but low accuracy. The prefetch on miss will perform better and is the method of choice for I-caches. However, for D-caches it has in general lower coverage than a *tagged* prefetch. An implementation of tagged prefetch is to associate a tag bit with each line. The tag is set to 0 initially and reset to 0 upon replacement. When a line is referenced or brought into the cache on demand, the tag is set to 1, but it retains its 0 value if the line is brought in via a prefetch. A prefetch to line $i + 1$ is initiated when the tag bit of line i is changed from 0 to 1. As can readily be seen, the tagged scheme will perform much better than prefetch on miss on a series of references to consecutive lines.

OBL can be enhanced for D-caches by allowing prefetching forward (line $i + 1$) or backward (line $i - 1$), at the cost of an extra tag bit. In processors with ISA that implement auto-increment of index registers, the prefetching can be done after the auto-increment step. That is, if the effective address is the sum of some register R_j and offset k, then the line at address $R_j + k +$ (auto-increment constant) will be prefetched if it is not already in the cache.

The most detrimental aspect of OBL and its variants is that their timeliness is often poor, especially if the prefetch has to percolate through levels of the memory hierarchy. OBL can be adaptive in the sense that several consecutives lines are prefetched rather than one, with the number of lines being prefetched depending on the success or failure of prefetches. This feedback mechanism is not very reliable, because its own timeliness is in question. An interesting twist to adaptive prefetching has been implemented in the IBM Power4 (see the sidebar in this chapter), whereby, upon a miss on line i, lines $i + x$ are prefetched with different x's and different numbers of lines depending on the level in the cache hierarchy.

In order to prevent cache pollution in adaptive prefetching, the sequential lines can be brought into *stream buffers*. These buffers are FIFO structures of fixed size corresponding to the maximum number of lines that one would prefetch in adaptive sequential prefetching. Upon a memory address reference, both the regular cache and the head of the stream buffer are checked. In case of a hit in the stream buffer, the line is transferred into the cache, and another prefetch to sequentially fill the buffer is initiated. If there is a miss both in the cache and at the head of the stream buffer, the latter is flushed. Starting a new stream buffer filling can be initiated as in the OBL tagged scheme. A single stream buffer of (say) four to eight entries is sufficient for enhancing significantly the performance of I-caches. For D-caches, not only is there a need for more than one stream buffer, but also the technique, which caters solely to improvements due to enhanced spatial locality, is not as comprehensive as it could be.

Stride Prefetching

In a program segment with nested loops indexed by $i_1, i_2, \ldots, i_m$, memory access patterns can be classified as:

- Scalar: These are simple variable references such as to an index or a count.
- Zero stride: These are accesses to indexed variables in outer loops whose subscript expressions do not change while executing inner loops; for example, $A[i_1, i_2]$ while in the inner loop of index i_3, or $B[i_1]$ while in the inner loop of index i_2.
- Constant stride: These are accesses to variables whose subscript expressions are linear with the index of the loop; for example, $A[i_1, i_2]$ while in the inner loop of index i_2.
- Irregular: None of the above, as in pointer-based structures or array variables whose subscript expression contain other array variables; for example, $A[i_1, B[i_2]]$ in a loop of any nested depth.

Standard caches work well for scalar and zero-stride accesses. Caches with large block sizes and sequential prefetching can improve the performance of constant-stride accesses if the stride is small, but will be of no help, or even detrimental, if the stride is large. In order to cater simultaneously to the first three categories above, a more sophisticated scheme is needed.

Given a string of references $a, b, c, \ldots$ three references are needed to detect if it is a *stream*, that is, a string of references whose addresses differ by a constant, namely $b - a$, called the *stride*. Differences in hardware prefetchers that recognize strides will arise in the implementation, namely, (i) whether the prefetched data will be put in the cache or in stream buffers, (ii) the timing of the prefetches, (i.e., the amount of lookahead), and (iii) how much is prefetched. We present two schemes,

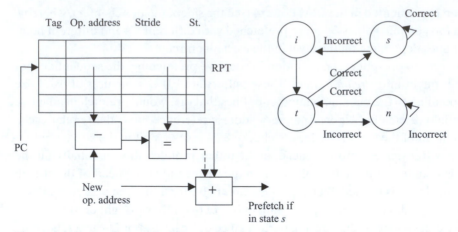

Figure 6.4. Reference prediction table (basic scheme) and its finite-state machine (adapted from Chen and Baer [CB95]).

one based on a reference prediction table and one that is an extension of sequential stream buffers.

As its name implies, the *reference prediction table* (RPT) method is based on the building, updating, and looking up of a table that will indicate whether prefetching should be done upon the recognition of a memory access operation. The RPT is organized as a cache. Minimally, each entry in the table will contain a tag related to the instruction address; fields to record the last operand address that was referenced when the program counter (PC) reached the instruction; the stride, (i.e., the difference between the last two addresses that were generated); and a state transition field as shown in Figure 6.4.

Prefetching using RPT proceeds as follows. For notational purposes, let an entry in the RPT be the tuple (*tag, op.address, stride, state*), and let *index* point to the entry in the RPT. When a memory access instruction is decoded, a check is made to see whether there is a corresponding entry in the RPT. If not, it will be entered in the RPT after the memory operand address has been computed with a *stride* of 0 and the state *initial*. On a hit, thus determining *index*, and also after the operand address has been computed, *stride* will be computed as the difference between the current memory operand address, *op.address*, and the address at *index*(*op.address*). Then, depending on the stride and the state, one of the following actions will take place:

- The state is *initial*. The entry at *index* becomes (*tag, op.address, stride, transient*). This corresponds to the second access to the memory instruction.
- The state is *transient*, and the computed *stride* equals *index*(*stride*).This corresponds to a third access and the detecting of a stream. The entry at *index* becomes (*tag, op.address, stride, steady*), and prefetching can start (prefetching could also start at state *transient* with better coverage and lower accuracy). Prefetching will be for the line at the address that is the sum of the instruction operand address and the stride. Of course, the cache is checked first to see

whether the line to prefetch is already present in cache, in which case it will be aborted; this will occur often for constant- and zero-stride items.

- The state is *steady*, and the computed *stride* remains the same. Prefetching continues to occur, subject to the absence of the line in the cache, and only the address field is updated.

- The state is *steady*, but the computed *stride* becomes different. We have reached the end of the stream (in fact, we have overflowed it). The state is reset to *initial* with a stride of 0.

- The state is *transient*, and the computed stride is different from the one in the table. No stream has been detected. The state is set to *no-prediction*, and no prefetching is done, although *index(op.address)* and *index(stride)* are updated.

- The state is *no-prediction*. There will be no prefetching. The *stride* is recomputed at each reference, and in case it is equal to *index(stride)*, the state is set to *transient*, because a new stream might have been detected.

The basic RPT scheme's timeliness depends on the time interval between executions of the same instruction, which is the time to execute an iteration of the inner loop that contains the instruction. If the loop is tight, the prefetching will be initiated too late. A lookahead mechanism can be implemented whereby instructions ahead of the current PC are addressed using a lookahead program counter (LA-PC). Instructions accessed by the LA-PC that are neither memory nor transfer of control are ignored. The LA-PC is modified by branch instructions according to the status of the branch predictor at that time. Memory access instructions accessed by the LA-PC look up the RPT and generate prefetches when appropriate, that is, when the corresponding entry is in state *steady*. Memory instructions accessed by the PC look up and update the RPT. Since the LA-PC can be several iterations ahead of the PC, a new field per entry is needed, namely the number of iterations that LA-PC is ahead of PC. This counter is incremented by the LA-PC and decremented by the PC. A prefetch generated by LA-PC is for $(op.\ address) + (stride \times count)$. Since the LA-PC can be way ahead of the PC, a limit must be imposed on how far it can deviate from the PC. The limit is related to the latency to fetch an item from the next level in the memory hierarchy. When a branch instruction executes and gives a result opposite to its prediction, the LA-PC is reset to the value of the PC given by the branch execution.

The lookahead RPT scheme requires a double-ported RPT. In addition, as in all prefetching schemes, the regular cache is going to be accessed concurrently by regular requests and prefetch tests to see whether the item to be prefetched is already there. Either an additional port to the tag array is required, or some form of filtering is needed to limit the number of prefetch tests.

The second class of methods, which are extensions of stream buffers, is cheaper to implement, but their accuracy and timeliness are more difficult to control. One of the schemes was proposed as a replacement for off-chip L2 caches in high-performance processors, such as Cray machines, that were intended for scientific programs where there is a dominance of stride accesses. The stream buffer extensions consist of:

- More than one buffer: Then, of course, checking for a hit requires checking not only in the cache, but also at the head of each buffer. When a miss is detected, a new buffer is allocated. If there is no buffer available, the LRU one is replaced.
- Filtering: Instead of starting prefetching as soon as a buffer is allocated, prefetching will be initiated only when there are misses to consecutive blocks. Note that this is not really stride prefetching, but rather an extension of OBL.
- Nonunit stride: Since the PC is not available off chip, computation of the stride as in the RPT method is not possible. Instead, a possibility is to implement finite-state machines, similar to the one in the RPT, for regions of the addressing space. The size of the regions must be assigned statically by the programmer or compiler. Additional machinery can be used to be sure that the stride corresponds at least to consecutive blocks and to prevent overlapping addresses in prefetch buffers.

An alternative, when the PC is available, (i.e., for L1 caches), is to replace the unit-stride detection by a prediction table. The prediction table just predicts the stride associated with a particular memory instruction address and thus is slighter simpler than the basic RPT.

Prefetching for Pointer-based Structures

Hardware mechanisms for pointer-based structures are more complex and in the case of the L1–L2 interface are hampered, as mentioned earlier, by the tightness of loops in applications that use linked lists. Architectures that use a separate prefetch engine that executes a subset of instructions selected by the compiler or the user have been proposed. In contrast with the use of the RPT and/or stream buffer, this prefetch engine is statically controlled.

Correlation Prefetchers

Sequential and stride prefetchers, and the prefetchers for linked lists, rely on memory access patterns as defined by programming language concepts. An alternative is to use *address correlation* between misses as a basis for prefetching.

In Markov-based prefetching, the reference stream of misses to a given level of the memory hierarchy is used to build a Markov model where nodes represent missing addresses and where transitions among nodes, say between nodes A (the source) and B (the target), represent the probability (transition frequency) that a miss on A will be followed by a miss on B. A correlation table is built, indexed by source nodes, where each row gives addresses of the targets as well as their frequencies, which can be translated into probabilities. If there is a miss on A, if B has been entered with probability p, and if B is not cached, a prefetch is enqueued for node B in a prefetch queue ranked in decreasing order of probabilities, with actual misses having probability 1. Note that this model can only be approximated, for the table is limited in size both in number of rows (number of sources in the table) and in width of rows (number of potential targets following a given miss address). The concept is best applied after checking a stride detector or predictor.

There are several problems associated with Markov prefetching as presented here. In order to get good coverage, the number of targets for each source must be more than one. This requirement means that the limitation of the method may be in the bandwidth required between the level of the memory hierarchy where prefetching is initiated and the next level. Second, because the accuracy is restricted, cache pollution could ensue. Having small associative prefetch buffers outside the cache can remedy the situation. Accuracy can be enhanced by correlating a miss with two previous misses, at the expense of lower coverage. In all cases, though, timeliness is an issue that cannot be controlled.

An alternative that caters to the pollution and timeliness concerns is to base the correlation not on subsequent misses but on the presence of *dead lines* in the cache. A dead line in a cache is a line that will not be referenced before being replaced. If a predictor can detect the last touch to a line, say at address A, before its eviction and predict the line, say B, that will replace it, then prefetching of B can occur as soon as A has been detected to be dead. In general, this will be long before the miss correlating with A would occur. Moreover, because B will take the place of a dead line, there will be no cache pollution. It remains of course to predict accurately both the dead line and its replacement! Instead of relying on a miss stream, instructions addresses that precede the last touch of a block are recorded, and the same is done for the replacement. Because it is not practical to record strings of individual addresses, a *signature* of the string of addresses is formed and used as an index in a table that predicts whether a line is dead. If so, the same entry will give the address of the line to prefetch.

A significant drawback of correlation prefetchers in general is the amount of state that must be kept, that is, the overhead of storing the correlations. The tables for an L1 cache are orders of magnitude larger than the cache but, of course, don't have to be accessed as rapidly. For L2 caches, the storage required for the tables is of the same order of magnitude as the cache itself, thus raising the question whether just allocating the storage to the cache itself would not yield as good or better performance.

Stateless Prefetching

The timelessness of dead-line prefetchers is certainly an improvement on that of Markov prefetchers, but still does not have quite the controllability found in the lookahead RPT scheme. Besides the vast amount of state required for the correlation tables, a secondary inconvenience of correlation prefetchers is that it may take some time before the tables are warmed up.

Contentless prefetchers do not require any state. They answer the requirement of lookahead clearly needed in pointer-based applications and should be used in conjunction with a stride prefetcher. They are better suited for L2 on-chip caches in that the demand requests from L1 to L2 provide a feedback on the success of previous prefetches, whose accuracy could be a problem, and in that they require knowledge of physical addresses and thus access to the TLB. The basic idea is that when a line is fetched into L2, the line is scanned for the presence of virtual addresses close to that of the one that has generated the loading of the line. If some of these are detected and, once translated, if their corresponding lines are not in L2, they are prefetched in some prefetch buffer. The process continues recursively, thus forming a chain of prefetching, until either there is no candidate line to be prefetched or the depth of recursion is greater than a given threshold related to the depth of the buffers and the latency of the next level of the memory hierarchy. Feedback from L1 occurs when there is an L1 miss serviced by the L2 buffer. The contents of the buffer are transferred to L1 (partially if the line size of L2 is greater than that of L1) and to L2, thus freeing an entry in the prefetch buffer and decreasing the depth of the recursion.

The main implementation difficulty resides in uncovering virtual addresses in a cache line. The premise for the heuristic is that in pointer-based structures there is a good chance that the base address of the structure has the same high-order (virtual) bits as the fields in the structure. Therefore, comparisons between the n (a parameter of the method) high-order virtual bits of the address of the line just fetched (or prefetched) and the n high-order bits of address-sized values in the cache line are performed. On a match, the virtual-to-physical address translation is done and the prefetch is initiated. The depth of the prefetch serves as a priority for enqueuing requests to the next level of the memory hierarchy. If there is a TLB miss – not so rare an occurrence, according to simulations – the miss has to be resolved. Although the TLB miss certainly does not improve the prefetching timeliness, resolving the TLB miss in parallel with what the processor is doing on the regular program is certainly worthwhile if the prefetching is accurate. The feedback provided by the L1 misses helps improve the accuracy by reinforcing the chains of prefetches that have been successful.

A more greedy solution, which has been called *scheduled region* prefetching, is to prefetch many lines surrounding the missing one. For example, on a cache miss, the whole (physical) page that contains the line is brought into the cache. Of course, this greedy approach will be beneficial only if the cache is large and the bandwidth between the cache and the next level of the memory hierarchy is high. These criteria imply that the cache should be the one closest to main memory, (i.e., L2 or L3), depending on the overall system. A little intelligence in the method, besides not prefetching lines already in the cache, will help: prefetching only when the interface to memory (see Section 6.4 in this chapter) is idle, and placing prefetches in low priority in the cache, for example, close to the LRU position. Intelligence in the memory controller in scheduling the prefetches and giving priority to the real misses is also beneficial.

Prefetching Summary

Modern microprocessors have prefetch instructions in their ISA. However, standard compilers take little or no advantage of these instructions. Embedded systems with their customized programs are more prone to use prefetch instructions. All microarchitectures implement at the very least a variation of OBL for their L1 I-cache and some form of sequential or stride–stream prefetching for their D-caches. We have examined a number of prefetching schemes for irregular patterns that have not yet found their way in present microarchitectures. Because measurements and simulations have shown that sophisticated microprocessors could be idle as much as 50% of the time due to L2 or L3 misses, it should be simply a matter of time before some combination of software and hardware prefetching that caters selectively to all types of memory access patterns becomes more common in commercial products.

6.2.2 Lockup-free Caches

In in-order processors, instructions cannot proceed past a stalled instruction. In case of a D-cache miss on a load, all instructions starting with the first one having a RAW dependency on the load must wait till the miss is resolved before entering the back-end. We saw how this led to rollback mechanisms for processors such as the Alpha 21164. By contrast, in out-of-order processors, instructions that follow the load that missed can enter reservation stations and execute if their operands are ready. We saw how cache misses then could lead to misspeculation and reexecution of some instructions, but nonetheless computation could proceed until no instruction could be selected for execution. However, in view of the fact that the cache is busy waiting for the miss to be resolved, how do we resolve cache accesses?

Allowing cache accesses resulting in hits while a single miss is outstanding does not add much complexity to the design, for all information related to the cache miss is known. This *hit-under-miss* policy was implemented in the Hewlett-Packard PA 1700. Whereas allowing a simple hit-under-miss policy reaps most of the benefits that can be attained in the L1–L2 interface, more than one miss should be allowed with more powerful processors. Not only will that provide more opportunities for computation to proceed, but also mechanisms such as prefetching and policies such as relaxed memory models for shared-memory multiprocessors (cf. Chapter 7) depend on it. The design is more complex, for now the data coming back from higher levels of the memory hierarchy can arrive in an order different from that of the requests. Caches that allow several concurrent misses are called *lockup-free* or *nonblocking* caches. Many L1 D-caches[1] in current microprocessors, and the great majority of L2 caches, are lockup-free. Note that having several main memory requests outstanding will also affect the complexity of the memory controller. In the following, we assume that write misses and dirty line replacements are handled with write buffers, and we consider only the case of read misses.

The basic idea is to encode the information related to a miss in a *missing status holding register* (MSHR). When a cache read miss occurs, an MSHR is associated with it. Minimally, as shown in Figure 6.5, an MSHR for an L1 cache must contain:

- A bit indicating whether it is free or busy. If there is no free MSHR, we have an instance of a structural hazard. The processor must stall until an MSHR becomes free.

---

[1] In this section only L1 D-caches are of interest, and we will not mention the "D" part any longer.

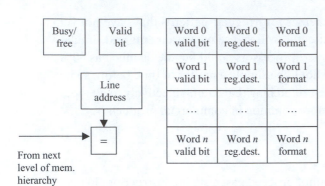

Figure 6.5. Basic layout of a simple MSHR (adapted from Farkas and Jouppi [FJ94]).

- Information regarding which missing line is attached to it. Assuming a physically indexed, physically tagged cache, the MSHR must contain the part of the address that is needed to bring in the missing line and store it in the cache, that is, all of the physical address except for the displacement bits. A comparator is associated with this information, and it is used in two ways. First, on a miss, all MSHRs are searched in parallel to see whether the missing line has already been requested. If it has, the MSHR is updated or the processor is stalled as discussed in the following, but no new MSHR is allocated. Second, when a line returns from the next level in the memory hierarchy, again all MSHRs are searched associatively, and one of them will necessarily match the returning address. Note here the requirement for both address and data to be returned via the memory hierarchy buses.
- A bit indicating whether the line is valid or not. This is a requirement imposed by cache coherency protocols in shared-memory multiprocessor systems, which will be discussed in Chapter 7.
- For each word (or basic addressable unit in the ISA) in the line, fields indicating to which physical register the data should be forwarded in case of a load, whether the data are valid or not (they could have become invalid because of the presence of store buffers and load speculation), and miscellaneous bits indicating the type of operation (e.g., load word or load byte).

When a missing line returns from L2, all destination fields of the associated MSHR and the cache line can be filled. In the most extreme case this would mean that the register file should have as many ports as possible words in a line. If this is not the case, the line must be buffered and the destination registers filled on consecutive cycles.

Note that stalls can still arise independently of those due to structural hazards if two load misses refer to the same word. This is not so unlikely an occurrence in string-processing programs where the basic unit of information is a byte. The basic layout could be expanded to replace the "word" fields by "position" fields within the line. Nonetheless, the same stall condition could still arise. A more costly design that would prevent these secondary misses would then be an inverted MSHR file whereby an MSHR is associated with each physical register. In view of the fact that current microprocessor can have more than a 100 of those, this is clearly overkill.

Simulations have shown that four MSHRs at the L1–L2 interface were more than sufficient. With prefetching, more could be advantageous, mostly at the L2–L3, or main memory, interface. The redeeming feature is that the MSHRs at the L2 level are slightly less complex, in that the destination fields are lines in the L1 cache.

6.2.3 Other Optimizations

Besides prefetching and lockup-free caches, other optimizations try to reduce the latency between levels of the memory.

Critical Word First

This optimization is intended for L1 caches. A miss to an instruction or a datum is not necessarily to the beginning of a line. Thus the cache controller at the L2 level can determine which part of the line is critical – for example, the next instruction to be executed in the case of an I-cache miss, or the byte, word, or double word to be loaded in the case of a D-cache miss. The line is logically rotated, and the critical word is sent first. It then can be forwarded directly to the instruction fetch buffer for an instruction miss along with the remainder of the physical lineup, or to the physical register that is awaiting it for a data read miss. Of course, the line is stored in the corresponding cache in its original form. The only resource requirements are a buffer and a shifter.

Write Strategies

We saw in Chapter 2 that one could implement any of the four strategies given by the Cartesian product {writeback, write-through} × {write-allocate, write-around}. Moreover, write buffers could be used to delay the writing to the next level of the memory hierarchy, thus allowing loads to bypass stores as seen from the memory hierarchy viewpoint. Furthermore, with load speculation, loads can bypass stores even before the latter have received the data that should be written. As we shall see (Chapter 7), this memory ordering, called *processor consistency*, violates the sequential consistency property for parallel programs but is of no correctness consequence in single-processor environments.

Reads (loads) are certainly more important to optimize than writes (stores), because they might prevent computations from proceeding. Reads occur twice as often as writes, and miss rates for loads and stores are about the same. Although scheduling priorities and speculation are thus directed towards loads, the performance of writes should not be neglected, because storing from one level of the memory hierarchy to the next uses a single communication resource, a bus, shared by reads and writes. Write buffers are one way to allow read misses to be served before write misses.

A succession of write misses will occur upon initialization of a data structure such as an array. In writeback write-allocate strategies, there will be a succession of write misses that will rapidly fill the write buffer, thus triggering a structural hazard that will most likely prevent the computation from proceeding, regardless of whether a write-allocate or a write-around policy is implemented. A policy called *write-validate* can be implemented whereby, upon a write miss, the data are written directly in the cache. This policy requires a valid bit per writable field in the line, because all other data in the line must be invalidated. The write-validate policy is therefore best with write-through caches. A possible variation, good for write-through direct-mapped caches only, is for all writes to write directly in the cache in parallel with checking the tag. In the case of a miss, the rest of the line is invalidated.

A mix of policies, writeback or write-through associated with write-allocate or write-around or write-validate, can be implemented page by page. Hints given by the compiler, with variations in the opcode if possible, could also help by letting the hardware know which policy is best for a given static instruction.

6.3 Design Issues for Large Higher-Level Caches

Multilevel cache hierarchies are now a given for personal computers and workstations and, of course, for servers. In the following we will generically talk about L2 caches as on-chip and closest to main memory. In some systems, we have off-chip L3 caches between L2s and main memory; most of what follows can easily be adapted to include the extra level if necessary.

6.3.1 Multilevel Inclusion Property

We saw in Chapter 2 the needed interactions, (e.g., invalidate or purge), between cache and main memory when I/O operations had to be performed. In the case of a cache hierarchy where L2 is closest to the memory bus on the processor side, it is convenient to design the L1–L2 interface so that L2 can shield L1 from all invalidation requests that have no effect on the contents of L1. In order to do so we can impose the *multilevel inclusion property* (MLI). For an L1–L2 hierarchy, the MLI property states that the contents of L2 are a superset of those of L1. In the case of a write-through L1 cache, the definition is unambiguous. If L1 is writeback, MLI is a *space* property, that is, there is a line in L2 that has been allocated to either have the same contents as a line in L1 if the latter is clean, or receive the dirty contents of L1 when the latter is replaced.

In the case of a single processor, imposing MLI is not difficult. As we shall see in Chapter 7, MLI becomes more complex if several L1s are backed up by a shared L2. Considering only the single-processor case and assuming a writeback L1, imposing MLI is simple if L1 and L2 have the same line sizes. Let a, a', and b be lines in L1 with corresponding lines A, A', and B in L2.

- On a miss to L1 and L2, the new line is allocated in both caches: a in L1, A in L2. The line a' replaced in L1 is written back in A' if it is dirty. If a line B different from A' is replaced in L2, then if there is an image b of B in L1, b must

a'	b

L1: the LRU set is on the left

B	A'

(a) Initial contents

L2: the LRU set is on the left

Figure 6.6. Illustration of imposing the MLI property.

a	Inv.

L1: the LRU set is on the right

A	A'

(b) contents after miss to a

L2: the LRU set is on the right

be invalidated and, if dirty, copied back in B before the latter is transferred to main memory. The initial situation is shown in Figure 6.6(a) with two-way set-associative L1 and L2. The final situation is in Figure 6.6(b).

- On a miss to b in L1 and hit to B in L2, the victim a that is going to be replaced by b in L1 is transferred to A in L2 if it is dirty. The contents of B in L2 are transferred to b in L1, and MLI is assured.
- On an invalidation request for a line, first a check is made to see whether the line is in L2. If not, L1 does not need to be disturbed. If the line is present in L2, a check must be made in L1 unless we provide some information in L2 stating that the same line is cached in L1 (a single bit suffices). If the bit is on, the line in L1 exists and must also be invalidated. If the bit is off (the usual case, because L2 is in general an order of magnitude larger than L1), there is no need for an L1 check. Adding an inclusion bit requires some action when a line in L1 is replaced, even if the line is clean, because the inclusion bit of the corresponding line in L2 must be cleared.

We have made two assumptions in describing how MLI can be enforced. First, we have assumed that L2 had a larger capacity than L1. It is difficult to envision the opposite. Second, we have assumed that different lines in L1 mapped to different lines in L2. In other words, the associativity of L2 must be at least as much as the associativity in L1.

Imposing MLI becomes slightly more stringent when the line sizes are unequal. Let B_1 be the line size for L1, and let B_2 be the line size for L2. We will consider only the usual case where $B_2 \geq B_1$ and B_2 is a multiple of B_1. Now, instead of a single inclusion bit associated with the tag of a line in L2, we need B_2/B_1 such bits, one for each line in L1 that is a subset of the line in L2. The handling of hits, misses, and invalidations in L1 and L2 proceeds almost as before. If the unit of coherence is the line size of L1, the latter will be disturbed for invalidation only when there is a corresponding line in L2 that has the inclusion bit on for the line in L1. The main difference is when a line in L2 is replaced. Now all lines in L1 that have the inclusion bit on must be purged.

Imposing MLI requires that the associativity of L2 be at least B_2/B_1 times as much as that of L1, that is,

$$A_{L2}/B_{L2} \geq A_{L1}/B_{L1}$$

EXAMPLE 2: MLI cannot be enforced with a 16 K direct-mapped L1 of line size 32 bytes and a 1 MB two-way set-associative L2 of line size 128 bytes. The ratio of associativity is 2, and the ratio of line sizes is 4. Lines at address 0, 512 KB + 32, and 1 MB + 64 map respectively to sets 0, 1, and 2 in L1 and to set 0 in L2. MLI in this case must be enforced by keeping only two of the three lines. Other schemes to impose MLI will be discussed when the cache hierarchy has shared components.

If the L1 and L2 capacities are close to each other, or if one does not want to impose MLI because of associativity constraints, then it is preferable to have *multilevel exclusion* so that a maximum of information is stored on chip. In this case L2 is nothing else than a huge victim cache for L1. In order not to disrupt L1 on all coherency requests, the caches are dual-tagged, with one set of tags used by processor requests and one set for coherency purposes. Interaction between the two sets of tags is needed only when dirty bits are set, or on misses, or on successful invalidations. A design of this type exists in the AMD Athlon processor with L1 I-cache and D-cache of 64 KB each and a unified 256 KB L2.

6.3.2 Replacement Algorithms

Variations on LRU

In Chapter 2 we downplayed the importance of replacement algorithms for set-associative caches. For two-way and four-way set-associative caches, the least recently used (LRU) algorithm has very good performance and is cheap enough to implement. However, with the large associativities, like 8-way or 16-way, that are encountered in large L2 or L3 caches, strict LRU is too expensive to implement (more than 100 bits per set for 16-way). Approximations to LRU are the norm, but start to deviate seriously from the (unrealizable in real-time) optimal algorithm.

Although approximations to LRU for paging systems can be fairly sophisticated because there is ample time to select a victim during a context switch, those for large caches must not lengthen the access time.

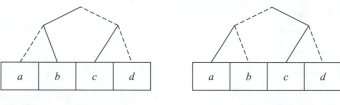

(a) Corresponds to a cache initially empty and the string of references "*bcad*"

MRU path

(b) The next reference is to *b*. If the next reference is a miss, *c* will be the victim

In this example, the algorithm gives the same result as true LRU. But the same tree would have been built if the original reference stream were "*bacd*", and *c* would still have been replaced, while in true LRU it would have been *a*.

Figure 6.7. Illustration of the tree-based approximation to LRU. The cache is four-way set-associative. In (a), when *d* is encountered, the right subset *ab* is MRU. In that subset *a* is MRU. In (b), a reference to *b* makes *ab* the MRU subset; hence the arc switches between *a* and *b* and at the root.

Two typical hardware-based approximations to LRU are the tree-based and the MRU-based algorithms. Both methods are fast and require little extra logic and hardware.

In the tree-based algorithm, used first in many L2 caches in IBM mainframes and now in the IBM Power4 (see the sidebar in this chapter), the *n* lines in a set are divided into two subsets recursively until the subsets contain only two lines. A binary tree with the *n* lines being the leaves is constructed. At each nonleaf node a bit indicates whether the MRU line is in the left or right subtree. Upon a hit, all nodes that lie on the path from the line that was hit, that is, the current MRU line, to the root have their bits set to indicate that the opposite direction of the path contains lines that are not as recently used as the one just hit. On a miss, the non-MRU links in the tree, as indicated by the setting of the bits, are followed from the root to a leaf, which becomes the victim. The latter is replaced with the missing line, which becomes the MRU line, and the tree is updated to that effect. This is illustrated in Figure 6.7 for a four-way set-associative cache. This scheme requires $n - 1$ bits per set for an *n*-way set-associative cache.

The MRU-based algorithm is even simpler. Each line has a *hit bit* associated with it. The hit bit is set initially when a line is brought in and on subsequent hits to the line because when all lines have their hit bits set, they are all reset. On a miss, the first one with its hit bit off is replaced. If that first one is chosen on a round-robin basis, we have the well-known *clock* algorithm used in paging systems. This scheme requires *n* bits per set for an *n*-way set-associative cache.

Reducing L2 misses is an important performance factor because of the high latency to access main memory. Measurements on various platforms have shown that during L2 misses, the whole processor engine can stall because either its instruction window or its reorder buffer becomes full. To illustrate this point, consider the following simplistic example.

EXAMPLE 3: Assume a processor and associated L1 caches with an *IPC* of 2 when there are no L2 misses. Numerous simulations have shown that this *IPC*

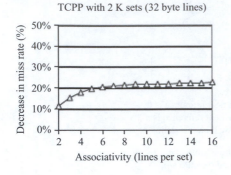

Figure 6.8. Performance of optimal and LRU replacement algorithms for various associativities. The application is TCPP, the cache is 256 KB with 32 byte lines, and the associativity varies from 2 to 16 (from Wong and Baer [WB00]).

could be achieved on a modern four-way out-of-order processor with 32 KB of L1 I-cache and 32 KB of lockup-free L1 D-cache with an L1–L2 latency of 6 cycles. Assume now that an L2 miss occurs once every 100 instructions, a reasonable figure for a number of applications, and assume an L2 of 1 MB. If the memory latency is 100 cycles, the *IPC* becomes 0.67 (it is easier to compute the new *CPI* as $CPI = 0.5 + 0.01 \times 100 = 1.5$, so that $IPC = 1/CPI = 0.67$). Now if we can improve the L2 miss rate by 10%, (i.e., to 0.009 misses per instruction rather than 0.01), then *IPC* becomes 0.71, a 6% increase. This demonstrates that improvements in L2 hit rates can yield substantial performance benefits.

The first question, though, that we should ask is whether there is an opportunity for improvement in the hit rate. Figure 6.8 shows that on some applications and for high associativities LRU can generate as much as 20% more misses than the optimal algorithm. Interestingly enough, a replacement algorithm that chooses randomly from the lower half of the set, (i.e., among the eight LRU entries for a 16-way associativity), performs as well as true LRU in this case. There are instances where LRU performs better than this half-random selection, and some instances where it performs worse, but this result gives some reinforcement to the notion that a tree-based LRU is quite sufficient if LRU-like performance is desired.

Inasmuch as there is an opportunity to do better than LRU, hardware and software schemes have been investigated to improve on the replacement. The basic idea in a hardware assist is to keep in cache those lines that exhibit some sustained temporal locality even if they fall to the bottom of the LRU cache. One possible scheme is to associate a *temporal bit* with each line in the cache. Upon a miss in L2, the line that is replaced is the LRU with its temporal bit off, with the exception that the most recently used (MRU) line is never chosen as a victim. Temporal bits are set when the same instruction references a line that is not the MRU one. The temporal bit of the line in the MRU position is reset if the next reference in that set is for the MRU line. Implementation of such a scheme requires a separate table of locality bits accessed in a cachelike fashion with the PC of the memory instructions. Because the PC is required to access the table, the scheme is best for on-chip caches. The real estate overhead is small (less than 10% of the cache's area). Simulations have shown improvements over LRU similar to those realized by adding a victim cache to L2 using the same amount of area as those required by the assist. The advantage over victim caching is a single-cache structure and consequent simpler mechanisms for cache coherence and lockup-free caching.

Reducing Hardware Requirements for Hit and Miss Detection

In a large-associativity cache, the replacement is a factor for performance, but realizing quickly whether there is a hit or a miss can take a significant amount of hardware and power, namely, comparators and levels of logic to decide which entry is the correct one. The hardware requirements can be reduced – at the cost, of course, of longer access times, making it reasonable only for L2s and L3s.

Several strategies are possible. The first one, which we call MRU-based, uses a single comparator per set to first check whether the reference is for the MRU line. The latter can easily be identified with a single bit in the tag array. In case of success, we are done, but if the MRU comparison fails, we have to look at the other tags in some linear fashion. Luckily, temporal locality, the motivation for the replacement algorithm discussed in this section, has been shown to exist in references to L2, so this is an adequate strategy. If p is the probability that the reference is to the MRU line, we have hits detected in one comparison with probability p. If the other entries in the set are hit with the same probability, then it will take on the average $p + (1 - p)(n - 1)/2$ comparisons to detect a hit, with n being the cache's associativity. For example, if the MRU line is hit 80% of the time, the average number of comparisons will be just over 2 for a 16-way set-associative cache. This translates into an average of one extra cycle per hit with only one comparator per set instead of the full-blown 16. It will take n comparisons to detect a miss, but this is of no great concern, for the time to resolve the miss is quite large, an order of magnitude more than the number of comparisons.

Another possibility is to perform the tag comparison in two steps. In the first one, k bits of the tag field in the reference address are compared in parallel with the corresponding k bits of the tags of all members of the set. In order to use the same amount of hardware as in the MRU strategy – that is, a comparator that can compare in one cycle two fields as large as a tag – the parameter k must be equal to t/n, where t is the length of the tag. This does not make much sense for a 32-bit architecture and a 16-way cache, and even for a 64-bit architecture one might want to add a few extra bits beyond t/n. If there is no match, we have a miss. If there are one or more matches, the remaining bits of the fields that matched must be compared in a linear fashion. In the best case it takes two comparisons to detect a hit, instead of one in the MRU-based method, whereas it takes only one comparison to detect a miss instead of n. However, it is the hit access time that we want to optimize and not the miss detection. Average cases depend on the selection of the k bits in order to restrict the possible matches in the first comparison of the two-step scheme. Because L2s are physically addressed and the tags are the high-order bits of the addresses, there is no incentive to try to be clever, and any subset of k bits should be fine.

Improvements on LRU are a first step towards reducing L2 misses. A bolder approach would be to make the cache fully associative and to use software-based replacement algorithms similar in spirit to those that have been successful in other contexts such as paging systems. Line tables, the equivalent of page tables, are totally impractical because of their enormous space requirements; an alternative is to use an *inverted index structure*. This type of indexing appeared first in the context of paging systems when physical memory was very small compared to the virtual address space. Instead of having large page tables directly indexed by the virtual page number, an associative table containing as many entries as there are possible physical pages can be used. The ith entry in the table contains the virtual page number currently mapped in the ith physical frame, that is, at the physical address starting at $i \times page\text{-}size$. Virtual address translation consists of an associative search in this *inverted page table*. On a hit, the position of the hit yields the mapping. On a miss, we have a page fault.

However, as soon as physical memory sizes became larger, this pure inverted table scheme had to be abandoned. The inverted structure can still be used, but now the mapping is kept in an open hash table. The hash table must contain more entries than the number of physical frames, and moreover there must be some room for chaining in case of collisions. Note also that the hashing, and the contents of each entry, must include the process PID (because we don't want to have one hash table per process), the virtual page number, and the physical page number. Still, the amount of physical memory needed for the mapping table is much less than that required by straightforward direct mapping. The discussions of the pros and cons of various implementations of direct mapping vs. inverted page tables in the context of paging in operating systems is outside the scope of this book, but the concept of inverted data structure can be applied to hit and miss detection in large caches.

In the case of a fully associative cache, each table entry in the index structure would not need to be as cumbersome as in a paging system. It would consist only of a tag, status bits, a pointer to the cache line (i.e., the index), and a pointer to the first entry in the chain table with the same hash function, if any. Some space could be saved by having each entry in the hash table be a row of m entries with the same hash function, and some time could be saved by comparing the tags in the same row in parallel.

It is easy to see that the inverted index structure will take more space than a conventional approach. At the very least, the tags are longer and the index has to be stored rather than subsumed. On the other hand, we have a fully associative cache, and the hit rate should be better. Of course, full LRU is not possible, but some implementation of the clock scheme becomes feasible.

Other techniques that have been proposed are similar to those found in garbage collection and use temporal locality, namely, lines are grouped in pools and are given priorities based on whether they have been referenced in some previous time interval. On a miss, the head and the tail in each pool are promoted or demoted, depending on their recency of reference, and the victim is chosen from the

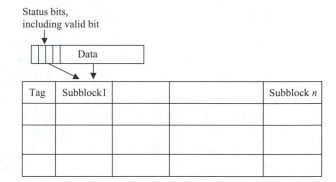

Figure 6.9. Sector cache organization.

lowest-priority pool. The number of pools is a parameter for both the performance of the replacement algorithm and the time it takes to move lines from pool to pool.

6.3.3 Sector Caches

The original implementation of caches in the IBM System 360/85 used a *sector cache* organization. Lines are divided into subblocks (see Figure 6.9) with each subblock having a valid bit attached to it. On a miss, only the subblock belonging to the missing line will be brought in; all other subblocks will have their valid bits turned off. A sector cache can be of any associativity. In the IBM System 360/85, the cache was fully associative with 16 lines of 4 KB each, each line being divided into 16 subblocks of 64 bytes.

The motivation for sector caches at the time they were introduced was twofold. First, the number of transistors one could put on a chip (in fact, a chip external to the processor) was limited, and therefore a small tag array was a necessity. Second, the processors were not pipelined and were executing one instruction at a time. On a cache miss the whole processor was stalled. Therefore, the time it took to bring a line in was critical, and lines (subblocks) had to be short.

Neither of these conditions exists today for L1 caches. For caches closest to the main memory, there is plenty of real estate to store tags, and the line size is not usually a main performance problem, although line sizes of, say, 4 KB are not the rule even for L3s. However, sector caches are used (see the sidebar) for L3s, for two reasons. First, there is never enough room left on the processor chip for very large L3s, but there can be room enough for an array of tags. Because L3s are enormous, even the tag array can be too large. Using a sector organization cuts the needed area by a factor proportional to the number of subblocks in a line. Second, very long lines may be detrimental in a multiprocessor environment in that they lead to an increase of false sharing (see Chapter 7). Hence, it is helpful to have the subblock as a unit of coherence. As an example, the L3 in the IBM Power4 is an eight-way set-associative sector cache, with lines of 512 bytes and four subblocks per line. The cache itself can be as large as 16 MB.

Before leaving the subject of sector caches, it is worth mentioning that the write-validate strategy of Section 6.2.3 has some flavor of sector cache organization.

6.3.4 Nonuniform Cache Access

Because larger portions of the on-chip area are used for caches, the question arises of how to organize the on-chip cache hierarchy. At the present time, L2 capacities are of the order of several megabytes. This (sometimes) leaves room for L3 tags and logic for the memory controller. With advances in technology, we can expect to have 16 MB available on chip with several on-chip processors (cf. Chapter 8). Though it is still reasonable to assume that all accesses to a 2 or 3 MB cache take the same time (namely, the worst-case time to access the bank furthest from the processor), this won't be true any longer with caches an order of magnitude larger.

A simple solution is to extend the hierarchy so that we now have an L2 and an L3 on chip. Because the L3 will be large, the area devoted to tags will be significant, even if we use a sector cache organization. Moreover, if we want to impose multilevel inclusion, the ratio of capacities between the L3 and L2, say 5:1 rather than the almost 50:1 between L2 and L1, can lead to significant replication of data on the chip. If multilevel exclusion is used between L2 and L3, then the large tag arrays in each cache must be duplicated for efficient cache coherence handling.

An alternative is to limit the on-chip hierarchy to two levels and recognize that latencies to access the L2 will be dependent on the physical location of the data in the cache. Having variable latencies is not an implementation problem, for lockup-free caches are well equipped to deal with the variations. However, there are design aspects that have to be taken into consideration, such as where to place data (statically or dynamically) and how to detect a hit or a miss.

We only sketch here a possible organization. The L2 cache is divided into banks, say of capacity 256 or 512 KB. Because of the potentially large number of banks, it is neither economical in chip area nor wise in terms of power to provide each bank with its own channel (bus) to the processor. Instead, a simple interconnection network such as a mesh (cf. Chapter 7) could be used to route requests and data to the correct bank as selected, for example, by the lower bits of the index part of the physical address as seen by the cache. Banks closest to the processor will be accessed faster than those farther. A simple mapping is to divide the cache into m columns of n banks of capacity c, for a total capacity of $C = mnc$ and an n-way set associativity. For example, we could have eight columns of four banks of 512 KB each for a total of 32 banks for a four-way set-associative cache of 16 MB. Each of the m columns contains a "way" from the n possible "ways" in a set. They have to be searched linearly, and this is the only difference between this organization and a conventional one. Note that there are different latencies between the first banks in different columns, because they are at different distances from the controller, and within banks of a column, for the same reason. One can design mappings to equalize search accesses over all columns at the expense of a slightly more complex routing mechanism. Other options include the sharing of the closest banks among multiple bank sets.

In the above scheme, the data placed in a bank remain in the same bank until replaced. It would be nice to have the most recently used lines in the closest banks.

Since implementing LRU might require too many data movements, a simple *promotion strategy* could be used whereby the line for which there is a hit is promoted one bank closer to the closest bank by exchanging it with its neighboring bank. The disadvantage is that on a miss, the incoming line is placed in the furthest bank because that is where the LRU line will tend to be.

Sidebar: The Cache Hierarchy of the IBM Power4 and Power5

The IBM Power4, introduced in 2001, and its successor the Power5, introduced three years later, implement the IBM PowerPC ISA. In addition to their extensive cache hierarchy, which we describe below, the Power4 and Power5 are out-of-order superscalars with very interesting characteristics that will be explored in more detail in the forthcoming chapters. Specifically, they both have two processors on chip and therefore are the first instance that we encounter in this book of chip multiprocessors (CMPs). Moreover, each processor in the Power5 has the capability of running two threads simultaneously. Multithreading, and simultaneous multithreading (SMT) as in Power5, will also be covered in forthcoming chapters.

The frequency at which these two IBM microprocessors can operate does not put them in the highest range of speed. The maximal frequencies are 1.7 GHz for the Power4 and 1.9 GHz for the Power5. It is interesting to note that IBM introduced in 2007 a much faster in-order processor, called the Power6, which runs at frequencies approaching 5 GHz while dissipating no more energy than its predecessors. Since the memory hierarchies of these three models are quite similar and the design of those of the Power4 and the Power5 is better documented, we will concentrate on them.

In each model, the two processor cores are identical. Each processor is an out-of-order superscalar with eight functional units. Up to eight instructions can be fetched from the I-cache at each cycle, and eight instructions can be issued per cycle. Branch prediction is performed in a way similar to that of the Alpha 21264 (cf. Section 4.1 sidebar), that is, it involves a local predictor, a global predictor, and a predictor of the predictors, as well as special mechanisms for call–return and iterative loop count predictions. Decoding, register renaming, and dispatching in issue queues are performed on basic blocks, or groups, of maximum size 5. If the last instruction is not a branch, the fifth instruction will be a no-op. Instructions are dispatched and committed group by group. Each type of functional units has its own issue queue (cf. Chapter 5, Table 5.1), for a total of 11 queues and almost 80 instructions that can be queued up. These issue queues function on a FIFO basis. There are 80 physical integer registers and 72 physical floating-point ones. The reorder buffer can hold up to 80 instructions, the actual number depending on the sequentiality of the program. Load speculation is performed along the lines of what was discussed in Section 5.2.2.

We now turn our attention to the memory hierarchy. The main differences between the Power4 and the Power5 cache hierarchies are in the placement of the L3 cache and of the memory controller. Although both microprocessors incorporate

Table 6.1 Geometries of the Power4–Power5 cache hierarchy (the notation *a/b* indicates the Power4/Power5 numbers. The Power6's L1 D-cache and L2 are twice as big as the Power5's)

Cache	Capacity	Associativity	Line size (bytes)	Write policy	Replacement algorithm	Comments
L1 I-cache	64 KB	Direct/2-way	128		LRU	Sector cache (4 sectors)
L1 D-cache	32 KB	2-way/4-way	128	Write- through	LRU	
L2 Unified	1.5 MB/2 MB	8-way/10-way	128	Writeback	Pseudo-LRU	
L3	32 MB/36 MB	8-way/12-way	512	Writeback	?	Sector cache (4 sectors)

the L3 directory on chip, the L3 data array is on the memory side in the Power4, (i.e., between the L2 cache and the memory controller), but on the processor side in the Power5, (i.e., adjacent to the L2). In the latter case, accesses to L3 do not share the same bus with accesses to the main memory. Moreover, the memory controller in the Power5 is on chip also.

An overall slightly simplified logical view of the Power4 cache hierarchy is shown in Figure 6.10.

The geometric parameters of the various caches are shown in Table 6.1. Their latencies are shown in Table 6.2. Note that the L2 latency of the Power5 is 13 cycles, vs. 12 cycles for the P4, but the clock frequency of the P5 is higher, so that in reality accesses to L2 are slighter faster in P5.

A fair amount of the design complexity of the L2 and L3 cache controllers resides in the way they handle cache coherency. We will fully examine this important

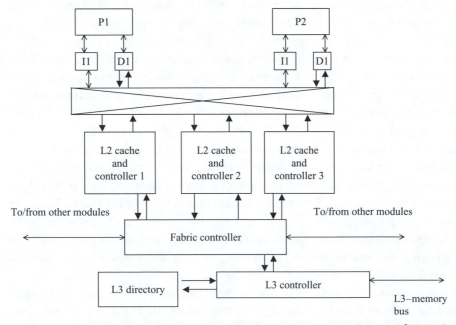

Figure 6.10 The IBM Power4 cache hierarchy (adapted from Tendler et al. [TDFLS02]).

Table 6.2 Latencies (in cycles) for the caches and
main memory in the P4 and P5

	P4 (1.7 GHz)	P5 (1.9 GHz)
L1 (I and D)	1	1
L2	12	13
L3	123	87
Main memory	351	220

feature in the next chapter. In this sidebar, we give details on the cache hierarchy as it pertains to a single processor.

L1 Caches

The L1 instruction cache is organized as a sector cache with four sectors (cf. Section 6.3.3 in this chapter). It is single-ported and can read or write 32 bytes/cycle. The 32 bytes thus correspond to one out of four sectors of the 128 byte line. 32 bytes also correspond to eight instructions, the maximum amount that can be fetched at every cycle on an I-cache hit.

A prefetch buffer of four lines is associated with the L1 I-cache. On an I-cache miss, the prefetch buffer is searched. If there is a hit in the prefetch buffer, the corresponding (partial) sector is forwarded to the pipeline as it would have been if the line had been in the I-cache. On a miss to the prefetch buffer, we have a real miss. The missing line is fetched from L2, critical sector first (i.e., the sector containing the instruction that was missed on). The missing line is not written directly into the I-cache, but rather in a line of the prefetch buffer, and the critical sector is sent to the pipeline. The missing line will be written in the I-cache during cycles in which the latter is free, for example, on a subsequent I-cache miss.

On a miss to the I-cache, sequential prefetching occurs as follows: If there is a hit in the prefetch buffer, the next sequential line is prefetched. If there is a miss, the two lines following the missing one are prefetched. Of course, if any of the lines to be prefetched already reside in either the I-cache or the prefetch buffer, their prefetching is canceled. The copying of prefetched lines to the I-cache occurs when there is a hit in the prefetch buffer for that line. Thus, all lines in the I-cache must have had at least one of their instructions forwarded to the pipeline.

The L1 write-through D-cache is triple-ported. Two 8 byte reads and one 8 byte write can proceed concurrently.

L2 Cache

The L2 cache is shared between the two processors. Physically, it consists of three slices connected via a crossbar to the two L1 I-caches and the two L1 D-caches. Lines are assigned to one of the slices via a hashing function. Each slice contains 512 KB of data and a duplicated tag array. The duplication is for cache coherence so that snoops, explained in the next chapter, can be performed concurrently with regular accesses. Among the status bits associated with the tag is one that contains an indication of whether the line is in one of the L1s and which one, thus allowing the enforcement of multilevel inclusion. The L2 is eight-way set-associative with four banks of SRAM per slice, each capable of supplying 32 bytes/cycle to L1. The replacement algorithm is tree-based pseudo-LRU (see Section 6.3.2 in this chapter). The tag array, or directory, is parity-protected, and the data array is ECC-protected (see Section 6.4.4).

Each slice contains a number of queues: one store queue for each processor corresponding to store requests from the write-through L1s, a writeback queue for dirty lines needed to be written back to L3, a number of MSHRs for pending requests to L3, and a queue for snooping requests. Each slice has its own cache controller, which consists of four coherency processors for the interface between L2s on one side and the processors and L1s on the other, and four snoop processors for coherency with other chip multiprocessors. Each of the four types of requests from the processor side, that is, reads from either processor or writes from either store queue, is handled by a separate coherency processor. The snooping processors implement a MESI protocol to be described in the next chapter.

In addition there are two noncacheable units at the L2 level, one per processor, to handle noncacheable loads and stores – for example, due to memory-mapped I/O operations and also to some synchronization operations that arise because of the relaxed memory model (again see the next chapter) associated with the multiprocessing capabilities of the Power4.

L3 Cache

The L3 cache directory and the L3 controller (including the coherency processors and queues associated with it to interface with main memory) are on chip. The L3 data array is on a different chip.

The L3 data array is organized as four quadrants, with each quadrant consisting of two banks of 2 MB of eDRAM each (eDRAM, that is embedded DRAM, allows higher operating speeds than standard DRAM but cost more). The L3 controller is also organized in quadrants, with each quadrant containing two *coherency processors*. In addition, each quadrant has two other simple processors for memory writebacks and DMA write I/O operations.

L3 is a sector cache with four sectors. Thus, the unit of coherency (512/4 = 128 bytes) is of the same length as the L2 line. It facilitates coherency operations. Note, however, that L3 does not enforce multilevel inclusion, which is not necessary, because coherency is maintained at the fabric controller level (cf. Figure 6.10) that is situated between the L2 and the L3.

Prefetching

We have seen already how instruction prefetching was performed at the L1 level. Hardware sequential prefetching is also performed for data caches at all levels. Eight streams of sequential data can be prefetched concurrently. Moreover, as we shall see, the prefetching takes into account the latencies at the various levels. A stream is conservatively deemed sequential by the hardware when there are four consecutive cache misses in various levels of the hierarchy. However, a *touch* instruction generated by the compiler can accelerate the detection and can ask for prefetching a sequential stream when executed.

Once a stream has been recognized as being sequential, when a new line, say B_0 (already prefetched in L1) is accessed for the first time, a prefetch of a single line, say B_1 at address $B_0 + 128$, occurs from L2 to L1. At the same time a new line is prefetched from L3 to L2, but instead of being the next line, it is one four lines ahead in order to take into account the order-of-magnitude jump in latencies between the two interfaces. Thus, B_5 at address $B_0 + 4 \times 128$ would be prefetched from L3 to L2. Similarly, the fourth line after B_5 would be prefetched from main memory to L3, but because the lines are four times as large in L3, this would correspond to B_{17} (and B_{18} B_{19} B_{20}). This last prefetching would be done only once every four times. Prefetching can be done either in ascending addresses or descending addresses, depending on the load address that generated the miss (low address in the line yields descending prefetch, and high address yields ascending prefetching).

Prefetching is stopped when (virtual memory) page boundaries are crossed. For the usual 4 KB page size this could happen fairly often, and therefore two page sizes are possible: 4 KB, and 16 MB for (technical) applications that use large amounts of data.

6.4 Main Memory

We have shown in the previous section of this chapter how computer architects are expending much effort in trying to optimize the lower levels of the memory hierarchy. Of course, the main reason is that the highest level, namely main memory, was getting relatively slower as processor speed kept increasing. With memory access times of the order of 40–100 ns as shown in Figure 2.11, the number of cycles to bring some data from main memory to a processor running at 3 GHz is between 120 and 300 cycles. So clearly, latency is a problem. Besides latency, the other two metrics that characterize main memory are capacity and bandwidth. Capacity growth has followed Moore's law, that is, the number of bits that can be stored on a chip quadruples every three years. Though this is good news in terms of the amount of storage, we shall see that it also poses some difficulties when expansion and bandwidth are to be considered. Finally, although there are means to increase bandwidth, care must be taken so that techniques to improve latency, such as prefetching, do not reduce unduly the amount of bandwidth available.

6.4.1 From DRAMs to SDRAM and DDR

A memory access (say, a read corresponding to the filling of the highest-level cache in the hierarchy, i.e., the cache closest to main memory) can be decomposed into four separate actions (recall the simplified example of Section 2.2.2):

- The address is sent over the memory bus to the memory controller.
- The memory controller converts the request into a series of commands for the device (DRAM).

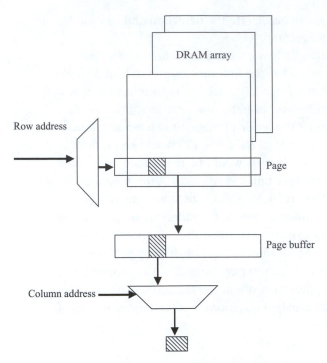

Figure 6.11. Basic page-mode DRAM.

- The data in the main memory device are read and stored into a buffer.
- The data are transmitted to the cache.

The times for the first and fourth actions depend on the speed and width of the memory address and data buses. In this section we are mainly interested in the third action, which is dependent on the design of the memory device. We shall touch upon the second one – the design of an intelligent memory controller – later on. Note that the first two actions can be delayed by contention and therefore queuing buffers are needed: the memory address bus can be busy when the request due to a cache miss is first uncovered, the memory controller can be busy when the request arrives, and commands are not necessarily sent to the device in FIFO order.

The simplest instantiation of a memory device is a collection of chips, each of which holds the same bit for all words stored in memory. Each chip is a rectangular array as shown in Figure 6.11. The number of rows does not have to be equal to the number of columns. For example, a 16 MB memory can be implemented using 32 4-Mbit arrays. Each bit in the array consists of a transistor and a capacitor that needs to be refreshed periodically; hence the term DRAM, for dynamic random access memory. This is in contrast with the six-transistor cell in the SRAM (S for static) technology used in higher-level caches.

The address lines are multiplexed into row access lines and column access lines. For a read operation, the main commands generated by the memory controller are:

- Row access strobe (RAS), which brings to sense amplifiers the contents of the whole row containing the bit of the array that is accessed; the time for this operation is t_{RAS}.

- Column access strobe (CAS), which selects the desired bit from the sense amplifiers; the time for this operation is t_{CAS}.

So, it appears that the time for the operation – the DRAM *access time* – is the sum $t_{acc} = t_{RAS} + t_{CAS}$. This is correct if the array was precharged beforehand. Otherwise a precharge time has to be included. Note that reading is destructive, and therefore the row that that was accessed must be written back. The access time plus the additional rewrite time yield the *cycle time*, that is, the minimum time between two row accesses. Typical timings show that the precharge time t_{pre}, t_{RAS}, and t_{CAS} are of the same order of magnitude.

The first improvement to the basic DRAM is to have it operate in *fast page mode* (the term "page" is, alas, a pretty bad one in that it has nothing to do with a virtual memory page; however, it is the standard commercial appellation). Instead of being deactivated at the end of the RAS probe, the whole row is kept activated. Subsequent accesses to the DRAM that have the same row addresses can then be fulfilled in t_{CAS} time. For example, if the line size of the lower-level cache is a multiple of what can be delivered by the DRAM in a single command, filling the cache line will require access to consecutive bits in each array, all of which share the same row address with the possible exception of a wraparound. All DRAMs nowadays operate in fast page mode. A further improvement is the *extended data out* (EDO) DRAM, where an additional latch between the page buffer and the data-out buffer allows more overlap between consecutive column accesses and data transfers.

Up to this point, the DRAMs that we have considered are asynchronous and are controlled by the memory controller. The latency to fulfill a request once a command has reached the DRAM is either

- t_{CAS} if the request is for the same row address,
- $t_{RAS} + t_{CAS}$ if the request if for a new row address and the DRAM has been precharged, or
- $t_{pre} + t_{RAS} + t_{CAS}$ if the device needs to be precharged.

In addition, there is the possibility that the row being accessed is in the process of being refreshed. In that case, there is an additional component to the latency.

The next step in the evolution of DRAMs is to have a synchronous DRAM, or SDRAM, that is, a device with an internal clock. The main advantage of the SDRAM is that it can include a programmable register that holds a *burst length*, which is the number of bytes requested. Instead of asserting CAS signals, the data are delivered at each clock cycle, in general in about half of the t_{CAS} time. Typically, the clock of an SDRAM in a given system will have a slighter smaller cycle time (higher frequency) than the memory bus to which it is connected, thus providing a small amount of error tolerance. Otherwise, the internals of the SDRAM are pretty much the same as those of a fast-page-mode DRAM. In a manner similar to that in the EDO DRAM, the SDRAM can be enhanced (ESDRAM) by having SRAM row caches (think of the sense amplifiers in Figure 6.11 being extended to a small cache). This feature allows precharging of the device and refreshing of rows that are cached on the device to proceed simultaneously with the access of a cached row. Finally, by transferring data on both edges of the clock, the data rate can be doubled, yielding the DDR SDRAMs (DDR stands for double data rate).

6.4.2 Improving Memory Bandwidth

Improving memory bandwidth means that we want to transfer as much information per (bus) cycle as possible. With a given memory data bus width, the DRAM chips should be organized optimally to provide a bus width of data per request. With current bus widths of 64 or 128 bits, the DRAM organization shown in Figure 6.11, whereby a chip yields one bit of output per request, needs to be revisited so that it yields a larger number of bits per request. Indeed, expansion is needed also so that the number of chips does not increase unduly and to ease the modularity of capacity expansion.

A first improvement is to allow more than one data output pin per chip, so that consecutive bits in a row can be delivered at each cycle from a single chip. Chips are organized into circuit board modules called *dual inline memory modules* (DIMMs), an improvement over SIMMs, where S stands for single, by doubling the number of connections on using the two edges of the physical connectors. As an example, a 256 Mbit SDRAM found in the marketplace could consist of four chips of 64 Mbit each. The 64 Mbit chips can be either (i) 8 K rows and 2 K columns of 4 bits (dubbed 16 × 4 in the commercial literature), or (ii) 8 K rows of 1 K columns of 8 bits (8 × 8), or (iii) 8 K rows of 512 columns of 16 bits (4 × 16). Generally, the cost of the module increases with the width it can deliver because of the larger number of data lines needed. Ideally, the number of bits that can be read on a read request should be equal to the number of bits that can be transmitted on the memory data bus. If the width is too narrow, a *reassembling buffer* must be included in the memory controller to concatenate the results of consecutive requests.

The number of chips that can be included on a DIMM is limited by physical constraints; 4 to 16 chips is a good order of magnitude. Because main memory is a resource that users will often want to expand, having very large capacity DIMMs means that jumping from one configuration to the next will involve large increments in capacity, and hence cost, thus also placing a user-motivated limit on the overall capacity of DIMMs.

Main memory is further divided into *banks* that can receive independent commands from the memory controller. Banks can be *interleaved* in several ways, depending on the mapping of memory addresses to banks. A popular mapping is to have banks interleaved by units of bus width. For example, if a memory has two banks and the data bus is 64 bits (8 bytes) wide, bank 0 stores all double words (8 bytes) at addresses 0, 16, 32, ..., while bank 1 stores those at addresses 8, 24, ... If the cache line size of the higher-level cache is greater than 8 bytes, then both banks can proceed in parallel to fulfill the request (except of course for the serialization on the bus). Alternatively, a bank can serve the whole request for a cache line, and the

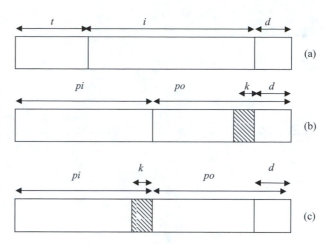

Figure 6.12. Interleaving of external banks: (a) address as seen from the cache, with d the line offset, i the set index, and t the tag; (b) line interleaving, with po the page offset, pi the page index, and k the bank index; (c) page interleaving.

next bank will then serve the next (addresswise) line. In the first case, because the bus is in general faster than the DRAM even in page mode, the number of banks should be larger than the number of cycles it takes to deliver data to the bus. Banks are also interesting for writes, for they allow writes in independent banks to proceed in parallel.

Banks can be grouped in banks of banks, or external banks. Within an external bank, the internal banks are interleaved so that they can deliver a request to the cache as fast as possible. The interleaving of the external banks is not as crucial, but some mappings are better than others. In Figure 6.12, we show how the address is seen from the cache's viewpoint and with two different natural interleavings of external memory banks.

As can be seen, in both types of interleaving the bank index overlaps with the cache set index. This will happen for all reasonable higher-level cache and DRAM page sizes. The consequence is that in case of cache conflict misses, the missing line will have the same bank number as the replaced line, and therefore the same bank will be accessed if there is line writeback (although this might be alleviated by the presence of write buffers) and also if the conflicting misses are occurring in a Ping-Pong fashion. In both cases, a full penalty of precharge and row and column access is likely, because the high-order bits in the addresses of the conflicting lines (those called pi at the left of the page offset) are likely to be different. A possible solution is to have the bank index be the result of a hashing (a single XOR operation is sufficient) of k bits in the *tag* field with the original k bits at the left of the page offset (those indicated in Figure 6.13). The advantage is that the cache conflicting misses will in all likelihood map to different banks and the contents of the pages remain the same (only the bank index changes). Moreover, because the original bank index is used in the hashing function, there is a uniform distribution of addresses in banks.

We have centered our discussion within the context of a single request from the processor, or rather the higher-level cache, to main memory. However, several

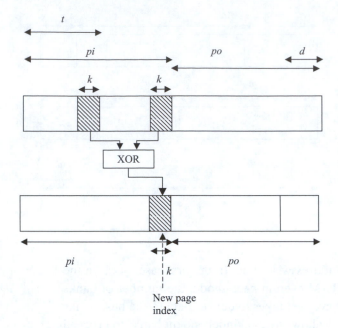

Figure 6.13. Interleaving scheme to reduce bank conflicts (adapted from Zhang et al. [ZZZ00])

requests could be pending, for the caches can be lockup-free. Moreover, I/O should be done concurrently, and main memory can also be shared by several processors. Holding the processor–memory bus busy during the whole latency of a request is not efficient in these conditions. Waiting times for the bus can be reduced by using a *split-transaction* bus. As its name indicates, with a split-transaction bus a request, for example a read transaction, can be decomposed into sending the address on the bus, releasing the bus while the DRAM reads the data, requesting the bus when the data are ready in the DRAM buffer, and, when this last request is satisfied, sending the data on the bus. While the data are read from the DRAM, other requests can be sent on the bus and queued at the memory controller, or data read from another transaction can be sent on the bus. If address lines and data lines of the bus are distinct, then two transactions can be in progress concurrently. The address for transaction A can be sent at the same time as the data for transaction B.

The presence of a split-transaction bus complicates the design of the memory controller. Buffering is needed for incoming transactions and possibly for read–write data. Of course, with this complication comes an advantage, namely, transactions do not have to be processed in order. An intelligent controller could, for example, delay prefetching transactions in favor of processing a real read miss as soon as possible. The controller could also take advantage of hits in row buffers, delaying temporarily a request that would destroy the locality of other transactions. However, because the read requests are processed out of order, they must be tagged so that the recipients can know when their requests are fulfilled.

Although interleaving and split-transaction buses improve the occupancy of the bus, they do not reduce the latency of single requests. Latency speedup requires faster devices and faster buses.

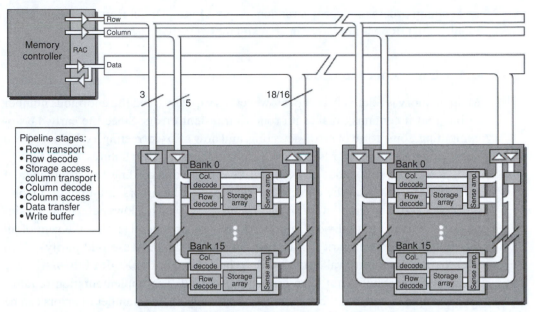

Figure 6.14. Direct Rambus and RDRAM microarchitecture (from Crisp [C97]).

6.4.3 Direct Rambus

A different DRAM interface has been proposed and manufactured by Rambus (see Figure 6.14). Now a narrow, very fast split-transaction bus carries the orders and transmits data to and from banks of DRAMs. The rationale is that the fast bus will provide more bandwidth for multimedia applications.

The bus is divided into row control lines (3 bits), column control lines (5 bits), and data lines (18 bits: 2 bytes plus 2 parity bits). Each external bank, or DRDRAM, comprises 16 internal banks that can deliver 16 bytes in 10 ns in the best conditions (open pages). The Rambus interface then takes these 16 bytes and transmits them 2 bytes at a time on the 400 MHz bus (1.25 ns for 2 bytes) with transfers occurring at both edges of the clock. Thus, peak bandwidth is 1.6 GB/s. Two adjacent internal banks share a 1 KB row buffer. The 17 half-row buffers may not be as efficient as the complete row buffers found in SDRAMs, but they occupy less space, which is at a premium in this organization. Note, however, that because of the split-transaction bus and decoupling of the row and column control lines, many operations such as refresh, precharge, and column access can occur simultaneously.

At the time of introduction of the Direct Rambus (circa 1997), SDRAMs were the norm and were running at best with 100 MHz internal clocks. With four banks, each providing 8 bits/cycle, the peak bandwidth was 0.4 GB/s, a far cry from the Direct Rambus's performance. With the improvements brought about by DDR DRAMs providing twice the bandwidth, a 64-bit bus, and a 133 MHz clock, the peak bandwidth becomes equal to that of Direct Rambus. Also, the latencies for a single access are about the same, of the order of 40 ns, because it takes several row and column orders to identify a random request in the Direct Rambus architecture. Finally, DRDRAMs are larger in area and more costly.

6.4.4 Error-correcting Codes

Main memory is relatively cheap. However, its capacity, (i.e., the enormous number of bits that it contains), makes it prone to transient errors. Since the early days of computing, some form of error-detecting, and now also -correcting, codes have been appended to memory words to increase mean times between failures.

Error-correcting codes (ECCs) can be classified according to the number of erroneous bits that can be detected (1 bit errors, 2 bit errors, multiple-bit errors) and corrected. The simplest form is *parity checking*, which allows detection of a single error. Given an n-bit word, an $(n + 1)$th bit is appended so that the sum of all bits is even (for even parity; of course, one could similarly use odd parity). With even parity, upon retrieval of the word, a check for 0 of the XOR of the $n + 1$ bits is done. If the result is not 0, an error has occurred. The implementation requires only a simple circuit, but the detection is weak: only an odd number of errors can be detected, and there is no means for correction.

Modern DRAMs and even some caches include more sophisticated error-correcting schemes. They are based on Hamming codes, which we present briefly.

The minimum number of bits that must be changed to convert one valid word to another is called the minimum distance of the code. For example, for n-bit words, an $(n + 1)$-bit word consisting of n data bits and a parity bit forms a code that has a minimum distance of 2. In general, a distance-k code will detect $k - 1$ errors.

Consider the case when we want to detect *and correct* one error. Detection implies a minimum distance of 2. If we create a code with a minimum distance of 3 by adding more error-correcting bits, a single error will result in a pattern that will be at distance 1 from the correct one and at distance 2 from all others. Hence, it will be possible to detect and correct a single error. If we were interested only in detection, the code of distance 3 would allow us to detect single and double errors. If we want to detect and correct a single error and detect two errors, then the code must have distance 4.

Let us see how a single error can be corrected and detected. We append m bits to the n-bit word. These m bits must identify which of the $n + m$ bits is in error, that is, 2^m patterns should identify one of the $n + m$ positions as well as the error-free condition. Thus, we must have

$$2^m > n + m + 1$$

or, for all practical purposes,

$$2^m > 2n \quad \text{and} \quad m = \lceil \log_2 n \rceil + 1$$

For example, let us see how to correct and detect one error in an 8-bit word. In this case we append $m = \lceil \log_2 8 \rceil + 1 = 4$ bits. Now we have a 12-bit word. Each index j in the 12-bit word can be represented as a sum of powers of 2, that is, $j = \sum a_i 2^i$, where a_i is either 0 or 1 and $i = 0, 1, 2, 3$. Each of the appended bits c_k will be a parity bit for all those indices that have 2^k in their representation. So if the original 8-bit word were $(x_0, x_1, \ldots, x_7)$, the new word is $(y_1, y_2, \ldots, y_{12}) = (c_0, \ldots, c_3, x_0, x_1, \ldots, x_7)$. Here y_1 is the parity bit for bits that have 2^0 in their representation, that is, $(y_1, y_3, \ldots, y_{11})$ or $(c_0, c_2, x_0, \ldots, x_6)$. Similarly, y_2 is the parity bit for bits that have 2^1 in their representation, that is, $(y_2, y_3, y_6, \ldots, y_{11})$ or $(c_1, c_2, x_1, \ldots, x_6)$, etc. Upon reading the word, the parity bits are computed, and if they are found different from those that were stored, we have an error whose index is given by $(c_0, \ldots, c_3)$.

> **EXAMPLE 4:** Assume that the bit x_4 corresponding to y_9 is in error. Then the computed values for c_0 (that is, y_1) and for c_3 (that is, y_4) will be different from those that are stored, yielding an error for the bit of index $2^0 + 2^3 = 9$.
>
> By adding a parity bit for the whole word, we increase the distance by 1 and can now detect (but not correct) two errors. For 64-bit words, as often delivered by DRAMs, we need to add 8 bits for single-error detection and correction and for double-error detection. This represents 12.5% extra storage requirement.

6.5 Summary

The disparity in speed between processors and main memory has given rise to a memory hierarchy, including several levels of caches. In modern microprocessors, there are an L1 I-cache and an L1 D-cache plus a unified L2 cache on chip. Many processors used for server applications have an off-chip L3 cache whose tag and status array can be on chip.

Since the goal of the memory hierarchy is to bring close to the processor the instructions and data that are going to be needed in the near future, a great deal of effort has been expended to minimize the latency of access at each level in order to minimize the average memory access time. The memory wall obstacle has been reduced to a series of still-challenging memory hurdles.

While the capacities of L2 and L3 caches have increased, access time requirements have limited the size and associativity of L1 caches. Techniques allowing parallel lookup of caches and TLBs, as well as schemes, such as victim caches, giving at low cost most of the benefit of larger associativities, have been implemented for L1 D-caches. Approximations to LRU for large-associativity L2 caches have minimized the amount of logic and power needed while retaining acceptable access times and miss ratios.

Prefetching, (i.e., bringing items into a cache before they are actually required), is a technique present at all levels of the memory hierarchy. Stride prefetching, an extension of the one-block lookahead technique, is particularly efficient for instructions and for data structures accessed according to a regular pattern. Stride prefetchers can be complemented by more sophisticated prefetchers catering to other data structures such as linked lists.

Out-of-order processors should not be hampered by stalling on a cache miss, for instructions further in program order could still execute. Similarly, prefetching implies that there could be several concurrent requests in the memory hierarchy. To that effect, caches are lockup-free, that is, mechanisms are implemented to allow more than one cache miss at a given time as well as return from higher levels of the hierarchy in any order.

In order to minimize the large tag arrays for high-level caches, the latter can be organized as sector caches with the unit of transfer between adjacent levels in the hierarchy being subblocks rather than entire lines. The capacity of these caches is such that uniform access times to all banks of the cache may not be possible any longer. Static routing assignments and dynamic interbank transfers may be needed to obtain better average access times.

The last level in the memory hierarchy, namely, main memory, has seen increases in capacity following Moore's law. However, latency and bandwidth have lagged behind, in spite of technological advances such as synchronous DRAMs (introduction of a clock on chip) allowing events on both edges of the clock (double data rate) and permitting the decomposition and scheduling of requests via split-transaction buses.

6.6 Further Reading and Bibliographical Notes

The literature on caches is very rich. We only provide a small sample of the major references in the area.

Smith's survey [S82] is the first paper to explain how the TLB and the cache can be searched in parallel. The various alternatives to access L1 caches are reviewed and analyzed in Peir et al. [PHS99]. Way prediction using an XOR technique was proposed by Calder et al. [CGE96] and used in the Alpha 21264. The use of page coloring is advocated in Kessler et al. [KJLH89].

An implementation and evaluation of column-associative caches can be found in Agarwal and Pudar [AP93]. Skewed caches were proposed by Seznec [S93]. Victim caches were introduced by Jouppi [J90], and the first industrial implementation, in the HP PA 7200, is reported in Chan et al. [CHKKSZ96].

The basic code-reordering algorithm is found in Pettis and Hansen [PH90]. Kalamatianos et al. [KKKM99] discuss possible improvements.

Software prefetching is covered in Mowry et al. [MLG92] and in Vanderwiel and Lilja's survey [VL00]. The simplest hardware sequential prefetching for instructions and data, (i.e., one-block lookahead), is proposed in Smith's survey [S82]. A variation taking into account the latencies of the various elements of the cache hierarchy has been implemented in the IBM Power4 and Power5, as indicated in the sidebar in this chapter. More details on these two microprocessors can be found in Tendler et al. [TDFLS02] and Kalla et al. [KST04]. Stream buffers were introduced by Jouppi [J90]. Palacharla and Kessler [PK94] showed that large stream buffers could advantageously replace higher-level caches in scientific applications. Many implementations and evaluations of stride prefetching, including those using a lookahead program counter, are presented in Chen and Baer [CB95]. Markov prefetchers were introduced by Joseph and Grunwald [JG97], and more sophisticated correlation prefetchers are evaluated in Lai et al. [LFF01]. Stateless prefetching is proposed in Cooksey et al. [CJG02]. The performance of greedy prefetching in the higher levels of the hierarchy can be found in Lin et al. [LRB01].

Lockup-free caches were first proposed by Kroft [K81]. Farkas and Jouppi [FJ94] discuss various implementations of MSHRs.

Baer and Wang proposed the multilevel inclusion property [BW88]. Wong and Baer [WB00] and Hallnor and Reinhardt [HR00] have developed alternatives to LRU replacement algorithms for L2 caches with large associativities.

Sector caches were the first caches ever implemented in the IBM 360/85, as recounted in Conti et al. [CGP68]. Nonuniform cache access has been proposed by Kim et al. [KBK02] among others.

A survey of various DRAM technologies as well as an evaluation of their timing parameters is found in Cuppu et al. [CJDM01]. Strategies for interleaving of memory banks are discussed in Zhang et al. [ZZZ00]. Direct Rambus is presented by Crisp [C97].

EXERCISES

1. (Section 6.1.1) In our presentation of the way prediction for physically addressed and physically tagged data caches, the predictive structure was accessed using an XOR of bits from the load PC and from the index register used in computing the effective address. Why is that a better idea than using the effective virtual address? How about waiting for the physical address?

2. (Section 6.1.1) For instruction caches, the way prediction can be embedded in the cache itself. How? Can the same technique be used for data caches?

3. (Section 6.1.1) Is page coloring adequate for L1 or for L2 caches? Discuss the various options.

4. (Section 6.1.1) Assume a page size of 4 KB and a direct-mapped virtual cache (virtual index and virtual tags) of 8 KB. On a cache miss:

   (a) How many lines have to be checked to see if the missing line has synonyms in the cache?
   (b) Generalize to the case of page size 2^k and a direct-mapped cache of capacity C.
   (c) Now consider the general case of page size 2^k, capacity C, and set associativity m.

5. (Section 6.1.2) In the column-associative cache (CAC), why should the high-order bit of the index be part of the tag when using flipping of the high-order bit of the index as a rehashing technique? What should be the setting of the rehash bit for an empty cache? Give examples of strings using references such as those defined as *a, b, c* in the text, whereby:

    (a) The miss ratio of the CAC is greater than that of a two-way set-associative cache.

    (b) The miss ratio of the CAC is smaller than that of a two-way set-associative cache.

6. (Section 6.1.2) Expand the formula given for the average memory access time in Section 2.2.2 in the following cases:

    (a) L1 is a column-associative cache.

    (b) L1 is a regular cache, and it is backed up by a victim cache.

7. (Section 6.1.3) In procedure reordering, when we merged two sets of procedures, *A* and *B*, we considered only the options whereby all procedures in set *A* were placed before those in set *B*. Does this mean that all procedures of set *B* will always be behind those of set *A* in the final layout?

8. (Section 6.2.1) In the text we state that we can trade off accuracy vs. coverage in prefetching. Discuss this assumption when varying the number of *useful prefetches* and the number of *prefetches generated*.

9. (Section 6.2.1) Accesses to I-cache lines often have a pattern such as i, $i + 1, i + 2, \ldots, i + n, j$ where each (sequential) reference is to a consecutive line until some branch is taken, as represented by reference j. What would be the accuracy and coverage for this string when one of the following variants of OBL is used?

    (a) Always prefetch.

    (b) Never prefetch.

    (c) Prefetch on miss.

    (d) Tag prefetch.

10. (Section 6.2.1) On a system using prefetching and a prefetch buffer, the following measurements were recorded during the run of some program:

- The total number of loads, N.
- The number of L1 misses due to the loads when there is no prefetching, m.
- The accuracy of prefetching, a.
- The coverage of prefetching, c.

Let l be the latency of accessing the L1 cache, $l + 1$ the latency of accessing a prefetch buffer, and L the latency of accessing the L2 and/or main memory when there is an L1 miss. Express the average memory access time for a load as a function of N, m, a, c, l, and L under the following assumptions:

    (a) The cost of a useless prefetch and the effect of prefetching on L are negligible.

    (b) A useless prefetch imposes an extra penalty of 1 cycle on the average memory access time.

(c) Now the prefetched lines go directly in L1, and a useful prefetch will not induce any cache pollution, whereas a useless prefetch will displace a line that will result in a miss with a probability p.

11. (Section 6.2.1) Consider the inner product program loop without prefetching shown in Figure 6.3. Each cache line can contain four elements, and initially none of the elements of arrays a and b are cached and they will not interfere with each other in the cache. Assume that the latency to access to the next level of the memory hierarchy is about the same as that of a multiplication followed by an addition. What would be the influence of the following hardware prefetchers on the time to execute the loop?

(a) A single stream buffer.
(b) Two buffers operating in stream mode (note that there is a single path between the cache and the next level in the memory hierarchy).
(c) A stride prefetcher using an RPT.

12. (Section 6.2.1) Consider straightforward matrix multiplication as implemented in the following segment of code:

```
Int A[100,100], B[100,100], C[100,100];
for (i=0; i<100; i++)
    for (j=0; j<100; j++)
      A[i,j] = 0;
      for (k=0; k < 100; k++)
      A[i,j] += B[i,k] × C[k,j];
```

Assume that the arrays A, B, and C start respectively at addresses $0 \times 0001\ 0000$, $0 \times 0004\ 0000$, and $0 \times 0008\ 0000$. In the body of the innermost loop, there are three load instructions, one each for the elements $B[i,k]$, $C[k,j]$, and $A[i,j]$ at respective addresses $0 \times 0000\ 0100$, $0 \times 0000\ 0104$, and $0 \times 0000\ 010c$. Show the contents of the RPT for these three instructions after iterations 1, 2, and 3 of the inner loop. The RPT is initially empty with all its fields initialized to 0.

13. (Section 6.2.2) Give the format of an MSHR for an L2–main-memory interface, assuming an L2 line is twice the size of an L1 line.

14. (Section 6.3.1) Prove that for the MLI property to hold we must have $(A_{L2} / B_{L2}) \geq (A_{L1} / B_{L1})$. You can assume that the capacity of L2 is much larger than that of L1 and that $B_{L2} \geq B_{L1}$

15. (Section 6.3.2) Show that true LRU can be implemented for an n-way set-associative cache using $n(n-1)/2$ bits per set.

Programming Projects

1. (Sections 2.2 and 6.1) Write application programs in some high-level language of your choice that enable you to discover the cache size, associativity, line size, and memory update policy of an L1 data cache. Check that your programs give the right answer by using a cache simulator (be sure that the cache simulator can use the output of the compilation of your programs!). The order in which you run your applications may be important, so think about this as you are designing them. You should only consider cache sizes, associativities, and line sizes that are powers of 2.

REFERENCES

[AP93] A. Agarwal and S. Pudar, "Column-Associative Caches: A Technique for Reducing the Miss Rate of Direct-Mapped Caches," *Proc. 20th Int. Symp. on Computer Architecture*, 1993, 179–190

[BW88] J.-L. Baer and W.-H. Wang, "On the Inclusion Properties for Multi-Level Cache Hierarchies," *Proc. 15th Int. Symp. on Computer Architecture*, 1988, 73–80

[C97] R. Crisp, "Direct Rambus Technology: The New Main memory Standard," *IEEE Micro*, 17, 6, Nov.–Dec. 1997, 18–28

[CB95] T.-F. Chen and J.-L. Baer, "Effective Hardware-based Data Prefetching for High-Performance Processors," *IEEE Trans. on Computers*, 44, 5, May 1995, 609–623

[CGE96] B. Calder, D. Grunwald, and J. Emer, "Predictive Sequential Associative Cache," *Proc. 2nd Int. Symp. on High-Performance Computer Architecture*, 1996, 244–253

[CGP68] C. Conti, D. Gibson, and S. Pitkowsky, "Structural Aspects of the IBM System 360/85; General Organization," *IBM Systems Journal*, 7, 1968, 2–14

[CHKKSZ96] K. Chan, C. Hay, J. Keller, G. Kurpanek, F. Shumaker, and J. Zheng, "Design of the HP PA 7200 CPU," *Hewlett Packard Journal*, 47, 1, Jan. 1996, 25–33

[CJDM01] V. Cuppu, B. Jacob, B. Davis, and T. Mudge, "High-Performance DRAMs in Workstation Environments," *IEEE Trans. on Computers*, 50, 11, Nov. 2001, 1133–1153

[CJG02] R. Cooksey, S. Jourdan, and D. Grunwald, "A Stateless, Content-Directed Data Prefetching Mechanism," *Proc. 10th Int. Conf. on Architectural Support for Programming Languages and Operating Systems*, Oct. 2002, 279–290

[FJ94] D. Farkas and N. Jouppi, "Complexity/Performance Trade-offs with Non-Blocking Loads," *Proc. 21st Int. Symp. on Computer Architecture*, 1994, 211–222

[HR00] E. Hallnor and S. Reinhardt, "A Fully Associative Software-Managed Cache Design," *Proc. 27th Int. Symp. on Computer Architecture*, 2000, 107–116

[J90] N. Jouppi, "Improving Direct-Mapped Cache Performance by the Addition of a Small Fully-Associative Cache and Prefetch Buffers," *Proc. 17th Int. Symp. on Computer Architecture*, 1990, 364–373

[JG97] D. Joseph and D. Grunwald, "Prefetching Using Markov Predictors," *Proc. 24th Int. Symp. on Computer Architecture*, 1997, 252–263

[K81] D. Kroft, "Lockup-Free Instruction Fetch/Prefetch Cache Organization," *Proc. 8th Int. Symp. on Computer Architecture*, 1981, 81–87

[KBK02] C. Kim, D. Burger, and S. Keckler, "An Adaptive, Non-Uniform Cache Structure for Wire-Delay Dominated On-Chip Caches," *Proc. 10th Int. Conf. on Architectural Support for Programming Languages and Operating Systems*, Oct. 2002, 211–222

[KJLH89] R. Kessler, R. Jooss, A. Lebeck, and M. Hill, "Inexpensive Implementations of Set-Associativity," *Proc. 16th Int. Symp. on Computer Architecture*, 1989, 131–139

[KKKM99] J. Kalamatianos, A. Khalafi, D. Kaeli, and W. Meleis, "Analysis of Temporal-based Program Behavior for Improved Instruction Cache Performance," *IEEE Trans. on Computers*, 48, 2, Feb. 1999, 168–175

[KST04] R. Kalla, B. Sinharoy, and J. Tendler, "IBM Power5 Chip: A Dual-Core Multi-threaded Processor," *IEEE Micro*, 24, 2, Apr. 2004, 40–47

[LFF01] A. Lai, C. Fide, and B. Falsafi, "Dead-block Prediction & Dead-block Correlation Prefetchers," *Proc. 28th Int. Symp. on Computer Architecture*, 2001, 144–154

[LRB01] W.-F. Lin, S. Reinhardt, and D. Burger, "Designing a Modern Memory Hierarchy with Hardware Prefetching," *IEEE Trans .on Computers*, 50, 11, Nov. 2001, 1202–1218

[MLG92] T. Mowry, M. Lam, and A. Gupta, "Tolerating Latency Through Software-Controlled Prefetching in Shared-Memory Multiprocessors," *Proc. 5th Int. Conf. on Architectural Support for Programming Languages and Operating Systems*, Oct. 1992, 62–73

[PH90] K. Pettis and R. Hansen, "Profile Guided Code Positioning," *Proc. ACM SIGPLAN Conf. on Programming Language Design and Implementation, SIGPLAN Notices*, 25, Jun. 1990, 16–27

[PHS99] J.-K. Peir, W. Hsu, and A. J. Smith, "Functional Implementation Techniques for CPU Cache Memories," *IEEE Trans. on Computers*, 48, 2, Feb. 1999, 100–110

[PK94] S. Palacharla and R. Kessler, "Evaluating Stream Buffers as a Secondary Cache Replacement," *Proc. 21st Int. Symp. on Computer Architecture*, 1994, 24–33

[S82] A. Smith, "Cache Memories," *ACM Computing Surveys*, 14, 3, Sep. 1982, 473–530

[S93] A. Seznec, "A Case for Two-way Skewed-Associative Caches," *Proc. 20th Int. Symp. on Computer Architecture*, 1993, 169–178

[TDFLS02] J. Tendler, J. Dodson, J. Fields, Jr., H. Le, and B. Sinharoy, "POWER4 System Microarchitecture," *IBM Journal of Research and Development*, 46, 1, Jan. 2002, 5–24

[VL00] S. Vanderwiel and D. Lilja, "Data Prefetch Mechanisms," *ACM Computing Surveys*, 32, 2, Jun. 2000, 174–199

[WB00] W. Wong and J.-L. Baer, "Modified LRU Policies for Improving Second-Level Cache Behavior," *Proc. 6th Int. Symp. on High-Performance Computer Architecture*, 2000, 49–60

[ZZZ00] Z. Zhang, Z. Zhu, and X. Zhang, "A Permutation-based Page Interleaving Scheme to Reduce Row-buffer Conflicts and Exploit Data Locality," *Proc. 33rd Int. Symp. on Microarchitecture*, 2000, 32–41

Multiprocessors

Parallel processing has a long history. At any point in time, there always have been applications requiring more processing power than could be delivered by a single-processor system, and that is still as true today as it was three or four decades ago. Early on, special-purpose supercomputers were the rule. The sophisticated designs that were their trademarks percolated down to mainframes and later on to microprocessors. Pipelining and multiple functional units are two obvious examples (cf. the sidebars in Chapter 3). As microprocessors became more powerful, connecting them under the supervision of a single operating system became a viable alternative to supercomputers performancewise, and resulted in cost/performance ratios that made monolithic supercomputers almost obsolete except for very specific applications. This "attack of killer micros" has not destroyed completely the market for supercomputers, but it certainly has narrowed its scope drastically.

In this chapter, we consider *multiprocessing*, that is, the processing by several processing units of the same program. Distributed applications such as Web servers or search engines, where several queries can be processed simultaneously and independently, are extremely important, but they do not impose the coordination and synchronization requirements of multiprocessing. Moreover, there are a number of issues, such as how to express parallelism in high-level languages and how to have compilers recognize it, that are specific to multiprocessing. We do not dwell deeply on these issues in this chapter; we are more interested at this junction in the architectural aspects of multiprocessing. However, these issues are becoming increasingly more important, and we shall touch upon them in Chapter 9.

If it were not for Moore's law (the increasing number of transistors on a chip) and the fact that clock cycle times are at the same level now as they were in 2003, we might not have considered including a chapter on multiprocessing in this book. However, the presence of a billion or more transistors on a chip, the multicycle access time of large centralized structures, the limitations on performance gains of ever more complex designs, and power issues that limit the clock frequencies have all converged toward the emergence of chip multiprocessors (CMPs), that is, the presence of two or more complete CPUs and their respective cache hierarchies on a single chip. The sidebar in the previous chapter (Section 6.3) gave one example of an IBM two-processor CMP. Intel is also producing dual and quad processor chips, and there is a Sun eight-processor CMP, with a 16-processor soon to follow. It is commonly acknowledged that a 64-processor chip should be available by the early 2010s.

We start this chapter with definitions of issues related to the structure of parallel computer systems. The forty-plus-year-old taxonomy due to Flynn is still useful. Because we are mostly interested in multiprocessors, we refine the category of multiple-instruction multiple-data (MIMD) systems and look at systems that address memory uniformly from the hardware point of view (uniform memory access (UMA) and symmetric multiprocessors (SMPs)), as well as at nonuniform memory access (NUMA). We then consider the interconnection of processors and memories, which plays an important role in this distinction.

The difference in memory addressing is also reflected in the cache coherence protocols that are required to preserve the integrity of the systems: snoopy protocols for the SMPs connected via buses, and directory protocols for the others.

Synchronization is essential for the correct behavior of parallel programs. We look at how synchronization is reflected in the ISAs of microprocessors and how atomic operations to acquire and release locks can be implemented. We then consider how the strict sequentiality enforcement of memory accesses can be relaxed.

We finish this chapter with a section that is part of the parallelism found in most contemporary general-purpose microprocessors but that does not really belong under the multiprocessor heading. It deals with the single-instruction multiple-data (SIMD) mode of operation, which is embedded in the many multimedia ISA extensions.

7.1 Multiprocessor Organization

7.1.1 Flynn's Taxonomy

As early as 1966, Flynn classified computer organizations into four categories according to the uniqueness or multiplicity of instruction and data streams. By *instruction stream* is meant the sequence of instructions as performed by a single processor. The sequence of data manipulated by the instruction stream(s) forms the data stream. Then, looking at the Cartesian product

(single instruction, multiple instruction) × (single data, multiple data)

we obtain the four architectures

Single instruction, single data (SISD).
Single instruction, multiple data (SIMD).
Multiple instruction, single data (MISD).
Multiple instruction, multiple data (MIMD).

The SISD category corresponds to the usual single processors that we have encountered so far. Granted, several instructions are executing concurrently in any pipelined machine, and moreover, superscalar processors have several functional units, but nonetheless the instructions are generated from a single stream and there is no streaming of data.

To our knowledge, there is no realization of the MISD concept, although some *streaming processors* can be construed to belong to this category. A streaming processor is composed of several processors of which each executes a dedicated set of programming kernels on a single stream of data. Research machines of this type are under consideration for applications such as image processing. One could also argue that the VLIW paradigm (recall Section 3.5), whereby an instruction word contains multiple instructions that are decoded and executed concurrently, is somewhat in between SISD and MISD in that the multiple instructions in the long word are determined at compile time.

In SIMD architectures, a single control unit fetches, decodes, and issues instructions that will be executed on processing elements (PEs), which are CPUs without control units. Transfer-of-control instructions are executed in the control unit, whereas arithmetic–logical and load–store instructions are broadcast to all PEs. PEs execute the broadcast instructions synchronously, and they have local data memories. Several supercomputers in the 1980s and 1990s, most notably the Illiac IV and the first Connection Machine CM-1, were built according to the SIMD model. Vector processors can also be considered to belong to the SIMD category. Although SIMD systems with full-fledged PEs are not cost-effective, the implementation of multimedia instructions in many microprocessors follows the SIMD model. We shall return to this topic in Section 7.5 of this chapter.

The MIMD organization is the most general. Several processors with their cache hierarchies operate in parallel in an asynchronous manner. Whether processors share a common memory and communicate via load–store instructions or whether they communicate via message passing is a major distinction. A further distinction for shared-memory systems is whether they access main memory in a uniform manner or whether each processor has associated with it a portion of a common distributed shared memory. Moreover, the number of processors in the system, their homogeneity, the interconnection fabric between processors and between processors and memories, means to assure cache coherence, and the way synchronization is handled all contribute to a vast design space for MIMD multiprocessor systems.

In this chapter, we are interested in the impact that multiprocessors have had on microprocessor and chip design. Therefore, we will limit ourselves to small to medium parallelism, that is, to a number of processors that could fit on a chip in the near future. This level of parallelism and the small distance between processors argue for a shared-memory organization. Large-scale parallelism and message-passing communication are certainly worthy of study, but they are beyond the scope of this book.

Before proceeding, it is worthwhile to remember Amdahl's law, which we saw in Section 1.2. Linear speedup in parallel processing is the exception rather than the rule. It happens only for "embarrassingly parallel" applications. Portions of the application that have to run sequentially, synchronization events where some

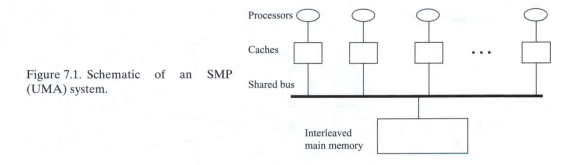

Figure 7.1. Schematic of an SMP (UMA) system.

processors may have to wait till some or all processors are finished with their portions of a task, and contentions for shared resources (e.g., the interconnection fabric) all limit the performance of parallel systems.

7.1.2 Shared Memory: Uniform vs. Nonuniform Access (UMA vs. NUMA)

In shared-memory systems, the parallel processes share a common address space. Data movement between the CPUs is achieved via the usual load–store instructions. Main memory can be at the same distance from all processors or can be distributed with each processor. In the first case, we have *uniform memory access* (UMA), and in the second, we have *distributed shared memory*, or nonuniform memory access (NUMA).

A schematic view of a UMA system where the interconnection fabric is a shared bus is shown in Figure 7.1. In some instances, processors can have an additional shared bus for control purposes, for example, for synchronization. Each processor–cache hierarchy in the figure could be a (chip) multiprocessor itself. The organization shown in Figure 7.1 is often referred to as a *symmetric multiprocessor* (SMP), although there is no need for the processors to be homogeneous as long as they have the same ISA, and although the caches can be of various geometries.

The use of a shared bus limits the number of processors in an SMP for at least two reasons: electrical constraints on the load of the bus, and contention for bus access. A second organization of UMA systems, often referred as *dance-hall* architecture, is shown in Figure 7.2. Now, the interconnection network can be a crossbar or an indirect network such as a butterfly network (cf. Section 7.1.3).

The drawback of the dance-hall architecture is that all noncached memory accesses are very far from processors, even those for variables that are private to the execution on a given processor. The alternative is to have nonuniform memory access.

In NUMA shared-memory architectures, each processing unit (or "processing element," not to be confused with the PEs of SIMD systems) consists of a processor, its cache hierarchy, and a portion of the global memory. On a load–store request that misses in the processor's cache hierarchy, a check is made first to see if the request can be satisfied in the local memory hierarchy attached to the processor. If so, the request is satisfied. If not, the request is sent to the appropriate local memory

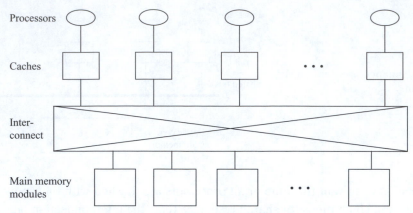

Figure 7.2. Schematic of a dance-hall (UMA) system.

of another processor through the interconnection network. The latter can either be centralized as shown in Figure 7.3 (closely resembling, from the interconnection viewpoint, the organization shown in Figure 7.2) or decentralized as in Figure 7.4. In this latter case, a "processing element" conceptually includes a switch that allows it to connect directly to some neighboring elements. Meshes and tori are typical interconnection fabrics in the case of decentralized networks.

In chip multiprocessors the local memory will not be on chip, but the L2s can be distributed in a manner similar to memories in UMA organizations or local memories in NUMA ones. Either buses, as in SMPs, or crossbars, as in NUMA with centralized networks, or meshes, as in NUMA with decentralized networks, can be the interconnection fabric.

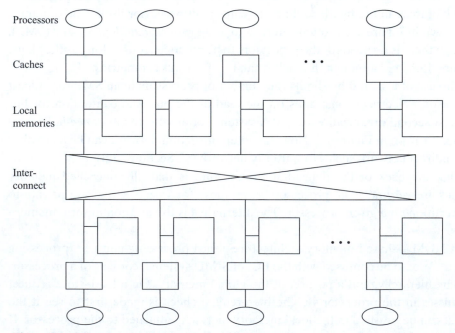

Figure 7.3. Schematic NUMA organization with centralized interconnection network.

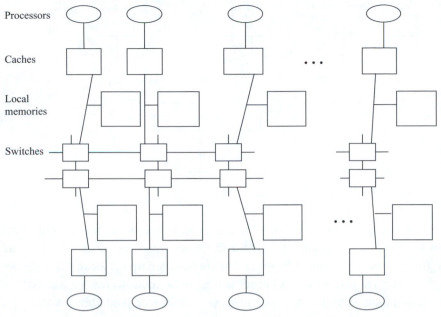

Figure 7.4. Schematic NUMA organization with decentralized interconnection network.

7.1.3 Interconnection Fabrics

We limit ourselves principally to three types of interconnection fabrics that might be used in CMPs: (i) shared bus, (ii) an example of a centralized switch, namely a crossbar, and (iii) an example of a decentralized one, namely meshes. There exist many more interconnection networks that have been used in MIMD and SIMD multiprocessors. The reader is referred to books and publications on such topics.

Shared Bus

The simplest form of interconnection is the shared bus as shown in Figure 7.1. It has several advantages in addition to its simplicity: low cost, ease of use, and, as we shall soon see, the possibility of simple cache coherence protocols because of the availability to broadcast information.

On the other hand, buses have severe limitations; in particular, they do not scale well. The lack of scalability stems from two sources. First, physical constraints (length, electrical loading) limit the number of devices that can be attached to a bus. Second, the longer the bus, that is, the larger the number of devices that can be attached to it, the slower it becomes. The loss of speed is due in part to the longer length and in part to the increased contention for the shared resource.

Contention is indeed a serious performance problem for shared-bus systems. If one defines bus utilization as

$$P = \frac{bus\ transaction\ time}{processor\ time + bus\ transaction\ time} \tag{1}$$

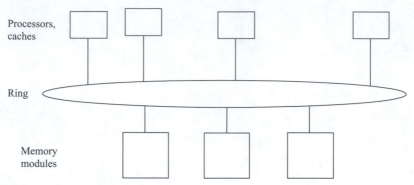

Figure 7.5. Ring interconnect.

then for a single processor we can estimate *processor time* as the average time between L2 misses. This is already quite a simplification, for it does not take into account the fact that there might be several misses queued up for lockup-free caches and the possibility of prefetching. In other words, some requests for the bus that are denied are resubmitted right away, and *processor time* as defined above is an upper bound.

The analysis becomes more complex for multiprocessors. In an extremely simplified manner, if we consider the quantity P from Equation (1) to be the probability that the bus is busy for one processor, then the probability that the bus is busy for n processors becomes

$$B(n) = 1 - (1 - P)^n$$

$B(n)$ is an approximation for the probability of bus occupancy. The point is that even with high cache hit ratios, the bus can become saturated quickly because of the long memory access times that are included in the bus transaction time.

We have seen in the previous chapter how split-transaction buses could remedy this situation somewhat by allowing releases of the data and address lines of the bus when they are not required by a given transaction. Thereby the bus transaction time can be reduced to the transfer times of addresses to memory and data transfers between caches and memory. Nonetheless, the bus cycle times are still much longer than processor cycle times, and the tendency to have large L2 lines that cannot be filled in a single bus transfer will increase bus data transfer times. Finally, contention is exacerbated by cache coherence transactions.

Early SMPs (circa 1985) consisted of up to 20 processors, with a maximum of about 30 a decade later. However, as processors became faster, bus saturation soon limited this number. Most SMPs based on a shared-bus interconnection have between two and eight processors (although these "processors" can themselves be two or four processors on a chip). The same limitation will arise in chip multiprocessors, but because the bandwidth on chip is more abundant, CMPs of up to eight processors may very well use a bus connection approach.

Rings are linear interconnects closely related to shared buses. In a ring, adjacent nodes of the network are directly connected (see Figure 7.5). The average distance for a ring of n modules is $n/2$ hops, but on the other hand, several transactions can be performed at the same time. The interconnect in the IBM Cell chip multiprocessor uses rings (see Chapter 8).

Crossbar

Crossbars provide maximum concurrency between n processors and m memories, that is, $\min(n,m)$, in the case of a UMA architecture as in Figure 7.2, and for n concurrent communications, (i.e., the mapping of one permutation of the n processors to another), in NUMA architectures. The cost – that is, the number of switches – grows as $m \times n$ in the first case and n^2 in the second. Logically, a crossbar switch for an n^2 connection is a set of n multiplexers. However, more control is needed in the case where several inputs are for the same output.

Crossbars are used extensively in specialized embedded processors such as network processors (see Chapter 8), where they provide the switch fabric for incoming and outgoing packets on different communication lines. If the number of lines is large, then the crossbar will be implemented on a separate chip. More often than not, capabilities for buffering and priority scheduling are included in the design. Some large multiprocessors have used crossbars, but quite often in a hierarchical way. For example, the Convex Exemplar, built in the 1990s, was composed of "hypernodes" connected via rings, where each hypernode was an SMP of eight processors sharing a common memory via a crossbar.

In the CMP arena, the squaring factor in a crossbar will limit the area that can be devoted to the interconnection network. We have seen examples of crossbars in our presentation of the IBM Power4 and Power5 (in the sidebar in Section 6.3). A crossbar connecting eight processors to four banks of L2 caches is present in Sun's Niagara (Chapter 8).

Crossbar switches are the building blocks for *direct interconnection networks* such as the Butterfly Network (cf. Figure 7.6) that have been used in some NUMA systems (IBM SP series). These multistage interconnection networks consist of $\log n$ stages of $n/2$ switches each. Each switch is a 2×2 crossbar, but actual implementations could use larger crossbars by merging several stages into one. The cost of such networks is proportional to $n \log n$, with the drawback that a connection takes $\log n$ time. An advantage is that fault tolerance can be included in the design at the cost of one or more extra stages.

Meshes

In direct connection networks, each processor is at the same distance from each memory or from any other processor. In *indirect interconnection networks* processing elements are connected to other processing elements at various distances. Quite often, these interconnection networks are differentiated by their dimension. For example:

- A ring (cf. Figure 7.5) is a unidirectional network;
- a 2D mesh (cf. Figure 7.7) where a processing element not at the edge is connected to four neighbors by a link of length 1 is a two-dimensional network;

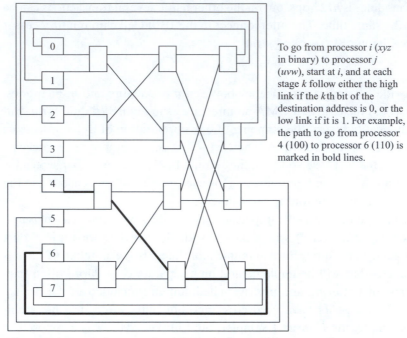

To go from processor i (xyz in binary) to processor j (uvw), start at i, and at each stage k follow either the high link if the kth bit of the destination address is 0, or the low link if it is 1. For example, the path to go from processor 4 (100) to processor 6 (110) is marked in bold lines.

Figure 7.6. Butterfly network of eight processors (three stages).

- a 2D torus, which is like a mesh but with links wrapping around at the edges, is also a two-dimensional network;
- an m-dimensional hypercube, where each processing element is connected by a link of length 1 to each of its m neighbors, is an m-dimensional network.

Many multiprocessors, and parallel processors using message passing, have been built using indirect networks. For example, a ring was used in the Kendall KSR machine and in the Sequent CC-Numa, where the ring connected shared-bus SMPs. The Intel Paragon used 2D meshes to connect up to 512 nodes, where each node

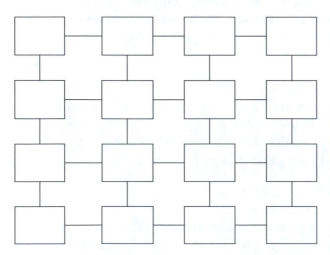

Figure 7.7. Schematic view of a 2D mesh. Each box is a processing element connected by a link of length 1 to its four neighbors.

consisted of an Intel i860 processor for computing purposes and one for switching purposes, along with DRAM memory. The Cray 3TD and 3TE use a 2D torus interconnection. The Connection Machine CM-2, an SIMD processor, used a 12-dimensional hypercube where each node had 16 1-bit processors.

Routing of a message from one processing element to another can be done in several ways. Higher dimension first is a common pattern. In a 2D mesh, this implies that the message travels first vertically, then horizontally. A more important question is *control flow*, that is, how messages make progress along the source–destination path. Various techniques, such as wormhole routing and virtual cut-through, have been developed. However, in the realm of CMPs, where "messages" are memory requests, control flow might simply require acknowledgments and retries. Although no commercial CMP uses indirect networks at this point, a number of research machines that can be classified under the rubric of grid processors use 2D meshes. The investigation of interconnection networks, which was a topic of high interest in the 1970s and 1980s, has seen a renewal of interest now that CMPs with more than eight processors, grid processors, and special-purpose processors with hundreds of ALUs on a chip are on the horizon.

7.2 Cache Coherence

The performance value of a well-managed uniprocessor cache hierarchy was documented in Chapter 6. In multiprocessors, main memory is even farther from each individual processor, for the time to traverse the interconnection network will be longer than that of access via the memory bus. Moreover, there will be more contention, both in the network and at the memory modules themselves. Finally, a new problem arises in shared-memory multiprocessors, namely, the consistency of shared data in the various caches, which is referred to as the *cache coherence problem.*

To illustrate the cache coherence problem, consider a three-processor system as abstracted in Figure 7.8. Each rectangular box represents a processor and its cache hierarchy. We show a UMA system, but the example would work similarly for a NUMA architecture.

EXAMPLE 1: Initially, all caches are empty. Then processor P1 reads some data A. After resolving the cache miss, the data are stored in P1's cache. In the next action involving A, let processor P2 read the same data A. On the cache miss, a copy of A – coming from either memory or P1's cache, depending on the cache coherence protocol – is stored in P2's cache. At this point, shown in Figure 7.8(a), P1 (or rather its cache), P2, and memory all have a valid copy of A, represented by a hatched box in the figure. Now let P3 have a write miss on the same data A. Once a copy of A is in P3's cache, there are two possible courses of action. In the first case, P3 writes a new value for A and sends it to all other caches that contain a copy of A as well as to main memory, so that all caches and main memory have the same value for A. Figure 7.8(b) shows the results

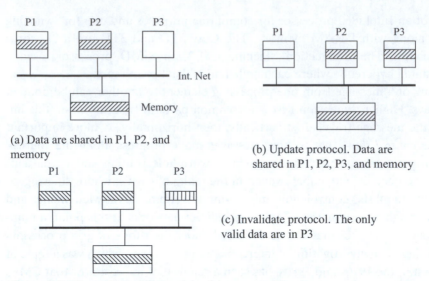

(a) Data are shared in P1, P2, and
memory

(b) Update protocol. Data are
shared in P1, P2, P3, and memory

(c) Invalidate protocol. The only
valid data are in P3

Figure 7.8. Illustration of the cache coherence problem.

of this *write–update protocol*, which resembles the write-through policy for
single-processor caches. The second case occurs when *A* sends an invalidation
message to all other caches containing *A* and to main memory. Now, as a result
of this *write–invalidate protocol*, P3's cache is the only one holding a valid copy,
as shown in Figure 7.8(c). The similarity with the single-processor writeback
policy is apparent.

In Example 1, we see that there is a requirement for cache lines to have some
state associated with them to indicate whether they are valid (for invalidate protocols), clean (i.e., unchanged from the image in main memory), or dirty (the opposite of clean). Also, cache controllers issue messages and must answer messages
from other controllers. The design and implementation of coherence protocols will
depend on whether the architecture permits easy broadcasts or not. In the case
where broadcast is as simple as a direct message, (i.e., in the case of a shared-
bus system), we have *snoopy protocols*; in the other cases, we rely on *directory
protocols*.

7.2.1 Snoopy Cache Coherence Protocols

Snoopy protocols are implemented for shared-bus systems. In these protocols all
messages sent on the bus are *snooped*, (i.e., intercepted and listened to), by all cache
controllers that answer in appropriate fashion if they have a copy of the line that is
being processed. In the following, we concentrate on invalidation-based protocols,
because in SMP systems the (L2) caches connected to the bus are writeback. We
leave the design of an update protocol, which could be important for future CMPs,
to the exercises.

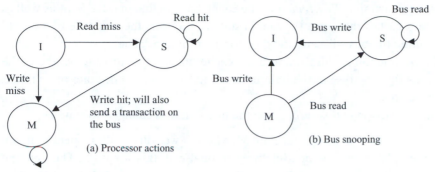

Figure 7.9. Basic three-state write–invalidate snooping protocol.

The most basic protocol requires that each line be in one of three possible states:

- Invalid (I): The line that was present in the cache has been invalidated.
- Shared (S): There is one or more copies of the line in the system, and they all have the same value.
- Modified (M), AKA dirty: The line is the single valid copy in the system.

Initially, all lines are in state I. We decompose the protocol into actions and state transitions due to processor requests (Figure 7.9(a)) and those due to bus snooping (Figure 7.9(b)).

Let us start with the processor actions.

- On a cache read hit, a line that was in either the S or the M state remains in the same state.
- On a cache read miss, a new line is brought into the S state via a *Bus_read* transaction. If the line was already present, it had to be in state I. If the line was not already there, a replacement is needed and the victim is written back to memory if it is (or has been – see discussion of next action) modified. The requested line will come from another cache if one of them holds a copy, and from memory otherwise.
- On a write hit, no state change occurs if the line is in state M, because it is already the only valid copy in the system. However, if the line is in state S, then it must be put in state M, because it is modified by the writing; and all other copies in the system must be invalidated. Hence, a *Bus_write* signal is sent on the shared bus along with the address of the line that is modified.
- On a write miss, the processor requests the line via a *Bus_read*, and as soon as the data arrive, it sends a *Bus_write* transaction. At that point, the line is put in state M. Replacement of a victim proceeds as in the read miss case.

We now consider the state changes due to the snooping on the bus for a cache that did not initiate the transaction.

- If the line addressed in the *Bus_read* or *Bus_write* transaction is not in the cache or is in the cache in state I, no action is necessary.

- If the transaction is *Bus_read* and the cache has the line in state S, it, as well as all other caches that have the line in state S, requests the bus. The first one to be granted the bus will send the data to the initiating cache.
- If the transaction is *Bus_read* and the cache has the line in state M, the cache requests the bus to send the data to the initiating cache. The state of its line is changed to S.
- If the transaction is *Bus_write*, then the line's state is changed to state I.

Note that a line can pass from state M, where it was dirty with respect to memory, to state S. We have two possible ways to deal with this situation. The first one is to retain the dirty bit that is set on a write hit or write miss, in addition to setting the state to M. Then, if the line that had passed from state M to state S is replaced, it will have its dirty bit on and will be written back to memory. The drawback is that the same data may be written back several times from different caches to memory; but this does not affect correctness. The second possibility is that when a line passes from state M to state S and sends the data to the initiating cache, the data are sent at the same time to memory. The dirty bit is not needed any longer, and on a replacement the victim will be written back to memory only if it is in state M. In this option, a *Bus_read* can be served from memory as well as from another cache. Since we are dealing with writeback caches, the dirty bit alternative seems more appropriate, although it requires an extra bit of state.

The cache controller's actions with respect to coherence actions are summarized in the pseudocode below.

SNOOPY CACHE CONTROLLER'S COHERENCE ACTIONS (THREE-STATE WRITE–INVALIDATE). We assume that there is a dirty bit per line. *victim* is the line to be replaced. *data_in* is a signal indicating that a line is being transmitted by a cache as an answer to *Bus_read* and will be recognized by the sender of *Bus_read* as completion of the transfer. The transfer from the bus data lines to the correct cache line is subsumed by the recognition of *data_in*. No action will be taken on *Bus_read* and *Bus_write* if the line is not in the cache.

```
case 'read_hit': exit
case 'read_miss': begin Request_bus;
                        when bus_granted send 'Bus_read';
                        if dirty_bit.victim then write back victim;
                        when data_in then state←S;
                  end
case 'write_hit': if state = M then exit
                  begin Request_bus;
                        when bus_granted send 'Bus_write';
                        state←M;
                        dirty_bit←true;
                  end
```

```
case 'write_miss': begin Request_bus;
                      when bus_granted send 'Bus_read';
                      if dirty_bit.victim then write back victim;
                      when data_in then begin Request_bus;
                                           when bus_granted send
                                           'Bus_write';
                                           state ← M;
                                           dirty_bit←true;
                                           end
                   end
case 'Bus_read': if state = I then exit
                    begin Request_bus;
                          when bus_granted send 'data_in';
                          if state = M then state←S;
                    end
case 'Bus_write': state←I
```

A question that is often asked is: "What happens if two processors want to write the same line at the same time?" The bus serves as a serialization device in that case. The cache controller to which the bus is granted first will perform the first write. If the writes are for the same data in the same line, then the result is not deterministic and the programmer should take account of that, either using synchronization explicitly in order to avoid this race condition, or developing the application in such a way that it does not matter which write is performed first. The latter option is quite all right for problems such as solving partial differential equations with relaxation methods, where the final result is obtained through some convergence criterion.

Although the three-state protocol is simple, its actual implementation is more difficult than it appears at first glance, especially when features such as split-transaction buses, lockup-free caches, and prefetching are present. The finite-state machine that is used to arrive in one of the three states defined above has in fact many more than three states. To show why this happens, consider the following example.

EXAMPLE 2: Processor cache P1 and processor cache P2 want to write to different words of the same line L, which is in state I in both caches P1 and P2, and in state S in cache P3. The shared-bus system uses a split-transaction bus. Assume that the two writes happen "at the same time" but there is no indeterminism, because the writes are to different words. A possible sequence of events among the many that can arise is as follows (we use the notation of the pseudocode above):

- Time t_0: P1 submits a *Bus_read* on the bus that is snooped by P3. P1 is in a state not indicated in the diagram and akin to "waiting for *data_in*."
- Time t_1: P2 submits a *Bus_read* on the bus that is snooped and queued by P3 (note that we have introduced a queue). P2 is also in the state "waiting for *data_in*."

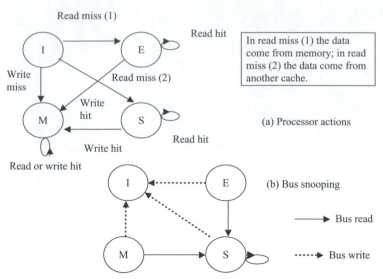

Figure 7.10. A four-state MESI protocol.

- Time t_2: P3 initiates a data transfer *data_in* for line L towards P1 (note that the transfer must be tagged with P1's "address" so that P1 knows it is the recipient; this is a requirement for split buses).
- Time t_3: P1 has received the data and sends a *Bus_write*. Both P2 and P3 must put line L in state I. In addition, P2 must pass in a state that will allow it to resend its *Bus_read* request, and P3 must dequeue the request from P2.

Although this situation is not difficult to analyze, it shows that the three-state machine requires refinement at the implementation level.

A second complexity brought up by snooping is that requests from the processor and snooping checks for different lines in the same cache should be able to proceed in parallel. This concurrency is critically important for CMPs, where L1s might be the caches on which coherence is applied and slowing access to L1 is not allowable. A common practice is therefore to duplicate the tag array, with one array for processor lookups (read and write hit or miss) and one for snooping lookups (*bus_read* and *bus_write*). Of course, both arrays must be kept consistent.

With these caveats on the simplicity of the three-state protocol, we now describe a slightly more complex protocol that has better performance than the three-state one in that it will reduce the number of bus transactions. The early motivation for introducing a fourth state was that it did not increase the number of bits required for the encoding (2 bits for both three and four states) and therefore came for free.

A fourth state, called *exclusive* (E), can be used to indicate that an unmodified line that is being cached is the only cached copy in the system. The advantage is that on a write hit to an E line, there is no need to broadcast an invalidation signal. Of course, the line will then transit to the M state. The presence of the E state is particularly useful for private variables (e.g., variables that are on the stack). A protocol using the M, E, S, and I states is shown in Figure 7.10.

On a read miss, if the data are in another cache, then they must come from there. Thus, the bus must have a special control line that indicates, as an answer to a *Bus_read* transaction, whether the data are transferred from a cache or from memory. When they come from another cache, the line will be loaded in state S. If they come from memory, they will be loaded in state E. On a *Bus_read* transaction, if a cache has the line in state E, it must transfer the data to the requesting cache and change the state of its line to S. Other transitions are similar to those in the three-state protocol, with the addition of raising an extra control line on transfers of lines in state E or S, as explained in this and the previous paragraphs.

An alternative to state E is an *ownership state* (O), whereby a distinction is made between a shared line (state S) and the latest shared line that has been modified, for example when there has been a transition from state M to state S (now state O). Only the lines in states M and O need to be written back, and one can dispense with the dirty bit.

The requirements of cache coherence introduce a new kind of miss, namely *coherence misses.* The three C's defined in Section 2.2 now become the four C's. As the cache sizes increase, the number of coherence misses will also increase, and therefore the assumption that we made, "the larger the cache, the better the performance," might not hold in multiprocessor systems. We shall return to performance aspects of cache coherence once we have presented protocols for non-shared-bus systems.

7.2.2 Directory Protocols

When the interconnection network is not a shared bus (or a ring), snooping is not a realistic option. Broadcast, or even multicast, (i.e., sending a message to several selected processing elements), is not easy, although it is certainly more convenient in centralized networks than in decentralized ones. Therefore, another mechanism for cache coherence is needed. The basic idea is to have a directory that indicates for each line in memory:

- whether the line is cached or not;
- where the line is cached (this could be only partial information);
- whether the cached line is clean or dirty.

In the *full directory* scheme, complete information is provided for all lines in memory. For an n-processor-cache[1] system, a Boolean vector of size $n + 1$ is appended to each memory line. If a bit i ($i = 1, \ldots, n$) is set, it indicates that the ith cache has a copy of the line. Bit 0 indicates whether the cached line is clean or dirty. A vector of all zeros means that the line is only in memory. If bit 0 is set, only one of the other bits can be set.

---

[1] Several processors and L1 caches could share an L2 cache to form a *unit of coherence*. Coherence would have to be maintained first among the L1s within a unit and then between the L2s of various units. We consider here coherence between the L2s, but we shall see examples where directory protocols can be used at the L2 and L1 levels.

In a distributed shared-memory NUMA system, each processing element has the part of the directory containing the information related to the lines stored in its memory. The processing element whose memory contains the initial value of a line will be called the *home node* of the line. Any other processing element will be a *remote node*. On a cache miss, the request will be sent to the home node's directory of the missing line. Replaced dirty lines will be written back to the memory of their home node.

The basic protocol for coherence is as follows. We assume writeback caches with each line having a clean–dirty bit. Consider actions emanating from the ith cache. Let L be the line that is being accessed, let j be the index of L's home node, and V the Boolean vector of the directory associated with L.

- Read hit on a clean or dirty line and write hit on a dirty line: Do nothing.
- Read miss: A request is sent to the directory of the home node.
  - The directory indicates that the line L is uncached or that the line is cached in the clean state (bit $V_0 = 0$). The data will be sent to cache i, and V_i, the ith bit in V, is set.
  - The directory indicates that the line L is cached and dirty (bit $V_0 = 1$), and it gives the index k of where the line is cached (bit $V_k = 1$, and it is the only bit except V_0 that is set).
    - If $k = j$, the line is cached in the home node. The data are written back from the home node's cache j to the home node memory. Line L's dirty bit is reset to clean in cache j. The data are then sent to cache i. Bit V_i is set to 1, and bit V_0 is reset to 0. This is called a one-hop process.
    - If L is cached in cache $k \neq j$, the home node asks cache k to write back the data and to reset its dirty bit for line L to clean. Then, once the data arrive at the home node, they are stored in the home node's memory and forwarded to cache i. Bit V_i is set to 1, and bit V_0 is reset to 0. This is called a two-hop process.
- Write miss: A request is sent to the directory of the home node.
  - The directory indicates that the line L is uncached: The home node sends the data, and bits V_i and V_0 are set to 1.
  - The directory indicates that the line is cached in the clean state: The home node sends an invalidation message to all caches whose bits are set in V (this is in fact a series of messages if multicast is not possible). Upon receiving an acknowledgment from a targeted cache, its corresponding bit in V will be reset. When all acknowledgments have been received, the home node forwards the data to cache i. Bits V_i and V_0 are set to 1.
  - The directory indicates that the line is cached in the dirty state in cache k ($V_0 = 1$ and $V_k = 1$).
    - If $k = j$, the home node, the data are written back from the home node's cache to the home node's memory. Line L is invalidated in cache j. The data is then sent to cache i. Bits V_i and V_0 are set, and bit V_j is reset (one hop).

- If L is cached in cache k, the home node asks cache k to write back the data and to invalidate its copy of line L. Then once the data arrive at the home node, they are forwarded to cache i. Bits V_i and V_0 are set, and bit V_k is reset (two hops).

- Write hit on a clean block: Proceed like a write miss on a clean block as described, except that the invalidation message is not sent to cache i, the requesting cache, and that the data do not need to be sent from the home node or any other cache.

When a dirty line is replaced, it is written back in the home node and its associated vector is reset to all zeros. When a clean line is replaced, we could just do nothing, as in a regular writeback cache, but then the directory would be slightly erroneous. At the very least, superfluous invalidation messages might be sent later on. A better solution is to have a message be sent to the home node asking for a modification of the directory, namely, a reset of the bit corresponding to the cache where the line is replaced.

The protocol is summarized in the following pseudocode:

FULL DIRECTORY PROTOCOL. We assume that there is a dirty bit per line. *victim* is the line to be replaced. *write_back(victim)* will write back *victim* to its home node if it is dirty and in any case change *victim*'s directory vector according to whether it is clean (reset a single bit) or dirty (reset to all 0's).

L is the line that is accessed in cache i. The home node is j. V is the directory vector associated with L. If L is dirty, its only copy is in cache k.

Request_read asks the home node j for line L, and *Request_write* does the same, but asks also for invalidation of all cached copies. *Request_invalidate* asks the controller at the home node to invalidate all copies except that from cache i.

Send_line sends a copy of line L from home node j to cache i. *Purge* is a request from the home node j to cache k to write back its copy of line L in the memory of j and *Invalidate* it in cache k. *Send_invalidate(m)* is a message from the home node asking a cache m to *Invalidate* its copy of L. It will be answered by an *Ack(m)*. We do not differentiate when $k = j$.

```
case 'read_hit': exit
case 'read_miss': begin Request_read; write_back(victim);   /*at i */
        if V0 = 0 then begin Send_line; Vi ← 1; end      /* at j*/
        else begin Purge;                                /*at j */
                            write_back(L); L.dirty ← 0;   /*at k */
                            Send_line;  V0 ← 0; Vi ← 1;   /*at j */
                end
end
```

```
case 'write_hit': if L.dirty = 1 then exit              /*at i, L is dirty*/
              else begin Request_invalidate;            /*at i, L is clean*/
                       for all m ≠ i s.t. Vm = 1            /*at j */
                            begin Send_invalidate(m);
                                Invalidate(L); Ack(m);      /*at m */
                                Vm ← 0;                     /*at j */
                            end{for}
                        V0 ← 1;                             /*at j */
                        L.dirty ← 1;                        /*at i */
                   end
case 'write_miss': begin Request_write; write_back(victim);   /*at i */
                     if (V0 = 0 and all Vi = 0) then
                          begin Send_line; Vi ← 1; V0← 1; end /*at j */
                     else if V0 = 0 then
                     begin for all m ≠ i s.t. Vm=1
                          begin Send_invalidate(m);           /*at j */
                                Invalidate(L); Ack(m);        /*at m */
                                Vm ← 0;                       /*at j */
                          end{for}
                          Send_line; V0 ← 1; Vi ← 1           /*at j */
                     end
                     else begin Purge;                        /*at j*/
                               write_back(L);                 /*at k*/
                               Send_line; Vi ← 1; Vk ← 0      /*at j*/
                     end
                     L.dirty ← 1                              /*at i*/
                end
```

A drawback of the full directory scheme is that the size of the directory grows linearly with the number of processing elements in the system. For example, the amount of memory overhead for the directory of an eight-processor system when the L2 cache lines (we assume that L2s are the caches on which coherence is applied) are 64 bytes would be less than 2% ($9/(64 \times 8) = 0.18$). If we have 64 processors, it becomes almost 13%. An alternative is to encode only partial information on the location of the cached lines.

The most memory-economical protocol must encode whether the line is uncached (state I), or, if it is cached, whether it is clean (state S) or dirty (state M). Recall that these requirements were those of the three-state snoopy protocol. Thus, two bits of encoding are necessary. A fourth state can be added for free, and the best choice is to have an exclusive state (state E) that has the same meaning as the one of the same name in snoopy protocols. However, this two-bit protocol is a directory scheme, and the states are encoded once per line in the directory memory, and not at each cache as in snoopy protocols. The drawback of this encoding relative to the full directory scheme is that there is no information on where the line is cached.

The main differences between this two-bit protocol and the full directory one are as follows.

- On a read miss:
  - If the line is in state I, the state in the directory becomes E. Of course, data are sent from the home node's memory.
  - If the line is cached and in state E, the data are sent from the home node's memory, and the state becomes S.
  - If the line is in state S, the data are sent from the home node's memory, and the state is unchanged.
  - (Major change:) If the line is in state M, broadcast a writeback message to all caches. Those that do not have a copy of the line will simply acknowledge. The one with a copy of the line will send it back to the home node memory, resetting its own clean–dirty bit to clean. The home node will then forward the data to the requesting cache. This can be either a one-hop or a two-hop process, depending on the location of the dirty line. The state becomes S.
- On a write miss:
  - If the line is in state I, the state in the directory becomes M. Of course, data are sent from the home node's memory.
  - (Major change:) If the line is in state E or S, broadcast an invalidation message to all caches. Caches with a copy of the line invalidate it. All caches acknowledge receipt of the broadcast. Data are sent from the home node's memory after all acknowledgments have been received and the state becomes M.
  - (Major change:) If the line is in state M, proceed as in the case of the read miss except that the line in the cache holding it becomes invalid and that the state in the directory becomes M.
- On a write hit to a clean block:
  - If the line is in state E, the home node acknowledges and changes the state to M.
  - If the line is in state S, proceed as in the case of a write miss for a line in state S (above), but do not send any data.

If the interconnection network is decentralized, broadcasts can be very expensive. In order to reduce their occurrence, a number of schemes have been proposed midway between the full directory and the two-bit protocols. The basic motivation is that quite often the lines are shared by a limited number of processors, say two or three.

Many variants have been proposed for these partial directories. In one class of protocols, instead of having $n + 1$ bits as in the full directory, each vector has $i \log n + 1$ bits, that is, the encoding for i cache locations. The protocols can be distinguished by whether they will use broadcast when more than i caches have a copy of a line (the so-called $Dir_i B$ protocols), or whether there will be some forced invalidation when more than i caches request a copy (the Dir_iNB protocols), or whether the directories can overflow in main memory.

An alternative is to have directories embedded in the caches themselves. All copies of a cached line are linked together by a doubly linked list. The list is doubly linked to allow easy insertions and deletions. The head of the list is in the home node. An insertion is done between the new cache and the home node. Deletions can be done in place. The amount of memory needed – two pointers of size $\log n$ per line in each cache – is proportional to the amount of memory devoted to caches, not to the total amount of memory. The drawback of this scalable scheme (its name is SCI, for "scalable coherent interface") is that invalidations require the traversal of the whole list.

In first-generation CMPs, like the two-processor IBM Power4 and Power5 or the eight-processor Sun Niagara, the L1 caches are kept coherent with respect to the shared L2 with a full directory protocol. The protocol is in fact easier because the L1 are write-through, write-no-allocate caches.

As was the case for snoopy protocols, directory protocols are more complex to implement than the description we have provided here. Of course, there is no atomic transaction, because it would lead right away to deadlocks. To see how this could be happening, think of two processors, each requesting a line from the other one's cache, with their home nodes different. In the same vein, only one transaction for a given line should be in progress. If a second one is initiated, it should be acknowledged negatively (beware of starvation) or buffered (beware of buffer overflows and hence deadlocks). This is of course even more important for protocols that use broadcasts. Solutions, besides imposing both positive and negative acknowledgments, might use duplicate interconnection networks, one for requests and one for replies, and/or buffer reservation schemes.

7.2.3 Performance Considerations

A number of issues have definite influences on the design and performance of coherence protocols. First, we have to revisit the multilevel inclusion (MLI) property that was introduced in Section 6.3.1, for now an L2 can be shared by several L1s, as in the *multicore* CMPs (see Chapter 8).

Recall that the MLI property in a hierarchy consisting of a *parent* cache and a single *child* cache – with the number of sets in the parent being greater than the number of sets in the child and the line size of the parent being at least as large as that of the child – holds if

$$A_{parent}/B_{parent} \geq A_{child}/B_{child}$$

where A is the associativity and B the line size. If the parent has k children (we assume they are identical, but the analysis can be carried out even if they are not), the MLI property holds if

$$A_{parent}/B_{parent} \geq k(A_{child}/B_{child})$$

EXAMPLE 3: A direct-mapped L1 of capacity 1 KB and line size 4 bytes has a parent L2 of capacity 32 KB and line size 16 bytes. In the case of a single processor, the MLI will hold if the L2's associativity is at least 4. If the L2 is now shared by four L1s, the L2's associativity must become 16.

As evidenced by Example 3, if the ratio between line sizes and/or the number of children caches becomes larger, meeting the required associativity of the parent cache becomes impractical. Instead of a strict MLI, the property has to be *partial MLI*, that is, invalidation of child lines must be performed even if there is no need for it from a strict coherence viewpoint. Some form of partial directory can be associated with each parent cache line in order to regulate the number of copies that can be cached.

A second performance issue directly associated with coherence misses, the fourth C in the taxonomy of misses, is that of *false sharing*. False sharing occurs when two (or more) processors write in an interleaved fashion two (or more) different subsets of the same line. As the line size increases, the probability of false sharing also increases. On the other hand, we saw previously that applications with good spatial locality have better performance with larger cache lines. In the same way that for each application on a single processor there is an optimal line size, there is also an optimal, and maybe different, line size in the case of multiprocessors. Various compiler and hardware protocol tweaks have been proposed to reduce the detrimental effects of false sharing.

Because of the long latencies to access memory, many techniques have been proposed to adapt cache coherence protocols to specific patterns and to prefetching. Speculative techniques have also been investigated. All these optimizations lead to more complex protocols with concomitant possibilities of race conditions and deadlock. In the realm of CMPs, all protocols have been kept simple so far, although in Chapter 8 we shall see some more sophisticated schemes when multithreading is implemented.

7.3 Synchronization

In single-processor multiprogramming systems, several processes appear to run concurrently although only one process at a given time can execute instructions because there is only one CPU. This concurrency has often been called *logical* or *virtual*. In multiprocessor systems, the concurrency can be both logical and *physical*, for now several processes can proceed concurrently on different processors. Concurrent processes may want to access shared data or acquire a physical resource "at the same time," where the time coincidence may be virtual or physical. Concurrent processes may also want to coordinate their progress relative to each other. Thus, concurrent processes must be synchronized. The synchronization may take on a competing aspect as, for example, in gaining access in a mutually exclusive way to critical sections where shared data must be modified in an orderly fashion, or global access to common shared data structures. In other cases, synchronization reflects the

```
Process P1                              Process P2

A ← A + 1                               A ← A + 2

ld    R1, A                             ld    R1, A
addi  R1,R1,1                           addi  R1,R1, 2
st    R1, A                             st    R1, A
              (a)  Original sequence

ld    R1, A                             ld    R1, A
                                        addi  R1,R1, 2
                                        st    R1, A

addi  R1,R1,1
st    R1, A
              (b) A timing sequence giving the result A + 1
```

Figure 7.11. Example showing the need for synchronization.

cooperation of processors as, for example, in producer–consumer relationships or the termination of all iterations of a loop in a parallel program. Many of the mechanisms used in single processors can be applied to multiprocessors. However, efficient implementations may differ.

Synchronization quite often implies the acquisition and release of locks. We start by presenting basic instruction primitives that allow the implementation of locks. We then describe some extensions that are geared towards multiprocessor systems. We also introduce a construct that is used for cooperation among processes, namely barriers.

There are numerous textbooks on operating systems that describe the creation of concurrent processes and their synchronization via higher-level primitives such as semaphores or monitors. Classical synchronization problems, such as the bounded buffer or producer-consumer problem and the five dining philosophers, are typically used to illustrate the concepts. We do not dwell on these problems, and instead we concentrate on the architectural aspects of locking and barrier mechanisms.

7.3.1 Atomic Instructions

Consider the very simple example of Figure 7.11, where two concurrent processes P1 and P2 update a common variable A. If the two increment operations were atomic, then the result would be $A + 3$. This corresponds to the execution of the three instructions (Figure 7.11(a)) of process P1 followed by the three instructions the of process P2 (or vice versa; there are several other sequences that would yield the same result). However, if the timing of the execution of instructions is as in Figure 7.11(b), where loading A in a register takes longer for P1 than for P2, then the result is $A + 1$. This situation could occur if, for example, variable A was cached in the processing element on which P2 executes and not cached for the one executing P1. It is not difficult to see that any of the three results $A + 1$, $A + 2$, and $A + 3$ can be the final one. Even if cache coherence mechanisms were present, we could have problems, for the invalidation of, say, processor P2 could arrive after the value of A computed by processor P1 was used by the latter.

In order to proceed in an orderly fashion, we must provide a lock for the variable A such that only one process is allowed to access A at a given time. The general paradigm for the use of a lock, including its *release*, is:

> while (!*acquire*(lock)) {waiting algorithm}
>
> computation on shared data
>
> *release* (lock)

Because several processes might want to *acquire* a lock simultaneously, the acquisition process must be atomic. Before proceeding on how to implement the acquisition, let us note that there are two main possibilities for the waiting algorithm that the processes that did not acquire the lock must execute. One is *busy waiting*, whereby the process repeatedly tries to acquire the lock, which in this case is called a *spin lock* (to be discussed). The other is *blocking*, whereby the process suspends itself and releases the processor on which it was running. The blocked process will be reawakened when the lock is released. Whether busy waiting or blocking or a combination of both (several attempts using busy waiting and then, if unsuccessful, the use of blocking) is best is often application-dependent. Since this distinction is more in the realm of operating systems, we do not consider it further.

Let us now return to the lock acquisition problem. In its simplest form, a lock will be a variable stored in memory that can have only the values 0 (lock is free) or 1 (lock is already acquired). The steps for *acquire* are therefore to test whether the value is 0 or 1 and, if it is 0, to set the value to 1. However, the test and the subsequent set must be indivisible; otherwise, two processes could test simultaneously that the lock has value 0 and both acquire the lock. What is needed is an instruction that can read, modify, and write a memory location without interference. Such an instruction, called *test-and-set*, was already part of the ISA of the IBM System/360. It was implemented by preventing the use of the memory bus by other instructions while it was being executed. All microprocessors today have some form of test-and-set in their ISA. Releasing a lock is of course much simpler. We just need to write the value 0.

Test-and-set is the simplest instance of an atomic exchange operation. It can be generalized to *exchange-and-swap*, which allows values other than 0 and 1 by exchanging the values of a register and a memory location. *Compare-and-swap* is a further generalization that allows the value in memory to be changed only if it is equal to the test value supplied. Both these instructions are present in the ISAs of the Intel IA-32 and Sun SPARC. In addition, in the Intel architecture, most integer arithmetic and logical instructions can be used with a lock prefix that makes them atomic.

For the example of Figure 7.11, none of the above instructions present an advantage over test-and-set, for a simple Boolean lock is all that is needed for synchronization. However, there are applications where more sophisticated atomic exchanges are useful, for example by using bits or bytes within a memory location (word) as individual locks for subsets of a data structure.

A second type of atomic operations is the *fetch-and-Θ* operation, which is a generic name for fetch-and-increment, fetch-and-add, fetch-and-store, and so on. The basic idea, for example for fetch-and-increment, is that the two operations of

```
loop:   test-and-set    R2,lock     /* test and set the value in location lock*/
        bnz             R2, loop    /* if the result is not zero, spin*/
        ld              R1, A       /*the lock has been acquired*/
        addi            R1,R1,1     /*increment A*/
        st              R1, A       /*store A*/
        st              R0, lock    /*release the lock; R0 contains 0*/
```

(a) Use of test-and-set. This instruction returns the value of lock in R1 and sets the value in lock to 1.

```
        fetch-and-increment     A
```

(b) Use of fetch-and-Θ, in this case fetch-and-increment

```
loop:   ll      R1, A       /*A loaded in R1 and its address loaded in link register*/
        addi    R1,R1,1     /*increment A*/
        sc      R2, A       /*test of the link register with address of A; if equal, sc returns 1*/
        bz      R2,loop     /* if failure try again; memory was not modified*/
```

(c) Use of ll-sc

Figure 7.12. Example of the use of three synchronization primitives.

fetching a value from memory into a register and then incrementing the value in memory are indivisible. Thus, in the example of Figure 7.11, process P1 would simply use the instruction "fetch-and-increment A." Process P2 would use "fetch-and-add A, R1," where R1 would have been previously loaded with the value 2. We shall see further examples of the use of fetch-and-Θ when we look at spinning locks and barriers.

Instead of atomic exchange, we can have an instruction pair that can be deduced to have operated in an atomic fashion. The DEC Alpha ISA provides such a pair, namely, *load-locked* (*ll*) and *store-conditional* (*sc*). With the *ll* instruction, a value is loaded into a register. This is the read part of the read–modify–write cycle. Instructions that follow *ll* can modify the value in the register. The last part of the cycle, the write, is provided by the *sc* instruction. *sc* checks whether the value in memory that was loaded by *ll* has been modified by another process. If it has not been modified, the atomic operation was successful. For implementation a special register, often called a *linked* register, is needed. It contains the address of the memory location whose contents have been loaded by *ll*. If this link register was not modified, *sc* writes the contents of the register in memory and returns the value 1. If the link register has been modified, for example because of an invalidation in a cache coherence protocol or a context switch, then *sc* fails, returning the value 0.

Figure 7.12 gives three corrected versions of Figure 7.11 for process P1, using respectively test-and-set, fetch-and-increment, and the pair *ll–sc*.

The pair *ll–sc* is in fact easier to implement in that it does not require the indivisibility of the atomic exchanges. It was first used in some MIPS and Alpha processors and is now part of the ISA of the IBM PowerPC and Intel IA-64.

7.3.2 Lock Contention

One of the waiting algorithms that we mentioned above, namely, spinning locks, is to repeatedly try to acquire a lock when the latter is already held by another process. We consider now how lock contention can degrade performance and how to enhance the atomic instructions of the previous section so that spinning locks can still be a viable tool in cache-coherent shared-memory multiprocessors.

Let us first look at the simplest mechanism, namely, test-and-set – or, as we are simply dealing with a lock, any of the atomic exchanges of the previous section. The first processor that wants to acquire a lock succeeds and caches the lock in a line in the modify (M) state. The first processor that requests the lock subsequently will get a copy of the lock and test it (unsuccessfully), but because the "set" part always writes a value, it will invalidate the copy in the cache of the holder and keep its cached copy in the M state. If there are other processors wishing to acquire the same lock, the last one that requests it will have the sole copy of it in the M state. However, since all tests are unsuccessful until the holder releases the lock, all requesters are repeatedly trying to read and modify the lock, which is in the M state in another cache. These attempts will result in heavy utilization, or even saturation, of the common bus in a snooping environment, or result in a "hot spot" in the case of a directory protocol, because all requests will be directed to the directory that contains the state of the lock. Moreover, the processor that holds the lock and wants to release it will have to contend with all the requesters before having the right to write it back.

In addition to the contention, which will slow down all other memory references, the test-and-set primitive does not allow a fair selection of the next lock holder. Worse, if there are more than two processors that request the lock and some of these want to reacquire the lock, then the request for acquisition of a particular processor can be permanently denied, leading to the *starvation* of the requesting process. In order to mitigate these effects, a mechanism called *exponential back-off*, used in another context in the Ethernet protocol, is advocated. When, after a few attempts, a processor has been denied the acquisition of the lock, instead of asking for it again immediately, it waits for some time t. If the attempt is again unsuccessful after a few renewed attempts, it waits for time $2t$, and then $4t$, $8t$, and so on, until finally it succeeds.

Rather than taking advantage of the caching process, the acquisition and release of spinning locks are hindered by it. In order to alleviate the number of requests to memory, a new primitive, *test-and-test-and-set*, has been proposed. The first part of the primitive tests the value of the lock, and if the lock has already been acquired, the procedure will spin without attempting to overwrite it. If it finds that the lock is available, it then performs a test-and-set. The spinning can be expressed as follows: "while $((lock = 1)$ and test-and-set$(lock))$" with the provision that the second part of the Boolean expression need not be tested if the first part is true. Now, copies of the busy lock can be cached in the shared state in all caches. Spinning will be done on a shared variable without the need to communicate with other caches or memory.

Although this new primitive certainly helps when a lock is already acquired, the competition upon the release of the lock is worse than for test-and-set. To see why, consider the scenario when the holder of the lock releases it. The write transaction of the holder will invalidate all copies, and the requesters will start competing to

```
init:    flag[0] := 0;                        /*initially; 1st processor can have the lock*/
         for (i :=0; i < n; i++)              /* all other processors will see a busy lock*/
                 flag[i] := 1;
         tail := 0;
acq:     myindex := fetch-and-increment (tail);   /* the increment is modulo n*/
         while (myindex = 1);                 /*spin while the lock is held elsewhere*/

         flag[myindex] := 1;                  /*I got the lock. Make it busy for next round*/

rel:     flag[(myindex + 1) mod n] :=0        /* release the lock and pass it on to the next processor*/
```

Figure 7.13. Software implementation of queuing locks.

acquire the lock. All requesters first attempt to acquire a shared copy via the "test" part. All requesters will succeed in the case of a shared bus and a round-robin bus-granting mechanism. Many of them will succeed, even if the interconnect is not a bus or there is some other scheme to grant the bus. The successful processes will then attempt to do a test-and-set. The problem then is that the test-and-set writes the value of the lock, thus invalidating all shared copies. All requesting processes that were not yet attempting a test-and-set will have to perform a read ("test") again. This will go on as long as there are test-and-sets in progress. For each test-and-set that is attempted, the number of pending test-and-sets is decreased but the number of test attempts will increase. When all test-and-sets have been attempted, the test will not have to be redone, and spinning will occur without bus or interconnection network contention. Note that test-and-test-and-set does not solve the starvation problem.

Locking using the two primitives above considerably slows down normal access to memory, especially in shared-bus systems, if there are a substantial number of processors competing for a lock. The problem has a negative feedback effect. Because the critical section of code protected by the lock will most likely involve accessing shared variables in memory, those accesses to memory are slowed down by the remaining transactions due to the locking process after the lock has been acquired. Although critical sections are generally meant to be short, the slowed-down memory references make them last longer, thus allowing more processors to contend before a new one gets the nod.

Queuing Locks

Memory contention can be reduced and at the same time starvation can be eliminated by having requesting processors enter a FIFO queue. We start by showing a software implementation of *queuing locks* (cf. Figure 7.13). Elements of an array are used to enqueue circularly the identities of the requesting processors. Initially the first element of the queue contains a flag indicating that the lock is free while all other elements contain a busy flag. A processor requesting the lock will perform a *myindex* = fetch-and-increment(*tail*), that is, position itself at the end of the queue and increment the queue counter (we omit the modulo operations needed for the circular queue implementation). It will then read the array element of index *myindex*, cache it, and either spin in cache if the corresponding flag is busy, or enter the critical section otherwise. While in the critical section, it will reset the flag at *myindex* to busy. At the end of the critical section, the release operation will reset the element at *myindex* + 1 to free. The write operation will invalidate the line containing the lock in the cache of the processor corresponding to *myindex* + 1. This will generate a read miss for the latter, and upon reading of its flag, its test will be successful.

Note that this implementation has several drawbacks. First, it relies on the presence of a fetch-and-increment instruction. If this instruction is not present in the ISA of the processor, then it must be simulated, that is, it requires the use of a lock to access the queue. Of course, the critical section for updating the queue is very short, but nonetheless contention can also arise there. Second, obtaining a lock may take longer when there is no contention, because instead of a single test-and-set there is now the task of incrementing a counter, reading a location, testing it, and writing another location. Third, each lock must be in a different cache line. The array is therefore an array of cache lines. This is somewhat wasteful of memory. The main disadvantage, however, is that one cannot coallocate shared data with the lock, because the lock is distributed. Coallocation has proved quite beneficial with test-and-set synchronization whenever it is possible, that is, when there are a small number of shared data in the critical section protected by the lock. Finally, if the process holding the lock is suspended (context switch), then all processes depending on the lock must wait till the suspended process is reactivated and releases the lock. This is true of all synchronization mechanisms. Queuing locks exacerbate the problem, for in that case, if a process that is queued but not holding the lock is suspended, its successors on the queue must wait till it is reactivated. Nonetheless, measurements have shown that queuing locks are beneficial in heavy contention. They were implemented in the shared-bus Sequent multiprocessor.

A hardware implementation of queuing locks, which in fact antedates the software one, was also proposed. The QOLB (queue on locked bit) scheme maintains a hardware queue of waiting processors. A succinct and not completely accurate description is as follows. The *enqueue* operation allocates a shadow copy of the line containing the lock in the processor's cache and enqueues the processor in the hardware queue. Spinning is performed in cache if the lock bit is set to busy. When the processor holding the lock releases it, it performs a *dequeue* operation that directly sends the freed lock and the data in the same line to the next waiting processor. In this scheme, coallocation is possible. Simulations show that it outperforms other mechanisms, but at a significant complexity cost. For example, it requires direct transfer from one cache to another, more cache coherence states, and the ability to perform some operations outside the cache coherence protocol.

Full–Empty Bits

In the *full–empty* bit scheme, each memory location can be used for synchronization purposes by looking at a special synchronization bit. If the synchronization bit is 0, it means that no value has been written in the memory location; if the bit is 1, a value has been produced. A read will stall until the synchronization bit is 1, that is, no value can be consumed until it has been produced. The read will reset the synchronization bit to 0. Similarly, a store to a location will stall until the bit is 0, because otherwise it would overwrite a previous value that has not been used yet. When the synchronization bit is 0 and the value is stored, the synchronization bit is reset to 1. As can be seen from this description, full–empty bits are extremely convenient for producer–consumer problems. Of course, not all load–store instructions should follow the convention of the full–empty bits; the ISA should be extended with special load–store instructions. An implementation of this concept was first done on the Denelcor HEP computer and later on the supercomputer Tera.

How important is the ability to resolve lock contention efficiently? It really depends on the scale (number of processors) of the system and on the applications. For example, investing in hardware queuing locks does not seem justifiable for CMPs with a limited number of processors. Choosing between regular and software queuing locks might be done application by application, or even critical section by critical section.

Transactional Memory

With the number of processors expected to increase in CMPs and the clock remaining at the same frequency, improved performance will be achieved through expanded parallelism. However, more parallelism implies more synchronization. Adequate locking may become difficult to achieve because (i) it might restrict unduly the amount of parallelism because some locks needed to ensure correctness are nonetheless superfluous for the great majority of program executions, and (ii) overabundance of locks might make ensuring program correctness or debugging much more strenuous.

To circumvent these difficulties, a new programming model has been proposed, based on the concept of *transactions*. The basic idea is that a critical section, or any section of code protected by locks, behaves in the same way as a transaction in the database sense. In a database transaction all state changes within the transaction are considered to be atomic, that is, either they are all executed or none of them are. This is indeed what is required of accesses to shared variables within a critical section, although transforming all critical sections in such a way that they become transactions can lead to deadlock in admittedly contrived examples. A second important property of transactions is that their execution does not depend on what other concurrent processes are doing, that is, transactions provide isolation.

One of the concurrency control mechanisms used in transaction-oriented systems is an optimistic scheme. When the beginning of the transaction is recognized, all state change actions are buffered. When the end of the transaction marker is reached, if there was no conflict in shared-variable access with another transaction, then all the state changes are committed at once. If there were conflicts, then the transaction is aborted and it has to be retried. The implementation of such a scheme could be purely in software (with a significant performance degradation compared to a lock-based implementation), purely in hardware, or in a combination of both.

The requirements of the optimistic scheme are that the beginning and the end of the transactions be recognized and that all state changes occurring during the transaction be buffered and subsequently either committed or aborted.[2] Recognition of the boundaries of a transaction is not complex. Either the denotations of the beginning and the end of the transaction will be incorporated in the programming language, or the hardware can detect instructions corresponding to *acquire* and *release* of locks. Although there is not yet any microarchitectural support for transactions, some of the existing mechanisms could be expanded in the buffering and in the detection of whether there have been conflicts or not. We do not present a formal approach, because transactional memory is still at a research stage but indicate some options that might be considered.

State changes are activated by stores to registers and memory. Because the optimistic control of transactions is another instance of speculation, we can rely at least partially on some of the same mechanisms as in other speculative schemes. In particular, registers can be saved (at the beginning of the transaction), committed, or restored (at the end of the transaction), in the same way as is done for branch (mis)prediction. In the case of stores to memory, we can try and piggyback on the actions of cache coherence protocols. The state of a cache line can be expanded to indicate whether the line has been read-accessed (R) or write-accessed (W) during the transaction. No line that was write-accessed can be written back to memory during the transaction's execution. Now, when the end of the transaction is reached, the processor sends coherence messages for all lines that have a W bit on. If no other cache has the same line with either an R or a W bit on, the transaction can commit. This is done by resetting all R and W bits, which can be done in a single gang-reset-like instruction. If at least one other cache has a line with an R or a W bit, the transaction is aborted.

The cursory description in the previous paragraph leaves several questions unanswered, such as what happens if a line with an R or W bit becomes a victim in a cache replacement, and whether one should allow nested transactions. The reader is referred to the current literature for this topic, which is generating a lot of interest.

7.3.3 Barrier Synchronization

A synchronization operation that requires concurrent processes to wait until all of them have reached a given point is called a *barrier*. A typical use of a barrier is when iterations of a loop can be executed in parallel on several processors, that is, each loop iteration is independent of all others. However, all processors must cooperate so that it is known when all loop instances have completed.

A software implementation of a barrier uses a counter that needs to be incremented atomically and a spin lock for those processors that have reached the barrier and are waiting for the last one to arrive to release the lock. The counter can be

---

[2] This is called a *deferred update* policy. The optimistic control scheme can also be implemented using an early conflict detection mechanism.

```
mycount := fetch-and-add (counter);
if (mycount = 0) then spin := 0;      /* if first to enter barrier, set the spin lock to busy*/
if (mycount = n) then                 /*last to enter barrier*/
        begin counter := 0;           /*not atomic but no processor should access counter, because they*/
                                      /*are all spinning*/
            spin := 1;                /*release the spin lock*/
            end
    else
        while (spin = 0);             /*spin*/
```

Figure 7.14. Centralized barrier implementation.

incremented by using either a short critical section or a fetch-and-add instruction if available in the ISA. Figure 7.14 shows sample code for this latter implementation.

There is a slight problem with the pseudocode in Figure 7.14. If the algorithm uses several barriers consecutively:

some computation
code for barrier (counter, spin)
some computation
code for barrier(counter, spin)

with the same arguments for the barriers, then we might have a deadlock.

Consider the case when one of processes, say A, is suspended while spinning (maybe because it has been spinning too long). All other processes have entered the barrier, so the last one sets the spin variable to 1, and then one of them will enter the second barrier, resetting the spin variable to 0. When process A is reactivated, it will continue spinning in the code of the first barrier, thus preventing it from completing, and will not enter the second barrier, thus preventing its code from completing as well, because there the counter will never reach the total number of processes. The reason for the deadlock is that we have counted the number of processes entering the barrier and we should also count the number of processes exiting it. Another possibility is to have several (counter, spin) pairs. A more elegant solution, called *sense reversal*, is to initialize the value of the spin alternately at 0 and 1 between consecutive barriers.

Contention will occur at the beginning of the barrier and usually at the end when processors are released. In order to avoid bus overload in shared-bus systems or hot spots in interconnection networks, the barrier can be implemented as a tree of barriers. For example, if there are 32 processors, they can be grouped in eight groups of four with each group having its own barrier. The groups can themselves belong to two supergroups, each with its own barrier. Finally, a last barrier would be needed for the two supergroups.

7.4 Relaxed Memory Models

In out-of-order single processors, we let operations proceed independently of the program order. This is true even for memory operations. We showed how we could even go further by allowing load speculation (Section 5.2). As long as results are committed in program order and as long as recoveries exist in case of misspeculation, all execution orderings are permissible. In particular, speculative values can be

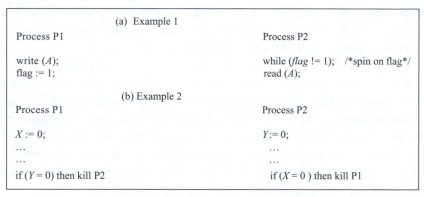

Figure 7.15. Two examples to illustrate potential lack of sequential consistency.

loaded into registers, thus permitting faster progress. The only requirement is that when a process is interrupted and has to relinquish the use of the single processor, all instructions that have started execution must complete, including all stores that are in the write buffers. At context switch, the states of the processor and of the memory are stable. When the process is woken up and reassumes the ownership of the processor, all values that were stored in memory are still there, although some of them that were in a given cache can be in a lower level of the memory hierarchy or even on secondary storage. Nonetheless, from a consistency viewpoint, the values have not changed.

The situation is quite different when multiple processors and concurrent processes are present. Although current cache-coherent systems impose some form of consistency, they fail to guarantee the model of memory semantics that programmers are accustomed to. We illustrate this point with the two examples shown in Figure 7.15

In the first example, the programmer intends to have a producer–consumer relationship by having process P2 read the value generated by process P1. Assume that the write to A is "seen" by process P2 later than the write to the variable *flag*. Process P2 then does not spin any longer and might read the old value of A. Such a situation could happen in a NUMA environment if the write and/or invalidation to A take longer to propagate to memory than that of *flag*.

In the second example, the intent of the programmer is to prevent P1 and P2 from both being killed. Either one of them, or both, should progress. However, if we allow reads to bypass writes or if X and Y are kept in write buffers, or even if in a cache-coherent system the invalidations of X and Y are both delayed, then the two "if" statements will see the old values of X and Y, and thus both processes will be killed.

The behavior of the processor and memory system that the programmer expects is what is called *sequential consistency*, namely:

- The result of any execution is the same as if the instructions of each process were executed in some sequential order, and
- the instructions of each process appear in that sequential order in program order.

The reader can easily verify that any interleaving of the statements in the two processes of each example with the requirement that each instruction complete before its successor will yield the results intended by the programmer.

Another way to state the properties of sequential consistency is that operations, or at least memory operations, should proceed in program order and that all writes should be atomic, that is, seen by all processors at the same time. Does this imply that structures such as write buffers should be forbidden, that there should be acknowledgments from all caches that invalidations or updates have been received before an instruction following a write can proceed, that loads should not bypass stores (and certainly not be speculative)? Enforcements of all these requirements would in many cases lead to tremendous losses in performance.

There are two ways to prevent those performance losses. The first one is to keep the sequential consistency model and to rely on techniques we have seen before, prefetching and speculation, adequately modified or supplemented so that the performance degradation can be alleviated. The second is to provide a *relaxed consistency* memory model.

We first look at ways to improve performance in the environment of a strict sequential consistency model. Let us assume an invalidation-based cache-coherent multiprocessor with out-of-order processors and a snoopy cache coherence protocol. The main goal is to avoid delays in loads and stores when there are cache misses. To that effect, we introduce new commands in the cache access and cache coherence protocols. If a load is encountered that is possibly conflicting with a previous memory operation, then a *read–prefetch* is performed for the missing line. As a consequence of this command, the line is put in the shared state. When the load is allowed to proceed, according to the sequential consistency constraints, the value is in the cache (or in progress towards the cache) unless it has been invalidated by another processor. In the case where it was not invalidated, the latency of the miss was (partially) hidden. If the read–prefetch hits in the cache, then the penalty is that the cache was accessed twice for the same operation. This penalty can be avoided by using the value speculatively. When the instruction is ready to commit, (i.e., is at the head of the reorder buffer), a check is made to see if the line holding the speculated value has been invalidated. If there was no invalidation, the computation can continue; otherwise, recovery has to proceed back to the load instruction in the program in a way similar to what happens for a wrong branch prediction. This recovery is not unduly onerous, because all the hardware mechanisms are present. Note that if the prefetched line has to be replaced before ensuring that speculation was correct, then it is treated as a misspeculation.

In the case of a store that should be delayed, a *read–exclusive prefetch* is performed whereby, in the case of a miss, the line is prefetched in the exclusive state. When it is time to perform the actual store, if the line is still in the exclusive state, the value can be written and the line enters the modified state.

In sequential consistency, even with the additions of the previous paragraph, the effects of loads and stores are as if they were *totally ordered* according to the program order. In relaxed memory models, the ordering will become a *weak ordering* whereby some of the loads and stores will become synchronization points, in a manner equivalent implicitly or explicitly to acquiring and releasing locks. How "relaxed" the model is depends on how much freedom there is in concurrency between acquires and releases. As an example, in one such model, when a synchronization point is reached, all memory operations preceding it in program order must complete before the process can proceed. This requires new instructions, such as *fences* or *barriers* (not to be confused with the barriers of the preceding section) as well as the introduction of these instructions either by the compiler or by library synchronization routines. The definitions and implementations of relaxed models are quite subtle, and the programmer and compiler writer must be aware of them.

One reason why we do not deal more with this topic is that it has been shown that one of the simplest relaxed models, namely *processor consistency*, in conjunction with the optimizations to sequential consistency already described, yields performance results comparable to those of more sophisticated models. Under processor consistency, writes have to be performed in program order, but loads can bypass writes. "Performed" in the preceding sentence means that all processors see the writes in the same order. Thus, FIFO write buffers are admissible. Under this model, Example 1 of Figure 7.15 will behave in the same way as if the system were sequentially consistent. On the other hand, Example 2 will not. Therefore, programmers and compiler writers must still be careful and insert the right synchronization operations. For example, the rules given for the Intel Itanium, whose performance depends heavily on the quality of the compiled code, include the following (there are other rules, but these are sufficient to show that careful programming is needed):

- Loads are not reordered with other loads, and stores are not reordered with other stores.
- Stores are not reordered with older loads, and in a multiprocessor stores to the same location have a total order.
- Loads may be reordered with older stores to different locations, but not to the same location.

EXAMPLE 4: Using these rules, with $x = y = 0$ initially, the sequences

```
P1              P2
R1 ← x          R2 ← y
y ← 1           x ← 1
```

disallow $R1 = R2 = 1$ (stores cannot be reordered with older loads), whereas the sequences

```
P1              P2
x ← 1           y ← 1
R1 ← y          R2 ← x
```

allow $R1 = R2 = 0$. This happens when both loads bypass their stores or when the performance of the writes is not seen until the loads have executed. If this was not the programmer's intent, explicit synchronization is required.

Processor consistency with the optimizations described previously improves performance over sequential consistency by about 10% for scientific programs that exhibit a fair amount of parallelism (the best case to show the advantages of relaxed consistency). A more sophisticated relaxed model could gain another 10% at the cost of more complex hardware implementations and software sophistication.

7.5 Multimedia Instruction Set Extensions

Since the mid 1990s, multimedia applications have become an important component of the computational loads of desktops, laptops, and embedded processors in smart appliances. These applications require what has been called *media processing*, that is, the creation, encoding and decoding, processing, display, and communication of digital multimedia information such as images, audio, video, and graphics. A subset of these applications can perform very well on embedded processors found in cell phones, digital cameras, PDAs, and the like; but providing a full range of applications with real-time constraints requires a large amount of computational power. To answer this demand, the ISAs of microprocessors have been enhanced by what we will call *multimedia instructions*, and microarchitecture designs have been adapted to cater to these new instructions. Even with these modifications, general-purpose microprocessors and a standard cache hierarchy are not sufficient for games that require, for example, very fast geometric and perspective transformations. Special-purpose on-chip processors, (e.g., graphic accelerators), are needed. The reader is referred to the specialized literature on this subject; we consider here only the impact of multimedia applications on general-purpose processors.

There are two characteristics of multimedia data that have strongly influenced the expansion of ISAs, namely: (i) the range of values is often limited (for example, pixels in images and videos need only 8 bits), and (ii) the data sets are large, and the same operations have to be performed on each element of a data set. The first characteristic has led to the packing of several data in a single word, and the second one has motivated the use of SIMD instructions. These instructions will operate on all operands packed in a single word.

The first ISA that was expanded with multimedia instructions was that of the Hewlett-Packard PA-RISC in 1994. Only nine instructions were added, because a design constraint was that these new instructions should fit within the already well-advanced design of the chip without additional hardware and without affecting the clock cycle. In contrast, the SUN Visual Instruction Set (VIS), introduced a year later, was comparatively complete. It included 121 new instructions, which have remained as part of the UltraSPARC ISA. As mentioned in Chapter 3, the ISA of the Intel IA-32 was expanded first by providing 57 additional instructions (the MMX set) to the Pentium II, then another 13 for the SSE extension with the Pentium III, and the extension comprised a total of 144 instructions in the SSE2 for the Pentium 4, although this last count is inflated in that many instructions that were designed for 64-bit-wide registers are replicated for 128-bit-wide registers. Another 13 instructions were added for SSE3 in 2004.

Multimedia instructions fall into four categories:

- SIMD instructions that operate on data packed in a single word. Each datum is considered as an integer. Typical instructions are add, subtract, multiply, multiply and add, multiply and accumulate, compare, and shift. For example, if a 64-bit word is divided into eight 8-bit data, eight adds can be performed concurrently. Similarly, four multiplications can be performed (only four because the result can be longer than 8 bits). However, some instruction sets can have both a regular multiply and a truncated multiply where only the low-order bits are kept, and in that case eight multiplications can be performed simultaneously in the previous example. Similarly, both modulo addition and saturated addition can be present, the latter seeming more adequate in many situations. For example, if "adding" two images yields a resulting pixel overflow because it is larger than the 8-bit value, its modulo might be very close to 0, which would be at the opposite end of the spectrum of colors. Saturation would leave its value at 255 ($2^8 - 1$).
- Conversion instructions to pack and unpack. Packing will, for example, convert regular integers into smaller values, most often through truncation. Unpacking does the opposite and transforms a datum from a low-precision data type to a higher precision using sign extension.
- Data communication instructions. For example, bytes from two 32-bit registers can be interleaved into a 64-bit result register, or a particular byte can be inserted in a specific position within a register.
- Memory transfer instructions such as block copy of 64-byte blocks and prefetch instructions.

In implementation, a deliberate choice can be made to dedicate part of the on-chip real estate to multimedia. This was the case for the design of the Sun Ultra-SPARC I processor and the VIS instruction set extension. The decision was to implement these instructions, as well as some for other functions helping the operating system and networking, rather than to use the transistors for the cache hierarchy. The instructions that were selected had to fulfill three criteria: (i) execute in a single cycle or be easily pipelined, (ii) be applicable to several multimedia algorithms, and (iii) not affect the cycle time. The graphic unit that implemented the instructions was added to the floating-point unit so that multimedia instructions could use the floating-point registers. Of course, this prevented concurrency between multimedia instructions and floating-point ones, a factor that was not deemed important, because few multimedia operations deal with real numbers.

On the other hand, the multimedia MMX instructions for the Pentium II were implemented with compatibility of the IA-32 architecture in mind. As was the case for the UltraSPARC, the floating-point registers were used, but no new functional unit was added. No new architectural state had to be introduced, so that applications using the MMX instructions could run with existing operating systems. This meant that upon exiting the multimedia operations the floating-point stack had to be in the same state as it was before the multimedia operations had begun. This constraint was removed when SSE was introduced. New architectural states were allowed, because the newer operating systems were aware of the extensions.

Have these extensions really improved the performance of multimedia applications? The question is difficult to answer, because there is no compiler that uses the SIMD instructions effectively. If the software calls library routines, then one must be careful that the overhead of the calls does not destroy the benefits of the new instructions. If the algorithms are hand-tuned for the SIMD instructions, the comparison is not quite fair, and certainly, the outcome is biased towards the multimedia extensions. With this caveat, it has been reported that in carefully tuned benchmarks the use of the multimedia extensions can on the average halve the execution time.

When looking at the characteristics of multimedia applications, the first myth that has to be dispelled is that data caches will not work effectively. This misstatement is based on the premise that there are a large number of streaming data that will not have temporal locality. However, on the contrary, media applications have kernels of high computational intensity that reuse data significantly, and the emergence of streaming processors lends credit to that observation. L1 data caches are often very efficiently utilized, and miss rates for multimedia applications are slightly lower than those of the SPEC integer applications. In many multimedia applications, the L1 caches can be small and remain efficient, thus making them more suitable for mobile devices. Making them larger does not improve the hit rates. Prefetching into L2 helps significantly, and when that is done judiciously, the result is that the multimedia applications are compute-bound if the SIMD instructions are used in a proper manner.

Because one SIMD instruction replaces a number of integer instructions, the number of instructions executed will decrease. Not only will loops be shorter, but the number of iterations will be smaller, thus reducing the overhead due to increment indexing. On the other hand, there is a need for packing and unpacking instructions, which reduces the instruction count advantage. The number of executed branches is also slightly smaller than that in regular integer applications, and the prediction accuracy is similar.

Overall, the combined reduction in the number of instructions, the number of branches, and the number of memory operations has a positive effect on performance that outweighs the penalties due to the packing–unpacking effects. However, a word of caution is necessary: the multimedia instructions are applicable to only a portion of a given multimedia application, and we should always remember Amdahl's law, which limits the possible performance gains.

7.6 Summary

In this chapter, we have introduced general concepts related to multiprocessor systems. As we shall see in the next chapter, CMPs are the present and future computing commodities. However, we are not yet sure of many aspects of their architectures, as the number of processors on a chip is going to increase. According to

Flynn's nomenclature, they will be shared-memory MIMD, but will they be UMA or NUMA? What will be their interconnect structure: shared bus, direct network, indirect network? We have examined definitions and alternatives in the first section of this chapter.

The form of interconnect, or rather the ability to broadcast messages and data easily, dictates the implementation of cache coherence, a must to ensure program correctness. In the case of easy broadcasts, as in a shared bus, write–invalidate four-state snoopy protocols are the rule. When the interconnection prevents easy broadcasts, directory protocols are preferred. The memory-costly full-directory protocols can be advantageously replaced by partial-directory schemes that require less memory and bring little degradation in performance.

Parallel programs running on multiprocessors need to be synchronized. The basic mechanism is that of a lock that protects portions of code and data structures so that they cannot be accessed simultaneously. Locks must be acquired through an atomic read–modify–write operation whose most basic instantiation at the ISA level is the test-and-set operation. We have presented other ISA instructions and alternative schemes that fulfill the same role but that do not present as much overhead contention in the presence of cache-coherent architectures.

Programmers are implicitly assuming a sequential consistency model. Many of the optimizations in out-of-order processors that we have examined in previous chapters do not follow this model. This is fine in the context of single processors, but can lead to erroneous programs, or interpretations of programs, when applied in a multiprocessor environment. In this situation, in order not to impede performance as much as is done by a strict enforcement of sequential consistency, relaxed memory models have been proposed and implemented in some commercial processors. In this case, programmers and compiler writers have to be aware that memory operations – loads and stores – do not have to follow the total order of sequential consistency. Among the relaxed memory models, one of the less relaxed is processor consistency, and it has been shown that it offers performance benefits almost as good as more complex models.

We closed this chapter with a brief overview of multimedia instructions, the only SIMD type of operations found in general-purpose microprocessors.

7.7 Further Reading and Bibliographical Notes

Flynn's taxonomy [F66] appeared in 1966. The term "dance-hall architecture" was coined by Robert Keller in the early 1970s. The book by Culler at al. [CSG99] is an encyclopedic view of parallel processing up till 2000. It does not include either a chapter on vector processors (see Hennessy and Patterson [HP07], Fourth Edition, Appendix F) or any mention of streaming processors (cf. [KRDKAMO03]). It does describe in detail interconnection network topologies, routing, and control flow. For the last, the key papers are Kermani and Kleinrock [KK79] (originally intended for wide-area networks) and Dally [D90] (intended for message-passing parallel computers). Among the many shared-memory multiprocessors, a typical SMP shared-bus system is the Sequent Symmetry, described by Lovett and Thakkar

[LT88], which was later extended into a ring of SMPs as described in Lovett and Clapp [LC96]. A hierarchy of rings was used in the KSR machine [K92]. The Convex Exemplar is described in Baetke [B95]. Information on IBM SP series switching can be found in Stunkel et al. [SHAS99] and in IBM manuals. The Intel Paragon is well described in Culler's book [CSG99], and further details can be found in Intel manuals. Scott describes the Cray 3TE [S96]. The SIMD Connection Machine CM-2 is presented in Tucker and Robertson [TR88].

Snoopy cache coherence protocols are described in Archibald and Baer [AB86], and the MOESI framework in Sweazey and Smith [SS86]. The particular four-state protocol of Section 7.2 is due to Papamarcos and Patel [PP85]. The full-directory protocol is due to Censier and Feautrier [CF78]. The two-bit solution can be found in Archibald and Baer [AB85]. The notation Dir_iB and Dir_iNB is due to Agarwal et al. [ASHH88]. The MLI for multiprocessors is developed in Baer and Wang [BW88]. A good study on how to mitigate the effects of false sharing can be found in Jeremiassen and Eggers [JE95].

Test-and-test-and-set was proposed by Rudolf and Segall [RS84]. Hardware queuing locks were first introduced by Goodman et al. [GVW89]; Anderson [A90] and Graunke and Thakkar [GT90] presented software implementations. Performance comparisons can be found in Anderson [A90] and in Kagi et al. [KBG97]. Full–empty bits were first proposed by Smith [S78]. Issues related to transactional memory are surveyed by Larus and Kozyrakis [LK08].

Sequential consistency was formally defined by Lamport [L79]. A comprehensive survey on relaxed models of memory consistency is given by Adve and Gharachorloo [AG96], two of the main contributors in the area. Hardware optimizations for the sequential consistency model were proposed by Gharachorloo et al. [GGH91]. Weak ordering was first introduced in Dubois et al. [DSB86]. Hill [H98] advocates the use of processor consistency with prefetching and speculative execution.

The original multimedia extensions for the Sun (VIS) and the Intel IA-32 (MMX) are presented respectively in Tremblay and O'Connor [TO96] and Peleg and Weiser [PW96]. Slingerland and Smith [SS05] survey multimedia extensions; Ranganathan et al. [RAJ99] is one of several papers assessing the performance of these extensions.

EXERCISES

1. (Section 1.1) Describe an application that would benefit from a streaming processor. Does this make a case for a streaming processor to be classified as MISD?

2. (Section 1.1) Do you consider vector processors to be SISD or SIMD? Discuss the pros and cons for each classification.

3. (Section 1.1) Does a split-transaction bus present any advantage over a regular bus in a single-processor environment? Justify your answer.

4. (Section 2.1) Consider a shared-bus multiprocessor with three processors C1, C2, C3 whose respective direct-mapped caches *C1*, *C2*, and *C3* are attached to the bus. Lines at addresses *A* and *B* will conflict in each of the three caches. Initially, the entries in the three caches (say X1, X2, and X3) corresponding to *A* (and therefore *B*) are in state invalid (I). Assume that it takes less than 500 cycles to complete a miss and associated transactions on the bus. In the case of the write–invalidate three-state protocol, show the events that occur (*read_miss*, etc.), the transactions on the bus (*Bus_read*, etc.), and the states of and the values stored in X1, X2, and X3 when the processors execute the following instructions:

> At time 0, C1 reads *A*.
> At time 1000, C2 reads *B*.
> At time 2000, C3 reads *B*.
> At time 3000, C3 writes *B*.
> At time 4000, C2 writes *A*.
> At time 5000, C3 reads *A*.

5. (Section 2.1) Repeat the previous exercise in the case of a MESI protocol with the additional instruction

> At time 1500, C1 writes *A*

6. (Section 2.1) Draw the state diagrams, one each for processor actions and bus snooping, for a MOSI protocol. Find an example similar to that of Exercise 4 that shows the role of state O.

7. (Section 2.1) Define a three-state protocol with states E, S, and M that combines properties of write-through and writeback caches and a write-update protocol. On a *Bus_read*, caches answer on a special line MS whether they have a copy of the line or not. (Hint: Recall that *Bus_write* is always preceded by a *Bus_read*; also, only lines in state S should see a *Bus_write* command, and memory must be updated on writes emanating from lines in state S.) Repeat Exercise 4 for this protocol.

8. (Section 2.2) Compare the memory overhead for the full directory with that required for ECC. You should consider both line sizes and the number of processors.

9. (Section 2.2) What simplifications occur in the full directory protocol if the system uses a centralized memory, that is, a UMA architecture rather than a NUMA one?

10. (Section 2.2) Show that deadlock could easily occur if the transactions in directory protocols were atomic.

11. (Section 2.2) Design a full directory protocol where the caches are write-through, write–no-allocate.

12. (Section 2.2) What partial directory implementation would you choose if it were known that most shared variables are either shared by two processors or by many processors?

13. (Section 3.1) If a lock cannot be acquired, the process can either busy-wait or block. An alternative is for it to spin for a few times and then, if the lock is still not acquired, be blocked. This latter option is called a *competitive* algorithm, and the difficulty is to know when to switch (this is out of the scope of this book). Define a snooping protocol using a competitive algorithm between write–update and write–invalidate commands.

14. (Section 3.2) Consider n processors in a write–invalidate snooping cache-coherent multiprocessor contending for a lock. They use a test-and-test-and-set primitive. Show that there can be $O(n^2)$ bus transactions after release of the lock by one processor before another processor can acquire the lock.

15. (Section 3.2) Implement the test-and-set and the test-and-test-and-set primitives using ll and sc.

16. (Section 4) Consider a shared-memory multiprocessor with the processors connected by a shared bus. The processors do not have caches, and there are no write buffers. Consider the following fragments of program run on two different processors (initially, the variables *flag1* and *flag2* both have the value 0):

```
Process 1          Process 2
flag1 = 1;         flag2 = 1;
if (flag2 = = 0)   if (flag1 = = 0)
Critical section   Critical section
```

(a) Show that under a sequential consistency model, the processes will never be simultaneously in their critical sections.
(b) Assume that both processors have write buffers. Is sequential consistency sufficient to ensure that both processes will never be simultaneously in their critical sections?
(c) Now processors have writeback caches, and the cache coherence protocol is write–invalidate. Is sequential consistency sufficient to ensure that both processes will never be simultaneously in their critical sections?

REFERENCES

[A90] T. Anderson, "The Performance of Spin Lock Alternatives for Shared-Memory Multi-processors," *IEEE Trans. on Parallel and Distributed Systems*, 1, 1, Jan. 1990, 6–16

[AB85] J. Archibald and J.-L. Baer, "An Economical Solution to the Cache Coherence Problem," *Proc. 12th Int. Symp. on Computer Architecture*, 1985, 355–362

[AB86] J. Archibald and J.-L. Baer, "Cache Coherence Protocols: Evaluation Using a Multiprocessor Simulation Model," *ACM Trans. on Computing Systems*, 4, 4, Nov. 1986, 273–298

[AG96] S. Adve and K. Gharachorloo, "Shared Memory Consistency Models: A Tutorial," *IEEE Computer*, 29, 12, Dec. 1996, 66–76

[ASHH88] A. Agarwal, R. Simoni, J. Hennessy, and M. Horowitz, "An Evaluation of Directory Schemes for Cache Coherence," *Proc. 15th Int. Symp. on Computer Architecture*, 1988, 280–289

[B95] F. Baetke, "The CONVEX Exemplar SPP1000 and SPP1200 – New Scalable Parallel Systems with a Virtual Shared Memory Architecture," in J. Dongarra, L. Grandinetti, G. Joubert, and J. Kowalik, Eds., *High Performance Computing: Technology, Methods and Applications*, Elsevier Press, 1995, 81–102

[BW88] J.-L. Baer and W.-H. Wang, "On the Inclusion Properties for Multi-Level Cache Hierarchies," *Proc. 15th Int. Symp. on Computer Architecture*, 1988, 73–80

[CF78] L. Censier and P. Feautrier, "A New Solution to Coherence Problems in Multicache Systems," *IEEE Trans. on Computers*, 27, 12, Dec. 1978, 1112–1118

[CSG99] D. Culler and J. Singh with A. Gupta, *Parallel Computer Architecture: A Hardware/Software Approach*, Morgan Kaufmann, San Francisco, 1999

[D90] W. Dally, "Virtual-Channel Flow Control," *Proc. 17th Int. Symp. on Computer Architecture*, 1990, 60–68

[DSB86] M. Dubois, C. Scheurich, and F. Briggs, "Memory Access Buffering in Multiprocessors," *Proc. 13th Int. Symp. on Computer Architecture*, 1986, 434–442

[F66] M. Flynn, "Very High Speed Computing Systems," *Proc. IEEE*, 54, 12, Dec. 1966, 1901–1909

[GGH91] K. Gharachorloo, A. Gupta, and J. Hennessy, "Two Techniques to Enhance the Performance of Memory Consistency Models," *Proc. Int. Conf. on Parallel Processing*, 1991, I-355–364

[GT90] G. Graunke and S. Thakkar, "Synchronization Algorithms for Shared-Memory Multiprocessors," *IEEE Computer*, 23, 6, Jun. 1990, 60–70

[GVW89] J. Goodman, M. Vernon, and P. Woest, "Efficient Synchronization Primitives for Large-Scale Cache Coherent Multiprocessors," *Proc. 3rd Int. Conf. on Architectural Support for Programming Languages and Operating Systems*, Apr. 1989, 64–73

[H98] M. Hill, "Multiprocessors Should Support Simple Memory-Consistency Models," *IEEE Computer*, 31, 8, Aug. 1998, 28–34

[HP07] J. Hennessy and D. Patterson, *Computer Architecture: A Quantitative Approach*, Fourth Edition, Elsevier Inc., San Francisco, 2007

[JE95] T. Jeremiassen and S. Eggers, "Reducing False Sharing on Shared Memory Multiprocessors through Compile Time Data Transformations," *Proc. 5th ACM SIGPLAN Symp. on Principles and Practice of Parallel Programming*, 1995, 179–188

[K92] Kendall Square Research, *KSR1 Technology Background*, 1992

[KAO05] P. Kongetira, K. Aingaran, and K. Olukotun, "Niagara: A 32-way Multithreaded Sparc Processor," *IEEE Micro*, 24, 2, Apr. 2005, 21–29

[KBG97] A. Kagi, D. Burger, and J. Goodman, "Efficient Synchronization: Let them Eat QOLB," *Proc. 24th Int. Symp. on Computer Architecture*, 1997, 170–180

[KK79] P. Kermani and L. Kleinrock, "Virtual Cut-through: A New Computer Communication Switching Technique," *Computer Networks*, 3, 4, Sep. 1979, 267–286

[KRDKAM03] U. Kapasi, S. Rixner, W. Dally, B. Khailany, J. Ahn, P. Mattson, and J. Owens, "Programmable Stream Processors," *IEEE Computer*, 36, 8, Aug. 2003, 54–62

[L79] L. Lamport, "How to Make a Multiprocessor Computer that Correctly Executes Programs," *IEEE Trans. on Computers*, 28, 9, Sep. 1979, 690–691

[LC96] T. Lovett and R. Clapp, "STiNG: A CC-NUMA Computer System for the Commercial Marketplace," *Proc. 23rd Int. Symp. on Computer Architecture*, 1996, 308–317

[LK08] J. Larus and C. Kozyrakis, "Transactional Memory," *Communications of the ACM*, 51, 7, Jul. 2008, 80–88

[LT88] T. Lovett and S. Thakkar, "The Symmetry Multiprocessor System," *Proc. 1988 Int. Conf. on Parallel Processing, Aug.* 1988, 303–310

[PP85] M. Papamarcos and J. Patel, "A Low-overhead Coherence Solution for Multiprocessors with Private Cache Memories," *Proc. 12th Int. Symp. on Computer Architecture*, 1985, 348–354

[PW96] A. Peleg and U. Weiser, "MMX Technology Extension to the Intel Architecture," *IEEE Micro*, 16, 4, Aug. 1996, 42–50

[RAJ99] P. Ranganathan, S. Adve, and N. Jouppi, "Performance of Image and Video Processing with General-Purpose Processors and Media ISA Extensions," *Proc. 26th Int. Symp. on Computer Architecture*, 1999, 124–135

[RS84] L. Rudolf and Z. Segall, "Dynamic Decentralized Cache Schemes for MIMD Parallel Processors," *Proc. 11th Int. Symp. on Computer Architecture*, 1984, 340–347

[S78] B. Smith, "A Pipelined, Shared Resource MIMD Computer," *Proc. 1978 Int. Conf. on Parallel Processing*, 1978, 6–8

[S96] S. Scott "Synchronization and Communication in the Cray 3TE Multiprocessor," *Proc. 7th Int. Conf. on Architectural Support for Programming Languages and Operating Systems*, Oct. 1996, 26–36

[SHAS99] C. Stunkel, J. Herring, B. Abali, and R. Sivaram, "A New Switch Chip for IBM RS/6000 SP Systems," *Proc. Int. Conf. on Supercomputing*, 1999, 16–33

[SS86] P. Sweazey and A. Smith, "A Class of Compatible Cache Consistency Protocols and their Support by the IEEE Future Bus," *Proc. 13th Int. Symp. on Computer Architecture*, 1986, 414–423

[SS05] N. Slingerland and A. Smith, "Multimedia Extensions for General-Purpose Microprocessors: A Survey," *Microprocessors and Microsystems*, 29, 5, Jan. 2005, 225–246

[TO96] M. Tremblay and J. O'Connor, "UltraSparc I: A Four-issue Processor Supporting Multimedia," *IEEE Micro*, 16, 2, Apr. 1996, 42–50

[TR88] L. Tucker and G. Robertson, "Architecture and Applications of the Connection Machine," *IEEE Computer*, 21, 8, Aug. 1988, 26–38

8 Multithreading and (Chip) Multiprocessing

Parallel processing takes several flavors, depending on the unit of parallelism and the number of processing units. Early on in the development of computer systems, we saw the emergence of *multiprogramming* (Section 2.3), whereby several (portions of) programs share main memory. When the program currently executing requires some I/O processing, it relinquishes the use of the CPU via a context switch, and another program takes ownership of the CPU. Parallel processing occurs between the program using the CPU and the programs (there may be more than one) executing some I/O-related task. Here, the unit of parallel processing is a program, or process, and the parallelism is at the program level. An efficient implementation of multiprogramming requires the use of an operating system with a virtual memory management component. At the other extreme of the spectrum of granularity, we have the exploitation of *instruction-level parallelism*. Several instructions of the same program are executing simultaneously. *Pipelining* (Section 2.1) is the simplest form of the concurrent execution of instructions. *Superscalar* and *EPIC* processors (Chapter 3) extend this notion by having several instructions occupying the same stages of the pipeline at the same time. Of course, extra resources such as multiple functional units must be present for this concurrency to happen.

In the previous chapter, we gave a strict definition of *multiprocessing*, namely, the processing by several processors of portions of the same program. Multiprocessors must include hardware and software to facilitate the creation of concurrent processes and their synchronization, as well as protocols to ensure the consistency of data across the memory hierarchy. Multiprocessors can also be used to execute different programs simultaneously, thus becoming an extension of multiprogramming. In multiprocessors, the granularity of parallelism ranges from the instruction level within one processor to complete applications running on different processors under the supervision of a common operating system.

In this chapter, we consider *thread-level* parallelism and its implementation, *multithreading.* To differentiate between processes and threads (also called lightweight processes), we use the operating system terminology in which a *process* is an executing program along with its state, represented by the values of the program counter, registers, and settings, which are found in a data structure of the operating system often called a *process table*. Two examples among many of entries in the process table are a pointer to the beginning of the table that holds the virtual–physical page mappings of the process, and the process PID that prevents complete flushing of TLBs during a context switch. We can contrast this dynamic definition of a process with the more static one of a *program*, which consists of the encoding of an algorithm, the layout of its data structures, and the input–output files it will use. With these definitions, multiprogramming is somewhat ill named and should be called multiprocessing, and multiprocessing then should be called multiprocessoring to indicate that there are several processors. However, leaving aside this hair-splitting terminology for historical reasons, we consider a *sequential process* to be defined as we have done and to have a single thread of control. However, we can allow a process to have several threads of control, whereupon *threads* will have the same properties as processes, but with the distinction that threads within a process share the same address space. Performing a switch from a thread to another thread in the same process is not as costly as a context switch, because, for example, the virtual memory mappings are not modified. The interleaved execution of threads belonging to the same process is called *multithreading*. Recently, the definition of multithreading has been expanded to include the same concepts as multiprogramming, but with the understanding that a context switch, or thread switch, is much cheaper in a multithreaded organization, because part of the process state is replicated for each thread.

Multithreading can be implemented on one or on several processors. The *granularity* of multithreading is defined by the events that mandate a change in thread execution. At the finest grain, the change can occur on every cycle, or even several threads can share the same stage of the pipeline at the same time, as in *simultaneous multithreading* (SMT). At a coarser grain, a thread switch can happen on an event where the current thread would be obliged to wait a number of cycles much larger than the number of cycles needed to switch threads. A typical example would be a miss in the whole cache hierarchy, requiring an access to main memory. In the first section of this chapter, we will present several implementations of multithreading on a single processor.

As indicated in the previous chapter, chip multiprocessors (CMPs) are becoming increasingly common in servers and high-end workstations. In the second and third sections of this chapter, we will show how multiprocessing and multithreading can be integrated to provide increased performance. We will differentiate between general-purpose CMPs, with the Niagara Sun and Intel Core Duo as prime examples, and special-purpose CMPs, with brief introductions to the IBM Cell Processor and the Intel IAX 2400 Network Processor.

8.1 Single-Processor Multithreading

8.1.1 Fine-grained Multithreading

Multiprogramming came about so that the main resource in the system at the time, namely the processor, would not remain idle when I/O tasks were performed.

Multithreading's intent is similar, that is, its goal is to tolerate high-latency operations. In fine-grained multithreading, as soon as an instruction stream in a thread is going to be delayed even for as little as one cycle (as in a RAW hazard), the control of the processor is given to another thread. Evidently, such thread switching should take "no time."

The first implementation of fine-grained multithreading (it was not called that at the time) had a thread switch at every cycle. In the sidebar of Section 3.2, we introduced the CPU of the CDC 6600 and its scoreboard. The CPU handled all program computations, but input–output tasks were performed by ten peripheral processor units (PPUs). These ten processors were sharing a common ALU and associated logic as well as a common memory. Each of the ten processors had its own set of registers and program counter. They took ownership of the ALU on a round-robin basis (in the original documents it was said that they formed a "barrel") with ownership changing every *minor cycle*. This is equivalent to saying that there was a thread switch at every cycle. A minor cycle was sufficient to execute a register operation. If some variable had to be loaded from memory, it took a major cycle that was equal to 10 minor cycles so that the value would be present the next time that the PPU that was performing the load would have ownership of the ALU. Note that all instruction executions took at least one major cycle, because the instruction itself had to be fetched from memory.

The PPU example shows that in fine-grained multithreading, each thread must have its own register set and program counter. Moreover, the number of threads ready to execute at a given time must be able to hide the latency of the longest operation. This longest operation must be pipelined so that several threads can be in the process of executing an instance of it. Since thread switching can occur cycle by cycle, instructions must be processed so that there is no need to flush the pipeline. Each instruction must carry a tag identifying the stream to which it belongs.

These concepts were incorporated in the design of the supercomputer Tera MTA (MTA stands for multithreaded architecture). Tera is a multiprocessor. Each processor can execute multiple threads (called streams in early papers) simultaneously. Each processor has a provision for 128 program counters, and thus up to 128 independent instruction streams can be active concurrently. Each stream has its own set of 32 64-bit registers, as well as eight target registers that are used to specify branch addresses and allow prefetching of instructions. There are no caches in the system, but instruction stream buffers are present. Virtual memory per se is not implemented, but each processor can have up to 16 domains that are relocatable, and therefore 16 different applications can run concurrently on a single processor. The longest operation is a memory fetch, and not only the processor but the interconnection network leading to the memory modules is pipelined.

If the PPU model were strictly adopted, there should be as many streams ready to execute at each cycle as the number of cycles required to perform a memory fetch, of the order of 70 in Tera's first implementation. Tera circumvents part of the problem by including in each instruction a field (3 bits) that indicates how many instructions (i.e., a maximum of 7) will execute before a potential data or control hazard may occur. Thus, stream switching is not theoretically necessary at every cycle, and the number of ready streams can be reduced. In the best of cases, it would appear that if the compiler can organize code in independent chunks of eight instructions, then 9 streams instead of 70 might be sufficient. However, this analysis does not take into account the delay due to instruction latency between consecutive instructions from the same thread, and in reality, more streams are necessary. Some instruction-level parallelism in each stream can be exploited by an ISA having VLIW characteristics (cf. Section 3.4) – namely, a load–store operation, an arithmetic operation, and a control operation can be present in the same instruction. Although this presents a distinct advantage for the execution of a thread, it makes it even more difficult to find independent VLIW instructions in the same thread, and hence might require a larger number of ready streams.

Fine-grained multithreading aims to increase throughput and relies on the assumption that there are enough threads available. It is therefore a good match for "embarrassingly parallel" applications, which constitute a fair amount of the workload of supercomputers. However, a Tera-like implementation is not viable if there are very few threads so that the high-latency memory operations cannot be overlapped with processor computations. In the specific case of Tera, the lack of caches is a great concern, especially for the performance of single-threaded applications, but it can be alleviated in other implementations – with some additional complexity due to the uncertainty about when a particular memory operation will terminate. Another drawback is the lack of virtual memory support; virtual memory features could be added, again with a more complex design. We shall deal with this issue in the next section, on coarse-grained multithreading. On the other hand, any application that would incur a lot of cache misses and that could be parallelized would be favorable to a Tera-like fine-grained multithreading implementation, because the accesses to memory would be pipelined and would not incur the overhead of checks for hits or misses.

In summary, fine-grained multithreading is a good architectural model for running applications on which one can extract a large number of threads, as in some scientific applications, or for running multiprogramming loads where each process requires significant memory bandwidth and low processor computational power. Tera is a system for the first type of applications, and Niagara, introduced in Section 8.2.1 of this chapter, is meant for Web servers whose applications fit the second characterization.

8.1.2 Coarse-grained Multithreading

In coarse-grained multithreading a thread switch will not occur at every cycle, but only when the currently executing thread encounters a long-latency operation. Here, "long" is relative and depends on the processor implementation, the hardware support given to each thread (that is, the time it takes to perform a thread switch), and the timings of accesses to various parts of the memory hierarchy such as caches and TLBs.

In the following, we consider a microprocessor system with a cache hierarchy and running under the control of an operating system with a paged virtual memory and TLBs. Let us assume first an in-order processor where caches are physically tagged. Because several threads can have outstanding cache misses, the cache hierarchy must be lockup-free. TLBs use PIDs because we want to consider both threads belonging to the same program and threads belonging to different programs. With the number of registers available on current machines, it is evident that an efficient implementation of multithreading requires that each thread have its own register set; otherwise, the saving and restoring of registers might take longer than the latency that is supposed to be hidden. In addition, a number of control registers, such as those indicating the addresses of the page tables and the respective tops of the stacks or the actions to be taken on some exceptions, have also to be saved and restored. The amount of processor state that identifies a thread is often called a *context*. A thread switch is not, however, as extensive as a context switch that occurs on an exception or interrupt in a conventional multiprogrammed machine, because the contexts are replicated in hardware.

In an in-order processor, several threads can occupy different stages of the pipeline as long as instructions carry a tag identifying the set of registers attached to their thread. So, in theory, a coarse-grained multithreaded processor would take "no time" for a thread switch, as was the case for fine-grained multithreading. One of its problems, though, is that all instructions in the pipeline after the instruction that triggers the thread switch must be voided, and the instruction buffer must be filled with the instructions of the thread taking over the processor. This latter performance impediment can be avoided by having one instruction buffer per context. Nonetheless, there will be a definite start-up cost to fill up the pipeline.

The number of contexts is necessarily limited, not only because of the additional hardware that they require, but also because the threads are sharing a number of resources such as caches, TLBs, and branch predictor tables. Moreover, there is an overhead in choosing among the ready threads, and this overhead should be kept as small as possible. A naive rule of thumb on the number of hardware contexts that should be provided could be: "If the longest latency to be hidden by multithreading is n cycles and operations with this longest latency occur on the average every m cycles, then there should be n/m hardware contexts." For example, if the latency to main memory is $n = 200$ cycles and L2 cache misses occur every $m = 50$ cycles, then there should be four hardware contexts if thread switches are to occur on L2 misses. However, the value 50 cycles for m might involve the assumption that its measurement was taken when a thread had total occupancy of the L2 cache. With four contexts, m might be lower, thus arguing for more contexts. The other side of the coin is that with more contexts, L1 and TLB misses as well as branch prediction errors would occur more frequently than with a single thread of control, for these structures are shared, and therefore the intervals between L2 cache misses would be greater, and the need for contexts reduced.

The first implementation of coarse-grained multithreading was done on a research multiprocessor, the Alewife machine at MIT, in the early 1990s. Each processor was a modified in-order SPARC processor with four hardware contexts, but an unlimited number of threads could be generated. Thread switching was triggered by either cache misses (there was a single off-chip cache) or failed synchronization attempts. A thread switch was implemented via a trap and took about 10 cycles. In order to simplify the implementation, the pipeline was flushed on a thread switch. Although Alewife was supposed to support virtual memory, the prototype did not do so.

A commercial and more complete implementation of coarse-grained multithreading can be found in a variation of the IBM PowerPC microprocessor. The multithreaded processor was intended for commercial workloads that have large working sets and therefore are subject to significant cache miss rates. In order to be able to run existing software, threads were considered as if they were running on a multiprocessor, a concept similar to the one that guided the design of Alewife. The in-order processor supported only two contexts, so a single bit was sufficient to indicate which thread was running in any part of the short five-stage pipeline. Instruction buffers were replicated, that is, there was one for each thread. Thread switching occurred on L1 cache and IERAT misses. IERAT is an IBM acronym for "instruction cache effective [i.e., virtual] to real address translation," meaning an array that contains virtual-to-real address translations for recently referenced instructions, which can be seen as a first-level I-TLB. The 128-entry IERAT was evenly split between the two threads, with provision for being totally dedicated to a single thread if multithreading was not in use. In case of an L1 D-cache miss (at least 8 cycles to get a line from L2) that was detected in the last stage of the pipeline, the switching penalty was to fill the pipeline. Since instructions of the new thread were already in an instruction buffer, the start-up time was only 3 cycles. In the case of an IERAT miss (at least 8 cycles to find the translation in the TLB), new instructions could start filling the pipeline at the next cycle.

The rule for thread switching was as follows. On an L1 miss or IERAT miss, a switch occurred unless the other thread was servicing an L2 miss or a TLB miss. The rationale for the latter case is that an L1 miss or IERAT miss is most often resolved in the L2 or the TLB, so switching from a thread waiting for a short-latency resolution to a thread waiting for a long-latency resolution is counterproductive. If the L1 or IERAT miss results in an L2 or TLB miss, then the switch will occur.

Performance results showed an improvement in throughput by up to 30% for commercial workloads, although the miss rates in the shared L1 D-cache were significantly higher than in the single-thread case. However, those in the L1 I-cache, L2, and TLB were not much affected, and multithreading allowed hiding the long latency to main memory.

The thread switching time becomes longer if the processor is out of order. Now all instructions preceding in program order the instruction that triggers the thread must complete, that is, be committed. With current designs, this will most likely take longer than the time to resolve an L1 miss. Therefore, thread switching should occur only on L2 misses.

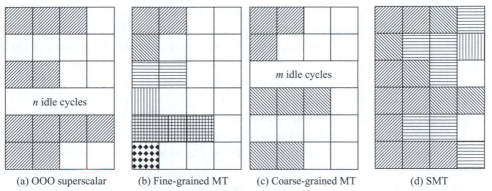

(a) OOO superscalar	(b) Fine-grained MT	(c) Coarse-grained MT	(d) SMT

Figure 8.1 Typical occupancy of pipeline issue stage for (a) out-of-order superscalar (n is the latency of an L2 cache miss that cannot be hidden), (b) fine-grained multithreading (six threads, occupying the six-stage pipeline), (c) coarse-grained multithreading (m is the start-up cost for a new thread; m n), (d) simultaneous multithreading with four threads. (Adapted from Eggers et al. [EELLST97]).

8.1.3 Simultaneous Multithreading

In Figure 8.1(a) we show an example of the occupancy of the issue stage of the pipeline of an out-of-order four-way microprocessor. A row of the figure represents occupancy of the stage at a given time (a blank square represents a vacant issue slot), and consecutive rows represent consecutive cycles. As can be seen, not all slots are occupied in a given cycle. The causes may be that there is contention for some functional units or that a data hazard prevents the issuing of some instructions. For example, it could be that only loads and adds are ready to be executed and there is only one adder and one load unit. Second, a whole row, (i.e., a whole cycle), might pass with no instruction being issued. The causes of that could be again data hazards, for example, waiting for data to come from the L2 cache, or cycles spent in recovering from a mispredicted branch. In one row, we have collapsed n consecutive rows to represent stalling due to an L2 miss. The number of empty cycles, n, should be less than the latency of accessing main memory (of the order of hundreds of cycles), but can be quite significant.

The intent of multithreading is to reduce the loss in performance due to these n empty cycles. In the fine-grained multithreading shown in Figure 8.1(b), there are no empty rows – if there are enough threads to cover the n empty cycles. This might be a tall order if n is of the order of several hundred cycles, even if we switch from one thread to the next only on a data hazard occurrence. Because fine-grained MT implies an in-order processor, the rows are less filled than with the superscalar.

Coarse-grained multithreading is represented in Figure 8.1(c). It has a pattern similar to that of the superscalar except that the number of empty rows on the occurrence of a long-latency event is smaller. Here m is the number of cycles needed to refill the pipeline on a thread switch if the processor is an in-order one, or to flush and refill if the processor is out of order. m is always less than n, but – as we saw previously – there are some additional hardware costs to implementing multi-threading, and also the gains may not be quite as great as expected, because some hardware data structures have to be shared among threads, thus diminishing their performance benefits.

In order to fill up both the horizontal slots (i.e., those that are left empty because there are not enough instructions to issue in a single thread) and the vertical slots (i.e., empty rows due to latencies, caused mostly by cache misses and mispredictions), we need to have several threads occupying the front end and the back end of the pipeline at the same time. This new organization is called *simultaneous multithreading* (SMT). Its effects are shown in Figure 8.1(d). As can be seen, almost all slots are filled now. The vacant issue slots (including some possible totally empty cycles that we have not shown) might be due to structural hazards – for example, all eligible threads requesting the same resources, or all threads waiting for cache misses.

How much more hardware and logic is needed to implement SMT features on top of a conventional out-of-order microprocessor? Not as much as one would think, if the number of threads that can execute simultaneously is limited. Commercial implementations of SMT are limited to two threads, as in the Intel Pentium 4 and Intel Core (where SMT is called *hyperthreading*) and the IBM Power5. A four-thread implementation was planned for a successor to the DEC Alpha 21364, but the company was sold to Intel before the processor was fabricated. It is estimated that a two-thread Pentium 4 requires 5% additional logic, and the prediction was that the inclusion of a four-thread SMT in the Dec Alpha would have added 8–10% to the amount of hardware needed for the processor.

In an SMT processor some of the hardware resources need to be replicated, and some can be totally shared, as could be done for coarse-grained multithreading. However, because several threads can be using the pipeline concurrently, some resources that were totally devoted to the currently executing thread in the coarse-grained implementation must now be either shared or partitioned among the threads.

Recall that in coarse-grained multithreading, the architectural registers, program counter, and various control registers need to be replicated. SMT imposes the same replications. In the same vein, the execution units and the cache hierarchy can be totally shared, as well as some other resources such as physical registers and branch predictors. As we saw earlier, TLBs can be either shared, with the inclusion of PIDs, or partitioned.

We can analyze the requirements for the remaining resources by walking through the main stages of the pipeline. The first decision is instruction fetching. There is no practical difficulty in sharing the I-cache or, in the case of the Intel Pentium 4, the trace cache, although in that latter case each thread must have its own trace-cache pointer. Each thread nonetheless must have its own instruction buffer. Sharing an instruction buffer among active threads is impractical when filling is performed with prefetching and when flushing occurs on a branch misprediction. Even with per-thread instruction buffers, some additional decisions that were not required for either superscalars or coarse-grained multithreading must be taken, such as which instruction buffer to fill on a given cycle, and from which instruction buffer instructions should proceed down the front-end. The first choice is fairly easy, for most likely a single instruction buffer will be empty in a given cycle. If not, any kind of round-robin access will be fine. In the IBM Power5, which restricts SMT to two threads, instruction feeding of the front-end alternates between the two threads. A more sophisticated algorithm in case there are more than two threads is to favor the thread(s) that have fewer instructions in the front-end. Once an instruction is in the pipeline, it must carry a tag identifying the thread to which it belongs.

As we have mentioned, branch predictors and branch target buffers can be shared except for the return stack predictors. Even with tagging, mixing returns from various threads in the return stack would quickly become unwieldy. In a similar vein, the logic needed to treat exceptions and interrupts should be replicated for each thread.

Moving down the front-end, the next stage that requires attention is the one where register renaming occurs. Whereas physical registers can be shared, the renaming tables must be individualized with each thread. A shared renaming table could be envisioned, with some tagging indicating to which thread a given physical register belong, but the difficulties in storing the table on a branch prediction and restoring it on a branch misprediction make the sharing solution quite unpalatable.

At the conclusion of the front-end, in-flight instructions join queues, or an instruction window, where they wait for free execution units and/or operand availability. In an SMT processor, these queues should be shared among active threads. Having separate physical queues for each thread is not the best solution, because of the dynamic nature of computation whereby threads advance often in spurts and have varying needs for instruction queuing. Moreover, a tenet of SMT processing is that one should be able to run a single thread using all available resources, and thus the entireties of the queues should be available to single-thread execution. The queues are therefore shared. The sharing does not prevent equal partitioning, but a better solution than that is to allow a variable number of entries with a maximum for any given thread, so that one thread does not occupy the whole queue and prevent other threads from progressing while it is itself waiting for a long-latency event. Dispatching instructions to execution units happens in the same fashion as in a superscalar – for example, based on the age of ready-to-dispatch instructions in the queue. This scheduling can be done independently of thread ownership of the instructions.

At first glance, the execution units do not seem to require any changes. However, one must be careful when designing forwarding units so that comparisons are performed between register names of instructions of the same thread. Because forwarding units require very simple logic, replicating them, one per thread, is the easiest solution. Similarly, the logic to restore state after a branch misprediction should be replicated.

Finally, we have to look at the structure of the reorder buffer and the commitment of instructions. On the one hand, the reorder buffer should be shared by all

Table 8.1. Replicated, partitioned, and shared resources in a
typical SMT design

	Resources
Replicated	• Architectural registers • Program counter • Various control registers • Instruction buffer • Return stack predictor • Register-renaming logic • Forwarding and recovery logic • Interrupt controller
Partitioned	• Issue queues for execution and load–store units • Reorder buffer
Shared	• Physical registers • Cache hierarchy • TLBs • Branch predictor and branch target buffer • Execution units

threads, so that in the case of single-thread execution it can be used in its entirety.
On the other hand, interspersing instructions from various threads in the reorder
buffer leads to difficulties when voiding instructions in the event of branch mispredictions or exceptions. A reasonable solution, adopted in the Intel (two-thread)
hyperthreaded Xeon (Pentium 4), is to statically partition the reorder buffer equally
among threads. Instructions can commit in the same cycle from either partition. A
different approach is taken in the IBM Power5, because there instructions are clustered in sequential groups when sent from the instruction buffer to the front-end
of the pipeline and thereafter when allocation is performed in the reorder buffer.
This allocation is consistent with the alternate fetching of instructions between the
two threads, as mentioned earlier. It also allows commitment of instructions to be
done group by group, that is, whenever all instructions in the oldest group in a
thread have completed. Two groups, one from each thread, can commit in the same
cycle. Although this design is satisfactory for two threads, it is unsuitable when more
threads are allowed, and in that situation, partitioning is the solution of choice.

A summary of the various SMT requirements is shown in Table 8.1. SMT certainly enhances resource utilization and yields better throughput than superscalar
and coarse-grained multithreading. High-priority or deadline-driven applications
can be run on an SMT machine if single-thread execution can use entirely all the
partitioned and shared resources. Thread selection and scheduling can be included
in the hardware and the operating system with little added cost compared to a conventional multiprogrammed environment.

On the other hand, the number of threads executing simultaneously in an SMT
processor is limited because of resource sharing and resource contention. Resource
sharing implies that some hardware data structures, such as L1 caches and branch
predictors, must be larger so that individual threads have adequate performance.
The same is true of the physical register file so that register spilling can be as rare

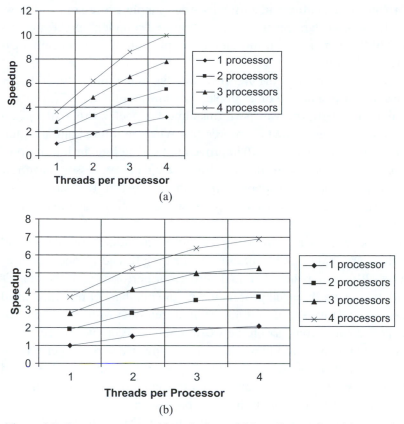

Figure 8.2. Improvements achieved via multithreading and multiprocessing: (a) "simple" processors and (b) "complex" processors (adapted from Chaudhry et al. [CCYT05]).

as in single-thread execution. Because larger resources imply longer access times, it might be that some stages in the pipeline that take only one cycle in a superscalar will need to take two in an SMT processor. Resource sharing also implies concurrent access to the shared structures, hence requiring a larger number of read–write ports. Resource contention will result in more frequent structural hazards on an individual thread, which is another way to say that SMT is engineered for enhancement of throughput and not of single-thread latency.

Finally, the design and verification of an out-of-order processor is already a challenge. SMT increases the difficulties. In view of these considerations, it is not a surprise that industrial implementations have been limited to two concurrent threads. However, a two-thread SMT is cheaper than a two-processor CMP, and combination, on a small scale, of SMT and CMP is already on the market with the two-processor (or four-processor) SMT Intel Core and IBM Power5.

8.1.4 Multithreading Performance Assessment

In the previous sections of this chapter we have stressed how multithreading helps in improving *throughput*. Figure 8.2(a) and (b) show respectively the (simulated)

relative performances of multithreading for in-order simple processors and powerful out-of-order superscalars (in these simulations a "complex" processor was
between 4 and 10 times more powerful than a "simple" one). The benchmark is
a large database application.

It is interesting to observe that the improvement due to multithreading is larger
when the processors are simple. For example, as shown in Figure 8.2(a), a single four-way multithreaded processor performs almost as well (within 10%) as a
multiprocessor with four single-threaded processors. When multithreading and multiprocessing are combined, a factor-of-10 improvement can be found with four processors and four threads, that is, 16 threads. Because simple processors have low
utilization of resources, they can support several threads before the performance
per thread diminishes. The nonlinear rise in performance is mostly due to synchronization requirements.

When the processors are more complex, resource utilization per thread
increases and there are fewer opportunities for competing threads. Nonetheless, as
shown in Figure 8.2(b), a four-threaded single processor performs as well as a multiprocessor with two single-threaded processors. As the numbers of processors and
threads increase, the relative speedup is less pronounced than with simple processors. Absolute performance comparisons between simple and complex processors is
difficult in that we would have to know the area and power dissipated per type of
processor so that we could establish equivalences between a complex processor and
several simple ones. As we shall see soon, there are commercial chip multiprocessors with either simple or complex multithreaded processors.

In the case of SMT, simulations of an eight-thread SMT processor that can
fetch eight instructions per cycle have shown throughput improvements on database
workloads between 150% and 300% compared to an out-of-order superscalar. More
realistic measurements on the IBM Power5 showed that out of eight workloads,
seven were improved using SMT. Under single-thread execution a copy of each
program was bound to each processor. In SMT mode, a copy of the program was
bound to each SMT context. The performance range was from a degradation of
11% (an exception due to very high miss rates in the L2 and L3 caches in both
single-thread and SMT modes) to an improvement of 41%. Higher efficiency was
achieved when the number of L2 and L3 cache misses was small. Measurements
on a hyperthreaded (two threads) Intel Pentium 4 reported performance improvements between 15% and 27% over a single Pentium 4 processor, both for multithreaded multimedia applications and for a set of three independent applications
such as Word, Acrobat, PowerPoint, and Virus Scan running simultaneously.

We have also mentioned that a good design for any variety of multithreading
should not impede best performance for single-thread execution. Since most current
applications are single-threaded, as exemplified by the IBM Power5 experiment of
the previous paragraph, the question arises of whether one can use multithreading
to improve on single-thread execution in the absence of languages and compilers
that will make multithreading explicit. As we have seen repeatedly in this book, one
possibility is to rely on speculation.

8.1.5 Speculative Multithreading

In the previous section, we have assumed that threads were explicitly exposed by either the programmer or the compiler or the operating system. In this section we show possible applications of the concept of multithreading when applied speculatively at run time. We start by the case of a single-processor environment.

Run-ahead Execution

When an instruction with a long latency, in all likelihood an L2 or L3 cache read miss, reaches the head of the reorder buffer and cannot commit because its result is not available, the instruction window and/or issue queues fill up. When no more instructions can be fetched and all the instructions sitting in the windows and queues are waiting for the oldest instruction to commit, the processor must stall. For some workloads, this situation can be severe enough that the processor stalls 70% of the time. Increasing the size of the instruction window (or reorder buffer) and issue queues is an option, but not a pleasant one, for these resources are addressed associatively and therefore are of high cost both in area and in power dissipation. A larger L2 cache would of course alleviate the problem, but most of the time the on-chip caches are already at the maximum size permitted by the chip's total area.

Taking its cue from multithreading, *run-ahead execution*, also called *hardware scouting*, is a technique that is used to implement some form of cache prefetching and of warming up of branch predictors. When a processor stall is detected and the oldest instruction is an L2 cache miss (we assume L2 to be the cache farthest from the processor), a *bogus* value is given to the result of the operation so that execution can continue. At this point, the context is saved, namely, the architectural registers, the return address stack, and possibly some register maps and history-based structures related to branch prediction. Execution continues in run-ahead mode (see the following paragraphs). When the blocking instruction yields its actual result, the context will be restored and execution will proceed normally from the point where run-ahead execution was initiated.

In order to detect and propagate bogus values, registers have an extra invalid bit per register indicating whether the result that is generated is bogus (invalid) or not. Invalid bits from registers are propagated so that a result register has its invalid bit set if any of its source operands is invalid. Run-ahead execution proceeds faster than normal execution, because when invalid computations are detected, they are not performed and the back-end of the processor is not used. An invalid instruction is also retired immediately from the instruction window, providing another means to speed up run-ahead execution. Note that during run-ahead, an invalid register might be redefined and become legal again. However, neither legal nor bogus stores can be put in cache and in memory; instead they are stored in a small run-ahead cache so that dependent loads in run-ahead execution can get the values they need (this is in fact slightly more complex, but we skip some technical details such as the fact that evicted lines from the run-ahead cache are just dropped).

The main goal of run-ahead execution is to discover loads and stores that will potentially generate cache misses and to prefetch the corresponding lines. When a valid store instruction completes during run-ahead, the data cache is checked, and if the check results in a miss, the corresponding line is prefetched. If a load is deemed valid after checking the source register and potential conflicts with invalid stores, then it proceeds as a regular load, except that if it misses in L2, then its result register is marked invalid. The rationale is that this cache miss will return after the one that spurred the run-ahead execution. However, the prefetch of the missing line is performed.

Various solutions can be implemented with respect to the branch predictor structures. First, branch prediction is performed as in normal execution. If any of the sources for the branching is invalid, run-ahead execution may proceed on the wrong path until the next correct – and valid – branch without ever being corrected. Because difficult-to-predict branches are quite often in short if–then–else constructs, the correct path will be soon followed again. The worst outcome would be some extraneous prefetching. More open to question, though, is the updating of the branch prediction apparatus. Simulations have shown that updating the branch predictor tables as in normal execution does not yield performance significantly worse than the expensive option of duplicating the branch predictor when run-ahead is initiated. Overall, the correct paths are followed in run-ahead execution with almost the same prediction rate as in normal execution.

Because instructions executed in run-ahead mode do not commit to architectural state, the technique is mostly a prefetch mechanism with another potential beneficial effect, namely, training the branch predictor. Although we have centered our discussion on the initiation of run-ahead due to an L2 miss halting normal execution, other structural hazards, such as a full store buffer, could also be used to start run-ahead execution. In multiprocessor environments, run-ahead could also be used when locks are encountered.

Run-ahead execution requires a minimal hardware investment: a shadow register file, 1 extra bit per register, a small run-ahead cache, and some temporary storage for various small components of the branch predictor and store buffer. Simulation evaluations of run-ahead added to an aggressive Pentium 4-like processor and hardware scouting associated with a Sun-like processor show significant improvements in performance, and, quite interestingly, almost the same results are obtained on the two platforms. *IPC* improves more with run-ahead than with a stream prefetcher. Even on benchmarks that do not exercise the memory hierarchy much, like SPECint2000, the benefits are evident: up to 12% with a 512 KB L2 cache. For more memory-intensive workloads, the improvement can reach 40%. Another interesting way to look at these results is that run-ahead is equivalent to putting extra cache on chip. For example, the same *IPC* results can be obtained for SPECint2000 with a normal processor and a 1 MB L2 cache and with the same processor, a run-ahead engine, and half (512 KB) of the L2 cache. In the case of SPECfp2000, the run-ahead with a 512 KB L2 attains the same result as if a 4 MB cache were present without run-ahead. Clearly these savings overshadow the run-ahead area requirements.

Speculative Multithreading

Run-ahead execution achieves impressive results with limited hardware and no software intervention. Only one run-ahead thread executes when the main thread stalls. Even with this restriction, some work done while in run-ahead mode is wasted. When the main thread resumes execution, instructions are refetched and their results recomputed even if they were correct.

With *speculative multithreading*, threads are spawned ahead of the time they would execute in a purely sequential process. In some sense it is an extension of run-ahead execution except that (i) the initiation times are not controlled by a stalling processor, (ii) several threads execute simultaneously, and (iii) some of the work performed by the speculative threads, and hopefully most of it, does not have to be redone. Of course, because several threads run concurrently, the platform on which they execute must be either an SMT processor or some multiprocessor architecture.

We can distinguish between control-driven and data-driven multithreading. In control-driven multithreading, new threads are spawned at specific control points in the flow of the program. The detection of these control points could be facilitated by the compiler or a profiler. Although there is growing interest in the matter, there has been little effort in that direction to date. However, in the absence of software support, the hardware can speculatively generate threads at easily recognizable control flow constructs. Some examples, which can be combined, are:

- When the beginning of a loop is encountered: The following loop iterations can be started simultaneously.
- At procedure calls: The main thread is the one that executes the procedure. A speculative thread can be started at the instruction following the call.
- When a backward branch is encountered and predicted taken: The main thread is the one that follows the backward branch. A speculative thread can start at the instruction following the branch.

The main difficulty with control-driven speculative multithreading arises in the recognition and execution of producer–consumer relationships. Here also the compiler can help by flagging the variables that are defined in a thread and that are used in a subsequent thread. Communication can be done through memory or through general- or special-purpose registers. However, the compiler cannot always be certain that the addresses of loads and stores are different. This so-called *memory disambiguation* problem is a well-recognized impediment to the automatic parallelization of programs. We saw a flavor of how it can be resolved in an out-of-order processor when we looked at load speculation (Section 5.2.2). In a multithreaded environment, temporal versions of stores can be used to check and potentially recover from load–store dependencies. Overall, though, the mechanisms required for this type of multithreading are rather complex, and, to our knowledge, the only industrial implementation of the concept has been that of the Sun MAJC (Microprocessor Architecture for Java Computing) chip. In MAJC the speculation is helped by the Java language virtual machine structure, which helps differentiate between stack and heap operations; nonetheless, several versions of a given heap variable may have to be kept.

The finest-grained data-driven multithreaded architecture is a *data-flow machine*. The pure data-flow concept is based on two premises:

- An instruction executes when and only when all the operands required are available.
- Instructions are purely functional and produce no side effects.

The second requirement, highly favored by mathematicians in particular in that it facilitates proofs of correctness, imposes a *single–assignment rule*: no variable should be assigned more than once. The first one imposes some machinery for the matching of the source operands of instructions with already generated results. In some sense, a data-flow implementation could be realized with an instruction window that contains the whole program, and matching could be performed by having each operand carry a token identifying the instruction for which it is a source. Some research data-flow machines were realized in the late 1970s and early 1980s, but their performance has suffered from the requirements of token matching and from lack of locality in the programs' execution. Moreover, the need to transform customary imperative programming languages into some single-assignment language has been another roadblock.

Speculative data-driven multithreading has been proposed. Helper threads that accompany the main thread of computation are not spawned at specific control points, but instead contain operations that are predicted to be of long latency, like cache misses, or not well predictable, like some branches. When the main thread recognizes the proximity of these long-latency operations, it spawns a helper thread, which executes faster because it can be pared down to the operations that are critically important (recall Section 5.3.2 for a possible definition of these critical operations). When the main thread's execution requires data computed by the helper thread, it can integrate the results obtained by the latter or reexecute the computation, hopefully much faster in that, for example, the helper thread might have moved data in the lower level of the cache hierarchy. The difficulties in this approach lie in the recognition of the long-latency operations and the building of the helper threads. To date, no practical implementation of this concept has been realized.

8.2 General-Purpose Multithreaded Chip Multiprocessors

We have mentioned several times already the emergence and current ubiquity of chip multiprocessors (CMPs). We have referred to the multiprocessing and multithreading capabilities of the dual-processor IBM Power4 and Power5 and of the dual-processor Intel Pentium 4. The Power5 and the dual Pentium 4 are instances of SMT, with the SMT level limited at two concurrent threads. Other dual (or quad) CMPs have been delivered and/or announced by Intel (the Core architecture), AMD, and Sun. In all these cases, each of the processors on the chip is a full-fledged complex out-of-order superscalar, although the Intel Core microarchitecture is more of a descendant of the Pentium III and Pentium M than of the Pentium 4. The Intel Itanium is a VLIW in-order processor (cf. Section 3.4.2), and the dual-processor Itanium is far from simple; when it was announced, it had the largest number of transistors on a chip, namely 1.7 billion (recall Figure 1.2). At the other end of the complexity spectrum, Sun's Niagara has eight simple processors, each of which can support four threads concurrently in a fine-grained multithreading fashion.

There are several characteristics that are pertinent to the categorization of general-purpose CMPs:

- The number of processors. The first CMPs had two processors on a chip. By 2006, four-processor and eight-processor CMPs were delivered. There have been predictions that, following Moore's law, the numbers of processors on a CMP will double every 18 months, but that has not yet happened, maybe because of the software challenges (see the next chapter).
- The amount of multithreading. There can be none, there can be SMT as mentioned above, or there can be coarse-grained or fine-grained multithreading. The Sun Niagara is an instance of the latter, with the possibility that each processor will support 8 threads (16 threads in the Sun Niagara 3 announced in 2008).
- The complexity of each processor. The dual and quad processors we listed at the beginning of this section are full-fledged out-of-order superscalars (except for the Itanium). In contrast, the Sun Niagara processor is a simpler in-order processor. We describe Niagara and Intel multicores in more detail below.
- The homogeneity of each processor. There have been proposals for a combination of simple and complex processors on the same chip. However, to date only homogeneous general-purpose CMPs have been realized. Along the same lines, we should mention that the identical processors on the chip do not all have to run at the same frequency. Slowing down of some processors might be needed in order to reduce power requirements and heat dissipation (we will return to the important topic of power in the last chapter of this book).
- The cache hierarchy. In all current general-purpose CMPs, each processor has its own L1 I- and D-caches. The L2 cache can be either private, that is, one per processor, or shared among processors. When there are two processors on chip, if the L2 is shared, we have *dual cores*; if they are private, we have *dual processors* (see Figure 8.3). This terminology expands to more than two processors, and almost all current CMPs are multicores.
- The interconnection between processors and L2 caches. L2 caches are divided into banks, and the connection between the n processor–L1 caches and the m memory banks is currently via buses or crossbars, that is, a uniform (cache) memory access structure. However, if the prediction about the doubling of cores

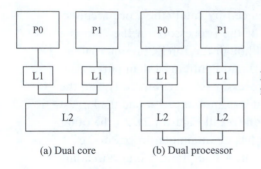

Figure 8.3. Generic dual-core and dual-processor configuration.

holds true, other interconnection schemes such as those described earlier (Section 7.1.3) will be needed, and sharing of the L2 cache will present even more challenges.

We illustrate some of these characteristics first with a description of the Sun Niagara and then the Intel Core Duo.

8.2.1 The Sun Niagara Multiprocessor

The Sun Niagara is an eight-processor multicore CMP. Each processor implementing the SPARC ISA is four-way fine-grained multithreaded so that 32 threads can be active at any given time. Niagara is meant to be used in applications that do not require high computational rates and that exhibit potential for parallelism. Web servers and database applications fit into these categories: their computational loads are not extensive, and the Web and/or database queries exhibit only a small number of synchronization requests, thus lending themselves well to multithreading. Performance speedups relative to a single-threaded uniprocessor should be close to those exhibited in Figure 8.2(a).

In Niagara each processor has its own L1 instruction cache (16 KB, four-way set-associative, line size 32 bytes, random replacement algorithm) and data cache (8 KB, four-way set-associative, line size 16 bytes, write-through), which is quite small by today's standards. The rationale is that the applications that we just mentioned have large working sets and would need much larger L1 D-caches to reduce significantly the miss rate, assumed to be of the order of 10%. Moreover, the fine-grained multithreading can hide much of the latency of L1 misses. The unified L2 is 3 MB and 12-way set-associative, and has 64 byte lines. It consists of four banks. The Niagara on-chip architecture is of the dance-hall variety, the interconnection between processors and L2 being an 8×4 crossbar switch. The I/O subsystem is also connected to the crossbar, and DMA accesses are routed via the L2 banks and four memory channels to and from main memory. An overall block diagram of Niagara is shown in Figure 8.4.

The processor is simple. It has a six-stage pipeline and issues a single instruction per cycle. In addition to the five stages of the pipeline described in Section 2.1, a sixth stage between IF (instruction fetch) and ID (instruction decode) performs thread selection (TS). Each of the four thread contexts has its own program counter (PC)

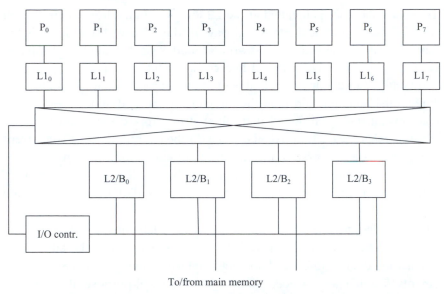

Figure 8.4. Sun Niagara block diagram (adapted from Kongetira et al. [KAO05]).

and register file. Each thread also has its own instruction buffer and store buffer. When all threads are available, each thread occupies the pipeline in a round-robin fashion as explained in Section 8.1.1 of this chapter. The front-end feeds a back-end with four integer functional units and a load–store unit. Two integer functional units, adder and shifter, have single-cycle latencies; the other two, multiplier and divider, have long latencies. A hit in the L1 D-cache returns the value after 3 cycles.

The first two stages of the pipeline, namely instruction fetch and thread selection, are replicated for each thread. The thread selection logic is the same for these two stages, so that if it is an instruction from thread i that is selected to be passed on to the decode stage, then it is the PC from the same thread i that will determine the I-cache and I-TLB access to load two instructions in the ith thread instruction buffer. The selection logic takes its inputs from the instruction type via predecoded bits in the I-cache that indicate long-latency operations, resource utilization, cache misses, and traps. When more than one thread is ready, the thread selection logic gives priority to the least recently used thread, thus avoiding starvation. As usual, loads are speculatively assumed to hit in the L1 cache with a latency of 3 cycles. However, the thread that issued the load is considered to have lower priority than the other ready threads.

Forwarding is implemented for the single-latency operations, although it is not needed if there are four threads sharing the pipeline, for then the writeback to the register file will occur 2 cycles before the same thread is in the execute stage again. However, long-latency operations such as multiply, divide, branches, and cache misses will stop temporarily the progression of a given thread. Therefore, in these cases the forwarding logic is needed. Furthermore, if the whole complement of threads is not available, a load becomes a *long* operation.

L1 D-cache coherence is handled at the L2 level via a directory scheme. Each L2 line has associated with it the tags and ways of the L1 lines for which it is the image. Since L1's are write-through and write-around, a single valid bit is sufficient for the L1 lines. On a load miss to the L1 D-cache and a hit in L2, the L1 tag address and way are entered in the directory and data are forwarded to the L1. On a store, the L2 line is first updated, and then the directory is checked and corresponding L1 lines are invalidated. The thread that initiated the store can continue without waiting for the coherence actions to take place. In the case of multiple concurrent stores, the updates are delivered to the caches in the same order, thus making sure that transactions are completed in order. L2 is writeback and write–allocate; on an L2 miss all L1 lines mapping into the L2 victim are invalidated, thus implementing partial MLI.

Sun Niagara designers chose simplicity in order to have more processors and more contexts. Notice, among other decisions, the short pipeline, the absence of branch predictors, and the absence of floating-point execution units and SIMD-type enhancements. Though we consider Niagara to be general-purpose, it would not perform well in scientific and data-streaming applications. The goal is to enhance thread throughput, not single-application latency, and hence the cycle time is not of utmost importance (the Niagara is supposed to run at a maximum of 2 GHz).

8.2.2 Intel Multicores

Intel has developed CMPs in each of the two architectural types shown in Figure 8.3. In the case of the two cores having private L2 caches, each core is on a separate die and there are two dies on the chip. When the two (or more) cores share a common L2 and are on the same die, we have so-called *monolithic multicores*.

Looking first at the architecture of Figure 8.3(a), there have been dual Intel Pentium 4 processors (or similar renamed processors such as Pentium D and Pentium Extreme) intended for servers with each processor running close to 4 GHz with its own private L2 cache. Power dissipation has prevented extensions to a larger number of cores, and it appeared at the end of 2008 that this product line had been discontinued. At that time, there were imminent announcements for dual, quad, and even octo processors with hyperthreading, also intended for servers and desktops, based on the Intel Core architecture. As we have already seen, the Core architecture is more of a descendant of the Pentium III and subsequent Pentium M processors than of the Pentium 4. We have also mentioned significant improvements in the Core architecture, such as microinstruction fusion, load speculation, and mini trace cache. The most powerful multicores will have private L1 and L2 caches and a shared L3 cache.

In this section, we describe some aspects of the Intel Core Duo architecture, intended mostly for laptop and mobile markets (the Centrino line), whose architecture belongs to the class represented in Figure 8.3(b). The processor is based on the Pentium M, thus still belonging to the complex category contrasting with the simple Niagara, and has even more significant design efforts to reduce power

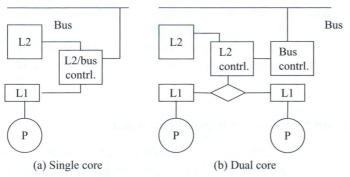

(a) Single core   (b) Dual core

Figure 8.5. Cache hierarchy: from single core to dual core.

dissipation. We shall return to this aspect of the design in Chapter 9. There are also some minimal microarchitectural improvements over the original Pentium M, such as more sophisticated hardware for SSE instructions, a decoder for SSE instructions that allows three of them to be decoded in the decode stage instead of a single one, a faster nonpipelined integer divide unit, and a slightly more sophisticated stream prefetcher between the L2 and main memory.

Our focus here is on the CMP aspect of the Core Duo and on the design of the cache hierarchy. Once the decision of having a shared cache has been taken, there still remains another major choice: Should the two L1 caches remain coherent via a directory scheme with the directory hosted in the L2 cache, as in the IBM Power5 and Niagara, or should they use a snoopy protocol? Simulations showed that there was no clear winner performancewise. The snoopy protocol was adopted, for two reasons: (i) it is closer to the design of the single-core Pentium M, and (ii) it requires less logic (no directory), and therefore less leakage power will be dissipated.

We elaborate a little more on the first reason. Figure 8.5 shows schematic diagrams of a single-core (Pentium M) and dual-core (Core Duo) cache hierarchies. When running in a multiprocessor shared-bus environment, the Pentium M follows a MESI cache coherence protocol. Because mutual level inclusion (MLI) is not imposed, snoops are performed in parallel in both the L1 and L2 caches. This function is diagrammed by the L2–bus-controller box.

When passing from single to dual cores, on a *Bus_read* from one of the L1 caches a snoop is performed on the second L1 cache first, because that is faster than looking at L2. In case of a hit in the second L1, the data are passed to the first L1. In case of a miss in L1, the request passes to L2 via the L2 controller. These functions are summarized in Figure 8.5(b) by the diamond box. Now if L2 has a copy of the line, it will pass it to the requesting L1. Otherwise, the request in sent on the bus via the bus controller, and when the data return the line is stored in both L2 and the requesting L1. Of course, on a *Bus_write* invalidations are sent to the other L1 and the L2 and, if needed (depending on the various L1 and L2 states), on the bus. The bus request to invalidate is avoided when the dual core is working in a standalone environment.

How scalable is this design? It is interesting to note that the quad-core member of this family is in fact two dual cores of the type shown in Figure 8.3(a), each on its own die with two dies on the chip, with communication between the private (per dual core) L2s through the external bus as in Figure 8.3(b).

As the number of cores continues to grow, it is not difficult to see that interconnect structures and cache coherence will become challenging issues to the computer architect.

8.3 Special-Purpose Multithreaded Chip Multiprocessors

There are many different ways of assembling special-purpose multiprocessor systems, mostly for embedded applications. In this section, we show two examples of multithreaded CMPs that are indeed specialized for some form of computation but that are also user-programmable and therefore not as tightly coupled to a particular application as a purely one-application-of-a-kind embedded system. The two examples are the IBM Cell Broadband Engine Architecture, commonly called Cell, originally intended for the Sony 3 game station but also useful for scientific applications, and the Intel IXP 2400 Network Processor, which can be used as an edge or core router in high-performance networks.

Although these two CMPs are used in completely different environments, they present similarities in their overall architecture, namely:

- A general-purpose processor.
- Specialized multithreaded engines that are simple (compared to an out-of-order superscalar) and whose ISAs are limited.
- Local memories associated with each of the engines rather than caches.
- Fast access to global memories.
- Simple interconnects between the various processors.
- Lack of good compiler support requiring extensive use of assembly language or libraries for good performance.

8.3.1 The IBM Cell Multiprocessor

The Cell Broadband Engine Architecture is a joint project of IBM, Sony, and Toshiba that started in 2000. The intent was to define an architecture for the Sony PlayStation 3 that would be two orders of magnitude faster than the PlayStation 2. More generally, the architecture was envisioned for a digital entertainment center, therefore emphasizing game and multimedia applications as well as real-time response for the user. The designers felt that they needed more thread-level parallelism than could be achieved by replicating a conventional superscalar like the IBM Power5, as well as processors that could efficiently compute on stream and vector data. Since the chip would include several cores and each of them would process large data sets, solutions that provided large memory bandwidth were sought. Of course, as is true of all designs in this century, the resulting product needed to be power-efficient. The first instantiation of the architecture, the Cell processor, became available in 2005.

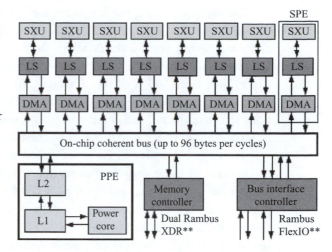

Figure 8.6. IBM Cell multiprocessor (from Kahle et al. [KDHJMS05]).

A block diagram of the Cell processor is shown in Figure 8.6.

If we consider the list of features that we listed at the beginning of this section, we see that Cell has a general-purpose processor, called the power processor element (PPE in the figure) with its own cache hierarchy; eight synergistic processor elements (SPEs), each with its own local storage (LS); and an interconnection network (on-chip coherent bus) between the PPE, the eight SPEs, a memory controller, and a bus controller. Let us look in more detail at some of these components.

The power core processor in the PPE implements the IBM power ISA in a manner that has significant differences from the IBM Power4 and Power5. First of all, the design is simpler. It is a single processor, not a dual core. Although it is still two-way SMT like the Power4, only four instructions are fetched on each cycle, alternately from each thread, as compared to eight for the previous models. The lowering of the instruction fetch bandwidth is reasonable in that the power processor in the PPE is an in-order (almost; see the following discussion) two-way processor whereas the Power4 and Power5 are four-way out-of-order. On the other hand, the Cell power processor is much faster: it runs at 3.2 GHz, almost twice as fast as the Power4 (1.7 GHz) and its contemporary the Power5 (1.9 GHz). Among the other simplifications, besides of course those that result from the in-order microarchitecture, we mention two important ones:

- A much less sophisticated branch predictor that uses a 4 KB 2-bit counter addressed by the global histories of the last six branches of each thread rather than the tournament predictors of the other two processors.
- A smaller cache hierarchy with 32 KB L1 I- and D-caches (lockup-free) and a 512 KB L2 cache (the reader should compare with the figures given in the sidebar of Section 6.3). An interesting point here is that the TLB and L2 can be managed by software tables that allow data in a given range to be *pinned* in L2. Because the Cell power processor is a single core and because it is not part of a multiprocessor system, the coherency controllers are not needed.

On the other hand, the resources for floating-point and multimedia computations are much more extensive. The processor contains not only a floating-point unit and a load–store unit for the floating-point registers, but also an SIMD component with two units: one that can perform operations on 128-bit vectors of various sizes from 128×1 bits to 2×64 bits, including all powers of 2 in between; and one used for word or subword permutations such as those mentioned in Section 7.5. Instructions that use the floating-point and SIMD units are queued at issue time and can be issued out of order with those using the integer units.

The eight synergistic SPEs are designed to optimize SIMD and short-vector processing. An SPE consists of an execution unit SXU, a local store LS (not a cache), and global memory and bus interfaces (DMA). The execution unit SXU has 128 (vector) registers of 128 bits with the data types ranging from a quadword (16 bytes) to a bit vector organized in the same way as the SIMD unit of the power processor. Instructions are RISC-like, that is, register to register. The SXU has four functional units: a vector integer unit, a vector floating-point unit, an SIMD-like data permute unit, and a load–store unit. All data paths are 128 bits wide. As can be seen, there is no scalar processing unit. However, the programmer, or the compiler, can optimize scalar processing in the vector units by placing the scalar variables in their leftmost natural positions in the 128-bit register. If need be, this positioning can be accomplished with the help of the permute unit. All subsequent vector instructions using the scalar variables in these positions will yield the intended results.

The SXU can issue two instructions per cycle, one to either of the vector units and one to either the permute or the load–store unit. Instructions are prefetched from the local store in 128-byte chunks to an instruction buffer. Since the Cell engine runs at high frequency, the pipeline of the SXU is relatively long: about 13 stages in the front end for instruction fetch, buffering, decode, and register read (the register file has six read ports and two write ports). The back-end functional units have latencies ranging from 2 to 6 cycles, but the writeback stage is such that all functional units access it in the same stage, 8 cycles after the last register read cycle. Predication is used as much as possible on a vector-wide basis. The load–store unit can read and write 16 bytes (i.e., a register width) per cycle directly to the local store. There is no provision for reading or writing units of smaller size, but, as we just explained, scalar processing is optimized within the vector units. If alignment of data is necessary, it will be performed via the permute unit.

The local store in the current implementation is 256 KB. A programmable local memory is used instead of a cache for several reasons. First, it can be better optimized for streaming purposes, that is, for getting large numbers of sequential data via programmed block transfers from main memory. Second, the chip area used by the local store is about half of what would be used by a cache of the same capacity, because there is no need for tags and the access and control logic is simplified. Third, the programmable DMA allows more concurrency and a larger variety of programs than would be possible with a cache. The local store has both narrow (16 bytes) and wide (128 bytes) ports. The narrow path is for direct load–store communication with the SXU; the wide path is for instruction prefetch and DMA transactions with main memory, the PPE, and other SPEs.

The on-chip interconnect between the PPE, the eight SPEs, the memory controller, and the I/O interfaces is called the element interconnect bus (EIB). This is something of a misnomer in that the EIB is made up of four circular rings, two in each direction. Each ring can cater to three transactions simultaneously if they are spaced appropriately. The EIB is clocked at half the processor speed. Each ring transaction carries 16 bytes of data. So, in theory, the bandwidth on the EIB is $16 \times 4 \times 3/2 = 96$ bytes per processor cycle. In practice, this bandwidth will not be attained, because of conflicting transactions or because the memory controller and I/O interfaces cannot sustain that rate. Note that each "unit," (i.e., each of the 12 elements connected to the EIB), is at a maximum distance of 6 from any other. The EIB can be seen as a compromise between a bus and a full crossbar.

Before leaving the description of the Cell processor, we want to emphasize the challenges faced by the user or the compiler to exploit such an architecture and thus the reasons why we consider it to be special-purpose.

- Applications must be decomposed into threads, with the additional constraint that some threads might be better suited for the PPE and others (hopefully more) for the SPEs.
- SIMD parallelization must be detected for the SPEs and to a lesser extent for the PPE. This is not a simple task, as evidenced by the difficulties encountered by compiler writers who want to use MMX-like instructions efficiently.
- Not only SIMD but also code for short vectors has to be generated for the SPEs, with special attention to making scalar processing efficient.
- Because the SPEs have no cache, all coherency requirements between the local memories of the SPEs have to be programmed in the application. In other words, all data allocation and all data transfers have to be part of the source code.
- Because there is no hardware prefetching or cache purging, all commands for streaming data from and to memory have to be programmed for the memory interfaces.
- Because the pipelines of the PPE and the SPEs are long and their branch predictors are rather modest, special attention must be given to compiler-assisted branch prediction and predication.

Granted, some of these challenges – for example, vectorization and message-passing primitives – have been studied for a long time in the context of high-performance computing. Nonetheless, the overall magnitude of the difficulties is such that, though the Cell can be programmed efficiently for the applications it was primarily intended for (namely, games and multimedia), it is less certain that more general-purpose scientific applications can be run effectively.

8.3.2 A Network Processor: The Intel IXP 2800

Wide-area networks, such as the Internet, require processing units within the network to handle the flow of traffic. At the onset of networking, these units were routers whose sole role was to forward packets in a hop-to-hop fashion from their origin to their destination. The functionality required of routers was minimal, and their implementation in the form of application-specific integrated circuit (ASIC) components was the norm. However, with the exponential growth in network size, in transmission speed, and in networking applications more flexibility became a necessity. While retaining the use of fast ASICs on one hand and dedicating general-purpose processors on the other hand had their advocates for some time, it is now recognized that programmable processors with ISAs and organizations more attuned to networking tasks are preferable. These processors are known as *network processors* (NPs).

The workloads of network processors are quite varied and depend also on whether the NP is at the core or at the edge of the network. Two fundamental tasks are IP forwarding at the core and packet classification at the edge. These two tasks involve looking at the header of the packet. IP forwarding, which as its name implies guides the packet to its destination, consists of a longest prefix match of a destination address contained in the header with a set of addresses contained in very large routing tables. Packet classification is a refinement of IP forwarding where matching is performed on several fields of the header according to rules stored in relatively small access control lists. The matching rule with highest priority indicates the action to be performed on the packet, e.g., forward or discard. Among other tasks involving the header we can mention flow management for avoiding congestion in the network and statistics gathering for billing purposes. Encryption and authentication are tasks that require processing the data payload.

To understand the motivations behind the design of network processors, it is worth noting several characteristics of the workload:

- In the great majority of cases, packets can be processed independently of each other. Therefore, NPs should have multiple processing units. For example, Cisco's Silicon Packet Processor has 188 *cores*, where evidently each core is much less than a full-fledged processor.
- The data structures needed for many NP applications are large, and there is far from enough storage on chip to accommodate them. Therefore, access to external DRAMs should be optimized. To that effect, and because processing several packets in parallel is possible, coarse-grained multithreading with the possibility of process switching on DRAM accesses is a good option. The Intel IXP 2800 that we present in more detail below has 16 cores, called microengines, which can each support eight hardware threads.
- Access to the data structures has little or no locality. The tendency in NPs is to use local data memories rather than caches, although some research studies have shown that restricted caching schemes could be beneficial.

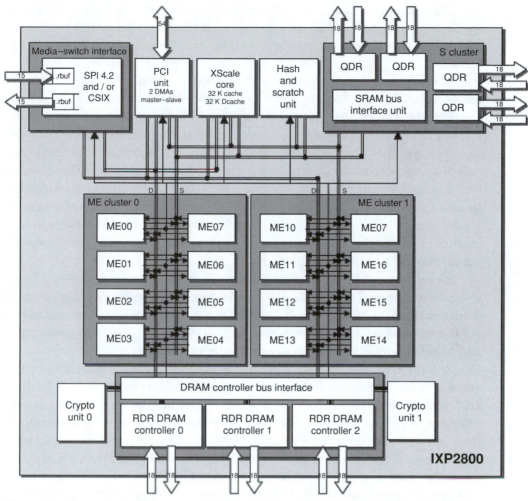

Figure 8.7. The Intel IXP 2800 network processor (from Adiletta et al. [ARDWW02]).

- Programs running on the microengines are short, both statically and dynamically. Source code can be downloaded on small memories attached to the microengines rather than using instruction caches with potential conflicts.
- There is no need for providing floating-point arithmetic. The ISA of the microengines should be biased towards integer and character (byte) processing. Special-purpose instructions, and hardware, can be present for functions such as cyclic redundancy check (CRC) or encryption.

We use the Intel IXP 2800 as an example NP. As will be seen, the general features of special-purpose multiprocessors that we listed at the beginning of this section are present, and the design objectives just listed have been followed.

Figure 8.7 shows the general architecture of the Intel IXP 2800. The main building blocks are a general-purpose processor, the Intel XScale; two clusters of eight microengines with their own local memories; interfaces to fast SRAM and to DRAM; and some special-purpose functional units.

The XScale processor, whose ISA is that of the ARM microprocessor, is used for packet exception handling and management tasks. It has a 32 KB I-cache and a 32 KB D-cache. It can communicate with the microengines through the external SRAM.

Each microengine has eight hardware contexts. Coarse-grained multithreading can be initiated under user (or compiler) control when external memory accesses are performed. Therefore, $16 \times 8 = 128$ packets can be processed concurrently. Each microengine has its own 4 K words control store, (i.e., instruction memory), to store application programs, and 640 words of local data memory. A context consists of a program counter, 32 general-purpose registers, 16 registers to communicate with a neighboring microengine, and four sets of registers for either input or output to either SRAM or DRAM. The neighbor registers facilitate communication for pipelined algorithms often used in NP applications, by means of a technique reminiscent of stream processing where each stage consists of several instructions or a kernel that will be applied to all packets.

Microengines have a six-stage pipeline. They are in-order, provide single-instruction issue, and run at 1.4 GHz. Standard memory operations access the local memory; SRAM and DRAM are accessed through I/O operations. A special feature is a 16-entry content-addressable memory (CAM) that allows multiway comparisons and is quite useful in many packet-processing applications.

In many NP applications, the SRAM is used for storing control information about packets and flow control in the form of queue descriptors or linked lists. The IXP 2800 has four SRAM programmable controllers that can operate concurrently. They can be programmed to synchronize processes through synchronization primitives very much like those we have encountered in general-purpose multiprocessors. The controllers are optimized for fast linked-list and circular-list insertions and deletions. There are also three controllers for access to DRAM banks. The amount of real estate devoted to SRAM and DRAM controllers emphasizes the importance of concurrent and fast access to memory.

Finally, there are two special-purpose functional units for encryption and authentication that are critically important at the edge of the network, but also in its core if applications are to perform some processing in the network – the so-called active network paradigm. There is also a hashing unit that computes a sophisticated hashing function quickly.

As can be seen, the IXP 2800 is built for packet parallelism and fast memory access, and includes some functional capabilities geared toward very specific applications. Its programmability ensures that it will not be obsolete when it needs to support new applications. On the other hand, it is far from being a general-purpose engine, and therefore its deployment is limited.

8.4 Summary

On-chip parallel processing at the thread level is now available in commodity processors. We have introduced three flavors of multithreading that can complement the multiprocessing capabilities described in the previous chapter, namely fine-grained, coarse-grained, and simultaneous (SMT). In all cases, each thread requires its own context, which is, at least, a set of general-purpose registers and a program counter.

In fine-grained multithreading, thread switching can occur on every cycle. In the coarse-grained case thread switches will occur on long-latency events, that is, events that will take noticeably longer than a thread switch. The typical example is an L2 miss. In SMT, several threads will occupy the pipeline concurrently, thus filling instruction issue slots lost to either hazards or lack of instruction-level parallelism. Coarse-grained multithreading concepts can also be applied to single-thread execution with the goal of warming up caches.

In the microprocessor environment, fine-grained multithreading will be restricted to "simple" processors. Coarse-grained multithreading is rare, and the complexities of SMT have limited its implementation to two concurrent threads (also called hyperthreading in Intel products).

Chip multiprocessors (CMPs) are now the commodity computational engines in commercial microprocessor systems. We have presented the characteristics of general-purpose and special-purpose CMPs. In general-purpose CMPs we have made a distinction between architectures where each core, (i.e., a processor and its on-chip L1–L2 cache hierarchy), has a private L2 (multiprocessors) and those where all cores share their L2 (multicores).

We have described two families of general-purpose multicores. The first one, Sun Niagara, is based on simple fine-grained multithreaded processors connected via a crossbar switch to a shared L2. The second one, Intel Core Duo, is based on complex processors sharing an L2 cache and whose L1s remain coherent through a snoopy protocol.

To show a vivid contrast between general-purpose and special-purpose microprocessor systems, we have also described two special-purpose CMPs: the IBM Cell, intended for game and multimedia processing, and the network processor Intel IXP2800.

8.5 Further Reading and Bibliographical Notes

Multithreading in one of its three flavors, namely fine-grained, coarse-grained, and simultaneous, is now a feature of most high-performance microprocessors. Fine-grained multithreading has its origin in the design of the peripheral processors of the CDC 6600 as described in Thornton's book [T70]. Fine-grained multithreading for central processors was proposed and then implemented by Burton Smith for the HEP multiprocessor [S78]. The Tera supercomputer [ACCKPS90] is a direct descendant of HEP. Coarse-grained multithreading has its roots in software threads and was first introduced for NUMA multiprocessor systems, whereby long-latency events were accesses to global memory. Agarwal and his students at MIT [ALKK90, ABCJKKLMY95] built the Alewife multiprocessor prototype using modified SPARC processors with four hardware contexts. The multithreaded characteristics of the IBM PowerPC processor that we described can be found in [BEKK00]. Simultaneous multithreading (SMT) was developed at the University of Washington by Eggers, Levy, and their students [TEL95, EELLST97, LBEGLP98]. Commercial implementations exist for the Intel ISA (where SMT is called hyper-threading) [KM03] and the IBM Power5 [KST04, MMMEK05], among others. The relative performance benefits of multithreading and multiprocessing when proces-sors are in order or out of order are discussed in [CCYT05].

Coarse-grained multithreading concepts can be applied to the execution of a single application without explicitly defining threads at compile time. On a long-latency event, the application can continue speculatively, thus warming up caches as in run-ahead execution [MSWP02], hardware scouting [CCYT05], or dynamic mul-tithreading [AD98]. The Multiscalar project headed by Sohi [SBV95] is the seminal precursor of many speculative multithreading studies, whose challenges and poten-tial benefits are discussed by Sohi and Roth [SR01]. Sun's MAJC was an attempt at a commercial implementation of these concepts [TCCCT00]. At the limit, multi-threading, or a superscalar with an "infinite" instruction window, can lead to data flow [DM74], an elegant paradigm for (functional) program execution. Data flow has a long history and fervent advocates, but has not yet been shown to be compet-itive with the contemporary optimized von Neumann architectures.

All major microprocessor manufacturers have introduced CMPs, some (like AMD, IBM, and Intel) with the same ISA and overall microarchitecture complexity as their previous top-of-the-line single processors (for example, the Intel Core Duo [MMGSCNK06]), and some (like Sun) with a larger number of simpler processors. Niagara [KAO05] is an example of the latter design.

There are many flavors of special-purpose CMPs. The IBM Cell is introduced in [KDHJMS05, GHFHWY06]. The Intel IXP 2800 [ARBWW02] is one example among many of network processors.

EXERCISES

1. (Section 1.1) Give two examples of nonscientific programs for which a fine-grained multithreading approach would be good. Assume that there is no cache in the system.

2. (Section 1.1) What type of branch prediction mechanism would you advocate for a Tera-like system?

3. (Section 1.2) In our simplistic analysis of the number of coarse-grained threads needed (on average) so that long latencies can be hidden, we did not include the time needed to switch hardware contexts. Let n_{sat} be the number of threads so that saturation occurs (i.e., long latencies are tolerated), m be the run length, that is, the (average) number of cycles between context switches, c be the time for a (hardware) context switch, and L be the long latency that is to be tolerated. Express n_{sat} as a function of m, c, and L. What is the value of n_{sat} if $m = 50$, $c = 5$, and $L = 200$?

4. (Section 1.2) What are additional steps that must be taken in coarse-grained multithreading if the processor is out of order?

5. (Section 1.2) Are there any additional complexities in the implementation of caches, TLBs, and branch predictors when coarse-grained multithreading is added to a (multiprogrammed) processor?

6. (Section 1.3) Show a scenario where having a single queue without maximum threshold for instruction issue in an SMT can lead to loss of performance.

7. (Section 1.3) The hyperthreaded Intel Pentium 4 Xeon replicates the I-TLB, so that each of the running two threads has its own I-TLB. The IBM Power5 does not, that is the I-TLB is shared between the two threads. Discuss pros and cons of these choices, considering the way instructions are fetched in the two implementations.

8. (Section 1.3) Which of the two main possible ways of register renaming – using a distinct physical register file, or using the reorder buffer – is most attuned to an SMT implementation?

9. (Section 1.4) What policy should be followed if there is an exception during run-ahead execution? How should an interrupt be handled?

10. (Section 2) Find advantages and drawbacks to homogeneous general-purpose CMPs in contrast with heterogeneous ones.

REFERENCES

[ABCJKKLMY95] A. Agarwal, R. Bianchini, D. Chaiken, K. Johnson, D. Kranz, J. Kubiatowicz, B.-H. Lim, K. Mackenzie, and D. Yeung, "The MIT Alewife Machine: Architecture and Performance," *Proc. 22nd Int. Symp. on Computer Architecture*, 1995, 2–13

[ACCKPS90] R. Alverson, D. Callahan, D. Cummings, B. Koblenz, A. Porterfield, and B. Smith, "The Tera Computer System," *Proc. Int. Conf. on Supercomputing*, 1990, 1–6

[AD98] H. Akkary and M. Driscoll, "A Dynamic Multithreading Processor," *Proc. 31st Int. Symp. on Microarchitecture*, 1998, 226–236

[ALKK90] A. Agarwal, B.-H. Lim, D. Kranz, and J. Kubiatowicz, "APRIL: A Processor Architecture for Multiprocessing," *Proc. 17th Int. Symp. on Computer Architecture*, 1990, 104–114

[ARBWW02] M. Adiletta, M. Rosenbluth, D. Bernstein, G. Wolrich, and H. Wilkinson, "The Next Generation of Intel IXP Network Processors," *Intel Tech. Journal*, 6, 3, Aug. 2002, 6–18

[BEKK00] J. Borkenhagen, R. Eickemeyer, R. Kalla, and S. Kunkel, "A Multithreaded PowerPC Processor for Commercial Servers," *IBM Journal of Research and Development*, 44, 6, 2000, 885–899

[CCYT05] S. Chaudhry, P. Caprioli, S. Yip, and M. Tremblay, "High-Performance Throughput Computing," *IEEE Micro*, 25, 3, May 2005, 32–45

[DM74] J. Dennis and D. Misunas, "A Preliminary Data Flow Architecture for a Basic Data Flow Processor," *Proc. 2nd Int. Symp. on Computer Architecture*, 1974, 126–132

[EELLST97] S. Eggers, J. Emer, H. Levy, J. Lo, R. Stamm, and D. Tullsen, "Simultaneous Multithreading: A Platform for Next-Generation Processors," *IEEE Micro*, 17, 5, Sep. 1997, 12–19

[GHFHWY06] M. Gschwind, H. Hofstee, B. Flachs, M. Hopkins, Y. Watanabe, and T. Yamazaki, "Synergistic Processing in Cell's Multicore Architecture," *IEEE Micro*, 26, 2, Mar. 2006, 11–24

[KAO05] P. Kongetira, K. Aingaran, and K. Olukotun, "Niagara: A 32-way Multithreaded Sparc Processor," *IEEE Micro*, 24, 2, Apr. 2005, 21–29

[KDHJMS05] J. Kahle, M. Day, H. Hofstee, C. Johns, T. Maeurer, and D. Shippy, "Introduction to the Cell Multiprocessor," *IBM Journal of Research and Development*, 49, 4/5, Jul. 2005, 589–604

[KM03] D. Koufaty and D. Marr, "Hyperthreading Technology in the Netburst Microarchitecture," *IEEE Micro*, 23, 2, Mar. 2003, 56–65

[KST04] R. Kalla, B. Sinharoy, and J. Tendler, "IBM Power5 Chip: A Dual-Core Multithreaded Processor," *IEEE Micro*, 24, 2, Apr. 2004, 40–47

[LBEGLP98] J. Lo, L. Barroso, S. Eggers, K. Gharachorloo, H. Levy, and S. Parekh, "An Analysis of Database Workload Performance on Simultaneous Multithreaded Processors," *Proc. 25th Int. Symp. on Computer Architecture*, 1998, 39–50

[MMGSCNK06] A. Mendelson, J. Mandelblat, S. Gochman, A. Shemer, R. Chabukswar, E. Niemeyer, and A. Kumar, "CMP Implementation in Systems Based on the Intel Core Duo Processor," *Intel Tech. Journal*, 10, 2, May 2006, 99–107

[MMMEK05] H. Mathis, A. Mericas, J. McCalpin, R. Eickemeyer, and S. Kunkel, "Characterization of Simultaneous Multithreading (SMT) Efficiency in Power5," *IBM Journal of Research and Development*, 49, 4, Jul. 2005, 555–564

[MSWP02] O. Mutlu, J. Stark, C. Wilkerson, and Y. Patt, "Run-ahead Execution: An Alternative to Very Large Instruction Windows for Out-of-order Processors," *Proc. 9th Int. Symp. on High-Performance Computer Architecture*, 2003, 129–140

[S78] B. Smith, "A Pipelined, Shared Resource MIMD Computer," *Proc. 1978 Int. Conf. on Parallel Processing*, 1978, 6–8

[SBV95] G. Sohi, S. Breach, and T. Vijaykumar, "Multiscalar Processors," *Proc. 22nd Int. Symp. on Computer Architecture*, 1995, 414–425

[SR01] G. Sohi and A. Roth, "Speculative Multithreaded Processors," *IEEE Computer*, 34, 4, Apr. 2001, 66–73

[T70] J. Thornton, Design of a Computer: The Control Data 6600, Scott, Foresman and Co., Glenview, IL, 1970

[TCCCT00] M. Tremblay, J. Chan, S. Chaudhry, A. Coniglaro, and S. Tse, "The MAJC Architecture: A Synthesis of Parallelism and Scalability," *IEEE Micro*, 20, 6, Nov. 2000, 12–25

[TEL95] D. Tullsen, S. Eggers, and H. Levy, "Simultaneous Multithreading: Maximizing On-chip Parallelism," *Proc. 22nd Int. Symp. on Computer Architecture*, 1995, 392–403

9 Current Limitations and Future Challenges

Since 2003, the peak frequency at which single processors and chip multiprocessors have operated has remained largely unchanged. One basic reason is that power dissipation effects have limited frequency increases. In addition, difficulties in extracting more parallelism at the instruction level, design complexity, and the effects of wire lengths have resulted in a performance plateau for single processors. We elaborate on some of these issues in this chapter.

While improvements in clock frequency and in ILP exploitation have been stalled, Moore's law is still valid, and the amount of logic that can be laid out on a chip is still increasing. Adding more cache memory to a single processor to fill all the on-chip real estate has reached a point of diminishing return, performance-wise. Multithreaded processors, which mitigate the effects of the memory wall, and multiprocessors on a chip (CMP, also called multicores) are the current approach to attaining more performance. A question that is of primary importance to computer architects and to computer users in general is the structure of future CMPs, as mentioned in the previous chapter.

In a conservative evolutionary fashion, future CMPs might look like those we have presented in Chapter 8, with naturally a slightly larger number of cores. Questions of whether there should be many simple cores vs. fewer high-performance ones, and of whether the cores should be homogeneous or not, have already been touched upon previously. Although speed is still the primary metric, other aspects such as reliability and security have gained importance. Looming very large in the picture is how to take advantage of the many cores available, that is, how to exploit parallelism at a coarse granularity. Although parallel programming is not a topic for this book, we would be remiss not to consider it along with the other challenges for the next generation of computing systems.

A more aggressive evolution would imply changes in the ISA. Current CMPs have essentially the ISA of their single-processor counterparts. Additions such as support for transactional memory do not constitute an enormous leap and, if deemed profitable, could happen very soon. More radical architectures are those that derive from dataflow concepts. Inasmuch as they are still in the research stage and no clear winning direction for them has been agreed upon, we will not elaborate on these interesting options.

Finally, there is a revolutionary way that we will not touch upon, that of nanostructures: quantum computing, synthetic biological engines, nanotubes, DNA computers, etc. It is left to the reader to explore these fascinating topics.

9.1 Power and Thermal Management

9.1.1 Dynamic and Leakage Power Consumption

The reader should look one more time at Figure 1.4, which illustrates in a striking manner the power dissipation issue. It affects all computerized devices, from those powered by batteries such as cell phones, PDAs, and laptops to the very large data centers that require extensive and expensive power and cooling.

Recall that power = work/time is expressed in watts, whereas energy = power × time = work is expressed in joules. In the context of computers, work is program execution (CPU, memory, and I/O operations), power is the rate at which the computer consumes electrical energy, including the amount it dissipates in heat, and energy is the total amount of power over a certain amount of time. *Power management* is a set of techniques that reduce power consumption without sacrificing much performance. For a device that operates with a battery storing a given maximum amount of energy, reducing the power will allow work to be performed for a longer period of time. For servers and data centers, it will lead to savings in electricity and cooling. Moreover, for the latter another primary concern is reducing peak temperatures through *thermal management* techniques so that the devices do not overheat. An additional challenge is that temperatures are not uniform on the chip and *hot spots* have to be detected.

Although conserving power is important in main memory and I/O devices, we focus on means to reduce power consumption and detect hot spots on processors and on-cache chips. Of the two components of power dissipation, the main one, namely, the *dynamic*, is due to circuit activity that occurs when input data to a circuit are changed. The second one, the static or *leakage* power consumption, results from the imperfection of transistors and the fact that current leaks even when a transistor is not switching.

In first approximation, dynamic power consumption can be expressed as

$$P_{dyn} \sim aCV^2 f \qquad (1)$$

where

- V is the supply voltage,
- f is the clock frequency,
- C is the physical capacitance,
- a is an activity factor related to the number of $0 \to 1$ and $1 \to 0$ switchings.

Power reduction techniques can be applied to each of these factors, either individually or in groups, at both the circuit and microarchitectural levels.

Leakage power can be expressed as

$$P_{leakage} \sim V I_{leak}$$

where V is again the supply voltage and I_{leak} is the current that flows through transistors even when they are off. $P_{leakage}$ increases with the number of transistors on a chip. Because Moore's law is still applicable, it would appear that it is more of a long-term threat than P_{dyn}. So far, technological improvements at every new generation of chips, such as using other materials than silicon, and circuit-level techniques have limited the effects of leakage. We will therefore concentrate on means to reduce the dynamic power, some of which, as we shall see, also reduce the leakage power.

Modeling thermal effects on a chip is made more difficult by the fact that what is important is not the average temperature but the detection of hot spots. There is not much correlation between power dissipated over some time interval and the temperatures at various locations on the chip. Nonetheless, power management techniques and thermal management techniques have a lot in common.

We will not give any detail on circuit level techniques. Most often, the techniques are meant to reduce switching activity by, for example, ordering transistors in circuits so that the amount of switching is minimized and, similarly, ordering the states in finite-state machines for the same reason. Variations in gate logic, for example, a tree vs. a cascade, and in bus encodings produce similar effects.

9.1.2 Dynamic Power and Thermal Management

Since power and thermal management became a vital issue in modern microprocessor designs, research in the area has blossomed. Analytical models have been devised, and power and thermal simulators have been implemented, with the primary intent of identifying the structures that would benefit most from power reduction. For some microprocessors, mostly of the embedded type, the models and simulators can guide operating systems and compilers to modify the voltage through specialized instructions. Heuristics to manage power at run time have been proposed and evaluated, often in the context of real-time systems.

In this subsection, we present only a small sample of these activities. Our focus is on microarchitectural techniques to reduce two factors in the previous formulas: voltage supply and activity. Note that reducing activity and/or supply voltage will influence both dynamic and leakage powers. The techniques that we present are mostly adaptive. They consist in:

- *monitoring* the state of the processor and of its memory activities;
- detecting whether some potential action should be taken – the so-called *triggering* step;
- *deciding* on the action to take.

The *monitoring* step depends on whether the intent is power management or thermal management. In the latter case, the temperature readings are performed via thermal sensors whose output can be digitized. The sensors must be on chip, because otherwise there is a significant delay between the rise of temperature on chip and the off-chip readings. The difficulty is in choosing where to put the sensor(s), for the hot-spot locations may vary with the application. In the Intel Pentium 4, for example, the location was chosen after extensive simulations of various applications.

Monitoring for power cannot use direct sensorlike instruments. In essence, monitoring for power consists in assessing performance. The basic idea is to record the performance of the processor during some time interval using some appropriate metric and to predict what the performance requirements are for the next interval, a common speculative pattern that we have encountered numerous times before. The activities of the whole processor or of the most power-hungry parts of the chip – such as the instruction issue mechanism (instruction queue or window, reservation stations, reorder buffer, scheduler) and the caches – can be monitored and assessed in several ways. For example, during a time sample interval, one can:

- Assess the proportion of idle time.
- Count the number of instructions that have been fetched; this may be slightly better than the number of instructions committed (a metric akin to the IPC), in that it takes into account the work done while speculating.
- Assess the location in the instruction queue of the issued instructions. If the most recently fetched instructions are not issued often, then the instruction queue may be too long; thus, not all of it needs to be searched at every cycle.
- Assess whether the instruction queue is full. If so, that might indicate that it is too short and that performance could be enhanced by having a larger window.
- Assess the cache miss rates, both on chip and off chip. If the count of off-chip misses is significant, it might mean that the processor is often idle. This metric is particularly easy to monitor in that most microprocessors have performance counters that can be programmed specifically for this type of measurements.
- Assess the *decay* of a cache line, that is, the amount of time since it was last accessed.
- Detect *phases* in an application, with the goal of using the characteristics of recurrent phases when a phase change is detected. Such a scheme implies recognition of phases, (e.g., through some signature of the working set), and storing their characteristics.

Triggering of an action to be performed is generally induced by comparing a measurement with some threshold. For example, the digitized output of a thermal sensor can be compared with values stored in some hardware registers indicating the low and high ends of the range of operating temperatures. Similar thresholds can be stored for the metrics that we have listed in the previous paragraphs. More qualitative criteria can be used, such as whether a laptop is plugged in or operates under battery power, or whether a display screen has been modified in the last x minutes.

There are two main techniques that can be used once the triggering step has been detected and it has been decided that an action should take place: *dynamic voltage and frequency scaling* (DVFS) and *resource adaptation.*

Dynamic Voltage and Frequency Scaling

We start our discussion of DVFS in the context of power management. Because voltage is a quadratic factor for dynamic power and because reducing the supplied voltage will also reduce the clock frequency, a decrease in voltage could have theoretically a cubic effect on power reduction. As a result of slowing the clock, there will be a linear loss in performance according to the *execution time* formula (2) in Section 1.2.1.

While theoretically correct, neither the cubic decrease in power nor the linear loss in performance is necessarily encountered in practice when voltage is scaled down. As an example for each case:

- The formula (1) we gave is true for CMOS transistors and therefore is a good approximation for the processor and on-chip caches. However, DRAM memories and I/O devices such as disks also draw power, and sometimes significantly more than the processor chip. Moreover, there can be different power supplies for the processor chip and the other components of the system.
- Slowing down the processor should not matter when the processor is idle because, for example, it is waiting for the resolution of a cache miss. Therefore, there are periods of time where the frequency can be lowered without impact on the total execution time.

Nonetheless, reducing the voltage selectively can have beneficial effects, because most systems are designed for continuous peak performance, which is not always needed. This is particularly true in a number of real-time systems that are designed for the worst case. If there is a possibility to assess that some part of an application can be run at slower speed without affecting the outcome, (i.e., without missing deadlines), then the power can be reduced effectively.

DVFS can be applied at various levels of granularity. Depending on the implementation, there can be a limited number of possible voltages, or it can be possible to vary the voltage in a continuous fashion, as for example in the Intel XScale processor, which we encountered when we discussed network processors (Section 8.3.2). Most implementations allow a privileged software instruction to set a mode register to modify the voltage. However, it is important to be aware that scaling up or down of the voltage or frequency is not instantaneous. It can take tens of microseconds before the clock network is stabilized anew.

At the coarsest grain, the voltage can depend on whether a mobile device is plugged in or is battery-operated (lower voltage). Some laptops with an Intel Pentium 4, Pentium M, or Intel Core processor operate thus in order to prolong the battery's lifetime. Granted, this "threshold" that we mentioned previously is hardly "dynamic"! A more interesting distinction is whether the scaling is done task by task (e.g., via the O.S.), or within a task. A further distinction is whether the monitoring step is offline, for example via profiling, or online.

Offline DVFS techniques have been mostly applied to real-time systems that run a limited number of applications. Platforms are generally mobile devices that have relatively simple processors. For a given application, voltage schedules to meet deadlines can be devised offline, and, theoretically, optimal power reduction can be achieved. Naturally, optimality is not really achievable, because of the variations in the workload even within an application. Nonetheless, one can see why it might be useful to have different speeds of execution for widely different applications such as deadline-driven audio and leisurely consulting one's calendar.

Online DVFS techniques are more general. Like offline techniques, they are often meant for real-time systems, but they can also be used for desktops or servers. The first DVFS algorithms monitored the proportion of processor idle time during a given time interval. Triggering occurred if either this proportion was smaller than some minimum threshold or larger than some maximum threshold. Upon triggering, the processor was either slowed down or speeded up. An easy improvement on the method is to use an average of the last n intervals before comparing with thresholds in order to reduce the possibility of thrashing due to peak computational periods followed by mostly idle ones. Better yet is to have a probability distribution of a given task's computational requirement based on past executions of the task or of similar ones, or some *phase* signature that indicates how to set the voltage or frequency for the next interval.

In the case of thermal management, an alternative used in the Pentium 4 is to stop execution for a short period of time. The interrupt for STOPCLOCK has high priority, and idleness can be achieved in about 1 μs.

Resource Adaptation

Every laptop user is cognizant of the *hibernation* feature of her computer. Hibernation at that level is an operating system (O.S.) feature that dumps the processor state and the contents of volatile memory on the hard disk before powering off the system. Restarting after hibernation will result in a state similar to the one before hibernation and is faster than a complete restart. A generalization of this feature is to hibernate some of the resources selectively.

Resource hibernation, which can be considered as a subset of such hibernation processes, is aimed at whole components, such as the disk or the display, that consume a significant portion of the power in portable devices (but not so in servers and workstations, where processor(s) and memory dominate). In the case of the disk on a laptop computer, the O.S. can monitor disk usage and prevent disk rotation, a major source of the power dissipated by the disk, when it has observed a given period of idleness. It will power it up again when there is a disk request. This simplistic approach, even with the use of adequate thresholds to mitigate up and down thrashings, can fail to reduce power if the workload is irregular, because restarting the rotation is more power-consuming than regular operation. Moreover, the technique cannot be used in a server, where there is practically always a request for disk access. In this case, the rotation speed can be regulated according to the demand, again using thresholds for the number of requests in the disk access queue, because power consumption is proportional to rotation speed. In the case of displays, the O.S. can dim or totally darken the display when there has been no user activity for some time.

Selectively turning off partially or totally some resources in a general-purpose processor has been advocated as a means to conserve power. In the same way as DVFS is used to take advantage of variations in workload and reduce power when peak performance is not needed, *resource adaptation* (the term that is most often used in this context) can be performed when (a phase of) an application is assumed not to need a complete set of resources. The resources that are targeted in such an approach are those that consume significant proportions of the total processor chip power, namely, the instruction issue apparatus (windows, reservation stations, reorder buffer, decoders, and schedulers/dispatchers) and caches.

At the beginning of this section, we saw some examples of how performance could be monitored and how a resource adaptation could be triggered. We now expand on some of the adaptations that can be performed for the instruction issue mechanism and the caches. It should be noted that additional logic is needed for the partitioning of resources – at the very least, gating of the clock in some portions of the circuit. Care should be taken that this extra logic does not consume too much power and/or real estate.

In the case of the instruction queue, downsizing or upsizing can be done on step by step. We list some options that have been implemented or proposed, from the most stringent to the least disruptive, and also from the easiest to implement to one that requires (slight) modifications to the microarchitecture.

- Prevent fetching of new instructions. This could be done for thermal management, where significant slowdowns can be required. Instruction fetching can resume when appropriate cooling has been reached.
- Fetch instructions every other cycle.
- Limit the number of instructions issued or decoded per cycle. In the case of an m-way issue, it can be temporarily reduced to $(m - 1)$-way or further down if needed.
- Split the queue into several partitions, and remove or add one partition at a time.

If caches are the adaptation targets, power savings are obtained by shutting down parts of them. Not only dynamic power, but also leakage power is decreased if large chunks of the caches are gated off. From the coarsest granularity down, bank(s), set(s), and line(s) are possible targets. In the case of writeback caches, care must be taken to save dirty lines prior to the shutdown so that there is no loss of information. An alternative is to have so-called *drowsy caches* whereby the energy supplied to a line or a set is lower than that needed to access the data but sufficient to keep the integrity of data. Another possibility is to partition the cache so that only part of it is first accessed, using some form of MRU approximation on a way-by-way basis.

Before leaving the topic of power consumption and reduction, it is worth emphasizing that the DVFS and resource adaptation can be combined. This combination is particularly attractive in workstations that are used for multimedia applications; thereby resource adaptation can be used as an additional benefit to DVFS. In addition, other microarchitectural techniques can be used at design time to reduce power consumption.

Examples of processors designed specifically for mobile devices, where battery life is at a premium, are Intel's Pentium M and the dual-processor Centrino Duo Mobile. In both cases, the trade-off between performance and power was of primary concern at design time. The Intel IA-32 ISA is kept for compatibility, and the processors are out of order for performance's sake. A sophisticated branch predictor is implemented because accurate branch prediction means fewer instructions executed, which means it yields both performance improvement and power savings. *Micro-op fusion* (recall Section 4.3) saves accesses to the instruction issue queue and retirement buffer, thus saving some energy. The reader might recall that a similar technique is present in the IBM Power4, whereby instructions are dispatched in groups for reasons of simplicity of implementation, but also with the side effect of limiting power consumption (cf. the sidebar of Chapter 6). Pentium M also has a DVFS feature that allows it to expand on the *lowest frequency mode* (LFM) and *highest frequency mode* (HFM) found in earlier Intel mobile processors. In the Centrino Duo, some microarchitectural design decisions were added, and, of course, this is a dual-core CMP (cf. Section 8.2.2). Both resource adaptation, mostly to decrease leakage power dissipation, and DVFS, for dynamic power, are implemented with a concerted hardware–software effort.

Resource adaptation is achieved by providing each processor with its own power-saving states for smaller savings and combined chip-set states for larger savings. The idea is to use the techniques and mechanisms of the Advanced Configuration and Power Interface (ACPI), a standard for O.S. power-directed management, to enter various forms of idleness. When a given core is active, it is in a state named C_0, but when it is idle for some time, the O.S. will make it enter a state C_i. ($i = 1, \ldots, 4$) with the goal of balancing power saving with the overhead of coming back to state C_0 when the processor becomes active again. States C_1, C_2, and C_3 are per processor and correspond to various clock stoppages: processor only, processor and bus, and clock generator. State C_4 is reduced voltage, but because both cores share the same power plane, it must be applied to the whole chip set (in fact, there is an additional state for further voltage reduction). Note that because multilevel inclusion is not implemented, shutting off L1 means that its dirty lines, which have to be written back to L2, might imply replacements in L2 and flushing of L2 lines to memory. Dynamic sizing of the L2 cache while in state C_4 is also a possibility, with reduction when the cores have been idle for a long time or there is low activity (e.g.,

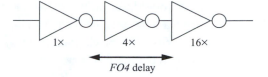

Figure 9.1. Illustration of the *FO4* metric.

handling only interrupts that do not require the L2 cache) and expansion when there is a new burst of activity.

Dynamic power reduction in the Centrino is performed by monitoring the computational needs of the executing application when in state C_0. Several *operational points*, (i.e., frequency–voltage combinations), are defined with the aim for the O.S. to make each processor run at the lowest operational point that meets the required performance.

9.2 Technological Limitations: Wire Delays and Pipeline Depths

Power dissipation and thermal concerns that we have introduced in the previous section are the major reasons for the standstill in clock speed that we have observed since 2003. However, there are other technological reasons for which performance would not gain as much from higher frequencies. We elaborate on two of them: wires and pipeline depths.

In this section we will use the metric that has been adopted to quantify gate and wire delays, namely *FO4*, (i.e., the delay for an inverter driving four identical copies of itself), as shown in Figure 9.1. The advantage of this metric is that it acts as a normalizing factor. Any delay in a combinational circuit can be divided by *FO4*, and the ratio will remain constant over a wide range of technologies.

Wires

In the late 1990s, picking up on the political slogans of the time, the outcry was "It's the wires, stupid" when discussing the impact of Moore's law and speed increases on performance growth. In other words, the concern was not putting more transistors on a chip, nor cranking up the clock, but mitigating the delays that would be incurred in communication. Today, even though the clock cycle has essentially remained constant, it is small enough that sending signals from one part of the chip to another cannot always be done in a single cycle. Furthermore, as feature size continues to decrease, *absolute* wire delays may increase slightly. The counterargument to that effect is that with smaller feature sizes, the wires can be shorter.

Without dwelling in the physics of delays in wire, let us just state that the delay can be viewed in a first approximation as proportional to the product of the resistance and the capacitance of the wire, in symbols RC. As technology improves, that is, feature sizes decrease, R increases significantly, and so does C, although to a much lesser extent. Thus, the *absolute delay* increases, and wire delay relative to gate delay could have skyrocketed if the frequency had kept increasing at the same rate. In addition to the delay on the wire, there is an overhead if a gate is used to drive a wire; this overhead can be assumed to be equal to *FO4*.

Wires can be characterized by their lengths and the entities that they connect. We can distinguish between:

- *Local wires*, such as those found in standard cells, for example, in an adder. These wires connect entities that are close to each other. Improved technologies will make them even shorter. They do not present a performance problem.
- *Global wires*, such as those connecting *modules*, for example, the wires connecting the register file to the inputs of the functional units. Global wires do not scale in length, and they are the wires that present a challenge.

Global wires that do not scale in length arise as a consequence of decreases in feature size that are at the basis of Moore's law. More logic on the chip results in more modules, and some of these modules' capacities get larger. We have seen that sophisticated superscalars have more functional units than their simpler counterparts; their branch predictors consist of several tables rather than the unique branch predictor table of two-bit counters; second-level caches are larger, and there can be a hierarchy of TLBs, etc. The multiplicity of modules implies an explosion in the number of wires. For example, forwarding the results of functional units to the other n functional units implies an n^2 growth in the number of wires. So, architects are confronted with more wires and the certainty of more delays in communication relative to computation speed. Luckily, for some global wires such as those for clock propagation, one can use repeaters, which in essence make their delays scalable.

Nonetheless, there are instances where wire delays influence the design and performance of modern processors. It cannot be taken for granted that on-chip distances do not count. A typical example is the use of clustered microarchitectures (cf. Section 5.3.3). Pushed a step further, clustered processors become CMPs. Another frequently cited example is that of the Intel Pentium 4, where reading a register takes two stages of the pipeline, the trade-off being that forwarding is done in a single cycle.

Optimal Pipeline Depth

The previous paragraph is an excellent motivation for this topic. In an ideal computational world, (i.e., one without hazards), a pipeline stage should be as short as possible to yield maximum throughput. If need be, extra stages in the pipe may be inserted, but this is of no consequence performancewise, because the throughput is the number of instructions executed per cycle and does not depend on the depth of the pipeline.

In reality there are constraints on the depth of the pipeline; some are technological, and some are due to the nonideality of computations, namely the presence of hazards. First, the pipeline stages are separated by pipeline registers that must provide stable storage. It has been estimated that writing and then reading the contents of these registers takes slightly less than $2FO4$ time. Second, the trick of spending extra pipeline stages to access data structures such as registers, caches, and branch predictors does not always work. For example, in recent microprocessors with deep pipelines and fast clock, the successful prediction of a branch taken along with a hit in the branch target buffer – that is, the perfect scenario – still imposes a one-cycle bubble. This extra cycle is needed because a data structure, the BTB, has to be accessed; the value of its entry has to be read and used as an index to the I-cache, which itself must be read; and the I-cache line which was read has to be transferred to the instruction buffer. Clearly, all these actions cannot be performed in the same cycle if the cycle time is associated with the time to read a register. Third, there are some RAW hazards that cannot always be circumvented even with fast forwarding and speculation, because of the latency of some operations. As a consequence of short stage times, the latencies of some units (for example, the L1 data cache and the floating-point units) become larger and hence counteract the benefits of pipeline depth. Finally, and most importantly, the deeper the pipeline is, the costlier the recovery from misprediction will be. As we have seen, the branch misprediction penalty, computed as a number of stages, almost doubled when passing from the 10-stage Intel Pentium III to the 20-stage Pentium 4, while the clock frequency increased only by a factor of 1.67. Therefore, *IPC* might suffer from longer pipelines.

In essence, what the previous two paragraphs say is that the execution time of an application is the sum of three components that are respectively:

- independent of the number of stages, p, in the pipe, for example, the proportion of instructions in a program that will cause hazards;
- inversely proportional to the number of stages (so that, in an ideal world without hazards, we should have as many stages as possible in order to increase throughput);
- proportional to the number of stages, because mispredictions are more costly when the number of stages that need to be recomputed increases.

Therefore, very abstractly, we can write

$$Exec.\ Time = a + b/p + cp$$

where a, b, and c are constants. Differentiating the above equation with respect to p and setting the resulting formula equal to 0 will yield a (noninteger) value for p. Granted, there is difficulty in finding the values of the constants, but the model shows that for a given application and a set of hardware parameters there is an optimal value. Simulations have indeed confirmed that there is a range of values of p that lead to "best" performance. That there is no single value of p is not surprising. The reader might recall a similar type of result: there is no single value for the cache line size that benefits all applications (recall Figure 2.18).

Another way to look at the same problem is to find, via simulation, the "optimal" logic depth per pipeline stage, expressed as a multiple of *FO4*. We put "optimal" in quotes for the same reason that we put "best" in quotes in the previous paragraph, namely because optimality will be different for various ISAs, capacities of structures such as register files and caches, and sets of applications. Nonetheless,

Table 9.1. Parameters in the evolution of CMPs

Parameter	Simplest	Most complex
Number of cores	Small (2–8)	Large (100–1000)
Multithreading	No	SMT
Core structure	Simple (in order, short pipe)	Complex (OOO, deep pipe)
Homogeneity	Yes	No
Cache hierarchy	Shared L2	Private L2
Interconnection network	Bus	Indirect network (mesh)
Hardware assists	None	Several (e.g., for transactions)

the *FO4* abstraction allows ignoring variations in technology in that the variations due to feature size may be less than the accuracies of the simulations. Finding the optimal depth of a pipeline stage, including the overhead of the pipeline registers, gives an indication that increasing frequency will not yield performance improvements after a certain limit has been reached. The simulation methodology must include ways to assess the number of cycles needed to access hardware structures as well as the latencies of functional units as multiples of *FO4*.

Results from two papers conducting somewhat different studies show that indeed there is a "sweet spot." In the study looking at the number of stages, the best p was about 20 stages. In the study looking at the depth of a stage, the best value was between 6 and 8 times *FO4*, that is, the amount of time allotted to computation should be between 2 and 3 times that of the stable storage overhead between stages.

9.3 Challenges for Chip Multiprocessors

The increasing power demands accompanying faster processor frequencies, the practical limit on how much ILP can be exploited, and the design complexity needed for improving performance, even slightly, in out-of-order superscalars have helped in clearing the way for chip multiprocessors (CMPs). Small-scale CMPs are now the rule. However, what will be the microarchitectural evolution of CMPs is not clear. In Table 9.1 we show the main parameters in the design of chip multiprocessors with extremes (simplest, most complex) for each parameter. These parameters were discussed in Section 8.2 except for the last one, which was mentioned in Section 7.3.2.

Challenges that exist in the design and performance of high-performance superscalars are also present for CMPs, and new ones arise because of the added coarse-grain parallelism. We consider very succinctly some of these challenges from the technology level up to the level of applications.

Technology: Because Moore's law is still viable, the number of transistors on a chip will continue to grow. Leakage power dissipation, which has been contained by recent technological advances for CMPs with a small number of processors, might become more of a problem when this number is scaled up. Dynamic power dissipation controls, such as DVFS, will have to be implemented on a core-by-core basis. The amount of activity will have to include that of transmitting data from one core to another, independently of the chosen methods of data transfer and interconnection. Technology trends will favor simpler processors that are more area- and energy-efficient. A looming problem is how to handle I/O bandwidth, for this factor will be exacerbated by the presence of more requests per unit time because of the larger number of active processors.

Microarchitecture: The multithreaded multicore paradigm will be successful only if fast and inexpensive launching of new threads is possible and if the synchronization of these threads can be done efficiently. Should there be new instructions in the ISA to perform these tasks? Should there be any hardware assists to do so? With the increased amount of data transfer on chip, shall we see a renewed debate on message passing vs. shared memory in that message passing can be done on chip whereas the use of shared memory might require frequent accesses to off-chip DRAM? Inasmuch as neither shared buses (because of contention) nor cross-bars (because of cost) scale well, what type of interconnection will be most useful? How will the cache hierarchy be managed; for example, where will (partial) directories be stored, and will there be replication and/or migration of data close to the producers or consumers? Of course, there are many more challenges that will arise, including those of homogeneity of processors and associated caches, and variations in clock frequencies among the cores.

Programming Languages, Compilers, Debuggers, etc.: Creating a large number of threads is a must if multicore computing is to be a success. This is the greatest challenge as CMPs become the norm. Although automatic parallelization via compilers can be successful for array-based scientific applications, this method is not a scalable answer for many other applications. Similarly, programming languages used for high-performance computing (HPC) cater mostly to scientific applications. What is needed is not only programming languages that explicitly create threads or that give compilers directives for where threads can be spawned, but also a new *philosophy* of programming, where the underlying model is not sequential but parallel programming. This paradigm shift requires a severe mind change in programmers' education. Functional languages such as those that were favored by advocates of dataflow machines are maybe too far off the model that programmers are accustomed to be practical. In imperative languages, parallel programming will create new, subtle rules such as relaxed models of memory consistency (recall the relaxed models sketched in Section 7.4). Not to be ignored is the increased difficulty in debugging that will arise because parallelism will result in nondeterministic timings.

Operating Systems: The challenges here might not be as great, in that operating systems for multiprocessors already exist. Scaling to more processors will require performance optimizations, but maybe no fundamental changes if the onus of creating threads is placed on the programmer.

Applications: CMPs are best suited for increased throughput. Applications that fall within the appellation of *distributed services* – for example, responses to queries to Web servers – will benefit from the increased parallelism brought about by CMPs, for these applications exhibit a very small amount of sharing and synchronization. "Embarrassingly" parallel applications can also benefit from a large number of cores. However, in some applications of this type – for example, those dubbed RMS (recognition, mining, synthesis) by Intel – the transfer of data between threads can be frequent although the number of data transferred each time is small. The CMP microarchitecture will have to deal with reducing overhead in these cases. In general, though, whereas in single processors increasing throughput was generally synonymous with reducing latency, this is no longer the case with CMPs. Increased throughput can be achieved with a large number of simple processors, but the absence of high-performance processors hurts the latency of single-thread applications. We saw that in multithreaded processors, there was always a provision to give (almost) all the resources to a single thread in case only one thread was running. The analog in CMPs is not possible unless there is a way to create a substantial number of threads in an application, that is, the challenge we just mentioned in the *Programming Languages* paragraph.

Finally, we should mention another challenge: how does one predict the performance of CMPs? Simulation has been used successfully in the design and evaluation of complex single processors. Multiprocessor performance has also been simulated – but, alas, with simulation programs running on single processors and taking hours if not days of computer time. The situation becomes untenable when the single processor's performance does not improve but the number of processors (or threads) increases dramatically.

Can these challenges be met by a straightforward evolution of current CMPs? Are new architectural paradigms needed, or should old ones, such as dataflow, be revisited? For example, a number of research projects investigate arrays of simple processors, often called *tiles*, on a chip connected via meshes. The distinctions among them include the underlying programming model, how accesses to memory are serialized, how code is placed or brought in on the various tiles, etc. One such architecture with 64 tiles, called Tilera, is being commercialized, but only for specific applications. In essence this is similar to the Cisco Network Processor with 188 microengines. Will future generations of CMPs be split into (i) those with a large number of very simple processors for applications that can use them, (ii) those with a limited number of complex processors, and (iii) some hybrid heterogeneous combination?

9.4 Summary

We have examined the two forms of power dissipation that have prevented increases in speed in current microprocessors: Static, or leakage, power dissipation is proportional to the number of transistors on chip and to the voltage; dynamic power consumption is related to the activity of switching devices, is proportional to the square of the voltage, and is linear in frequency. We have introduced two run-time techniques to reduce power consumption that require microarchitectural mechanisms and O.S. cooperation, namely, dynamic voltage and frequency scaling (DVFS) dissipation and resource adaptation.

Other factors that we have briefly introduced that can limit performance or clock frequency are wire lengths and pipeline depth.

We have concluded this chapter with an outline of the challenges that will face computer architects, basic software writers, and application designers when confronted with the scaling of the number of processor cores on a single chip.

9.5 Further Reading and Bibliographical Notes

A comprehensive survey of power reduction techniques can be found in Venkatachalam and Franz [VF05]. The first DVFS interval-based algorithm is due to Weiser et al. [WWDS94]. There are numerous online DVFS algorithms, mostly for portable devices, some of which are criticized in Grunwald et al. [GLFMN00]. Quite often DVFS algorithms are linked with scheduling policies to meet hard deadlines. The interested reader should consult the literature on real-time systems and embedded processors.

Albonesi et al. [ABDDFHKMSSBBCS03] presents a methodology and a survey of techniques for resource adaptation on a general-purpose processor. Instruction queue dynamic sizing is investigated in Ponomarev et al. [PKG01] and Folegnani and Gonzales [FG01]. Cache and TLB reconfigurations for better performance and energy savings are investigated in [BABD00]. Drowsy caches are introduced in Kim et al. [KFBM02], and cache line decay in [KHM01].

Thermal management is investigated in Brooks and Martonosi [BM01] and Skadron et al. [SSHVST03].

An analysis of the effect of improved technology on wire delays and the resulting performance aspects are described in [HMH01]. The two studies that we referred to for optimal pipelines are by Harstein and Puzak [HP02] and Hrishikesh et al. [HJFBKS02].

Design decisions relative to power and thermal management for the Intel Pentium 4 are described in [GBCH01], those for the Intel Pentium M in Gochman et al. [GRABKNSSV03], and those for the Intel Centrino Duo Mobile in [NRMGCKK06].

REFERENCES

[ABDDFHKMSSBBCS03] D. Albonesi, R. Balasubramonian, S. Dropsho, S. Dwarkadas, E. Friedman, M. Huang, V. Kursun, G. Magklis, M. Scott, G. Semeraro, P. Bose, A. Buyuktosunoglu, P. Cook, and S. Schuster, "Dynamic Tuning Processor Resources with Adaptive Processing," *IEEE Computer*, 36, 12, Dec. 2003, 49–58

[BABD00] R. Balasubramonian, D. Albonesi, A. Buyuktosunoglu, and S. Dwarkadas, "Memory Hierarchy Reconfiguration for Energy and Performance in General-purpose Processor Architectures," *Proc. 33rd Int. Symp. on Microarchitecture*, 2000, 245–257

[BM01] D. Brooks and M. Martonosi, "Dynamic Thermal Management in High-Performance Microprocessors," *Proc. 7th Int. Symp. on High-Performance Computer Architecture*, 2001, 171–182

[FG01] D. Folegnani and A. Gonzales, "Energy-effective Issue Logic," *Proc. 28th Int. Symp. on Computer Architecture*, 2001, 230–239

[GBCH01] S. Gunther, F. Beans, D. Carmean, and J. Hall, "Managing the Impact of Increasing Power Consumption," *Intel Tech. Journal*, 5, 1, Feb. 2001, 1–9

[GLFMN00] D. Grunwald, P. Levis, K. Farkas, C. Morrey, and M. Neufeld, "Policies for Dynamic Clock Scheduling," *Proc. 4th USENIX Symp. on Operating Systems Design and Implementation*, 2000, 73–86

[GRABKNSSV03] S. Gochman, R. Ronen, I. Anati, A. Berkovits, T. Kurts, A. Naveh, A. Saeed, Z. Sperber, and R. Valentine, "The Intel Pentium M Processor: Microarchitecture and Performance," *Intel Tech. Journal*, 7, 2, May 2003, 21–36

[HJFBKS02] M. Hrishikesh, N. Jouppi, K. Farkas, D. Burger, S. Keckler, and P. Shivakumar, "The Optimal Logic Depth per Pipeline Stage is 6 to 8 FO4 Inverter Delays," *Proc. 29th Int. Symp. on Computer Architecture*, 2002, 14–24

[HMH01] R. Ho, K. Mai, and M. Horowitz, "The Future of Wires," *Proc. of the IEEE*, 89, 4, Apr. 2001, 490–504

[HP02] A. Harstein and T. Puzak, "The Optimum Pipeline Depth for a Microprocessor," *Proc. 29th Int. Symp. on Computer Architecture*, 2002, 7–13

[KFBM02] N. Kim, K. Flautner, D. Blaauw, and T. Mudge, "Drowsy Instruction Caches – Leakage Power Reduction Using Dynamic Voltage Scaling and Cache Sub-bank Prediction," *Proc. 29th Int. Symp. on Computer Architecture*, 2002, 219–230

[KHM01] S. Kaxiras, Z. Hu, and M. Martonosi, "Cache Decay: Exploiting Generational Behavior to Reduce Cache Leakage Power," *Proc. 28th Int. Symp. on Computer Architecture*, 2001, 240–251

[NRMGCKK06] A. Naveh, E. Rotem, A. Mendelson, S. Gochman, R. Chabuskwar, K. Krishnan, and A. Kumar, "Power and Thermal Management in the Intel Core Dual Processor," *Intel Tech. Journal*, 10, 2, May 2006, 109–122

[PKG01] D. Ponomarev, G. Kucuk, and K. Ghose, "Reducing Power Requirements of Instruction Scheduling through Dynamic Allocation of Multiple Datapath Resources," *Proc. 34th Int. Symp. on Microarchitecture*, 2001, 90–101

[SSHVST03] K. Skadron, M. Stan, W. Huang, S. Velusamy, K. Sankararayanan, and D. Tarjan, "Temperature-Aware Microarchitecture," *Proc. 30th Int. Symp. on Computer Architecture*, 2003, 2–13

[VF05] V. Venkatachalam and M. Franz, "Power Reduction Techniques for Microprocessor Systems," *ACM Computing Surveys*, 37, 3, Sep. 2005, 195–237

[WWDS94] M. Weiser, B. Welch, A. Demers, and S. Shenker, "Scheduling for Reduced CPU Energy," *Proc. 1st USENIX Symp. on Operating Systems Design and Implementation*, 1994, 13–23

Bibliography

N. Abel, D. Budnick, D. Kuck, Y. Muraoka, R. Northcote, and R. Wilhelmson, "TRAN-QUIL: A Language for an Array Processing Computer," *Proc. AFIPS SJCC*, 1969, 57–73

M. Adiletta, M. Rosenbluth, D. Bernstein, G. Wolrich, and H. Wilkinson, "The Next Generation of Intel IXP Network Processors," *Intel Tech. Journal*, 6, 3, Aug. 2002, 6–18

S. Adve and K. Gharachorloo, "Shared Memory Consistency Models: A Tutorial," *IEEE Computer*, 29, 12, Dec. 1996, 66–76

A. Agarwal, R. Bianchini, D. Chaiken, K. Johnson, D. Kranz, J. Kubiatowicz, B.-H. Lim, K. Mackenzie, and D. Yeung, "The MIT Alewife Machine: Architecture and Performance," *Proc. 22nd Int. Symp. on Computer Architecture*, 1995, 2–13

A. Agarwal, B.-H. Lim, D. Kranz, and J. Kubiatowicz, "APRIL: A Processor Architecture for Multiprocessing," *Proc. 17th Int. Symp. on Computer Architecture*, 1990, 104–114

A. Agarwal and S. Pudar, "Column-Associative Caches: A Technique for Reducing the Miss Rate of Direct-Mapped Caches," *Proc. 20th Int. Symp. on Computer Architecture*, 1993, 179–190

A. Agarwal, R. Simoni, J. Hennessy, and M. Horowitz, "An Evaluation of Directory Schemes for Cache Coherence," *Proc. 15th Int. Symp. on Computer Architecture*, 1988, 280–289

A. Aggarwal and M. Franklin, "Scalability Aspects of Instruction Distribution Algorithms for Clustered Processors," *IEEE Trans. on Parallel and Distributed Systems*, 16, 10, Oct. 2005, 944–955

H. Akkary and M. Driscoll, "A Dynamic Multithreading Processor," *Proc. 31st Int. Symp. on Microarchitecture*, 1998, 226–236

D. Albonesi, R. Balasubramonian, S. Dropsho, S. Dwarkadas, E. Friedman, M. Huang, V. Kursun, G. Magklis, M. Scott, G. Semeraro, P. Bose, A. Buyuktosunoglu, P. Cook, and S. Schuster, "Dynamic Tuning Processor Resources with Adaptive Processing," *IEEE Computer*, 36, 12, Dec. 2003, 49–58

R. Alverson, D. Callahan, D. Cummings, B. Koblenz, A. Porterfield, and B. Smith, "The Tera Computer System," *Proc. Int. Conf. on Supercomputing*, 1990, 1–6

G. Amdahl, "Validity of the Single Processor Approach to Achieving Large Scale Computing Capabilities," *Proc. AFIPS SJCC*, 30, Apr. 1967, 483–485

D. Anderson, F. Sparacio, and R. Tomasulo, "Machine Philosophy and Instruction Handling," *IBM Journal of Research and Development*, 11, 1, Jan. 1967, 8–24

S. Anderson, J. Earle, R. Goldschmitt, and D. Powers, "The IBM System/360 Model 91: Floating-point Execution Unit," *IBM Journal of Research and Development*, 11, Jan. 1967, 34–53

T. Anderson, "The Performance of Spin Lock Alternatives for Shared-Memory Multiprocessors," *IEEE Trans. on Parallel and Distributed Systems*, 1, 1, Jan. 1990, 6–16

J. Archibald and J.-L. Baer, "An Economical Solution to the Cache Coherence Problem," *Proc. 12th Int. Symp. on Computer Architecture*, 1985, 355–362

J. Archibald and J.-L. Baer, "Cache Coherence Protocols: Evaluation Using a Multiprocessor Simulation Model," *ACM Trans. on Computing Systems*, 4, 4, Nov. 1986, 273–298

D. August, D. Connors, S. Mahlke, J. Sias, K. Crozier, B. Cheng, P. Eaton, Q. Olaniran, and W.-m. Hwu, "Integrated Predicated and Speculative Execution in the IMPACT EPIC Architecture," *Proc. 25th Int. Symp. on Computer Architecture*, 1998, 227–237

T. Austin, D. Larson, and D. Ernst, "SimpleScalar: An Infrastructure for Computer System Modeling," *IEEE Computer*, 35, 2, Feb. 2002, 59–67

J.-L. Baer and W.-H. Wang, "On the Inclusion Properties for Multi-Level Cache Hierarchies," *Proc. 15th Int. Symp. on Computer Architecture*, 1988, 73–80

F. Baetke, "The CONVEX Exemplar SPP1000 and SPP1200 – New Scalable Parallel Systems with a Virtual Shared Memory Architecture," in J. Dongarra, L. Grandinetti, G. Joubert, and J. Kowalik, Eds., *High Performance Computing: Technology, Methods and Applications*, Elsevier Press, 1995, 81–102

R. Balasubramonian, D. Albonesi, A. Buyuktosunoglu, and S. Dwarkadas, "Memory Hierarchy Reconfiguration for Energy and Performance in General-purpose Processor Architectures," *Proc. 33rd Int. Symp. on Microarchitecture*, 2000, 245–257

L. Belady, "A Study of Replacement Algorithms for a Virtual Storage Computer," *IBM Systems Journal*, 5, 1966, 78–101

A. Bernstein, "Analysis of Programs for Parallel Processing," *IEEE Trans. on Electronic Computers*, EC-15, Oct. 1966, 746–757

D. Bhandarkar, *Alpha Implementations and Architecture. Complete Reference and Guide*, Digital Press, Boston, 1995

D. Boggs, A. Baktha, J. Hawkins, D. Marr, J. Miller, P. Roussel, R. Singhal, B. Toll, and K. Venkatraman, "The Microarchitecture of the Pentium 4 Processor on 90nm Technology," *Intel Tech. Journal*, 8, 1, Feb. 2004, 1–17

J. Borkenhagen, R. Eickemeyer, R. Kalla, and S. Kunkel, "A Multithreaded PowerPC Processor for Commercial Servers," *IBM Journal of Research and Development*, 44, 6, 2000, 885–899

D. Brooks and M. Martonosi, "Dynamic Thermal Management in High-Performance Microprocessors," *Proc.7th Int. Symp. on High-Performance Computer Architecture*, 2001, 171–182

W. Bucholz, Ed., *Planning a Computer System: Project Stretch*, McGraw-Hill, New York, 1962

B. Calder and D. Grunwald, "Fast & Accurate Instruction Fetch and Branch Prediction," *Proc. 21st Int. Symp. on Computer Architecture*, 1994, 2–11

B. Calder and D. Grunwald, "Next Cache Line and Set Prediction," *Proc. 22nd Int. Symp. on Computer Architecture*, 1995, 287–296

B. Calder, D. Grunwald, and J. Emer, "Predictive Sequential Associative Cache," *Proc. 2nd Int. Symp. on High-Performance Computer Architecture*, 1996, 244–253

B. Calder and G. Reinmann, "A Comparative Survey of Load Speculation Architectures," *Journal of Instruction-Level Parallelism*, 1, 2000, 1–39

R. Canal, J.M. Parcerisa, and A. Gonzales, "Dynamic Cluster Assignment Mechanisms," *Proc. 6th Int. Symp. on High-Performance Computer Architecture*, 2000, 133–141

J. Cantin and M. Hill, *Cache Performance for SPEC CPU2000 Benchmarks*, Version 3.0, May 2003, http://www.cs.wisc.edu/multifacet/misc/spec2000cache-data/

R. Case and A. Padegs, "The Architecture of the IBM System/370," *Communications of the ACM*, 21, 1, Jan. 1978, 73–96

L. Censier and P. Feautrier, "A New Solution to Coherence Problems in Multicache Systems," *IEEE Trans. on Computers*, 27, 12, Dec. 1978, 1112–1118

K. Chan, C. Hay, J. Keller, G. Kurpanek, F. Shumaker, and J. Zheng, "Design of the HP PA 7200 CPU," *Hewlett Packard Journal*, 47, 1, Jan. 1996, 25–33

S. Chaudhry, P. Caprioli, S. Yip, and M. Tremblay, "High-Performance Throughput Computing," *IEEE Micro*, 25, 3, May 2005, 32–45

T.-F. Chen and J.-L. Baer, "Effective Hardware-based Data Prefetching for High-Performance Processors," *IEEE Trans. on Computers*, 44, 5, May 1995, 609–623

I-C. Cheng, J. Coffey, and T. Mudge, "Analysis of Branch Prediction via Data Compression," *Proc. 7th Int. Conf. on Architectural Support for Programming Languages and Operating Systems*, Oct. 1996, 128–137

D. Christie, "Developing the AMD-K5 Architecture," *IEEE Micro*, 16, 2, Mar. 1996, 16–27

G. Chryzos and J. Emer, "Memory Dependence Prediction Using Store Sets," *Proc. 25th Int. Symp. on Computer Architecture*, 1998, 142–153

D. Citron, A. Hurani, and A. Gnadrey, "The Harmonic or Geometric Mean: Does it Really Matter," *Computer Architecture News*, 34, 6, Sep. 2006, 19–26

R. Colwell, D. Papworth, G. Hinton, M. Fetterman, and A. Glew, "Intel's P6 Microarchitecture," Chapter 7 in J. P. Shen and M. Lipasti, Eds., *Modern Processor Design*, 2005, 329–367

T. Conte, K. Memezes, P. Mills, and B. Patel, "Optimization of Instruction Fetch Mechanisms for High Issue Rates," *Proc. 22nd Int. Symp. on Computer Architecture*, 1995, 333–344

C. Conti, D. Gibson, and S. Pitkowsky, "Structural Aspects of the IBM System 360/85; General Organization," *IBM Systems Journal*, 7, 1968, 2–14

R. Cooksey, S. Jourdan, and D. Grunwald, "A Stateless, Content-Directed Data Prefetching Mechanism," *Proc. 10th Int. Conf. on Architectural Support for Programming Languages and Operating Systems*, Oct. 2002, 279–290

R. Crisp, "Direct Rambus Technology: The New Main Memory Standard," *IEEE Micro*, 17, 6, Nov.–Dec. 1997, 18–28

D. Culler and J.P. Singh with A. Gupta, *Parallel Computer Architecture: A Hardware/Software Approach*, Morgan Kaufman Publishers, San Francisco, 1999

V. Cuppu, B. Jacob, B. Davis, and T. Mudge, "High-Performance DRAMs in Workstation Environments," *IEEE Trans. on Computers*, 50, 11, Nov. 2001, 1133–1153

H. Curnow and B. Wichman, "Synthetic Benchmark," *Computer Journal*, 19, 1, Feb. 1976

Z. Cvetanovic and D. Bhandarkar, "Performance Characterization of the Alpha 21164 Microprocessor Using TP and SPEC Workloads," *Proc. 2nd Int. Symp. on High-Performance Computer Architecture*, 1996, 270–280

Z. Cvetanovic and R. Kessler, "Performance Analysis of the Alpha 21264-based Compaq ES40 System," *Proc. 27th Int. Symp. on Computer Architecture*, 2000, 192–202

W. Dally, "Virtual-Channel Flow Control," *Proc. 17th Int. Symp. on Computer Architecture*, 1990, 60–68

P. Denning, "Virtual Memory," *ACM Computing Surveys*, 2, Sep. 1970, 153–189

J. Dennis and D. Misunas, "A Preliminary Data Flow Architecture for a Basic Data Flow Processor," *Proc. 2nd Int. Symp. on Computer Architecture*, 1974, 126–132

J. Dongarra, J. Bunch, C. Moler, and G. Stewart, *LINPACK User's Guide*, SIAM, Philadelphia, 1979

J. Dongarra, P. Luszczek, and A. Petitet, "The LINPACK Benchmark: Past, Present, and Future," *Concurrency and Computation: Practice and Experience*, 15, 2003, 1–18

M. Dubois, C. Scheurich, and F. Briggs, "Memory Access Buffering in Multiprocessors," *Proc. 13th Int. Symp. on Computer Architecture*, 1986, 434–442

A. Eden and T. Mudge, "The YAGS Branch Prediction Scheme," *Proc. 31st Int. Symp. on Microarchitecture*, 1998, 69–77

J. Edmondson, P. Rubinfeld, R. Preston, and V. Rajagopalan, "Superscalar Instruction Execution in the 21164 Alpha Microprocessor," *IEEE Micro*, 15, 2, Apr. 1995, 33–43

S. Eggers, J. Emer, H. Levy, J. Lo, R. Stamm, and D. Tullsen, "Simultaneous Multithreading: A Platform for Next-Generation Processors," *IEEE Micro*, 17, 5, Sep. 1997, 12–19

B. Fagin and K. Russell, "Partial Resolution in Branch Target Buffers," *Proc. 28th Int. Symp. on Microarchitecture*, 1995, 193–198

D. Farkas and N. Jouppi, "Complexity/Performance Trade-offs with Non-Blocking Loads," *Proc. 21st Int. Symp. on Computer Architecture*, 1994, 211–222

B. Fields, R. Bodik, and M. Hill, "Slack: Maximizing Performance under Technological Constraints," *Proc. 29th Int. Symp. on Computer Architecture*, 2002, 47–58

M. Flynn, "Very High Speed Computing Systems," *Proc. IEEE*, 54, 12, Dec. 1966, 1901–1909

D. Folegnani and A. Gonzales, "Energy-effective Issue Logic," *Proc. 28th Int. Symp. on Computer Architecture*, 2001, 230–239

M. Franklin and G. Sohi, "A Hardware Mechanism for Dynamic Reordering of Memory References," *IEEE Trans. on Computers*, 45, 6, Jun. 1996, 552–571

K. Gharachorloo, A. Gupta, and J. Hennessy, "Two Techniques to Enhance the Performance of Memory Consistency Models," *Proc. Int. Conf. on Parallel Processing*, 1991, I-355–364

S. Gochman, R. Ronen, I. Anati, R. Berkovits, T. Kurts, A. Naveh, A. Saeed, Z. Sperber, and R. Valentine, "The Intel Pentium M Processor: Microarchitecture and Performance," *Intel Tech. Journal*, 07, 2, May 2003, 21–39

M. Golden and T. Mudge, "A Comparison of Two Pipeline Organizations," *Proc. 27th Int. Symp. on Microarchitecture*, 1994, 153–161

J. Goodman, M. Vernon, and P. Woest, "Efficient Synchronization Primitives for Large-Scale Cache Coherent Multiprocessors," *Proc. 3rd Int. Conf. on Architectural Support for Programming Languages and Operating Systems*, Apr. 1989, 64–73

G. Graunke and S. Thakkar, "Synchronization Algorithms for Shared-Memory Multiprocessors," *IEEE Computer*, 23, 6, Jun. 1990, 60–70

D. Grunwald, P. Levis, K. Farkas, C. Morrey, and M. Neufeld, "Policies for Dynamic Clock Scheduling," *Proc. 4th USENIX Symp. on Operating Systems Design and Implementation*, 2000, 73–86

M. Gschwind, H. Hofstee, B. Flachs, M. Hopkins, Y. Watanabe, and T. Yamazaki, "Synergistic Processing in Cell's Multicore Architecture," *IEEE Micro*, 26, 2, Mar. 2006, 11–24

S. Gunther, F. Beans, D. Carmean, and J. Hall, "Managing the Impact of Increasing Power Consumption," *Intel Tech. Journal*, 5, 1, Feb. 2001, 1–9

L. Gwennap, "Brainiacs, Speed Demons, and Farewell," *Microprocessor Report Newsletter*, 13, 7, Dec. 1999

E. Hallnor and S. Reinhardt, "A Fully Associative Software-Managed Cache Design," *Proc. 27th Int. Symp. on Computer Architecture*, 2000, 107–116

E. Hao, P.-Y. Chang, and Y. Patt, "The Effect of Speculatively Updating Branch History on Branch Prediction Accuracy, Revisited," *Proc. 27th Int. Symp. on Microarchitecture*, 1994, 228–232

A. Harstein and T. Puzak, "The Optimum Pipeline Depth for a Microprocessor," *Proc. 29th Int. Symp. on Computer Architecture*, 2002, 7–13

J. Hennessy and D. Patterson, *Computer Architecture: A Quantitative Approach*, Fourth Edition, Elsevier Inc., San Francisco, 2007

J. Henning, Ed., "SPEC CPU2006 Benchmark Descriptions," *Computer Architecture News*, 36, 4, Sep. 2006, 1–17

M. Hill, *Aspects of Cache Memory and Instruction Buffer Performance*, Ph.D. Dissertation, Univ. of California, Berkeley, Nov. 1987

M. Hill, "Multiprocessors Should Support Simple Memory-Consistency Models," *IEEE Computer*, 31, 8, Aug. 1998, 28–34

G. Hinton, D. Sager, M. Upton, D. Boggs, D. Carmean, A. Kyker, and P. Roussel, "The Microarchitecture of the Pentium4 Processor," *Intel Tech. Journal*, 1, Feb. 2001

R. Ho, K. Mai, and M. Horowitz, "The Future of Wires," *Proc. of the IEEE*, 89, 4, Apr. 2001, 490–504

M. Hrishikesh, N. Jouppi, K. Farkas, D. Burger, S. Keckler, and P. Shivakumar, "The Optimal Logic Depth per Pipeline Stage is 6 to 8 FO4 Inverter Delays," *Proc. 29th Int. Symp. on Computer Architecture*, 2002, 14–24

J. Huck, D. Morris, J. Ross, A. Knies, H. Mulder, and R. Zahir, "Introducing the IA-64 Architecture," *IEEE Micro*, 20, 5, Sep. 2000, 12–23

W.-m. Hwu and Y. Patt, "HPSm, A High-Performance Restricted Data Flow Architecture Having Minimal Functionality," *Proc. 13th Int. Symp. on Computer Architecture*, 1986, 297–307

Intel Corp., A Tour of the P6 Microarchitecture, 1995, http://www.x86.org/ftp/manuals/686/p6tour.pdf

T. Jeremiassen and S. Eggers, "Reducing False Sharing on Shared Memory Multiprocessors through Compile Time Data Transformations," *Proc. 5th ACM SIGPLAN Symp. on Principles and Practice of Parallel Programming*, 1995, 179–188

D. Jiménez, S. Keckler, and C. Lin, "The Impact of Delay on the Design of Branch Predictors," *Proc. 33rd Int. Symp. on Microarchitecture*, 2000, 67–76

L. John, "More on Finding a Single Number to Indicate Overall Performance of a Benchmark Suite," *Computer Architecture News*, 32, 1, Mar. 2004, 3–8

D. Joseph and D. Grunwald, "Prefetching Using Markov Predictors," *Proc. 24th Int. Symp. on Computer Architecture*, 1997, 252–263

N. Jouppi, "Improving Direct-Mapped Cache Performance by the Addition of a Small Fully-Associative Cache and Prefetch Buffers," *Proc. 17th Int. Symp. on Computer Architecture*, 1990, 364–373

S. Jourdan, J. Stark, T.-H. Hsing, and Y. Patt, "Recovery Requirements of Branch Prediction Storage Structures in the Presence of Mispredicted-path Execution," *International Journal of Parallel Programming*, 25, Oct. 1997, 363–383

D. Kaeli and P. Emma, "Branch History Table Prediction of Moving Target Branches Due to Subroutine Returns," *Proc. 18th Int. Symp. on Computer Architecture*, 1991, 34–42

A. Kagi, D. Burger, and J. Goodman, "Efficient Synchronization: Let them Eat QOLB," *Proc. 24th Int. Symp. on Computer Architecture*, 1997, 170–180

J. Kahle, M. Day, H. Hofstee, C. Johns, T. Maeurer, and D. Shippy, "Introduction to the Cell Multiprocessor," *IBM Journal of Research and Development*, 49, 4/5, Jul. 2005, 589–604

J. Kalamatianos, A. Khalafi, D. Kaeli, and W. Meleis, "Analysis of Temporal-based Program Behavior for Improved Instruction Cache Performance," *IEEE Trans. on Computers*, 48, 2, Feb. 1999, 168–175

R. Kalla, B. Sinharoy, and J. Tendler, "IBM Power5 Chip: A Dual-Core Multithreaded Processor," *IEEE Micro*, 24, 2, Apr. 2004, 40–47

U. Kapasi, S. Rixner, W. Dally, B. Khailany, J. Ahn, P. Mattson, and J. Owens, "Programmable Stream Processors," *IEEE Computer*, 36, 8, Aug. 2003, 54–62

S. Kaxiras, Z. Hu, and M. Martonosi, "Cache Decay: Exploiting Generational Behavior to Reduce Cache Leakage Power," *Proc. 28th Int. Symp. on Computer Architecture*, 2001, 240–251

R. Keller, "Look-Ahead Processors," *ACM Computing Surveys*, 7, 4, Dec. 1975, 177–195

C. Keltcher, J. McGrath, A. Ahmed, and P. Conway, "The AMD Opteron for Multiprocessor Servers," *IEEE Micro*, 23, 2, 2003, 66–76

Kendall Square Research, *KSR1 Technology Background*, Waltham, MA, 1992

P. Kermani and L. Kleinrock, "Virtual Cut-through: A New Computer Communication Switching Technique," *Computer Networks*, 3, 4, Sep. 1979, 267–286

D. Kerns and S. Eggers, "Balanced Scheduling: Instruction Scheduling when Memory Latency is Uncertain," *Proc. ACM SIGPLAN Conf. on Programming Language Design and Implementation*, SIGPLAN Notices, 28, 6, Jun. 1993, 278–289

J. Keshava and V. Pentkovski, "Pentium III Processor Implementation Tradeoffs," *Intel Tech. Journal*, 2, May 1999

R. Kessler, "The Alpha 21264 Microprocessor," *IEEE Micro*, 19, 2, Mar. 1999, 24–36

R. Kessler, R. Jooss, A. Lebeck, and M. Hill, "Inexpensive Implementations of Set-Associativity," *Proc. 16th Int. Symp. on Computer Architecture*, 1989, 131–139

T. Kilburn, D. Edwards, M. Lanigan, and F. Sumner, "One-level Storage System," *IRE Trans. on Electronic Computers*, EC-11, 2, Apr. 1962, 223–235

C. Kim, D. Burger, and S. Keckler, "An Adaptive, Non-Uniform Cache Structure for Wire-Delay Dominated On-Chip Caches," *Proc. 10th Int. Conf. on Architectural Support for Programming Languages and Operating Systems*, Oct. 2002, 211–222

N. Kim, K. Flautner, D. Blaauw, and T. Mudge, "Drowsy Instruction Caches – Leakage Power Reduction Using Dynamic Voltage Scaling and Cache Sub-bank Prediction," *Proc. 29th Int. Symp. on Computer Architecture*, 2002, 219–230

A. KleinOsowski and D. Lilja, "MinneSPEC: A New SPEC Benchmark Workload for Simulation-Based Computer Architecture Research," *Computer Architecture Letters*, 1, Jun. 2002

P. Kogge, *The Architecture of Pipelined Computers*, McGraw-Hill, New York, 1981

P. Kongetira, K. Aingaran, and K. Olukotun, "Niagara: A 32-way Multithreaded Sparc Processor," *IEEE Micro*, 24, 2, Apr. 2005, 21–29

D. Koufaty and D. Marr, "Hyperthreading Technology in the Netburst Microarchitecture," *IEEE Micro*, 23, 2, Mar. 2003, 56–65

D. Kroft, "Lockup-Free Instruction Fetch/Prefetch Cache Organization," *Proc. 8th Int. Symp. on Computer Architecture*, 1981, 81–87

A. Lai, C. Fide, and B. Falsafi, "Dead-block Prediction & Dead-block Correlation Prefetchers," *Proc. 28th Int. Symp. on Computer Architecture*, 2001, 144–154

M. Lam, "Software Pipelining: An Effective Scheduling Technique for VLIW Machines," *Proc. ACM SIGPLAN Conf. on Programming Language Design and Implementation*, SIGPLAN Notices, 23, 7, Jul. 1988, 318–328

L. Lamport, "How to Make a Multiprocessor Computer that Correctly Executes Programs," *IEEE Trans. on Computers*, 28, 9, Sep. 1979, 690–691

J. Larus and C. Kozyrakis, "Transactional Memory," *Communications of the ACM*, 51, 7, Jul. 2008, 80–88

D. Lee, P. Crowley, J.-L. Baer, T. Anderson, and B. Bershad, "Execution Characteristics of Desktop Applications on Windows NT," *Proc. 25th Int. Symp. on Computer Architecture*, 1998, 27–38

J. Lee, "Study of 'Look-Aside' Memory," *IEEE Trans. on Computers*, C-18, 11, Nov. 1969, 1062–1065

J. Lee and A. Smith, "Branch Prediction Strategies and Branch Target Buffer Design," *IEEE Computer*, 17, 1, Jan. 1984, 6–22

W.-F. Lin, S. Reinhardt, and D. Burger, "Designing a Modern Memory Hierarchy with Hardware Prefetching," *IEEE Trans. on Computers*, 50, 11, Nov. 2001, 1202–1218

M. Lipasti and J.P. Shen, "Exceeding the Dataflow Limit with Value Prediction," *Proc. 29th Int. Symp. on Microarchitecture*, 1996, 226–237

J. Liptay, "Design of the IBM Enterprise System/9000 High-end Processor," *IBM Journal of Research and Development*, 36, 4, Jul. 1992, 713–731

J. Lo, L. Barroso, S. Eggers, K. Gharachorloo, H. Levy, and S. Parekh, "An Analysis of Database Workload Performance on Simultaneous Multithreaded Processors," *Proc. 25th Int. Symp. on Computer Architecture*, 1998, 39–50

G. Loh, "Advanced Instruction Flow Techniques," Chapter 9 in *J. P. Shen and M. Lipasti*, Eds., *Modern Processor Design*, 2005, 453–518

T. Lovett and R. Clapp, "STiNG: A CC-NUMA Computer System for the Commercial Marketplace," *Proc. 23rd Int. Symp. on Computer Architecture*, 1996, 308–317

T. Lovett and S. Thakkar, "The Symmetry Multiprocessor System," *Proc. Int. Conf. on Parallel Processing*, Aug. 1988, pp. 303–310

H. Mathis, A. Mericas, J. McCalpin, R. Eickemeyer, and S. Kunkel, "Characterization of Simultaneous Multithreading (SMT) Efficiency in Power5," *IBM Journal of Research and Development*, 49, 4, Jul. 2005, 555–564

R. Mattson, J. Gecsei, D. Slutz, and I. Traiger, "Evaluation Techniques for Storage Hierarchies," *IBM Systems Journal*, 9, 1970, 78–117

S. McFarling, "Combining Branch Predictors," WRL Technical Note, TN-36, Jun. 1993

H. McMahon, "The Livermore Fortran Kernels Test of the Numerical Performance Range," in J. L. Martin, Ed., *Performance Evaluation of Supercomputers*, Elsevier Science B.V., North-Holland, Amsterdam, 1988, 143–186.

C. McNairy and D. Soltis, "Itanium 2 Processor Microarchitecture," *IEEE Micro*, 23, 2, Mar. 2003, 44–55

A. Mendelson, J. Mandelblat, S. Gochman, A. Shemer, R. Chabukswar, E. Niemeyer, and A. Kumar, "CMP Implementation in Systems Based on the Intel Core Duo Processor," *Intel Tech. Journal*, 10, 2, May 2006, 99–107

G. Moore, "Cramming More Components onto Integrated Circuits," *Electronics*, 38, 8, Apr. 1965

A. Moshovos, S. Breach, T. Vijaykumar, and G. Sohi, "Dynamic Speculation and Synchronization of Data Dependences," *Proc. 24th Int. Symp. on Computer Architecture*, 1997, 181–193

T. Mowry, M. Lam, and A. Gupta, "Tolerating Latency Through Software-Controlled Prefetching in Shared-Memory Multiprocessors," *Proc. 5th Int. Conf. on Architectural Support for Programming Languages and Operating Systems*, Oct. 1992, 62–73

O. Mutlu, J. Stark, C. Wilkerson, and Y. Patt, "Run-ahead Execution: An Alternative to Very Large Instruction Windows for Out-of-order Processors," *Proc. 9th Int. Symp. on High-Performance Computer Architecture*, 2003, 129–140

A. Naveh, E. Rotem, A. Mendelson, S. Gochman, R. Chabuskwar, K. Krishnan, and A. Kumar, "Power and Thermal Management in the Intel Core Dual Processor," *Intel Tech. Journal*, 10, 2, May 2006, 109–122

E. Ozer, S. Banerjia, and T. Conte, "Unified Assign and Schedule: A New Approach to Scheduling for Clustered Register File Microarchitectures," *Proc. 31st Int. Symp. on Microarchitecture*, 1998, 308–315

S. Palacharla, N. Jouppi, and J. Smith, "Complexity-Effective Superscalar Processors," *Proc. 24th Int. Symp. on Computer Architecture*, 1997, 206–218

S. Palacharla and R. Kessler, "Evaluating Stream Buffers as a Secondary Cache Replacement," *Proc. 21st Int. Symp. on Computer Architecture*, 1994, 24–33

S. Pan, K. So, and J. Rahmey, "Improving the Accuracy of Dynamic Branch Prediction using Branch Correlation," *Proc. 5th Int. Conf. on Architectural Support for Programming Languages and Operating Systems*, Oct. 1992, 76–84

M. Papamarcos and J. Patel, "A Low-overhead Coherence Solution for Multiprocessors with Private Cache Memories," *Proc. 12th Int. Symp. on Computer Architecture*, 1985, 348–354

D. Papworth, "Tuning the Pentium Pro Microarchitecture," *IEEE Micro*, 16, 2, Mar. 1996, 8–15

S. Patel, D. Friendly, and Y. Patt, "Evaluation of Design Options for the Trace Cache Fetch Mechanism," *IEEE Trans. on Computers*, 48, 2, Feb. 1999, 193–204

D. Patterson and J. Hennessy, *Computer Organization & Design: The Hardware/Software Interface*, Third Edition, Morgan Kaufman Publishers, San Francisco, 2004

D. Patterson and C. Séquin, "RISC I: A Reduced Instruction Set VLSI Computer," *Proc. 8th Int. Symp. on Computer Architecture*, 1981, 443–457.

J.-K. Peir, W. Hsu, and A. Smith, "Functional Implementations Techniques for CPU Cache Memories," *IEEE Trans. on Computers*, 48, 2, Feb. 1999, 100–110

A. Peleg and U. Weiser, "Dynamic Flow Instruction Cache Memory Organized Around Trace Segments Independent of Virtual Address Line," U.S. Patent Number 5,381,533, 1994

A. Peleg and U. Weiser, "MMX Technology Extension to the Intel Architecture," *IEEE Micro*, 16, 4, Aug. 1996, 42–50

C. Perleberg and A. Smith, "Branch Target Buffer Design and Optimization," *IEEE Trans. on Computers*, 42, 4, Apr. 1993, 396–412

K. Pettis and R. Hansen, "Profile Guided Code Positioning," *Proc. ACM SIGPLAN Conf. on Programming Language Design and Implementation*, SIGPLAN Notices, 25, Jun. 1990, 16–27

D. Ponomarev, G. Kucuk, and K. Ghose, "Reducing Power Requirements of Instruction Scheduling through Dynamic Allocation of Multiple Datapath resources," *Proc. 34th Int. Symp. on Microarchitecture*, 2001, 90–101

M. Postiff, G. Tyson, and T. Mudge, "Performance Limits of Trace Caches," *Journal of Instruction-Level Parallelism*, 1, Sep. 1999, 1–17

S. Przybylski, *Cache Design: A Performance Directed Approach*, Morgan Kaufman Publishers, San Francisco, 1990

E. Pugh, L. Johnson, and J. Palmer, *IBM's 360 and Early 370 Systems*, The MIT Press, Cambridge, MA, 1991

P. Ranganathan, S. Adve, and N. Jouppi, "Performance of Image and Video Processing with General-Purpose Processors and Media ISA Extensions," *Proc. 26th Int. Symp. on Computer Architecture*, 1999, 124–135

E. Riseman and C. Foster, "The Inhibition of Potential Parallelism by Conditional Jumps," *IEEE Trans. on Computers*, C-21, 12, Dec. 1972, 1405–1411

T. Romer, D. Lee, G. Volker, A. Wolman, W. Wong, J.-L. Baer, B. Bershad, and H. Levy, "The Structure and Performance of Interpreters," *Proc. 7th Int. Conf. on Architectural Support for Programming Languages and Operating Systems*, Oct. 1996, pp. 150–159

E. Rotenberg, S. Bennett, and J. Smith, "Trace Cache: A Low Latency Approach to High Bandwidth Instruction Fetching," *Proc. 29th Int. Symp. on Microarchitecture*, 1996, 24–34

L. Rudolf and Z. Segall, "Dynamic Decentralized Cache Schemes for MIMD Parallel Processors," *Proc. 11th Int. Symp. on Computer Architecture*, 1984, 340–347

P. Salverda and C. Zilles, "A Criticality Analysis of Clustering in Superscalar Processors," *Proc. 38th Int. Symp. on Microarchitecture*, 2005, 55–66

M. Schlansker and B. Rau, "EPIC: Explicitly Parallel Instruction Computing," *IEEE Computer*, 33, 2, Feb. 2000, 37–45

S. Scott, "Synchronization and Communication in the Cray 3TE Multiprocessor," *Proc. 7th Int. Conf. on Architectural Support for Programming Languages and Operating Systems*, Oct. 1996, 26–36

A. Seznec, "A Case for Two-way Skewed-Associative Caches," *Proc. 20th Int. Symp. on Computer Architecture*, 1993, 169–178

H. Sharangpani and K. Arora, "Itanium Processor Microarchitecture," *IEEE Micro*, 20, 5, Sep. 2000, 24–43

J. P. Shen and M. Lipasti, *Modern Processor Design Fundamentals of Superscalar Processors*, McGraw-Hill, 2005

T. Sherwood, E. Perelman, G. Hamerly, S. Sair, and B. Calder, "Discovering and Exploiting Program Phases," *IEEE Micro*, 23, 6, Nov.–Dec. 2003, 84–93

D. Sima, "The Design Space of Register Renaming Techniques," *IEEE Micro*, 20, 5, Sep. 2000, 70–83

K. Skadron, M. Martonosi, and D. Clark, "Speculative Updates of Local and Global Branch History: A Quantitative Analysis," *Journal of Instruction-Level Parallelism*, 2, 2000, 1–23

K. Skadron, M. Stan, W. Huang, S. Velusamy, K. Sankararayanan, and D. Tarjan, "Temperature-Aware Microarchitecture," *Proc. 30th Int. Symp. on Computer Architecture*, 2003, 2–13

N. Slingerland and A. Smith, "Multimedia Extensions for General-Purpose Microprocessors: A Survey," *Microprocessors and Microsystems*, 29, 5, Jan. 2005, 225–246

A. Smith, "Cache Memories," *ACM Computing Surveys*, 14, 3, Sep. 1982, 473–530

B. Smith, "A Pipelined, Shared Resource MIMD Computer," *Proc. Int. Conf. on Parallel Processing*, 1978, 6–8

J. Smith, "A Study of Branch Prediction Strategies," *Proc. 8th Int. Symp. on Computer Architecture*, 1981, 135–148

J. Smith, "Characterizing Computer Performance with a Single Number," *Communications of the ACM*, 31, 10, Oct. 1988, 1201–1206

J. Smith and A. Pleszkun, "Implementation of Precise Interrupts in Pipelined Processors," *IEEE Trans. on Computers*, C-37, 5, May 1988, 562–573 (an earlier version was published in *Proc. 12th Int. Symp. on Computer Architecture*, 1985)

J. Smith and G. Sohi, "The Microarchitecture of Superscalar Processors," *Proc. IEEE*, 83, 12, Dec. 1995, 1609–1624

G. Sohi, "Instruction Issue Logic for High-Performance, Interruptible, Multiple Functional Unit, Pipelined Computers," *IEEE Trans. on Computers*, C-39, 3, Mar. 1990, 349–359 (an earlier version with co-author S. Vajapeyam was published in *Proc. 14th Int. Symp. on Computer Architecture*, 1987)

G. Sohi, S. Breach, and T. Vijaykumar, "Multiscalar Processors," *Proc. 22nd Int. Symp. on Computer Architecture*, 1995, 414–425

G. Sohi and A. Roth, "Speculative Multithreaded Processors," *IEEE Computer*, 34, 4, Apr. 2001, 66–73

S. Srinivasan, D.-C. Ju, A. Lebeck, and C. Wilkerson, "Locality vs. Criticality," *Proc. 28th Int. Symp. on Computer Architecture*, 2001, 132–143

J. Stark, M. Brown, and Y. Patt, "On Pipelining Dynamic Instruction Scheduling Logic," *Proc. 34th Int. Symp. on Microarchitecture*, 2000, 57–66

C. Stunkel, J. Herring, B. Abali, and R. Sivaram, "A New Switch Chip for IBM RS/6000 SP Systems," *Proc. Int. Conf. on Supercomputing*, 1999, 16–33

P. Sweazey and A. Smith, "A Class of Compatible Cache Consistency Protocols and their Support by the IEEE Future Bus," *Proc. 13th Int. Symp. on Computer Architecture*, 1986, 414–423

J. Tendler, J. Dodson, J. Fields, Jr., H. Le, and B. Sinharoy, "POWER 4 System Microarchitecture," *IBM Journal of Research and Development*, 46, 1, Jan. 2002, 5–25

J. Thornton, "Parallel Operation in the Control Data 6600," *Proc. AFIPS. FJCC*, pt. 2, vol. 26, 1964, 33–40 (reprinted as Chapter 39 of C. Bell and A. Newell, Eds., *Computer Structures: Readings and Examples*, McGraw-Hill, New York, 1971, and Chapter 43 of D. Siewiorek, C. Bell, and A. Newell, Eds., *Computer Structures: Principles and Examples*, McGraw-Hill, New York, 1982)

J. Thornton, *Design of a Computer. The Control Data 6600*, Scott, Foresman and Co., Glenview, IL, 1970

G. Tjaden and M. Flynn, "Detection and Parallel Execution of Independent Instructions," *IEEE Trans. on Computers*, C-19, 10, Oct. 1970, 889–895

R. Tomasulo, "An Efficient Algorithm for Exploiting Multiple Arithmetic Units," *IBM Journal of Research and Development*, 11, 1, Jan. 1967, 25–33

M. Tremblay, J. Chan, S. Chaudhry, A. Coniglaro, and S. Tse, "The MAJC Architecture: A Synthesis of Parallelism and Scalability," *IEEE Micro*, 20, 6, Nov. 2000, 12–25

M. Tremblay and J. O'Connor, "UltraSparc I: A Four-issue Processor Supporting Multimedia," *IEEE Micro*, 16, 2, Apr. 1996, 42–50

L. Tucker and G. Robertson, "Architecture and Applications of the Connection Machine," *IEEE Computer*, 21, 8, Aug. 1988, 26–38

D. Tullsen, S. Eggers, and H. Levy, "Simultaneous Multithreading: Maximizing On-chip Parallelism," *Proc. 22nd Int. Symp. on Computer Architecture*, 1995, 392–403

E. Tune, D. Liang, D. Tullsen, and B. Calder, "Dynamic Prediction of Critical Path Instructions," *Proc. 7th Int. Symp. on High-Performance Computer Architecture*, 2001, 185–195

R. Uhlig and T. Mudge, "Trace-driven Memory Simulation: A Survey," *ACM Computing Surveys*, 29, 2, Jun. 1997, 128–170

S. Vanderwiel and D. Lilja, "Data Prefetch Mechanisms," *ACM Computing Surveys*, 32, 2, Jun. 2000, 174–199

P. VanVleet, E. Anderson, L. Brown, J.-L. Baer, and A. Karlin, "Pursuing the Performance Potential of Dynamic Cache Lines," *Proc. ICCD*, Oct. 1999, 528–537

V. Venkatachalam and M. Franz, "Power Reduction Techniques for Microprocessor Systems," *ACM Computing Surveys*, 37, 3, Sep. 2005, 195–237

R. Weicker, "Dhrystone: A Synthetic Systems Programming Benchmark," *Communications of the ACM*, 27, Oct. 1984, 1013–1030

M. Weiser, B. Welch, A. Demers, and S. Shenker, "Scheduling for Reduced CPU Energy," *Proc. 1st USENIX Symp. on Operating Systems Design and Implementation*, 1994, 13–23

O. Weschler, "Inside Intel Core Microarchitecture," Intel White Paper, 2006, http://download.intel.com/technology/architecture/new_architecture_06.pdf

M. Wilkes, "Slave Memories and Dynamic Storage Allocation," *IEEE Trans. on Electronic Computers*, EC-14, Apr. 1965, 270–271

W. Wong and J.-L. Baer, "Modified LRU Policies for Improving Second-Level Cache Behavior," *Proc. 6th Int. Symp. on High-Performance Computer Architecture*, 2000, 49–60

K. Yeager, "The MIPS R10000 Superscalar Microprocessor," *IEEE Micro*, 16, 2, Apr. 1996, 28–41

T.-Y. Yeh and Y. Patt, "Alternative Implementations of Two-Level Adaptive Branch Prediction," *Proc. 19th Int. Symp. on Computer Architecture*, 1992, 124–134

T.-Y. Yeh and Y. Patt, "A Comprehensive Instruction Fetch Mechanism for a Processor Supporting Speculative Execution," *Proc. 25th Ann. Symp. on Microarchitecture*, 1992, 129–139

A. Yoaz, M. Erez, R. Ronen, and S. Jourdan, "Speculation Techniques for Improving Load Related Instruction Scheduling," *Proc. 26th Int. Symp. on Computer Architecture*, 1999, 42–53

Z. Zhang, Z. Zhu, and X. Zhang, "A Permutation-based Page Interleaving Scheme to Reduce Row-buffer Conflicts and Exploit Data Locality," *Proc. 33rd Int. Symp. on Microarchitecture*, 2000, 32–41

Index